Praise for Salesforce.com® Secrets of Success

"Salesforce.com is usually thought of as an SFA system, but it really needs to be thought of as a full-fledged CRM. For more than five years, I've headed up marketing teams trying to expand the power of SFDC for highly automated Internet customer interaction systems. *Salesforce.com® Secrets of Success* is required reading for the modern marketer, sales exec, or customer support professional."

—Mark de Visser, CEO of Sonatype

"*Salesforce.com® Secrets of Success* is terrific because it gives guidance to every major executive, as well as tactical recommendations to the implementation team. Using this book's methods ensures the high user adoption rate we achieved at Syneron. It also provides hundreds of tips that save time and money in the real world."

—Doron Gerstel, CEO of Syneron Medical

"*Salesforce.com® Secrets of Success* helps the busy executive figure out what to do—and not to do—when a Salesforce system is being built or extended. I appreciate the balance it provides, giving strategic guidance to the executive team and tactical tips to the implementers."

—Dave Kellogg, CEO of Mark Logic

"*Salesforce.com® Secrets of Success* focuses on the business processes that surround SFDC—the things that people do to leverage the system and become more effective. Any organization going through internal change in sales, marketing, or other customer-facing teams needs to see and work on the big picture. This book helps them do just that."

—Jon Lambert, CFO of Wombat Trading Systems division
New York Stock Exchange

"Mr. Taber takes a hard look at reality and CRM systems and finds the way to bridge the gap between the two using Salesforce.com. You are sure to succeed with your Salesforce.com initiative by reading this excellent book. This is the Salesforce.com 'manual' we were all looking for."

—Joshua Meiri, Salesforce.com User Group Leader

"*Salesforce.com® Secrets of Success* combines Agile with Salesforce.com, the most widely used, hosted SFA system. Taber takes it one step further by telling product marketers and product managers how to use SFDC and the latest Agile tools to do their jobs better. A must-read."

—Rich Mironov, CMO of Enthiosys

Salesforce.com® Secrets of Success

Salesforce.com® Secrets of Success

Best Practices for Growth and Profitability

David Taber

PRENTICE
HALL

Upper Saddle River, NJ • Boston • Indianapolis • San Francisco
New York • Toronto • Montreal • London • Munich • Paris • Madrid
Capetown • Sydney • Tokyo • Singapore • Mexico City

The publisher offers excellent discounts on this book when ordered in quantity for bulk purchases or special sales, which may include electronic versions and/or custom covers and content particular to your business, training goals, marketing focus, and branding interests. For more information, please contact:

U.S. Corporate and Government Sales
(800) 382-3419
corpsales@pearsontechgroup.com

For sales outside the United States, please contact:

International Sales
international@pearson.com

Visit us on the Web: informit.com/ph

Library of Congress Cataloging-in-Publication Data

Taber, David, 1956-
  Salesforce.com secrets of success : best practices for growth and profitability / David Taber.
     p.   cm.
  Includes index.
  ISBN 978-0-13-714076-3 (pbk. : alk. paper)
  1. Customer relations—Management. 2. Sales management. I. Title.
  HF5415.5.T32 2009
  658.8'10028553—dc22

                                         2009004576

Pearson Education, Inc
Rights and Contracts Department
501 Boylston Street, Suite 900
Boston, MA 02116
Fax (617) 671-3447

ISBN-13: 978-0-13-714076-3
ISBN-10:   0-13-714076-2
Text printed in the United States on recycled paper at RR Donnelley in Crawfordsville, Indiana.
First printing, May 2009

Editor-in-Chief Mark L. Taub	**Development Editor** Michael Thurston	**Project Management/** **Composition/Illustration** ContentWorks, Inc.	**Indexer** Ted Laux
Acquisitions Editor Trina MacDonald	**Managing Editor** John Fuller	**Copy Editor** Jill E. Hobbs	**Proofreader** Andrea Fox
Editorial Assistant Olivia Basegio	**Full-Service** **Production Manager** Julie Nahil		**Cover Designer** Alan Clements

To my wife, Jennifer, who makes everything possible.

Contents

Acknowledgments

If it takes a village to raise a child, it takes a lot of colleagues and good friends to write a book. I have a lot of people to thank for this one. Before I do, I have to apologize to Jennifer, Andrew, and Nicholas for my absenteeism these past months.

First and foremost, I have to thank the team at Prentice Hall. Trina MacDonald, my acquisitions editor, helped me sell the book idea in the first place. Michael Thurston, my development editor, helped shape my writing for the needs of the reader. Jill Hobbs, my copy editor, had to deal with my endless punctuation errors. Andrea Fox proofed the book and found hilarious examples where the automatic spell-checkers made silly substitutions. Finally, Olivia Basegio and Molly Sharp kept the draft organized and on schedule.

As this book covers a lot of ground, the text contained a ton of ideas that had to be organized and balanced. A raft of people helped me by bullet-proofing arguments and reviewing chapters from the perspective of different Enterprise organizations. To Todd Cawthron, Erin Kinikin, Dave Korba, Patricia Menadier, Steve Messino, Rich Mironov, Craig Stouffer, Michal Wachstock, and Chuck deVita of the Growth Process Group, thanks.

Thanks to my technical reviewers who read the whole manuscript and provided valuable input: Joel Martin at Salesforce.com, Joshua Meiri at Data Domain, and Daniel Weiss at Bell Microproducts.

I am indebted to industry analysts and gurus who publish survey results that I used to substantiate my points. In particular, Aberdeen Group, AMR Research, CSO Insights, GoToMarket Strategies, Inside CRM, and Sirius Decisions have provided valuable perspectives on the best interactions between sales and marketing departments.

I also owe a debt of gratitude to the readership of *The Taber Report,* for their feedback and positive arguments about controversial topics. Thanks, too, to my Sales*Logistix* customers for providing the technical and organizational challenges that were my inspiration for this book. I also want to acknowledge Meredith Rudof Weiss and Daniel Kushner for not saying anything bad about the content.

Finally, Dave Korba deserves special mention here as a comrade, source of inspiration, and friend.

Thanks to you all.

About the Author

David Taber is an internationally recognized marketing and management consultant in the IT industry, with more than twenty-five years of experience, including eight years at vice president or above.

When he first used Salesforce.com back in 2000, David saw the system's potential, even in that early version. His company, Sales*Logistix*, is a certified implementer of Salesforce.com solutions, with clients in the United States, Canada, Israel, and India. Sales*Logistix* has created two widely used applications published in Salesforce's AppExchange. He has personally worked on dozens of Salesforce.com implementations, from early-stage startups to larger companies such as Sun Microsystems and Symantec.

His experience as a marketing VP—working with the sales organization, engineering, customer support, finance, and corporate management—gives him unique insight into the habits and needs of the executive suite. Additionally, his background in IT makes it easy for him to translate insights into language that both business and technical people can understand.

As an accomplished writer and speaker, David has created and delivered presentations to audiences in 10 countries, and he coaches CEOs on VC pitches. He has been a guest lecturer in marketing at the University of California and Carnegie Mellon University, and he taught the Product Marketing class at the University of California Berkeley extension.

David is a fourth-generation Californian who still hasn't figured out how to leave the Bay Area.

Introduction

Everybody sells.
—Thomas Watson

The Promise of CRM

Salesforce.com (SFDC) is the world's leading on-demand system for salesforce automation (SFA), customer relationship management (CRM), and support operations. Used by more than 50,000 businesses worldwide, the SFDC community includes 100,000 external developers and 1,100,000 end users. This community grows by the hundreds of people every day.

From recent industry analyst reports and surveys, it's easy to see why SFDC is growing:

- According to CSO Insights, successful CRM customers see a 10% increase in sales representatives achieving quota, a 10% improvement in win rates for forecasted deals, and a 10% better conversion rate at every level of the waterfall (the more stages you have in your waterfall, the bigger the "compound interest" effect provided by SFDC).

- According to Aberdeen Group, 86% of CRM customers following "best practices" saw an average 24% increase in annual customer revenue. Nearly the same number of firms saw an increase in sales contribution margin, with the average increase being 25%.

- CSO Insights surveys show a 25% reduction in sales rep turnover rate with use of a good CRM system, which translates into fewer "learning curve effects" and an improvement in overall spending effectiveness. This translates into a deal or two more per rep per year, easily paying for an SFA/CRM system in a few months.

May not make business grow, but can provide confidence: accuracy

---

AVOIDING DEATH IN THE BOARD ROOM

It's week 12 of the quarter, and the board is wondering if you're really going to make your number. What's worse, your company is going to need some more capital soon, so you need the financial picture to look as solid as possible for investors.

You're sweating a bit as you prep for the meeting, because the forecast has been jumping around from week to week. Two weeks ago, the pipeline looked thin—there was no way to make the quarterly number. You chewed out your sales team, and they came back with a bigger forecast. But how could this extra business suddenly appear? Are the reps just trying to make you feel good? Is this forecast any more real than the last one?

The guys and gals in the factory are telegraphing that they don't believe the sales goal is reachable. They haven't shifted the production schedule because they don't see the orders yet. If they manufacture too much product, you'll be sitting around the first week of next quarter with a bunch of inventory to drag down your profits.

Terrific.

This is one of the nightmares that a solid SFA/CRM system will help you avoid. An SFA/CRM system won't necessarily make your business grow fast enough to make your investors happy, but if it's done right you'll *always* know where you are, and you'll have confidence indicators that will help you sleep well—even in week 12 of the quarter.

These are the generic industry data. In reality, SFDC has been able to achieve even better outcomes than these numbers, with its customers typically achieving industry-leading results.

There's only one problem with this rosy picture: most SFA/CRM customers *fail* to get meaningful results from their system. This isn't an SFDC problem, but rather an issue that's endemic to the whole SFA/CRM industry. Take a look at what industry analysts have said recently:

- In 2007, AMR Research surveys indicated that 35% of CRM implementations faced serious user adoption issues. This percentage was down from 47% of CRM customers in 2002, but is still higher than what customers expected.

- In 2007 and 2008 surveys by CSO Insights and GoToMarket Strategies, respondents indicated that the average CRM customer had adoption rates of less than 75% among members of its sales team, with even lower percentages among its marketing and customer support personnel.

- These two firms' surveys confirmed that only half of CRM customers are achieving significant sales performance improvements or believe they can get real-time information from their SFA/CRM system. Most customers use the system only for contact management and pipeline management; only 30% use it for forecasting.

- Approximately 75% of prospect business cards will never make it into the SFA system, according to CSO Insights (2006).

Issues caused by: people, policy, & process problems

- According to Inside CRM surveys, only half of sales managers who do use their SFA/CRM system for forecasting and opportunity management believe the system is effective.

- According to *Software* magazine, only 30% of companies that deploy SFA/CRM systems report significant increases in sales performance (e.g., shorter sales cycles, better win rates, or overall revenue increases).

These issues don't arise because of a technology or product problem. Instead, they're caused by *people, policy, and process* problems. This is the reason why I wrote this book.

Achieving the Promise of SFDC

The promise of SFDC is increased profitability *and* increased customer satisfaction at the same time, as shown in Figure I-1.

The key success factor for achieving either of these benefits is early and deep user adoption; everything else flows from this source. When the users naturally turn to the SFDC system because it makes them more efficient, they will fill the system with more credible data. Those data make reports more meaningful—and so the availability of good information attracts more users to the system. We'll discuss how to encourage this virtuous cycle throughout the book.

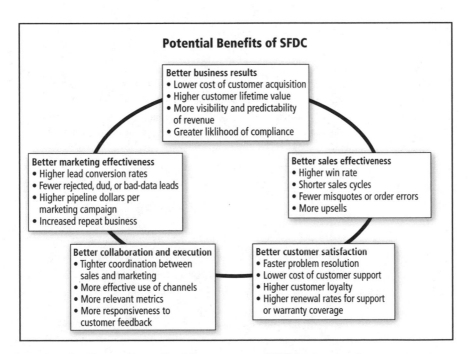

FIGURE I-1   Benefits that can be realized from a proper SFDC implementation

[Handwritten annotation at top: To achieve improvement → more disciplined / develop new processes / apply best practices]

[Handwritten annotation in left margin: Just slapping automation on top of an outdated business process merely makes you execute errors faster]

The promise of SFDC cannot be achieved just by buying some new software. Some change will also be needed in business processes and user behaviors. Most customers discover months *after* they buy an SFDC system that, to achieve real improvement in sales and operations, they need to be more disciplined, develop new processes, and apply best practices. Just slapping automation on top of an outdated business process merely makes you execute errors faster.

Real SFDC success depends on three factors:

- **Products** that extend SFDC and integrate it with other software so that the users can get a complete view of the customer's situation and do the right thing as smoothly as possible

- **People** who are fully indoctrinated on how to use SFDC *and* how to quickly solve customer problems

- **Business processes** that are "tuned" so that the *natural* way people work supports company objectives, best practices, and regulatory compliance

HOW TO BLOW UP TWO CAREERS AT ONCE!

A friend of mine was a VP of Marketing at a startup, and she walked into a board meeting ready to present her group's results for the quarter. She was walking into an ambush.

The VP of Sales hadn't made his number, and at the start of the board meeting he had made a long presentation about how the sales representatives *couldn't* make their numbers. They didn't have enough leads, and the ones they got were garbage. Marketing wasn't doing its job—that's why sales underachieved.

The board of directors confronted the VP of Marketing, who was totally blind-sided. Once she heard the complaint, she asked to be excused for 5 minutes. She went back to her office, pulled together some numbers, and came back to the board meeting. It turns out that marketing had delivered eight times as many leads as sales had said—and that 95% of the leads had never been contacted, not even *once*.

The board got it, and the VP of Marketing was off the hook.

Actually, no. The board ended up firing both the VP of Sales and the VP of Marketing. The twin functions—which really need to feed each other—were too disconnected, too dysfunctional.

This company had a basic SFA system. But all the *business processes surrounding its core system* were broken. Nobody agreed on the definition of a lead, or what it took for a lead to be qualified. Poor-quality data made reports misleading. Sales and marketing weren't communicating through the system. Politics were rampant. The business leverage just wasn't there.

Sometimes, the only way to fix the SFA/CRM problem is to fix the *people and the processes*. That's what this book is all about.

① Marketing
② Quoting/order entry

This stuff is hard. Big SFDC customers spend boatloads of money on consultants to extend the functionality, integrate the system, redesign business processes, and indoctrinate the users. Of course, most companies can't afford the time or money to follow this path. Most SFDC customers need shortcuts, "canned" procedures, and best-practices-in-a-box so they won't flail about and be frustrated. This book was designed to give you the information you need quickly and without a lot of Web searching or head scratching.

Do You Need an SFA System or a CRM System?

Industry analysts often treat SFA systems as a different product category than CRM systems. I'm going to make the case that the SFA–CRM distinction is really a continuum of functionality and business practices. I will also argue that SFDC can be used very effectively as *either* an SFA system or a CRM system: it all depends on how you invest and which behaviors your team takes on.

The term "salesforce automation system" is really a misnomer, because these systems don't automate the sales function. They *can* prevent things from falling through the cracks, streamline processes, accelerate the sales cycle, and provide clear metrics . . . but sales is still a very human process. From an image perspective, the SFA category was badly named: no sales rep wants to be automated. What the marketers at the time should have insisted on was "sales funnel acceleration"–a far more user-friendly positioning of what these systems do. Even so, the SFA moniker stuck.

SFA systems typically start out as software for direct sales or telesales people, providing simple contact and account management. Small companies tracking calls and managing lead maturation may be able to use Outlook, Excel, ACT, or Goldmine without a problem. Over time, however, those simple tools tend to run out of gas as the sales organization tries to manage opportunities and the pipeline. These customers may use SalesLogix software or another PC-based tool to provide this level of SFA functionality, but they're better off using SFDC.

All of these "SFA-only" systems are driven by the sales team and are basically stand-alone products. Consequently, they cannot fundamentally improve sales efficiency. To make a real difference in efficiency and follow-through, the business must start to integrate its SFA system into the rest of the enterprise. The first area for system expansion is the marketing function, as it is the source of the leads, programs, and collateral that feed the sales cycle. The next natural area for expansion is quoting or even order entry, because the objective of any sales team is to close deals faster. Given that this functionality is usually handled by other systems, the natural expansion strategy is to integrate the quoting or ordering screens into the SFA system. This incremental integration is a natural evolution for SFDC customers, and they tend to take this route at their own pace.

Of course, as the reach of the SFA system expands, sales reps' behaviors and business processes have to evolve as well. Marketing has to confer more frequently with sales to

SFA vs. CRM

make sure that the lead flow has both the quality and the quantity necessary to generate a sufficient pipeline. Marketing starts to work with sales to select and "tune" upcoming campaigns. In a similar way, as the sales reps begin using the system to create quotes, quote approval needs to be handled in a different way. Sales reps do *not* need to send out quotes until discounts have been approved, and they should *not* modify quotes once they've been approved. These process changes, although obvious, often take months to become standard operating procedure. Unfortunately, process failures in these areas are often blamed on the SFA system. This book will show you how to completely avoid the most common and troublesome problems, and rapidly recover from anything that does go off the rails.

The next expansion step is for the SFA system to be used by the customer support team. Because the customer's contact information and purchase history are already in the system, bringing the support team into the SFA system is a natural step. By the time customer support has adopted the SFA system, they have moved it incrementally toward becoming a CRM system—that is, the focal point for acquiring, retaining, and growing customer relationships.

CRM systems have a loftier set of goals than just sales productivity: the system should help convert your company's content (expertise) into customer conversations,[1] thereby moving customers into shared experiences (and values), proceeding to relationships, and finally creating a long-term revenue stream after the company has been established as a trusted advisor to the customer. A full CRM system ends up touching the customer from several angles: sales, marketing, support, consulting (if applicable), channels, Web, and, to a small extent, accounting (invoicing and accounts receivable)—so it must inevitably be integrated with several existing systems.[2] A full-blown CRM system also demands process and policy improvements, to avoid misuse and user dissatisfaction (as discussed in Chapters 8 through 13).

SFDC is one of the very few systems that can grow incrementally from a straightforward SFA tool into a serious CRM system. Thanks to its technically solid platform, SFDC can be extended with partner products and integration tools (as discussed in Chapter 7) to achieve an array of functions, from PR to HR. Indeed, at the end of the system evolution, SFDC may not only provide a 360-degree view of the customer, but also become the central executive application for managing the entire business.

Only you can decide whether you want an SFA system or a full-bore CRM. Here are some ways to think about the distinction at a high level:

- Do you want to monitor sales rep behavior (SFA) or customer behavior (CRM)?

- Are you trying to manage the transaction (SFA) or grow lifetime value (CRM)?

- Are you worried about quarterly revenue (SFA) or annual profitability (CRM)?

---

1. If you've never read *The Cluetrain Manifesto* about "how commerce is a conversation," I recommend it. The whole thing is available for free at http://manybooks.net/titles/variousother05cluetrain.html.
2. For all intents and purposes, there is no such thing as a stand-alone CRM system. The people at NetSuite are the exception that proves the rule, and it's interesting to note how many NetSuite customers use only accounting or only CRM functionality.

When Salesforce.com Is the Best Choice—an
It Isn't

SFDC is the pioneering SFA/CRM delivered in a hosted "software as a servi
Recent industry data from CSO Insights and other sources indicate dramatically ⸺ ⸺comes
can be achieved with on-demand (SaaS) CRM systems than with on-premises products:

- Much faster time to value

- Fewer budget overruns

- Higher end-customer satisfaction

- Better sales productivity

SFDC is best of breed for SaaS SFA/CRM systems. It's reliable, it's secure, and it performs well from anywhere in the world.[3] It offers the best compromise of features, flexibility, and usability. It can be quickly set up, and it's accessible from BlackBerry, Palm, and iPhone devices. Its Web user interface is one of the finest in the world of business applications, and I know of no competitor's product that is easier to use. SFDC is an ideal choice for companies that need to get their feet wet in an SFA system, try it out in one department, and ultimately expand use of the system to other areas. SFDC lends itself to incremental usage—in terms of both the number of users and the features enabled, giving your organization time to learn and optimize the way it uses the system.

It's important to understand that SFDC "out of the box" is really just an SFA system. As discussed in Chapter 1, SFDC's standard features cover most of what sales and marketing need for lead generation and pipeline management. For features involving quoting, order entry, or inventory management, SFDC must be extended or integrated with outside systems. Fortunately, SFDC has the industry's widest array of add-on products, and it integrates with those additions more easily than just about anything else on the market. If it turns out that you don't like the available third-party products, the SFDC system provides a development environment that lets you build custom applications that leverage the core system data. No matter where you are on the continuum of needs, there are several strategies for efficiently satisfying them via SFDC.

That said, there are some situations in which SFDC may not be the right approach:

- If you are doing a "greenfield" implementation that needs to include SFA, professional services automation, accounting, and inventory/distribution, all at once, a unified system from a single vendor could serve your purposes better. It will pro-

---

3. You *do* have to have a decent Internet connection. While the system can be used with a dial-up modem (56 Kbps), that is just not a good way to live.

duce less fingerpointing, and more of a known quantity out of the box. No incompatibilities.[4] If you like the SaaS model, this means NetSuite (but not Microsoft). If you prefer the on-premises model (where you own the software and it runs on your servers), this means Microsoft (but not NetSuite).

- If you already have one or more SFA/CRM systems in place and they cannot be removed, adding yet another SFA system to the mix is unlikely to improve the situation. That said, having a strategic plan to consolidate multiple SFA/CRM systems onto SFDC can make a huge amount of sense. Just be aware that getting everything really right in a multi-CRM environment—including external system integration and business process/user behavior changes—will take a while and require serious effort and tight management. This goes double if one or more of these systems is of the home-brew variety.

- If your corporation has a mandated enterprise application suite such as that offered by SAP or Oracle, getting another system in the door (even if it's "in the clouds") can be a bureaucratic nightmare. In this case, your only practical solution may be to use the suite vendor's SFA/CRM module. Generally speaking, the suite vendors' SaaS offerings are quite weak: you'll probably install their on-premises version—which the users will hate.

How to Use This Book

I wrote this book to provide specific answers for decision makers and users at every level of SFDC user organization:

- CEOs, presidents, and board members ("What's possible?")

- VPs of Sales or Marketing ("Which direction should we set?")

- IT, finance, or operations people ("How do we get it done?")

- Sales reps and managers ("How do *I* do it?")

Even though there's a lot of value in reading this book cover to cover, not everyone will have enough time to do so. At the very least, focus on the chapters that are immediately relevant to your role and those sections that answer questions pertinent to your immediate situation:

- If you are an executive, read the Executive Summary and the one chapter between Chapters 9 and 13 that comes closest to your job title. You might also want to scan Chapters 5 through 8 for topics that are relevant to you.

---

4. Although this is only a rhetorical advantage. Which is worse: incompatibilities *between* products or bugs *within* the single-vendor product you just bought to avoid incompatibilities?

- If you will be part of an SFDC implementation team, read Chapters 1 through 4, focusing on those sections that are most relevant to where you are now. You also should scan Chapters 5 through 8 looking for interesting topics.

- If you're a future user of SFDC, you'll want to understand how the system is best deployed across your organization. Read the one chapter between Chapters 9 and 13 that matches your role in the organization—so you can see what we've told the boss to do. Scan Chapters 5 through 8 to understand the people, products, politics, and process issues surrounding substantial SFDC implementations.

There are lots of updates, freebies, blogging, and user feedback at www.SFDC-secrets.com, so check it out.

See you there!

–David Taber
Palo Alto, California

Executive Summary

Don't solve problems; pursue opportunities.

—Peter Drucker

T HIS CHAPTER IS THE distillation of the best practices presented throughout the book, reframed from the perspective of VPs and CxOs (e.g., CEOs, COOs, CFOs, CMOs) of a company that plans to implement a Salesforce.com system, or radically expand one. We've designed this chapter so that it's the only one that every executive needs to read. **If you're not an executive, skip this chapter,** as you'll find the more detailed information you need in later chapters of the book (check out the "How to Use This Book" section at the end of the Introduction).

What Every CxO Needs to Know About Salesforce.com

Salesforce.com is *the* right choice for most companies who want an easy-to-use and flexible sales force automation or customer relationship management (SFA/CRM) system. Here are seven things *you* need to know about it.

- **User adoption is everything.** Without solid data in it, the SFDC system will be an empty shell. More users mean more data in the system, and more data mean a better view of the customer situation. So your *first* job is to make sure that users adopt the system. Communicate verbally and through behavior that *you* will be relying on the system to make management decisions—and you expect people at every level to do the same. A key success factor for your SFDC implementation will be the way employees perceive how *you* use the system and value its data. If they sense you don't care about it or don't believe in it, neither will they. Provide rewards for early adopters, and use the system yourself.

- **Bad data are your nemesis.** Duplicates, low-quality data, and lost entries are to be avoided at all costs, as they hurt user adoption, undermine system credibility, and can even undermine *your* credibility. The key here: don't skimp on data migration,

1

integration, and automation projects that stop bad data at the source. As much as you can, put all data relevant to the customer relationship inside, or make the data accessible from, the SFA/CRM system.

- **Visibility is your first benefit.** Once users are really on the system, SFDC will provide much more visibility into what's going on with prospects and customers. It will give you better early warning signals for forecast, pipeline, and customer satisfaction problems. It will also give you clear metrics and real-time dashboards for achievement versus goals. Invest in the integration that will give you a 360-degree view of the business. Provide incentives for predictability.

- **Management by exception is your goal.** The best way to manage your time is to manage by exception (MBE). By taking the "normal" for granted, you will be able to focus on the variances where you can make a difference. SFDC provides dashboards, alerts, and workflows that mean compliance and managing to a plan. Set realistic goals, relevant metrics, and clear employee incentives that match the desired behavior. Invest in business processes that can be streamlined and accelerated once you have a reliable, accurate base of information to work with—and then manage to them. Reward autonomy, so that your organization learns that management by emergency (the "squeaky wheel" effect) is *not* how you're running the company now.

- **Strategy is the crown.** Who are your most profitable customers, and why? Which products do they buy from you, and what are the reasons they prefer doing business with you? Where do you need to be investing more, and where can you economize on marketing and selling? These questions can be answered only when you have a database of customer purchase patterns and a history of behaviors. The answers will be just guesses, "gut feelings," and "garbage out" until your SFA/CRM system serves as the foundation for strategic analysis.

- **Be careful about what you say.** Everyone in your organization will be on the alert because SFA/CRM systems come with a bit of political baggage—the "Big Brother" effect. Sales reps aren't asking to be automated, and nobody wants to be micromanaged. If any personnel sense that your real goal is to more tightly monitor *them*, all the good things that an SFA/CRM system can do for your company will be delayed or even nullified. Even though the words below may have the same abstract meaning, what your people will *hear* from the two lists is drastically different:

Do talk about	*Don't talk about*
Bigger deals	Higher productivity
Happier customers	Tighter management
Less wasted effort	Automation
Improving business processes	Job elimination
Achieving goals easier	Leverage
Giving employees the tools that they need	Comprehensive system

If employees sense that you're using the SFDC system to unify your company and make it more coherent and coordinated, they will follow your example. But if they sense that you're going to use the system to lay blame or fuel political battles, they will subtly sabotage the system as they would any enemy.

- **Publicize the good news.** It's been proven many times that the organization will follow your lead in regard to the SFDC system. Celebrate the good things that the system is doing for the business every quarter while it's being built and extended. Tell the board about your successes, tell your subordinates about the benefits—get the news out about how effective CRM is reshaping your business.

Why Are You Looking at an SFA/CRM System?

There are dozens of good reasons to be investing in an SFA/CRM system. But to have clear communications with your organization and focus for the implementation team, it's best if you have a *small* number of goals. Prioritize the objectives so that people spend time and effort on things that will make a difference to the business.

You don't need me to tell you that the "good old days" of selling are gone—the easy money has already been made. Customers expect a much higher level of sales rep knowledge, tighter execution, and deeper post-sales support. Also, they want to do business on the Web, whether your operations are ready for it or not. If you want to achieve higher customer lifetime value, your sales, marketing, and customer support teams will need to collaborate much more effectively than they did in the past.

With SFA/CRM systems, the business case is all about *profits*. Those profits will come mainly from the *revenue* side: bigger deals, higher conversion ratios, more repeat business, and improved customer loyalty. Although SFA/CRM systems can also lead to cost reductions, putting the emphasis there starts the project out on the wrong foot.

Every executive reading this chapter needs to agree on the high-level business objectives you are trying to achieve with an SFA/CRM investment. While your company will have unique goals, some precepts are nearly universal for SFDC customers:

- The whole point of an SFA system is to get the most return from the amount you invest in marketing and sales (e.g., salaries, programs, travel, customer dinners). The purpose of the system should be *maximizing customer life-cycle profitability,* which entails a lot more than just "getting more sales." The SFDC system is designed to reduce the *cost of customer acquisition* and shorten sales cycles.

- While growth may come from getting new customers, *profit* definitely comes from milking existing customers. It is three to ten times more expensive to acquire new customers than it is to upsell and expand existing accounts. *Of course* you need new customers, but SFDC can help you do that while also getting more profit out of your customer base.

Here are the areas where an SFA/CRM system can make a decisive difference for company performance. While every one of these business objectives is within reach, in most cases you will **only achieve three or four** of them in the first year or two of SFDC system operation. And to actually get them, you have to keep the team focused *consistently* on those three or four objectives until they are achieved. So choose wisely.

Higher Business Leverage

- Lower costs for finding and closing new customers
- Larger order sizes
- Higher profit from existing customers
- Improved marketing and promotional effectiveness
- Fewer erroneous orders and product returns
- Lower customer support costs

Better Visibility, Better Decisions

- Deeper, broader view of customers and operations
- More realistic metrics of the customer relationship
- Ability to spot and react to market trends faster
- Better competitive intelligence and more effective responses
- Ability to see and predict customer behavior
- Tighter cross-organization collaboration
- More effective business processes
- Better partner management
- Tighter controls and improved compliance

Keeping the Big Picture in Focus

As desirable as these business goals are, before you even think about an investment in an SFA/CRM system, you have to think through how you want your organization to change. Putting in an SFDC system without optimizing the sales, marketing, and support business processes means missing a huge opportunity. Instead, you need to consider broader organizational, people, and process goals. Think about how you want to give the revenue engine a tune-up.

In some cases, you may need to completely rebuild your revenue engine, rather than just performing a tune-up. Typically, **a company's most unreliable business process is revenue generation.** This unreliability shows up as erratic forecasts, one-off contracts, excessive discounting, rocky customer satisfaction ratings, weak profitability, and other issues. You wouldn't let your production line be that unreliable. It's time to make your revenue process a consistent, predictable engine—one that's firing on all cylinders. While you're at it, make sure you replace the old carburetor of spreadsheets with the modern fuel injection of SFDC.

Change Management

Like business-level goals, business process changes must be prioritized because you can make only a few real changes during a year's time. Business process changes have too many organizational repercussions if you overdo them—and it's better to have a suboptimal business process that will be fixed soon than a broken one that will stay broken.

The first step for business process work is triage:

- Which two or three business processes will be replaced or rebuilt[1] from the ground up?

- Which business processes will be modified in small ways?

- Which business processes (the vast majority) will be kept the same?

The next step is to make sure that the people below you and in different organizations are committed to making improvements to the two or three business processes that will be undergoing major surgery, *before* you begin. Passive-aggressive resistance can destroy the chances of success, so deal with the political issues up front!

Next, establish baseline metrics of the business process's performance, both in terms of the things that basically work today (e.g., number of transactions, cost per transaction) and the areas that aren't working well (e.g., error rate, number of executive escalations). Don't skimp on these "as-is" metrics, as they become the baseline for your project's return on investment. If you don't know how much the broken process is costing your company, you don't know if some extra investment is a good business decision.

Next, define *achievable* and *meaningful* metrics for how the business process needs to perform. State these "to be" metrics in terms of absolutes (30 transactions per hour) and a percentage improvement (50% more transactions with existing staff), as each form dramatizes the required change in a different way.

---

1. Consolidated, eliminated, or automated.

Setting Metrics of SFDC Success

The metrics of success for your SFDC project will be a mixture of business process improvements and overall business performance. As a member of the executive team, you need to document these goals for the first year of the SFDC project *before* the project starts—and commit to not changing them:

- **Business performance:** a list of the three to four measurements, such as average deal size, customer retention rate, or cost per order.

- **Business process improvements:** a list of perhaps three metrics per business process that will be upgraded during the year.

- **New capability or system functionality:** a *short* list of big-picture items to be added from a business (not technical) perspective, such as "95% of quotes to be reviewed and generated automatically" or "all orders conform to discounting rules." Make the criteria as quantitative as possible.

Each of these goals should be envisioned as providing go/no-go criteria for the acceptance of the SFDC system. If things aren't that clear, change the statement of metrics so they are black-and-white. Note that some goals may work against each other (high growth versus high profitability, profit of support versus customer satisfaction), so make sure that your goals aren't self-contradictory.

It's a best practice for the executives to also set *nongoals:* things you want to avoid, as well as things that you acknowledge aren't economically feasible in the short term. Nongoals will be surprisingly useful to the team—and to you—in project reviews months down the line.

Driving Toward Project Approval

Before the SFDC project even begins, you'll be asked for money and political sponsorship. You need to directly participate in the process, or else appoint a delegate with decision-making power and some budgetary authority.

Championing

Industry analysts universally agree that executive championship is a key success factor for any SFA/CRM project, even while the business case is being prepared. Of course, not all executives are equally effective in filling this role. The best formula is to have the COO/VP of Sales be the champion and driver of the SFDC project. Nevertheless, if the CEO feels very strongly about SFDC, he or she can be an effective champion as well. See Chapter 6 if you want to understand the rationale behind the choice of champion.

To make an SFDC system successful deep within the many layers of a company, *every* executive must take on the following *personal* action items:

- When investing in SFA/CRM functionality, always give the users something that is intrinsically valuable—something that saves them time or makes *them* look smarter—before you ask users to put effort into the system. If individuals (particularly sales folks) don't get anything directly in return, they'll view the system as a burden and a tax—and, not surprisingly, the amount and quality of the data in the system will decline.

- Focus on system *credibility* over system functionality. The fanciest features in the world don't make any difference if they're based on garbage data. Be ready to put some serious time and money[2] into data quality, migration, and integration. In fact, it is almost impossible to spend too much on ensuring data credibility.

- Provide more reasons for users to stay in the system and fewer reasons to work outside it. Make sure to identify key user groups, and keep the team focused on tailoring the system to their needs. The goal is to make outboard spreadsheets and "insurance policy" steps disappear because they're a waste of effort and they prevent you from really seeing what's going on in the organization. The system needs to embody *all* of the steps and data for any business process it supports.

- Build the system incrementally, with features coming in phases rather than being delivered as a "Big Bang." In the implementation project, start small with a tight team and quick wins, grow incrementally, and show value to the business at least every 60 days. You'll asking users to change some of their behaviors for handling customer interactions. Making these changes will be for the better, but it will still take time. Users need time to learn and modify their behaviors if they're going to be really effective SFDC users.

- As an executive, you need to do five things for the SFDC team:

  - ➥ Set the business priorities.

  - ➥ Define the metrics of success.

  - ➥ Provide funding and dedicated staff.

  - ➥ Remove organizational obstacles.

  - ➥ Promote system usage and system users.

---

2. In most SFDC implementations, data massaging accounts for 20–50% of the total system cost—and an even larger percentage if you have a lot of messy historical data spread across several systems.

> ### DO'S AND DON'TS
>
> | *Don't focus on* | *Do focus on* |
> | --- | --- |
> | Technology for its own sake | Business process improvement |
> | Excessive measurement | Change management |
> | Cost control | Revenue/profit increase |

The Business Case

The business case for SFDC is pretty straightforward, at least on the cost side of the equation. On the benefits side, the tricky things to quantify are *opportunity costs*—expenses you can avoid, or lost deals you could win—and the team will need your help with questions like these:

- How much more revenue could you realistically get if you could close the trickiest 1% of customer deals? What about the trickiest 5%?

- What would be the impact of shortening the sales cycle by one week? Would that mean more revenue, or simply reps with more time on their hands?

- What would it mean to the bottom line if marketing could divert 10% of its programs from people who aren't likely to buy and instead spend that money on people who were more likely to buy?

- What would it mean for customer support personnel if they could handle each customer issue with one less phone call?

- What would it mean for your bottom line if customers were 5% more satisfied with your product or service? What would it mean if you achieved a 1% better upsell rate?

- How would it change your business if you could predict customer behavior better? How much more profitable would the company be if the sales forecast were 5% more accurate?

Of course, none of these improvements will be achieved the first day the SFDC system is running. Nevertheless, you want to think about the "big picture" to ensure that the team is pointed in the right direction and the investment you make in the system serves your real business objectives.

Requirements and Priorities

The majority of SFDC customers will need to make significant modifications to the "off-the-shelf" SFA/CRM system before it becomes truly effective for their business. The larger your

SFDC: THE GOLDILOCKS INVESTMENT

Enterprise software has been bedeviled with high costs, delayed deployments, and a surprising amount of outright failure. While nothing is perfect, SFDC is an amazing step forward for successful SFA/CRM deployments.

SFDC is a game-changer not because of features,[3] but because of its *incremental model* that lets you invest *just enough* to make business progress quickly. Once you've done an initial implementation, you can put the SFDC system into production and measure its initial results. From there, you'll rapidly discover the next area where some additional functionality will make a business difference. SFDC incremental improvements can happen in a matter of weeks, so you might even be able to identify and measure at least some benefits in the same quarter you pay for those changes.

This *Agile* style of development and investment makes your business case have a shorter range: it's a "by-the-drink model," rather than the "bet-the-farm model" followed by traditional enterprise software. Beyond a simpler business case, using an incremental style means you avoid investments that aren't really needed and you get increased business flexibility at every stage.

However, this "Goldilocks investment"[4] requires three behavioral changes on your part:

- Investment isn't a one-shot, fire-and-forget-it deal. You need to be more attentive over time to the incremental investment needs.

- You'll get the best results if you are consistent over time about priorities. Of course you have to respond to market and business changes, but excessive changes of direction are likely to be responded to . . . leading to waste.

- That said, don't expect a cast-in-concrete long-term feature roadmap. Decisions are made along the way with the incremental approach, so priorities, schedules, and expected results will change on at least a quarterly basis. If you're really keen on a specific feature, the way to make sure it happens sooner is to invest some of your own budget in it. Check out Chapters 4 and 12 if you want to know more about this topic.

company and the more complex your products and sales cycles, the deeper the modifications will need to go. SFDC makes most modifications really easy to implement and maintain, but don't be fooled: you'll need to invest time and money in the implementation.

While detail-level requirements won't be collected up front, you need to provide overall direction and priorities fogoldir the SFDC project. Which SFA/CRM problems do you need to solve? Which functional areas of the system will your team need to use? How many people will be on the system? Which other systems will need to be integrated with SFDC?

---

3. SFDC's sales reps curse me when I say this.
4. Not too big, not too small, but *just* right.

In stating requirements, do not telegraph a "sky's the limit" perspective. Be incredibly clear about what the "nice to have" features are and what the real priorities are. The biggest enemy of a successful SFA/CRM implementation is unclear or inconsistent priorities.

During the formative stages of the project, a few archetypal users need to be identified and interviewed, so that the system is designed around the needs of real people. It is imperative that the SFDC team interview a few sales reps and a person from order operations so that the user descriptions will reflect your real priorities.

In addition, you'll probably be asked to participate in some brainstorming around reports and dashboards that you *personally* need. At this stage, nobody is trying to design the specifics; they're just trying to see the "big picture" of what you need to drive the ship. This session—maybe 45 minutes huddled around a whiteboard—is intended to help the team understand what you manage to, and which information you need to see on a daily or weekly basis.

THE EXECUTIVE VIEW

What do you need from the SFDC system—*personally*? What is the *one critical report* you need to do your job, and what are the five to seven pieces of information you need (whether in the current system or not) to make key decisions? Here are example questions to think about:

- How often do you look at the SFA/CRM information?
- Why do you look there, and what are you trying to measure?
- How do these data affect the things that *you* are measured on?
- What action do you take on the basis of the data—which decisions do you make?
- What incentives do you have for the people below you to score well according to the metrics?
- If you question the data, how would you validate them? What would you compare the data to?
- If you found an error in the data, who would you talk to about getting the problem fixed?
- Which other items of information would be useful for you (i.e., would actually change your behavior or alter a decision)?
- Which comparisons (e.g., historical, comparative to industry norms) of these data would be meaningful?

Don't spend any time trying to figure out the answer to the question "What would be useful in addition?" The goal is to understand what will *really* make a difference to your decisions. Nail that answer before moving on to cool new ideas.

Terminology and Semantics

As part of your company culture, you have your own terminology for customer interactions, sales management, and marketing programs. One of the key factors for successful SFDC usage and interpretation is establishing a common vocabulary and a well-understood set of semantics for the sales process. Although the executive team shouldn't get bogged down in any of the details, it's amazing how much time can be wasted in a meeting when there isn't a common understanding of the word "customer" or "deal." Answers to all the following questions need to be documented:

- What's a lead, a contact, a sales cycle, and a customer?

- When is a customer no longer a customer?

- What's a partner? What are your channels?

- What are the stages of the sales cycle?

- What are the stages of the customer support cycle?

- What are the trigger events or conditions that move a prospect from one stage of the sales cycle to another, or a customer from one support status to another?

- What is the difference between booked deals and recognized revenues?

- What are the main product and service categories the company offers? Which services do you offer in the form of a product?

Make sure that these definitions are nailed down and agreed to by *all* departments early in the SFDC project.

Resource Commitments

When the management decision is made to go for SFDC, the company will be committing money to the project. *Every executive* who has any plans to leverage the system will need to be dedicating some time on the part of his or her staff to make sure that the system actually meets the organization's needs. Great systems happen only with the participation of people who care and put the time into the following tasks:

- Clearly spelling out the details of requirements and understanding the repercussions of decisions and tradeoffs

- Making sure that data are properly interpreted and prepared for the new system

- Identifying business rules and thinking through business processes, to make sure that they are unambiguously documented

- Reviewing user interface screens to make sure they're clean, clear, and usable

- Helping design reports and dashboards that highlight the issues that management really cares about

- Participating in acceptance testing of the system, while paying particular attention to the meaning and accuracy of results

Make sure that the right people on your team are assigned goals and dedicate time—your entire organization will benefit dramatically from the right level of participation.

Once the Project Is Under Way

As soon as the SFDC project starts, the team will come to you asking for your department's time—including some of your own time. The sections that follow cover things to expect during the project (particularly during the first quarter or two).

Detailed Requirements

Throughout the project, the SFDC team will need access to knowledgeable individuals in your organization to drill into the detailed requirements and "rules of the road" for the system. Fortunately, the team won't be asking for a bunch of time or effort—and every hour you invest has the potential to yield *very high leverage*. You will get better results faster if you make this small investment to ensure the team is building the things your organization really needs.

The implementation team needs three kinds of input, usually from three different levels in your organization:

- **Business process and policy knowledge.** This information lies at the heart of how your company does business, and the SFDC team will sometimes need to know the *why* behind a procedure or a tradeoff. This level of information is usually best obtained from a fairly senior manager in your organization.

- **Details about how things really work or how they need to change.** These data consist of the standard operating procedures, the wrinkles, and the exception-handling procedures that make everything really go. This level of information will usually come from people who have been around a while, but who work near the bottom of the organization.

- **The meaning and behavior of data.** This information consists of knowledge about data models, semantics, interactions, and integrations among systems. This level of information is best known by quasi-IT people (employees or consultants) in your organization, with titles like Business Analyst, System Administrator, Data Specialist, or Application Architect.

Business Process Changes

Although it's called an SFA system, SFDC is not focused solely on automating sales. In reality, the system is very flexible and powerful, and it can be the basis for making business process improvements in nearly every customer-facing aspect of your business. An SFDC system doesn't just speed things up; it helps you change the *way* you do business. Done right, SFDC can become the basis of competitive advantage and industry leadership.[5]

In thinking about business process changes, it's important to push the implementation team to follow these "Top Ten Best Practices":

1. **Focus on things that matter to the customer.** These issues should speed up the sales cycle or noticeably improve customer interactions. Don't let things get ridiculously complicated or let perfectionism creep in. Combine individual steps to make the process more sensible and systematic. The goal is to eliminate activities that are clumsy, out of order, patchwork solutions, or work-arounds.

2. **Work on a few high-leverage processes that are naturally linked.** Don't try to "boil the ocean." Fix things that are naturally related, not disparate elements from across the organization.

3. **Validate business rules.** First, make sure they're still relevant and meaningful. The *single most highly leveraged thing* you can do in business process reengineering is to eliminate obsolete or redundant rules, policies, or standards. If you must have a complex set of rules, make sure they provide something of beauty or value *to the customer*, rather than just avoiding a hypothetical negative.

4. **Remove paper from the process.** As innocent as paper might appear, it is nearly always indicative of wasted time, increased error rates, and manual labor. Many organizations still use manual data entry—from data on paper—to link data across business processes. Replacing paper with on-screen steps and system integration will lower costs, save time, and increase professionalism. The on-screen updates will make the workflows much easier to monitor, measure, and improve over time.

5. **Increase information sharing.** While being mindful of security and compliance issues, sharing information is the first step to effective collaboration. Better collaboration means faster identification of problems and unintended consequences, while creating more meaningful measurements at every level of the organization.

6. **Bake in measurements and thresholds.** These points of reference foster ongoing improvement. If there is a clear metric that is meaningful to the customer (e.g., "How long did it take for us to get back to the customer about a problem?"), add thresholds, alerts, and automatic escalations to the new process so that management can see problem areas before they boil over.

---

5. The SFDC sales reps love it when I say this. And it's true.

7. **Minimize manual exceptions.** While human judgment is what sets great businesses apart, exceptions need to be handled in a methodical way in your business processes. MBE forces you to systematize and streamline how you handle 95%[6] or more of the business process. Not every step of the exception-handling procedure can be automated, but the entire exceptions process should still be systematized and measured so that the organization doesn't spend too much time on the unusual cases.

8. **Optimize globally.** Keep your eye out for suboptimization and siloed thinking. Discourage "over-the-transom" behaviors because they don't help anybody and they usually hurt the customer. The point is to make the *entire system* (your company) work better, faster, and more pleasantly for the customer. That said, expect to find significant business process variations in your international operations, and know that the SFDC system will need to accommodate them.

9. **Keep it practical and immediate.** Even though business process engineering has to consider big-picture effects, focus your energy on improvements that can be measured in the here and now.

10. **Ask for workflows.** The whole point of BPM improvement is streamlining and workflows. By having a clear delineation of business processes, you establish metrics and thresholds for what's normal and what's a variance. In the SFDC system, business process workflows may be triggered by deadlines, customer actions, and thresholds. These workflows free up people from the mindless tedium of repetitive actions and allow them to start managing by exception. Workflows also make the important parts of your business more measurable.

The Touchy Side of Business Processes

Some of the requirements you'll be asked about imply business process changes. Ideally, the SFDC team will focus on improving a small number of business processes, rather than fostering a wholesale replacement. Refining or streamlining an existing business process involves a lot less stress and uncertainty than starting from scratch. Plus, if you are upgrading a business process that exists, it is easier to establish valid (and achievable) comparative metrics (e.g., 20% fewer errors or 10% decrease in labor costs).

There can be a lot of politics involved with a big business process change. In some cases, you'll be changing the daily tasks of workers—or even changing their jobs entirely. The uncertainty inherent in this kind of change can lead to a lot of questions, endless meetings,

---

6. The 95% value represents a two-sigma standardized process. In sales and marketing, anything beyond four-sigma (99%) automation almost always involves ridiculous investment, so the best bang for the buck in SFDC-relevant business processes is somewhere between 95% and 99% automation.

and user resistance—even if the workers are given orders from on high. You may even want to include HR issues in your thinking if jobs are going to be redesigned in a big way.

Sponsorship and Escalation Path

Probably *the* critical success factor in any SFA/CRM project is strong executive sponsorship—from day one—that propels the implementation team and the end users into action.

In prioritizing and trading off requirements, the SFDC project leader will need a set of executive sponsors who can act as champions for the project when political and resource issues arise. For project success, the champions *must* include the VP of Sales, but will also usually include the VP of Marketing, the CFO, and perhaps even the CEO. Championship is about making sure resource commitments and policy changes happen, so this responsibility can't be delegated very far down the organizational hierarchy. Fortunately, filling the champion role probably requires only a couple of hours per month for the key VPs.

As the project champion, you'll also need to break logjams on escalated issues. Because the SFDC implementation team will work fast, it will really make a difference whether you resolve issues this week versus next. Team members won't ask for your intervention often, but when an issue is escalated your way, please respond quickly.

Management Council

The corporate VPs cannot afford the time to personally participate in the SFDC project, but the team will need access to some senior knowledge and judgment on a regular basis. You will need to deputize a senior person on your staff to be a regular participant within the SFDC implementation team. The SFDC project leader will form a management council of these deputies to make priority calls, policy decisions, and tradeoffs. For simplicity of voting, the team needs to be small and contain an odd number of people (including the SFDC product manager). A small management council would include representatives from sales and marketing, plus the project leader. A larger council might add representatives from finance, customer care, international operations, professional services, channel operations, and business analytics. This council will need to hold *brief* meetings on a weekly basis.

The management council will probably need to handle most escalations. With luck, at least 80% of escalated issues can be decided there, but sometimes budgetary or policy variances will require the intervention of the sponsoring VP.

Team Members

Some individuals in the organization will need to devote significant time to the tasks mentioned in Chapter 1's "Getting the Right Resources Committed" section. These team members will be charged with delivering documents and making binding decisions at a detail level, so you'll want to assign individuals who know their stuff. Their effort on the team needs to be part of their "day jobs," so you need to dedicate a portion of their schedule and allocate some of their personal goals (MBOs) to this endeavor during the months of their project involvement.

Project Reviews

As an executive, you've been trained to look for a budget that's firm and a schedule that has a clear end-date. Unfortunately, large systems projects don't fit that model too often. High degrees of command and control just don't work with software projects. Also, Agile project management—which focuses on high-speed, quality deliveries of only features that are really needed—can create a frustrating uncertainty about exactly what will be delivered when. You need to give the project leader a little wiggle room so that he or she can deliver what matters, sooner.

SFA/CRM systems and processes must be highly adaptable to evolving business needs, so they are *never* implemented with a predetermined and fixed architecture the way a building would be constructed. Focus your attention on the cutover ("go live") date for the features your organization needs, and emphasize the absolute minimum acceptance criteria that must be met to achieve the go-live goal. Most significant SFDC implementations are replacements for previous systems, and it should be fairly straightforward to identify the criteria needed for the new system to be "good enough" to support the switchover. It is important to use terms like "good enough" or "acceptance criteria" to communicate the understanding that the system will continue to improve after the go-live date. In many areas, the company will need only 80% of the SFDC system's functionality on day one to support the business.

As always, perfectionism does not pay. By focusing the discussion on what is *really* needed to support a given business process on a day-to-day basis, you can get make realistic decisions and tradeoffs. For example, it might be acceptable to *manually* approve orders for the first month of operation, so as to double-check that the system's automatic order approval rules accurately reflect the business requirements.

Project Deliveries

Agile projects focus on frequent delivery of functionality, so that something of value is made available to the business **twice a quarter.** That doesn't mean that *your* organization will get wonderful new features all the time, but *somebody* in the corporation will get an important improvement on a regular basis.

When a new feature is being delivered to one of your groups, it's important that employees participate in its final testing (to make sure they're getting exactly what they need) and receive appropriate training. The training sessions will be short and nondisruptive, and they will save your employees a lot of time and misunderstanding. Make *sure* your organization knows that training is mandatory.

WHY CFOS SHOULD LOVE AGILE PROJECTS

Agile projects on the surface may look disorganized and chaotic. But let's face it, *all* large software projects tend toward disorganization and chaos—the Agile methodology just surfaces that reality. In doing so, Agile projects also make for *more efficient spending*, for the following reasons:

- They don't make big, long-term resource commitments. They spend in small chunks on the things that are most highly valued by the business at the time.

- Less-certain elements fail fast, rather than mushrooming into cost and schedule nightmares. If something isn't going to work out or won't be worth the effort, you'll know sooner; as a consequence, investment in that area will be abandoned earlier than with traditional software models.

- Agile projects give visibility sooner to the real costs and real benefits of a project or feature.

- Agile projects ruthlessly avoid features for which there is no passionate user or customer. Nice-to-have features are implemented only when they will be *used*. Perfectionism is almost unheard of in Agile projects.

Of course, SFDC is still software, which suffers from the "iceberg phenomenon": the toughest work in the project relates to infrastructure and data cleanup that has no visible feature, no immediate "win" for any department. Nevertheless, this infrastructure effort (particularly at the beginning of the SFDC project) lays the foundation for the features that will benefit the company as a whole. Solid, reliable data—which will give you visibility and automation you need—don't come for free.

Deployments and the Adoption Cycle

Success rates for SFA systems are generally quite low: most industry analyst surveys show that less than 50% of SFA projects are deemed a success by management. A core reason for this low percentage is that any SFA product—even if perfectly implemented—is only a tool with little intrinsic value. Without users and accurate data, SFDC will remain just an empty shell.

Clearly, getting users happily on board—and developing the value of the information asset—is more important than implementing any particular set of SFA product features. The single most important thing for you to do is to stimulate adoption and usage of SFDC, to get people on the bandwagon so that the system becomes a valuable data asset.

Your *personal* behavior over the entire deployment sequence really counts. Everyone must get the unambiguous message that SFDC is important to *you* and the way you want

> ## THE ENEMY: SCOPE CREEP
>
> Scope creep is one of the most dangerous things that can happen to any software project, and the danger grows with the size and length of the effort. The problem occurs whenever a requirement is stretched, an assumption is made that "we can fit that in," or an executive proposes an *even better idea*.
>
> The key warning sign of scope creep: the requirements list grows while the project is under way. Because items aren't removed from the list, the number of deliverables grows even though the budget and schedule remain unchanged (or worse, aren't being achieved by the project). When the project runs into trouble and needs a schedule or budget extension, there's a particular temptation to load up the requirements even further, even though it should be obvious the project is already at risk of under-delivering.
>
> Your behavior as an executive is a key part of the solution for scope creep. Don't let your staff propose new requirements without demoting or eliminating existing requirements. If you sense that some other VP is letting new requirements creep in, call him or her on it.

to do business. Your team knows you, and can read your nonverbal messages about what you *really* think. A few words carelessly thrown around when you're stressed out can set SFDC adoption back by months.

In addition to your consistent personal support, there must be a proactive "good news" campaign touting the SFDC system almost from day one.

Executive Mandates

As delivery of SFDC features begins, put some mandates in place so that your organization gets the right big-picture orientation about the system:

- The SFDC system is what executives will use as their only source for information about customer relationships. If other systems contain customer data (such as warranty registration), they'll need to be integrated with SFDC over time so that the company achieves a 360-degree view of the customer.

- SFDC is *not* to be used as a spying machine or micromanagement tool. You will not listen to people who try to use it that way, or who are trying to game the system for personal or political gain.

- The SFDC system is to be used as the command center or virtual war room for winning accounts and keeping customers happy. The data entered into the system need to be good enough to drive real decisions and allocate resources.

- SFDC is supposed to eliminate excessive emails, data reentry, and forgotten action items. Show users that requests made via email are given lower priority than requests made through the SFDC system.

- Paper reports and spreadsheets generated outside of SFDC will not be acceptable for use in management meetings. It's acceptable to "pretty up" the format of SFDC data, but it is not okay to prepare external spreadsheets independently of the official, system-of-record data.

- The organization will move toward an MBE policy, which means routine decisions should be handled "in process." People should be able to handle 90% of the work without invoking manual work-arounds or unusual decisions. SFDC's alerts, thresholds, workflows, and reports should be used to handle normal situations, and to automatically flag or escalate the unusual cases.

- The company is to be a learning organization, and you expect things to improve incrementally and consistently. SFDC follows that philosophy by delivering changes in increments, and adapting to feedback along the way. If problems occur, you expect feedback to be delivered candidly to the SFDC team, so that they can adjust and do better. Sniping does no good for anyone.

ADOPTION SEQUENCE

In an SFDC system rollout, there is a preferred sequence of user adoption that may seem quite counterintuitive: inside sales and marketing first, outside sales last.

Even though the phasing of the rollout is fairly fast (almost always within the same quarter), you probably wonder why the executive suite and other high-priority roles in the company come so late to the SFDC system. Why aren't they first?

The answer: data credibility and reliability are the foundation for adoption of SFDC. Anything that undermines system credibility—including having a user work the system before it's ready—must be avoided. When you've got a new system (or a cutover from an old, unreliable one), the quality, completeness, and relevance of the data in the system just aren't good enough during the early stages of the implementation. It takes a while for the data assets in SFDC to ripen to the point where you can bet the farm on them.

So hang on. You'll be getting the cool new stuff as soon as it's got the solidity you expect.

Adoption Metrics

The executive team should set up adoption metrics early on in the project, so that the organization can know how well the system is being accepted. Because you can't fix what you don't measure, make sure that the metrics you establish are *meaningful to the business*, rather than being trivial data points (e.g., the number of people who logged in to the SFDC system last week).

Here are examples of meaningful adoption metrics that should be used to judge SFDC acceptance and success:

- Number of times the average person logged in during the week

- Percentage of deals that have any meaningful data attached to them

- Percentage of deals that have complete data attached to them

- Average length of time since deals had an update to the data

- Percentage of "error-free" records

- Percentage of fields that are erroneous

- Percentage of users who are "totally into the system," "average users," and "Luddites" (resisters)

- Percentage of executives who trust the data in the system versus those who distrust the data or think the data are meaningless or misleading

The Politics of System Adoption

Unfortunately, some people will inevitably look for any excuse not to use the SFDC system. They will jump at the chance to criticize it, and will point to others' criticism as the basis for not bothering to log in. Your support is a key success factor in overcoming resistance.

Use both carrots and sticks to motivate the users. If you are an SFDC executive champion, clearly articulate why the system is important to the way you do business.

Champions

The champions of the system are the single most important force in driving SFDC usage, because it is their will and budget that make the system happen in the first place. It is also their organizational clout and enthusiasm that drive *fast* adoption.

It is incredibly important for champions to act consistently about SFDC, and to show people through their behavior that they will be depending on the system for their success. They need to say how often they'll rely on its data and reports to run management meetings. They need to have a dashboard named after them, and have that dashboard appear on the home screen of their organization. See Chapters 9 through 13 for more best practices in this area.

The champion should create a sequence of milestones for meetings that will depend on SFDC data and reports. For example, if the system will initially go live in January, the champion should ask that all lead reports at executive staff be based on the system by March, that all opportunity lists be driven off the system by April, and that all forecasting and pipeline reports be based only on SFDC data by May. As the year unfolds, the champion should issue an email stipulating that no deal will be discussed at any level of management review unless it is in the SFDC system first. Later, an email from this executive should clarify the requirement that deals won't be reviewed unless their SFDC data have been updated within the last two weeks. By *incrementally* and *repeatedly* emphasizing the importance of the system to every level of the management chain, the champion cements the right kind of thinking and behavior about SFDC.

It's incredibly important to maintain the illusion of the inevitability of system usage. It takes only a few negative or ambivalent words from the champion to halt the system's positive momentum. Rumors fly fast, and any frustration expressed by the champion will get around. When the misinformation shows up in a report or dashboard, the champion must have the discipline to say, "This information is no good. I rely on my team to keep the data in SFDC accurate and timely, and I don't want to see this happen again." If in a moment of frustration the champion says something like, "This system is no damn good—I can't use this garbage," the champion will be setting back SFDC adoption by months.

SETTING EXPECTATIONS FOR PERFORMANCE

SFDC is a hosted application, which means that none of the computing work is done within your company. SFDC spends millions every year to make sure its systems are reliable and perform on a 24 × 365 basis.

While the SFDC system has had virtually zero unplanned downtime for the last three years, there are planned (and carefully preannounced) maintenance windows. These windows are typically 4 hours long and occur during weekend evenings once every 6 weeks or so. Almost all customers have no problem coping with these maintenance windows, but if you have eCommerce or other 24 × 365 supporting systems, you need to make provisions for these interruptions.

SFDC's system responsiveness is consistently very good around the world, and the company proves it by publishing the measurements right on its Web site (http://trust.salesforce.com). While Google may look faster, that company isn't trying to do the customer-specific complex calculations that SFDC has to perform on every page.

However, if your network is busy, SFDC's screen updates may seem to take forever. If you hear noise along these lines, upgrading your company's internal network is the quick and easy fix. In most cases, you really needed to make the upgrade anyway, and SFDC usage just becomes the forcing function.

Sticks

Upper management always has the power to issue mandates. Of course, it is all too easy to issue overly grandiose management commands or to use sticks too early, only to have them be dismissed by workers as "another thing those executives will forget about next month." Obviously, this you need to avoid.

Because the SFDC system will be delivered incrementally, "sticks"—commands and requirements—should also be doled out gradually. In the very early days of the SFDC project, the system will not be functionally complete and—worse—it won't contain much interesting data. The trick is to get users on the system doing *something* that will add to the system data asset as a *natural part of their jobs*. The user representatives on the implementation team will find a part of the business process to serve as the beachhead for SFDC users. Once this step in the business process is identified, management should mandate that the users change to the new behavior on a specific date. After a few weeks, more user steps should be added to the mandatory SFDC activity.

Only after SFDC has the required functionality, data volume, and data quality to be a reliable asset should the big sticks come out. Any penalties (such as "No commission on deals will be paid unless . . .") should **not be even hinted** at for the first six months of system usage.

Carrots

"Carrots" are positive incentives for people to use the SFDC system. Carrots are typically more powerful and reliable than many of the sticks described in the preceding section.

The first carrots come from organizational incentives: procedures or activities that are more easily performed by using the system than by not using it. For example, if your sales team needs loaner equipment or travel authorization, make it easier to get these resources approved through the system than the old way. Management should make it clear that action items presented to them as SFDC tasks will be handled sooner and more predictably than requests presented by email or voicemail. Not surprisingly, users will rapidly acquire new habits when they realize you will stick to your guns.

The next carrots come from rewards. After the first few weeks, you can start contests with rewards and recognition for the users with the best data, the most frequent logins, and the most complete customer records. Make these contests and incentives as relevant to your business objectives as possible—awards for meaningless system metrics are about as lame as the ones for "tidiest office cube" or "most recycled coffee cups."

The last bunch of carrots comprises the benefits that are intrinsic to SFDC system usage: the users discover that by doing things through the system, they save time and streamline onerous tasks. These carrots become more important as the system becomes more functionally complete and has workflows, integrations, and data that make it *the* optimal way to carry out a task. When you discover some good news in this area, make sure to send out emails touting these highly leveraged behaviors, so that people can see the effects on their personal productivity.

After Deployment: Using SFDC to Help Drive the Ship

Once the SFDC system's data asset has become solid thanks to greater usage, it will serve as a key management tool. In addition to delivering good metrics on internal activities, it represents the repository for your customer intelligence. The system can be the command center for customer relationships—and here are best practices for how to use it in this role.

Be Careful What You Ask For

In a system with as much data and reporting as SFDC, it's easy to ask for things and get a nice-looking dashboard—and get it in short order. Unfortunately, you could ask for lots of meaning-less data on this dashboard, and subordinates aren't likely to say no to your requests.

For example, it's easy to ask for the number of leads each week. But leads are like Web site traffic: they are better indicators of visibility and vague interest than they are of a solid pipeline. Further, activity management indicators (such as "number of dials" or "customer support call volume") are very easy to "game," and the numbers won't mean anything.

Here are the best indicators of business health, particularly when compared over time:

Marketing

- Number of fully qualified or converted leads
- Number of converted leads accepted by sales
- Percentage of leads converted
- Percentage of free trials that converted
- Percentage of nonresponsive or stale leads

Sales

- Percentage of reps logging in on a weekly basis
- Number of sales cycles started
- Number of quotes issued
- Average time in stage (or, alternatively, number of stalled deals)
- Percentage of wins, losses, and no-decisions
- Number of new customers
- Average deal size, for new customers versus repeat customers

- Percentage repeat business
- Percentage renewals/retained customers

Pipeline

- Forecast sales versus quarterly goal
- Actual bookings versus weekly expected achievement[7]
- Percentage of opportunities "moving backward" (decreasing in size or probability, or moving out in time)
- Number and dollar value of disappearing opportunities (deals dropping out of the quarter, plus losses)
- Forecast accuracy
- Number and value of unforecasted deals

Customer Support

- Number of new problems identified
- Number of problems solved
- Customer-perceived "time to resolve"
- Percentage of satisfied customers
- Number of highly dissatisfied customers

Customer Base

- Cost of customer acquisition
- Percentage of revenue coming from repeat business
- Percentage of customer base that's still active/current
- Customer lifetime revenue
- Customer lifetime profitability[8]
- Customer loyalty

---

7. This statistic tells management, "By week 4 of the quarter, we normally expect 20% of the total target to be closed; this quarter, we have only 15% closed."
8. It is important that you look at this figure over time, not as a snapshot. If you decide to get rid of your least profitable customers without making changes to your company's overhead, you'll instantly create a new batch of customers who look unprofitable.

THINK ABOUT USERS BEFORE ASKING . . .

It's easy to ask for reports that you won't actually use, but it's *dangerous* to ask for reports that you *will* use to bad effect.

Before you ask the reps to enter any more data (which they'll view as a tax and an intrusion), figure out what you would *do differently* if you already had the report in front of you. Which decisions would you *actually* make differently? If you're just curious or not sure what you'd do differently, **don't ask** the reps to enter anything new.

If you ask the reps to do something new, walk a mile in their shoes first. Top-down edicts with measurements and incentives practically guarantee attempts to game the system, particularly if the edicts have clear penalties or rewards. If you're going to lay down the law, make sure that gaming the system carries the biggest penalties of all.

When reps game the system, it not only undermines SFDC's credibility (and data integrity), but also insidiously undermines *your* authority. Don't open the door to this behavior.

Don't get too fancy with the analytics too early. They scare the employees, and besides, half the time the data aren't any good early during the system implementation process. Gradually add a new report, dashboard, or analytic every six weeks or so.

SFDC also has a set of dashboards that can give you a great personal overview of the data. There's one key caveat: *any time* you see a Refresh button on a dashboard screen, click it! Dashboards are the only part of the system that do *not* display data in real time, so the information will be misleading if you haven't refreshed it recently.

Forecasting

SFDC is a real-time system that allows forecasts to be run at any time. For most companies, a weekly forecasting cycle is all that's needed. The forecasting cycle typically starts on Thursday evening (when the individual reps put in their commit numbers) and continues with a multilevel review and refinement process that culminates in a consolidated forecast ready for executive review on Monday morning. As discussed at length in Chapter 9, it is imperative that *all* qualitative and quantitative information about the forecast be stored in SFDC, and *only* in SFDC.

SFDC is the natural place to run sales forecasts, and there is no reason to look outside the system for *bookings* forecast information. When it comes to accounting data (adhering to Generally Accepted Accounting Principles [GAAP]) and *revenue* forecasts, however, you must look to the financial system for the best data. Only that forecasting system has the revenue recognition, inventory allocation, reserve accounts, and other special logic and calculations needed to prepare an accurate worldwide forecast of all channels' revenues.

We recommend that this bifurcation of forecasting roles be maintained: the SFDC system for bookings (which is usually what sales and marketing use to manage things) and the financial system for revenues (which is what the executive staff and the board need to see). Of course, the SFDC bookings forecast will need to feed into the revenue forecast, but the financial forecast should *not* be pushed back into the SFDC system. In addition to keeping things simpler, this division of roles ensures that only those with a need to know have access to the corporate financial forecast.

Executive Meetings

No one will ever run an executive staff meeting exclusively from an SFDC screen. Nevertheless, it is a best practice to have a couple of dashboards and reports that are available for executives first thing on Monday morning. Most management teams prefer that this kind of information be delivered on paper, but most of the power of these summaries is best delivered in color. Most color printers are slow, and color copiers are fairly expensive. If you want the report printed nicely, make sure that some lucky executive assistant produces these materials on Sunday night or early Monday morning.

Many executives have presbyopia, which makes the fine print of an HTML report unreadable. For ease of reading and nice formatting, SFDC reports should typically be exported to Excel, where they can be made far more legible using simple macros. Although it may take a while to get everything just right, these reports can be reproduced by clicking two buttons every week. Make sure that a lucky executive assistant knows where to find those two buttons, and is made responsible for printing the spreadsheets in preparation for your management meeting.

If the executive staff meeting takes minutes, any sales or customer-related items should be documented in SFDC records. SFDC's Notes area allows for notes to be made private, so that prying eyes won't see confidential remarks.

Compliance

Although SFDC is almost never the system of record for accounting or other auditable and regulated data, it does hold sensitive information and feeds business processes that draw government and legal attention.

Of particular interest are the Sarbanes-Oxley Act business process requirements relating to information controls and revenue forecasts. SFDC has very fine-grained access controls to make sure that only the right people can see certain fields, and that an even narrower group of people can make changes to sensitive data. SFDC also has workflows that can be configured to ensure that forecasts are modified by authorized people only, and that closed deals cannot be modified by anyone except individuals in the finance organization.

As a matter of best practices, you should deliberately discourage anyone in the organization from sending deal-related internal emails with any real content. The critical information should reside in the SFDC system, which serves as the central repository of all things customer—for all the authorized people to see. Emails have no inherent controls for (1) what's in the message, (2) when the email will be read or acted on, or (3) who will see the email (via random forwarding). SFDC's controls and workflows guarantee that the right people will have access to all the key data, while reducing the amount of internal email about current deals and customer situations.

Essential Tools for the Executive

If you are a hands-on executive and want to be quickly able to get information for individual customers, there's a nice tool for you. SFDC's Mobile edition lets you find key information right on your smartphone (BlackBerry, Palm, Microsoft Mobile, and iPhone) in real time. If you need this kind of information and access without having to lug a laptop around, take a look at the Mobile edition. In addition to the instant access it provides, the mobile support has great "wow value" with customers.

Most executives don't need to enter or modify data; instead, they want to see reports, dashboards, and scorecards for the organization. When sophisticated reports and analytics are desired, SFDC reports will typically be supplemented by outboard systems such as data warehousing, business intelligence, and scorecarding systems. It will take several months for SFDC's underlying data, integration process, and outboard databases to sufficiently mature to make such analysis worthwhile. Talk to your business analysts to get the analytics you need.

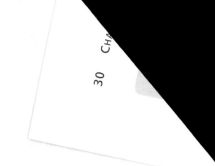

CHAPTER 1

Planning Ahead

"Intangible results" is just another way of saying "poor planning."

—Anonymous

T HIS CHAPTER IS INTENDED for executives, decision makers, business analysts, and project leaders who need to make decisions, set expectations properly, and budget the time, money, and people for an SFDC project. Readers will learn how to make planning decisions that give them the best chance of success and the quickest possible failure recovery.

Getting to Business Value

A truly effective Salesforce.com (SFDC) system can dramatically improve your business results in terms of customer satisfaction, executive decision making, smooth partner/channel interactions, and, of course, sales. But the benefits of increased visibility, streamlined operations, and faster cash-to-cash cycles are anything but automatic. The whole reason for this book is to guide you through a series of choices and actions to get you the best results with the least amount of cost, delay, and risk.

One of the key success factors in any sales force automation and customer relationship management (SFA/CRM) project is strong executive sponsorship that propels the implementation team and the end users. You'll want to check out Chapter 6 to learn about the best sponsors for your company's situation—but here we'll assume that you already have an executive with fire in his or her belly.

Peter Drucker wrote that the most important part of solving a business problem is a well-formed question. The same is true here: the best way to achieve results quickly is to clearly articulate and prioritize goals. This chapter focuses on understanding the requirements, schedules, and costs that are involved in completing any SFDC project successfully. You'll want to make sure the entire team understands the business drivers and the tradeoffs that will shape your SFDC implementation, its integration with surrounding systems, and the instantiation of business processes that will streamline the way your business runs.

Developing a Model of Your Customer Relationship

SFA/CRM applications are designed to improve the speed of acquiring new customers and to achieve the highest amount of revenue or profits from accounts, thereby raising the customer lifetime value. Before you start detailed planning for any SFA/CRM project, you need to develop a model for how your organization works, showing the basic organizational ownership for each stage of the customer cycle. Figure 1-1 depicts the customer cycle, showing how a company converts the initial investment in marketing and sales to a completed, invoiced order. In developing the customer cycle for your company, you'll need to identify which groups are responsible for each of these stages. Make sure the relevant groups have basic agreement on "who does what" to double-check your model.

Note the dashed lines at the qualifying, delivering/servicing, and upselling stages: these lines are meant to indicate where the current customer cycle "breaks"—where conversion or retention ratios tend to be too low, or where organizations squabble and opportunities fall through the cracks. It is very common to have breakage points in these three stages, but every organization is different and you should identify the perceived breakage points for your organization as early as possible in the project.

The right-hand side of the customer cycle is the sales cycle, in which sales and marketing activities generate all your company's revenues. Because the sales cycle is the principal domain of an SFA/CRM system like SFDC, you'll need to have a detailed model of what the sales cycle stages are, who "owns" them, how long they take, and what the conversion ratios at each step are expected to be. Figure 1-2 illustrates an example sales cycle for a business-to-business (B2B) direct sales operation.

The sales cycle may be viewed as a "waterfall" showing the conversion steps for each stage of the cycle. The diagram shows who owns each stage, what the expected conversion ratios are, and how much time each stage takes. Make sure that both sales and marketing executives concur with the basic data and relationships within this waterfall early in the project. Find out which stages represent the biggest problems and where the executives believe the SFA/CRM can help them the most.

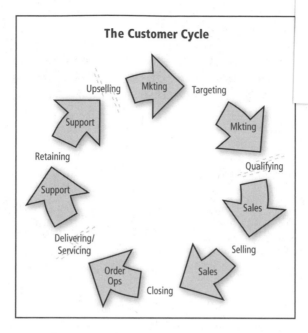

FIGURE 1-1   The customer cycle

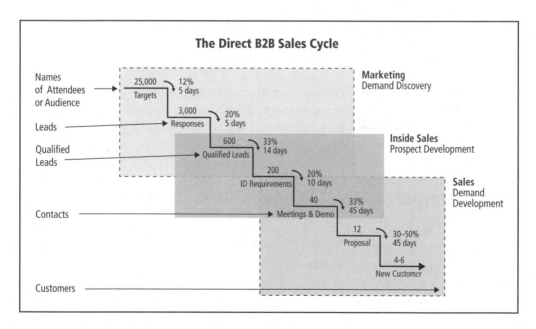

FIGURE 1-2   The direct B2B sales cycle (*Source: DOTnet Consulting, Inc. and Serious Decisions, Inc.*)

Setting Business Goals

Before you drill down into any of the details, it's important to define a set of business goals that transcend individual requirements. These goals are best stated as numerical performance objectives[1] that are not currently being achieved but are easily communicated to executives, such as these examples:

- Improving calls-per-day to 55

- Shortening the sales cycle by two weeks

- Increasing the conversion or close rate by 20%

- Lowering the cost of customer acquisition by 15%

- Increasing the average order size by $10,000

- Increasing revenues by 20%

- Increasing gross profitability by 10%

- Improving customer retention to 80%

- Increasing customer lifetime value by 10%

- Decreasing customer service complaints by 30%

- Decreasing incorrect orders to 1%

Of course, you can't have everything. Keep the list as short as politically feasible. But no matter how many metrics there are, upper management *must* prioritize them. These figures of merit will be important touchstones for prioritizing the features and process changes that will be done in the course of the SFDC implementation.

Setting Requirements: Who, Where, What, and Why

To make the business case for the SFDC project, you'll need to identify and prioritize requirements at an overview level. Even though the details of many individual requirements can't be known until several weeks or even months after the project go-ahead, you will need to have enough information to scope the cost and assess the benefits. You can't sell the project to management without identifying specific, concrete **pain points and potential advantages.**

---

1. Avoid vague or overly qualitative goals like "improve collaboration" or "gain visibility." This kind of goal statement is too mushy to drive a business decision.

The first step in requirements setting is to identify who will (and who won't) need to use the future SFDC system. It's easy to say "everybody," but that decision can mean big implementation, training, and ongoing costs. Worse, it means trying to make "everybody" happy, even if those people aren't critical users. In most companies, only a few departments directly touch the customer every day, so many people won't need direct access to the SFDC system. It's far better to have a narrow list of users, at least initially.

Create a spreadsheet with a list of user names, including the user's organization, job title, location, contact information, and expected SFDC interactions. From this list of users, group together the people who are expected to have similar SFDC interactions. Each of these types of user represents an *actor* (sometimes called a *persona*) in the system. For each of these archetypal actors, create a one-page description that provides overview information about them: location, educational level, job title, job responsibilities, preferences, habits, language, and so on. Almost any SFDC implementation will involve at least four actors, but this number will multiply quickly in large companies. To keep the number of actors to a reasonable level (more than 10 can be unmanageable), you'll probably need to generalize across similar actors. Descriptions of actors should cover their general *role and goals* in using the system: how often (and how long) they are expected to be on the system, what they are trying to achieve, which parts of the system they use, what they need to avoid, and what they expect in terms of usability (for example, users might need to do their job on a laptop while they're on the road).

Later in the project, team members will want to interview representative actors to get detailed requirements and feedback on the system. For now, however, these one-page summaries help provide some reality and context to the planning process. It's a good idea to give each actor a nickname and include a small photo on the description page to make the user seem more real. Log on to the *Salesforce.com Secrets of Success* book Web site (www.SFDC-secrets.com) to download a template Actor document.

Going beyond the list of people who will actually touch the system, it's important to create a list of people who will have an indirect dependence on the system. These individuals may never log in, but they will depend on some report or data flow that comes from the system. You don't really need to create a full persona description for these individuals (or roles), but it is important to understand which requirements they have for the system (e.g., a distribution center manager who might need the system to be fully operational on Saturdays, even if no users are logged in to it).

Get management involved early in the decisions regarding "how far do we want to go"— not the detailed requirements, but the general objective. Identify the executive champion, and engage that person in the process (see Chapters 4 and 5 for more on this topic). Use the SFA Maturity Model Level descriptions from Chapter 5 to guide this decision, which will provide an overall "scoping" of the project investment. Also go through the SFA Maturity Model questions in Chapter 5 to understand your organizational readiness, and note which actors are part of particularly advanced or immature organizations. In your project planning, avoid over-reaching! It kills both budgets and the likelihood of project success.

DO YOU NEED TO CALL IN OUTSIDE HELP?

This chapter assumes that the reader is part of a team that will be doing the project on their own. Many companies choose this path, but you should consider whether you need advisory help early on to prepare the business case, prioritize requirements, understand the implications of alternatives, and give guidance. The right advisor can save your company a bunch of time and money by avoiding blind alleys.

Consider an outside expert if you're feeling uncomfortable with the topics here or are looking for industry best practices from day one. An outsider can help you answer the following types of questions:

- What are your competitors doing with SFA and CRM? What's the customer expecting in this area?
- Which departments should be using the SFA/CRM system, and which ones really shouldn't?
- What are the high-payoff business processes to streamline, and which should be left alone (see Chapter 8 for more on this topic)?
- Should you try to enhance your existing SFA/CRM system, or should you do a wholesale replacement of it?
- What are the quantitative payoffs for your industry peers of a solid SFA/CRM system?
- What are the lessons learned and pitfalls to avoid in SFA/CRM projects for a company like yours?

Before you engage an outside consultant, check with the members of your own information technology (IT) team. They may have a list of preferred vendors and, at the very least, can help screen consultants for competence and value.

Once the objective and the actors are settled, identify the *scenarios* (also called *use cases* or *user stories*) for each of the ways the actors will use SFDC. For example, actors in order operations will be entering and reviewing orders all day long, but they may also need to approve exceptional discounts or other special cases every day or so. Given that this approval process involves different thinking and actions from ordinary orders, approvals must be described in a different scenario. The same person may need to do sales forecast reports to support executives, again requiring a different scenario. These scenario write-ups should *briefly* describe what the actors are trying to achieve, the data they need to see and modify, the approvals they need to proceed, and the other actors or business processes they need to interact with. Make sure to note whether the scenario requires direct access to the system, or whether the situation could be handled through indirect means such as interacting with another application (e.g., the accounting system) or viewing a Web page, spreadsheet, or report. Log in to www.SFDC-Secrets.com to see an example scenario.

From the scenarios, the team needs to distill a set of system requirements. In many cases, the scenarios will have overlapping needs that are stated from different perspectives. A key step is to identify and consolidate the near-duplicate requirements, and to map them to the features provided by SFDC and related systems. For example, one sales scenario is to create a quote for an opportunity. This is fairly similar to the sales operations' scenario of updating a quote as well as to the sales manager's scenario of reviewing and approving a quote. All these scenarios are the requirement to edit opportunity, forecast, and quote information in real time (with the proper access controls to protect privileged information). This requirement maps to stock features in SFDC's Enterprise edition, but adds the requirement to integrate quote approval with the accounting system. It's a smart idea to create a correspondence table showing which scenarios need each requirement. Check www.SFDC-secrets.com for an example of this kind of mapping.

Many users (particularly executives) don't really think in terms of discrete requirements. Instead, they simply visualize what they need to make a decision or take an action. For this reason, it's a good idea to do mock-ups of a few reports, forms, approval screens, and dashboards (using Excel, PowerPoint, or even pen and paper) and do a "day in the life" walkthrough of people's jobs to get them thinking. Creating these mock-ups can very rapidly elucidate hidden—and difficult—requirements. You'll be surprised how often a user will say, "Of course, I have to be able to see the customer's order history to make my decision . . ." To make sure you're being realistic, run through a couple of the exercises described in Chapter 2.[2]

Resist the temptation to speak in terms of product feature lists. Each requirement should be stated in terms of the business need (i.e., a step in a business process with a measurable result) rather than as a technical description (how the feature works). Each requirement description should be as brief as possible, and each should be stored in a separate document. (If your company is really into paper, the requirements document should be placed in a three-ring binder, with individual pages being inserted or updated on at least a monthly basis.)

In addition to user-driven features, make sure to cover "taken for granted" system characteristics in your requirements documents: system availability (e.g., 7 A.M.–10 P.M. EST five days a week), system response times (1 second during operating hours), administrative response times (e.g., 1 hour during operating hours, 4 hours on weekends), thresholds for data error (e.g., zero defects in records A, B, and C, but 4% in all other records), international language support, multi-currency support, unusual fiscal periods, and other "environmental items" that you discover from your requirements gathering.

In a large company with complex business processes, the scenarios and requirements will multiply quickly: their sheer number will soon be overwhelming. The best way to handle this issue is to create a short overview spreadsheet that organizes and summarizes the requirements

2. SFDC will have no problem complying with all these requirements, but you need to know about them so the system can be properly configured from day one.

in a hierarchical fashion and helps the team visualize them from a "top-down" perspective. This high-level spreadsheet should not provide the details of any one requirement, but rather should show how the requirements fit together to form the big picture of the project. (Check out www.SFDC-secrets.com for an example requirements overview spreadsheet.) The requirements spreadsheet needs to make it obvious to team members (and executives) the reasons why each line item is there, its scope, its schedule, its cost, its sponsor, and the line item(s) it could be traded off against.

Organizing and Publishing Project Documents

Even before the project begins, best practices call for storing, publishing, and organizing the project's documents online. Put them in an intuitive hierarchy, with all the project-related documents in one place that is scanned by an internal search engine or a desktop index (such as Google's free desktop search or X1's indexer) and is backed up regularly.

You can store these documents in a shared folder on a file server, but even better is to have them in an intranet site. Best of all would be a wiki[3] that's accessible to all team members (including contractors). Your top-level wiki "article" should include pointers to the project schedule, the current phase's goals and nongoals, project personnel, news, discussion forums, blogs, and user tips on the system. The wiki should also provide a hierarchical library that includes all of the requirements documents, discussions, rationales for priority calls, and the project requirements phasing spreadsheet.

The wiki should be "Information Central" for the project, so any relevant information should be available there, including team members' contact information, email aliases, email/discussion archives, cheat sheets, podcasts, WebEx sessions, screen cams, and internal success stories. By making it really easy to get to and find all the current project information, you'll be on the road to clearer communications, better expectations management, and a much lower chance of confusion throughout the project.

You should also put a short document into SFDC's Documents section describing how to get to the file server or wiki. Promoting what's there will allow any interested user or project team member to quickly become better informed.

It's usually best that these documents be editable Word files, with change tracking turned on. For Excel files, the first page of the spreadsheet should include a revision history indicating who changed what and when. The files should be downloadable by any authorized user, but should be *updatable* only by sending the changes through the project manager. In this way, the project manager can filter and prioritize input and manage the

---

3. What's a wiki? Time to catch up on your jargon! A wiki helps you present information in a *kiosk model*—where users are given information only when they care about it. This approach stands in contrast to a broadcast model like email—where users are given information at a time when the *originator* thinks it's relevant, rather than the receiver. Using a wiki properly can save dozens of emails, phone calls, and even the occasional status review meetings. To find out more, read the article on the topic of wikis at the grand-daddy of them all, wikipedia.org.

evolution of the requirements and other documents (which inevitably change throughout the project).

Documents should never be deleted. Obsolete documents should be marked as such and moved to an archive directory.

For certain kinds of files, it's useful to leverage the shared editing and shared access of Google Docs. Although the files have to be much simpler (no macros or heavy formatting), Google Docs sharing can improve collaboration in a distributed implementation team. This is particularly true for status documents, priority lists, or other highly collaborative content. SFDC has recently created an integration with Google Docs that makes this option even more tempting.

Prioritizing Requirements

One of the toughest tasks throughout the life of the project will be understanding the ramifications of requirements and making priority calls among them. With a system of any size, some requirements will have to be delayed or may even have to be abandoned as too expensive. Making these decisions can get interesting when interdependencies among the requirements exist, and things get even juicier when political overtones and competition among the requirement sponsors complicate matters.

Although this complexity sounds scary, there's a counterbalance. The overriding principle of prioritization for any SFA/CRM project is that it **doesn't matter how many requirements you've delivered on** if the users aren't adopting the system in droves. This is because the *value* of an SFA/CRM system—to sales, marketing, support, and executives—grows in proportion to the amount and quality of data the system holds. Make priority calls that cause users to get quality data in the system sooner and that persuade users to get on the system more often . . . and the rest will follow. Instill this overriding principle in the project sponsors as much as you can so everyone pulls in the right direction.

One way to guide prioritization discussions is to use the short list of the specific business problems that the executives defined earlier in this chapter. These specific improvements should be specific, unambiguous, and quantified—"reduce customer support response times by 20%," not "improve brand value." Estimate how the major features will affect these business goals, and from that calculate the return on investment (ROI) for the feature: lowering of costs, increasing revenues, or both. This overview page will help keep things in perspective as you try to make priority calls.

Like all complex decisions, the tough calls will be made in meetings where there is insufficient information. Your requirements summary spreadsheet is the tool the team will use to make those tradeoffs and priority calls. The goal of the project leader is to channel the discussions during these meetings down paths that are rational: all of the choices are achievable, and the final choice optimizes ROI.

PRIORITIZATION TOOLS

Appendix A describes several tools that can be used to prioritize requirements. Give at least one of them a try to find out which tool is most natural for your team and produces the most credible priority rankings.

The two groups that usually get the highest weight in the prioritization are sales representatives and executives. Things that are of direct, immediate benefit to them are assigned a lot of points. The specific points you give to other departments and user types are up to you, but an SFA implementation team forgets "who's the boss" at their peril.

There isn't a universal formula for prioritizing requirements: too much depends on the specifics of your company. For example, should the requirements from highly sophisticated users (as identified in Chapter 5's SFA Maturity Model) be prioritized *higher* than others (because those users can gain the most) or *lower* than others (because those users will be better able to cope with an incomplete feature set)? The answer to this question inevitably depends on your company and its management style.

You'll want to carefully plan out who will start using the system when, as the timing affects priorities. Put simply, the timing and order in which you deliver SFDC functionality and extensions can have a *big* impact on the total project cost and schedule. Some functional areas go together very easily; others can involve a lot of controversy, meetings, and rework. While the order of functions is fundamentally your choice, a good rule of thumb is to bring users onto SFDC in the order listed in Table 1-1.

Almost always, the revenue-focused business processes conducted at headquarters are implemented first. Later, other headquarters processes are brought online. Usually, business processes done in the field happen a bit later.

You might wonder why the executive suite and other high-priority roles in the company seem to come so late to the system. Why aren't their requirements satisfied first? Chapters 3 and 4 answer that question: the quality, completeness, and relevance of the data in the system just aren't good enough early on. Any reports or dashboards an executive wants won't be reliable, and they could even provide misleading information that would lower the credibility of the system. It's a big mistake to bet the farm on SFDC data assets before they are ripe.

Add groups and adjust priorities on the list in Table 1-1 to fit the realities of your business. No matter what the order selected, use the ordering to help prioritize requirements. Requirements coming from teams that will be coming on board early should be treated as having a higher priority (so they get done early).

A key issue in prioritizing requirements is the "squeaky wheel" phenomenon, where a noisy or politically powerful proponent causes great emphasis to be placed on a requirement that isn't really critical. All too often, a significant proportion of the effort in large projects is devoted to requirements that are "nice to haves" but that ultimately waste time and effort. Consequently *the* highest leverage thing a project leader or business analyst can do is

TABLE 1-1 General Sequence of Bringing Users into SFDC

Organization	Activity	Business Priority	Political Priority	Phase
Telesales/inside sales	Orders	High	Medium	I
Order operations	Approvals	High	Medium	I
Sales development	Appointments	High	Low	I
Telemarketing	Cold calls	High	Low	I
Marketing	Lead generation	Medium	Low	II
Sales analyst	Executive support	Medium	Medium	II
Product marketing	Purchase analysis	Medium	Low	II
Sales VP and Marketing VP	Management, forecasting	High	High	II
Executive team	Management	High	High	III
Legal	Contracts	High	Low	III
Sales engineers, consultants	Deal support	High	Low	IV
Shipping/receiving	Distribution	Low	Low	IV
Customer support	Customer care	Medium	Low	IV
Finance	Business analysis	Medium	Low	IV
Field sales managers	Sales management	High	High	V
Partner/channel manager	Channel management	Medium	Medium	V
Individual sales representatives	Selling	High	High	VI
International operations	Selling	High	High	VI

identify and deprioritize the uncritical. While avoiding confrontation, smoke out dubious requirements using gambits like these:

- "How much of *your* budget would you be willing to dedicate to solving the problem?"
- "Can you quantify how much waste this problem has been causing for you on a monthly basis?"
- "How much profit increase would the company see if this were done?"
- "How much more productive would you be if the problem were solved?"
- "Which other department needs this feature?"
- "How have you been able to succeed without this so far?"

- "What's the forcing function—the deadline beyond which we can no longer do business the current way?"

- "Which of your other requirements would you be willing to put on the back burner to get this one done?"

AVOIDING HAPPY EARS

Whenever a new system is being developed and people are interviewed about what they need, users start to hear hints about how things will work. Nearly everyone will assume that if they've heard about an issue, it's going to be solved by the new system. They'll even extrapolate, imagining all the wonderful new features that will become available to make their job easier. It's human nature to be optimistic, and that goes double for sales and marketing folks. But this "happy ears" phenomenon leads to spiraling expectations and scope creep that can kill a project.

Project leaders and especially project sponsors must continuously push to lower these expectations, even if they yet haven't seen overt signs of happy ears. The project goals must be simple—even minimalist—for the first phases, and "great ideas" must be explicitly pushed off in time. Even when things are going okay, *undersell* and be tentative about making the schedule. Even if the team has a way of delivering "something great," consider delaying it (ironically, see "The Art of the Quick Win" later in this chapter). When you *do* deliver this great thing, *do not publicize it until it's delivered,* so that you can provide pleasant surprises to users.

In prioritizing and trading off requirements, the project leader will need a set of executive sponsors who can act as champions for political and resource issues. For SFDC project success, the champions *must* include the VP of Sales, but usually include the VP of Marketing, the CFO, or perhaps even the CEO. These key supporters cannot afford the time needed to participate in the project, so they'll need to deputize a senior person on their staff to be a regular participant[4] on the SFDC implementation team. The project leader should form a management council of these deputies to make priority calls, policy decisions, and tradeoffs. For simplicity of voting, the team needs to be small and contain an odd number of people (including the product manager). A small management council would include representatives from the Sales and Marketing departments, plus the project leader. A larger council might add representatives from the Finance, Customer Care, International Operations, Professional Services, Channel Operations, and Business Analytics departments. This council will need to have *brief* meetings on a weekly basis, and it should devote a significant amount of time to analyzing business processes. Because a key factor in ensuring project success will be the availability of the right people for this team, get their (and their bosses') commitments early.

---

4. As we'll discuss later in this chapter, "participant" means an active worker who will be charged with the task of delivering documents and making binding decisions. Participants' effort on the team needs to be part of their "day job," so their boss needs to dedicate a portion of their schedule and allocate some of their personal goals (MBOs) during the months of their project involvement. Their effort needs to be measured and rewarded!

The challenge for the project leader is to keep one (and only one) priority list that encompasses everyone's needs, while clearly limiting the number of items that are "must do's" for each phase. Even so, maintaining a consistent, clear, tightly enforced requirements priority list is an invaluable tool for the project leader, and its existence will help fend off countless arguments during the project.

When Requirements Should Bend

It is common for requirements to be stated as absolutes, with intricate detail being provided about the way things must be done. But these "requirements" are often an interpretation of a business need, or an executive's preference, or even a legal regulation. Sometimes, the literal requirement is a poor interpretation of the underlying business need. It's important to be as creative as possible in requirements statements so that you don't over-specify or get locked into one particular approach. Identify alternatives and different ways of achieving the underlying goal.

For example, the Finance department may have an edict that an order cannot be shipped without a manual approval. So the requirement is stated as a mandatory human approval cycle. But if the approval cycle is there only to apply a set of strict rules, maybe the *manual* approval cycle isn't the real requirement. By restating the requirement as "no shipment will be made without applying the following rules," it becomes possible to have a fully automated approval, saving time and cost on every order.

Look for opportunities to restate "requirements" that are over-specified or arbitrarily complex. Requirements should be statements of business goals and criteria, rather than strict step-by-step procedures.

In some cases, the best path forward is to change the business process, rather than investing in automation of a silly or obsolete practice. In particular, look for opportunities to make things better by making subtle changes to the sales and marketing processes. Some of the most doctrinaire SFA/CRM requirements miss key opportunities for leverage. The SFA/CRM system will give sales reps and managers information and tools they never had before. Because the whole point of the system is to make it easier for the reps to make their numbers, why not take the blinders off? For example, better qualification of leads can mean fewer pointless sales calls and shorter sales cycles. Likewise, marketing personnel should be encouraged to think outside the box, looking for new ways to plan campaigns and execute events. Of course, you'll need to get the executives' approval before you formally recommend process changes or restate the requirement, but it's well worth the effort.

Bending and restating requirements in this way can make the system easier to implement, easier to use, and more beneficial to the business over time.

Knowing Your Boundaries

One of the most important issues in requirements setting is determining the "edges" of the system—that is, the boundaries beyond which users must log in to a different system if they want to do something. All users would like the system to encompass all of the things they need to access for their particular jobs, but it's impractical to deliver a single system that covers every business function for every employee.

When you first install SFDC, it has the following functional boundaries:

- **Order entry:** Anything having to do with bookings, invoices, or payments is in your accounting or enterprise resource planning (ERP) system, not SFDC.

- **Order management:** Anything having to do with shipments, order status, returns, or exchanges will be in the distribution or ERP system, not SFDC.

- **Marketing:** Leads, contacts, campaigns, and simple email blasts are fine within SFDC. Almost all of the details having to do with emails, marketing events, advertising, or other marketing initiatives, however, will be in your email blasting, marketing automation, or content management system, not SFDC. For example, SFDC tracks the outcomes and history of campaigns, but actual campaign management is external to the system.

- **Customer assets, inventory, and licenses:** Almost anything having to do with the customer's order history, shipments, downloads, or licenses will be in your accounting, ERP, or other corporate databases. SFDC has a very limited view of assets.

- **Defect reports or bug tracking:** Anything having to do with the technical side of customer problems will be in the defect management or bug tracking database; most companies already have an entrenched system for this purpose. SFDC can be configured to integrate with these systems, but out of the box it's really focused on "cases" or "incidents."

- **Documents:** Almost anything in your sales literature, marketing library, Web site content, proposals, customer specifications, or contracts is already stored outside of SFDC, often in a file system or in content management products. SFDC has an add-on product that helps present and organize document libraries in a clever way, but this product will usually be a supplement to existing external systems, rather than a replacement for them.

- **Business analytics:** Although SFDC provides an excellent set of built-in reports and dashboards, almost any business analyst will need to go beyond these features and use an external database and business analysis tool.

For a detailed view of business systems that touch on SFDC, see Figure 1-3. As shown in the diagram, several add-on products may be tightly integrated with SFDC to improve its functional coverage (see Chapter 7 for a discussion of these products). These extensions and external products are a huge strength of SFDC, because they allow the core system to be simple and easy to use, yet flexible and scalable enough to handle much broader requirements. Further, SFDC has a very open and well-documented set of external interfaces, presented as Web services. These "SOAP APIs" allow programmers to connect, integrate, and extend SFDC to almost anything.

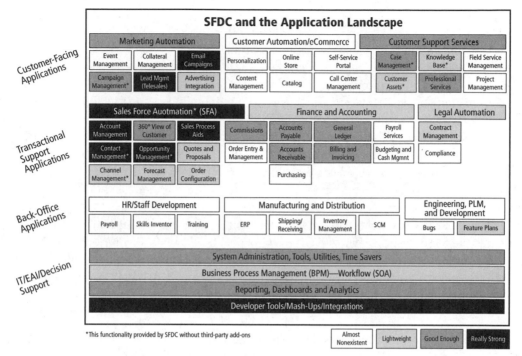

SFDC and the Application Landscape

FIGURE 1-3   SFDC and the application landscape (as of spring 2009)

Even though you *could* integrate SFDC with any external system, it's easy to overshoot the mark by trying to do too much in the initial implementation. In evaluating and prioritizing requirements, it's important to identify when a requirement crosses over into an external system. Any such requirement is inherently more complex and risky, so it should be assigned a lower priority than requirements that are entirely within SFDC's native functionality. Read the section on integration in Chapter 7 before you deal with any requirements for integration.

Thanks to the modularity of the SFDC architecture, almost all internal functions can be turned on in phases at the time of your choosing. For example, turning on the Campaigns or Forecasting function can be done the day you bring up the system or, alternatively, months later without involving significant rework. Many external add-ons act in the same way, allowing a very flexible deployment schedule. However, some of the more sophisticated add-ons (such as Eloqua marketing automation or Intacct accounting) will involve significant changes to your data, the user interface, and user behaviors. Consequently, the timing and sequence of deploying the more complex and expensive add-ons cannot be taken lightly.

As with all requirements, the extension of SFDC via add-ons and integration with other systems should be prioritized with a keen eye toward schedule and risk. Even though basic integration is of the "plug and play" variety, the interaction among systems and databases can cause subtle data corruption problems that won't discovered for several weeks. Consequently, it is usually a good idea to deploy basic SFDC functionality without external integration, get the users comfortable using it, and get some real data flowing through the system (even if

> ### WHEN OTHER PROBLEMS MUST BE SOLVED FIRST
>
> In large organizations, the political drivers for installing or replacing the existing SFA/CRM system will be executive visibility, customer reporting, or uneven execution of business processes. Unfortunately, merely upgrading to SFDC will not help in many of these situations. In large organizations, other problems need to be solved *before* the new system will function properly, let alone resolve any deep issues.
>
> The project manager should analyze the requirements and problem statements to understand which of them are actually caused by bad data, disconnected systems, unclear business rules, inconsistent business processes, and other "environmental" or infrastructure issues. These problems are typically scattered across several databases or applications, and fixing them will be a prerequisite to any successful SFDC deployment.
>
> If you discover this situation, it is important to get a project team started on analyzing and remedying those external problems even before your SFDC work starts. That project team should be chartered to work with your SFDC team, but typically it should be managed separately. If this team is chartered to work under the SFDC team, make sure that its focus doesn't become too broad (e.g., "rework this entire outside system") or distract the main SFDC implementation team.

only manually) in the early weeks. Later, new functional add-ons and integrations can be deployed on top of a stable baseline system, and users can gradually become used to the new features as the system expands. External integrations (particularly with complex systems such as accounting, ERP, and marketing automation) should be started early for testing purposes, but not turned on for full two-way data transfer until later phases.

Appendix B provides example requirements for both a small company and a large company. Of course, every company's needs and priorities will be different, but the examples show the level of detail that you will need (not much at this stage) and the kind of interdepartmental prioritization you'll need to think about when preparing your company's list of requirements.

The SFDC system will almost certainly be implemented over several quarters, with only the first two phases as "hard priorities." Later requirements will be reordered depending on perceived business priority after initial usage; technical issues or needed process changes will be discovered during the project. In addition, perceived business needs may change over the life of the project. It's important that the executive sponsors understand, however, that each major requirements change will cause some delay and wasted effort. Communicating this point clearly but pleasantly is one of the key challenges for the project leader, because the executives are as vulnerable to "happy ears" as anyone else.

Making the Business Case

Most companies will require a formal business case for an investment in SFDC. Even if yours doesn't have a formal review meeting for the decision, it's a good idea to go through the exercise of cost, benefit, and ROI analysis so that the team understands the financial implications of what they are doing. Understanding the things that really make a big financial difference—and the things that really don't—helps everyone make better decisions throughout the life of the project.

Estimating Costs

When evaluating Software as a Service (SaaS) systems such as Salesforce.com, it is tempting to think that cost analysis isn't critical. After all, it's just a monthly fee and you pay only as long as you're receiving value . . . right? That's what the salesperson wants you to think, if only to make you stop thinking. Life isn't that simple.

Procurement

The big three cost areas are procurement, implementation, and ongoing user expenses. Procurement costs for SFDC, like most SaaS products, consist of a monthly fee. The fee varies based on the following factors:

- The number of users (internal "full feature" users, platform users, partner users, and customer users)

- The version you buy (most readers of this book will purchase Enterprise edition, but many will also want the Mobile edition, the sandbox, or other extra-cost items)

- The length of the contractual commitment (one year is the minimum; more than three years seems to make little difference to the discount)

- Your willingness to prepay (prepaying one year makes a difference, but longer prepays seem to make less of a difference)

WHO SHOULD PAY?

The best decisions will happen when the departments that *benefit* the most *pay* the most for the system. This typically means sales should pay at least 50% of the total, with marketing and support sharing the remainder of the cost. Of course, this split depends entirely on your company's organizational structure and system usage.

Another funding formula is to have the project be financially sponsored by the executive suite—at the corporate or business unit level, which shows executives' level of commitment.

The only funding model that *doesn't* work is to have central IT foot the bill. While this works with infrastructure, in SaaS applications—and particularly those that directly benefit only a part of the company—this model doesn't work in either the short run or the long run. Check out Chapter 6 for more on this topic.

Because you're gong to be delivering the system in phases, make sure to activate only the number of seats you'll actually use at any one time. In the negotiations for a large deal, this aspect of incremental deployment may save your company a significant sum.

Include add-on products in your procurement cost estimates, thinking through phasing effects that will affect the number of users and timing of activation for each product separately. Most add-on products for SFDC are also SaaS, but a few are on-premises products with hardware requirements and perpetual licenses. For those products, don't forget to include the cost of hardware procurement.[5]

Do not neglect support fees. The basic support level that's included in SaaS products will be insufficient for at least your first year. You'll need speed of access to in-depth expertise that is available only through premium support. Your team members (particularly developers and system administrators) will also need technical training classes to become rapidly productive. Do *not* negotiate for these items piecemeal if you want the best discount.

If your company will have more than 100 users, the annual fees for SaaS can be a surprise. While it's true that you aren't paying for upgrades, patches, hardware, and operating staff, SaaS fees can easily exceed $100,000 per year, and the amount climbs to more than $1 million per year for the very largest deployments.[6] Don't assume that you'll have a lot of bargaining power once the deal is signed: the only way you can get a better discount is to buy even more or to commit for an even longer period. Downgrades are not allowed. The vendor knows you don't have a credible threat of changing the system, as the real cost of a changeover can be quite large even with the flexibility provided by SaaS's Web services technology. As your users grow accustomed to features and your developers become experts at using SFDC's APIs, you will be just as locked in to the vendor's technology as you would be with any Microsoft product.

To get a significant discount on the procurement, you'll need to get a budgetary allocation for the multi-year commitment. Work with your Finance department to develop the business case, making sure those personnel understand that the number of users will go up over time even if the per-seat price is stable.

Implementation

In contrast to "procurement costs," implementation costs for SFDC and other SaaS products are one-time fees. You will almost certainly need consulting and other services required to convert legacy data, integrate with other systems, write custom `APEX` and `VisualForce` software, test the system, deploy it, and train users. Do not assume that your internal IT

---

5. For both security and performance reasons, you'll almost certainly want any on-premises add-on products to run on dedicated servers.

6. Discounting on SaaS deals is much less than it is for traditional enterprise software. Discount levels for the very largest deployments (10,000 users or more) are a well-guarded secret, but it is unlikely that discounting exceeds 80% even at that level. If you have knowledge about the negotiated price of a large SFDC deal, feel free to email me at david@SFDC-secrets.com.

people are interested in SaaS projects or that they have the required skills and experience (but check out Chapter 13 anyway). Some of the implementation costs are easy to identify and are "fixed fee" in nature (e.g., training classes). Most of the big elements of implementation, however, are highly customized and can be brought to a fixed-price bid only after significant analysis by your vendor. Of course, every Finance department will want a fixed price, but there is *significant* gamesmanship in the bidding process. It is very easy to get caught up in the engineering change order (ECO) trap, where "fixed price" contracts create an avalanche of over-runs.

WHEN THE PRICE ISN'T RIGHT

At the beginning of a project, all you can see is price. At the end of the project, all you'll remember is the value of benefits, the quality of the work (or lack of it), the pain (or lack of it), and the over-runs (large or small). It's easy to be "penny wise and pound foolish." **It is far more important to choose a vendor that you can trust, rather than one that bids low.** You need to see proven experience, skills in project management, actionable communication, and references from other customers.

One of the advantages of the phased deployments we recommend in this book is that the vendors can give you a more accurate bid for the immediate phase (which will be very tightly defined) than they can for the project overall (which may suffer from scope creep and extensions). *Best practices are to use hourly rates with a tightly managed cap rather than fixed-price engagements* because this practice (1) exposes the scope creep that hurts overall chances of project success, (2) avoids the bickering, administrivia, and gamesmanship of fixed-price "change orders," and (3) prevents vendors from hiding large margins in their bid.

Explore your consultant's willingness to work using performance incentives. If they are designed properly, these types of contracts can yield the best possible deal for you because your goals and metrics are tightly aligned with the consultant's. As wondrous as pay-for-performance contracts are, they're equally rare. But give it a shot.

The first step in quantifying the implementation costs is drawing up the statement of work and development/integration requirements for each of the projects. The more homework you can do yourself, the more accurate the vendors' bids will be. Some of the project areas will require analysis that you can't do, and the bidding vendors will have to analyze this themselves. The vendors are unlikely to do enough "drill-down" analysis for free, but there's good news: this scoping project will be short and *should* be fixed-price. This is money well spent before you make a large commitment. Some vendors will do this scoping project only *after* you have signed on with them for the main project. My own experience with this kind of vendor is not good, but don't treat that issue as a show-stopper. If the vendor is very well qualified and you trust the consultant, proceed.

Note that the cost of implementation talent for serious SaaS projects isn't that much different from the corresponding costs of conventional on-premises software packages. Skills and deep experience in SaaS implementations are fairly rare (particularly outside the United States), and fees can be $300/hour or more for the best people. Many customers have experienced overall implementation costs that exceed the software fees they pay to their SaaS vendors in the first year. Although this amount is significantly fewer dollars than customers paid for classic enterprise software (where implementation was typically projected to be 1.5 or more times the cost of the software licenses), it may still come as an unpleasant surprise if proper allocation for it has not been arranged.

Do your cost estimates only for the initial implementation, but know that the happier your users are, the more likely they will be to ask management for further system enhancements. It is not uncommon for companies to have multiyear engagements before they reach the management nirvana of the 360-degree view of the customer.[7]

Don't forget the costs of your internal people. It's not unusual to have five people be involved on a full-time basis in an SFDC implementation (even with consultants), with another five involved intermittently. Even though these people's salaries are already budgeted for, the effort they put into SFDC will be time that won't be available for other company priorities.

Ongoing Costs

After estimating total first-year costs—first-year fees, add-on procurements, and implementation expenses—the ongoing costs for SaaS basically consist of the annual subscription fees. There may be some one-time costs in the out-years (such as a data recovery exercise or temporary use of SFDC's sandbox), so put a placeholder in those budgets. The more interesting ongoing costs are related to people: follow-on implementation or expansion work, training costs for new users or administrators, travel and fees for power users attending technical conferences (a good investment), and time for any consultants working on the system.

As with any large system, data pollution is an inevitability and is poisonous to the system's credibility. Business analysts and others will discover corrupted or duplicate data creeping into the system over time. Whether it's a temporary coder, a data-entry clerk, or overtime hours of internal people, some corner of the budget should be set aside for a health check and cleanup session at least once a year. You'll almost certainly want a deduping or data cleansing tool, which will cost at least $3,000 per year, which is money well spent (see Chapter 7 for discussion of this). Furthermore, identifying the source of the problem, rectifying it, and cleaning up the data are often tasks carried out in collaboration with contractors.

---

7. This refers to the ability to see all customer interactions with your company from all angles, from Web site visits to payment history to letters of complaint. This visibility lets management see which accounts are the most valuable versus which customers are noisy but just not profitable enough. While this 360-degree visibility is very powerful for marketing and management personnel, it involves extensive integration and changes to business processes that can take years to come to fruition.

These ongoing costs are likely to be most pronounced in year two of the system, but some budget should be set aside every year after the initial deployment.

Quantifying the Return

Any project this size has to be justified with improvements to the bottom line. The two components of achieving this goal—lowering costs and increasing revenues—are hard to quantify. But they can at least be modeled to provide a credible SWAG.

Lowered Costs

To counterbalance all of the costs outlined previously, it's important to identify areas of cost saving. Because SFDC is a salesforce *automation* system, you'd expect to find some. But that's rarely the way it works—after all, many of the expense areas are sunk costs that cannot be recovered or labor that is taken for granted. You may have to be a good detective to ferret out the labor savings.

The first obvious place to look is cost avoidance for the system SFDC is replacing. It won't be much, but at least it can be immediately quantified. Next, look at ancillary systems that can be decommissioned because SFDC makes them less relevant. For example, you may have a large number of spreadsheets for the marketing group with macros that won't need to be maintained or extended any more.

The next place to look is wasted labor. Whether the waste takes the form of contractors or employees, the hourly rate should be quantified. The first waste-avoidance item will be system administration and maintenance for software and hardware that can be retired. This will probably amount to at least 32 hours per month; for large systems, it can be much more. Another source of wasted labor is sales administrators who—even in small companies—may spend 8 or more hours per week preparing the weekly forecast, and order operations people who spend 20 hours or more in order entry, correction, and reconciliation. Some business analysts also have to spend huge chunks of time trying to piece together spreadsheets from fragments of customer data. In addition, order fulfillment people (license generation, shipping, distribution, and expediting) may spend their entire day doing things that could be 80% automated. Finally, customer support people can easily waste 10 minutes per call trying to find data, correct erroneous entries, or fix problems that could have been avoided by automation. These areas of direct waste add up, as they occur every week and may become much larger in the closing weeks of the quarter. Even though employees' time is a "sunk cost," quantify the savings as if those workers were paid by the hour.

See Table 1-2 for an example cost-savings matrix for a small company (as always, visit the book's Web site to find free downloads of Excel and other files that you can use on your project). Check out www.SFDC-secrets.com for other examples.

TABLE 1-2   Potential Cost Savings and Efficiency Improvements

Cost Savings	Units	Savings/Year
Hard Cost Savings		
Ongoing license fees for existing SFA/CRM system	n/a	n/a
Support fees for existing SFA/CRM system	n/a	$2,000
Hardware maintenance and support costs for SFA/CRM system	1 server	$1,500
Auxiliary software products for existing SFA/CRM system	3 licenses	$3,000
Potential Cost Savings/Efficiency Improvements		
Tradeshow and related travel expenses reduced	1 tradeshow/year	$30,000
Advertising and other marketing expenses reduced	n/a	$20,000
Avoiding unproductive on-site sales calls/demonstrations	1 meeting/year	$2,000
Avoiding low-probability "proof of concept" projects	1 POC/year	$2,000
Improved product marketing and engineering decisions	n/a	$10,000
Improved executive decisions	1 decision/year	$25,000
Internal Labor Savings		
System administration time for existing SFA/CRM software and hardware	16 hours/month	$20,000
Sales administrator time reconciling orders	32 hours/month	$30,000
Sales administrator time rolling up forecast	32 hours/month	$30,000
VP time investigating/adjusting weird forecast numbers	12 hours/month	$12,000
Missed Opportunities		
Lower cost of customer acquisition by 5%	50 new customers/year	$100,000
Prevent one lost sale[*]	1 new customer/year	$50,000
Ability to do one more upsell[*]	1 upsell/year	$20,000

[*]   This should be the revenue from the average first sale to new customers. Sophisticated finance types will tell you that this is an overstatement, and will try to get you to use the *profit* from a new customer instead. Don't do it: your fall-back position should be the **contribution margin** value from an extra transaction.

Opportunity Costs

The larger cost savings are more difficult to quantify because they involve missed opportunities or avoidance of wrong decisions. What would it mean if the cost of customer acquisition were 5% lower? How would it lower costs if the sales cycle were a week shorter? What would be the impact of reducing sales representative turnover by just *one rep* per year? What percentage of marketing dollars is spent on marketing to the wrong people or participating in the wrong events? How much could be saved if you could quantify which marketing activities really produced revenue, rather than just "visibility"? How much travel expense and labor could be saved by avoiding just one unproductive tradeshow, sales call, or proof-of-concept project? If you knew more about which prospects were (or weren't) going to yield the most profit, which other improvements could your company make?

Focus on quantifying **external waste** that could be reduced, rather than on internal jobs that could be eliminated, as the latter will bring the project nothing but political strife. You'll need to interview people in sales, marketing, and pre-sales support to make this determination. Nevertheless, as you develop an effective model for estimating the cost savings, the amount saved can turn into big money.

There is also value to the risk reduction that SFDC will bring. Hits to customer reputation, knocks to brand value, and even Wall Street embarrassment all cost the company money—and all can be improved by a really solid SFA system. Avoiding just one unreliable forecast or a few irate customers can save enough to pay for the whole of SFDC. The problem, of course, is quantifying this value.

HEAD'S UP!

Watch out for finance groups that try to use your estimates as a justification for cutting the budget of other departments. They may say, "Well, if you do such a great job detecting unproductive marketing activities, we'll just cut their budget by 10% now to make sure you actually achieve that goal." This kind of budgetary reasoning can get poisonous in a hurry, so always couch cost savings as potential and as a way of increasing the leverage of the money that will be spent anyway. In other words, describe the change in terms of improved ROI or getting more value for the company's money, not in terms of spending less money.

Increased Revenues

The flip side of lowering costs is increasing revenue. To develop credible estimates, it's important to interview several sales and channel managers, discounting the opinions of people who are not directly responsible for revenues. It is political suicide to present your revenue conclusions without having first reviewed them with the Sales VP.

Develop a spreadsheet that shows the value of extra deals that could be closed with the aid of better prospect and customer information, better lead quality, tighter qualification, and higher conversion/win rates. What if a hot prospect never "fell through the cracks"? What would be the value of the extra deals you could do if the sales cycle were shorter? What kind of extra revenue might the channel produce if leads were handed off and managed more effectively? What would be the value of doing one additional "upsell" per year or of closing a deal with one more customer? What if your customer loyalty or retention rate increased by 10%? For the sake of credibility, keep the estimates conservative.

It's also a good idea to identify opportunities to increase sales leverage—that is, getting more yield from the same cost structure. How would it change the company if a sales rep could manage twice as many deals without slip-ups? Or if a sales manager could manage 50% more sales reps? How would the company operations change if the forecast were *really* reliable in week 10 of the quarter? These issues could mean better scalability for the company and ability to respond to market changes more quickly. These speed and scalability advantages increase both the profitability and the value of the company.

Beware of politics surrounding revenue estimates. It's tempting to say something like, "We could increase revenue 10% if only . . ." Sales executives may be very sensitive about this topic, and ornery finance executives might say, "We'll approve this project if only the Sales department is willing to increase its quota by 10%." To avoid this downhill spiral, focus your estimates on quantifying the *increased probability* of making the revenue targets the company already has. This approach is a less direct way of making the business case for SFDC, but it avoids the political traps and still makes the point.

Finally, beware of blatant double-counting of cost savings or revenue improvements. While some double-counting is almost unavoidable, if it's too obvious it simply lowers your credibility (note that the example in Figure 1-4 on page 63 shows just "the right amount" of double-counting).

Developing a Straw-Man Schedule

Part of making the business case for SFDC involves answering the question, "How soon can we get the benefits?" Once the project is approved, the schedule will be the single most visible aspect of managing the implementation. While SFDC and other SaaS systems can be turned on in a day or so (the SFDC sales reps will have made *sure* to tell you that), the standard system that is delivered will be of no practical use until it is configured (somehow the SFDC reps may not have emphasized this point). The time to configure the system may be short, but the time required to think through and test precisely how you need the system configured will be just as long as it would be with enterprise software. And the biggest cost and schedule elements—integration and data import—are just as large and uncertain as they would be with a conventional system. In large companies with a sophisticated IT department, allocate time in your schedule for initial review meetings: even though SFDC is a hosted system, security and compliance reviews will be required before you're allowed to "go live." Given that unexpected delays may be tagged as "project failures" by upper management, estimating the schedule and setting executive/sponsor expectations appropriately are key success factors for delivering the project.

As with any complex project, the SFDC schedule estimate has to be based on a reasonable best-case scenario: you assume that you won't make wrong decisions, that the right resources will be available when needed, and that there won't be any unpleasant discoveries along the way. To counteract this structural optimism, buffer elements must be added to the schedule during the riskiest tasks (such as development of a new software element or integrating an external system). Buffer elements must also be added during weeks that are critically constrained for sales personnel and executive management (e.g., sales managers are unlikely to be responsive to an action item during weeks 12 and 13 of the quarter, and no executive can be expected to attend an SFDC management review during the week of quarterly results and the board meeting). One of the first things a project manager should do is collect the calendar of "blackout periods" for each key resource. Immediately after completing this task, the project manager should identify "forcing functions"—external events with firm deadlines—that will likely drive the deployment calendar. For example, an annual sales meeting will be an ideal time to roll out new functionality and do user training.

GANTT CHARTS, PERT DIAGRAMS, AND OTHER MANAGEMENT DELUSIONS

While developing the schedule estimate, it really helps to use a Gantt charting tool such as Microsoft Project. This kind of software is fairly straightforward to learn, and during the planning phase its nice charts can help persuade busy managers about resource commitments.

By contrast, it is a very rare project that will actually *use* the Gantt charting tool during the life of the actual project, because maintaining the data and updating the schedule require a tremendous amount of effort. Unfortunately, few project participants will be willing to update their own information, so maintaining an accurate Gantt schedule will usually fall to the project manager. Most of the time, the day-to-day schedule will take the form of a spreadsheet. Set expectations with management accordingly.

That said, when a new project phase starts (or, less optimistically, when a major rework of the schedule is required), it is a good idea to redo the Gantt charts. Store backup copies of the original chart files for comparison purposes, but develop new ones that show the expected work breakdown structure at an overview level. You can have hours of fun comparing the original schedule with reality, and develop lessons learned for later phases of the project.

Ironically, one of the major areas of schedule uncertainty is in requirements setting and prioritization. A very common problem of large IT projects is to over-specify at two levels: at the high level, creating requirements that have questionable or unknown business value, and at the low level, specifying things in too much detail. At both levels, over-specification creates a lot of extra work and often engages employees in a level of perfectionism that has limited payoff.

The idea behind "value engineering" is making sure that a requirement is going to be *worth* satisfying before you spend the resources to do so. The best possible investment you can make as a business analyst or project manager is time spent vetting and validating requirements, because every hour you spend can save days of effort later. Allocate double the amount of time you think you'll need for interpreting and prioritizing requirements, as "smoking out" a marginal or bogus requirement can cut overall wasted effort in half.

Although the iterative process of an Agile project (described in Chapter 4) helps to contain the risk, any significant project will require a large number of meetings to discover what the requirements really are, how to prioritize and sequence them, and what they really mean for the system implementation.

THE ART OF THE QUICK WIN

From the outset, it's important to develop a wide collection of user-visible features that can be liberally sprinkled through the schedule to maintain the perception that progress is being made and that the project is delivering business value on a frequent basis. This "quick win" list gives the project leader a tool to manage expectations and counteract a known negative (for example, "For the next two weeks, you can't do X, but we've given you this cool new feature Y to make your day go better"). Sometimes, a quick win is preventing a problem from ever occurring again. At other times, it's creating an alert to automatically flag unusual situations or adding a new "toy" that will keep users interested.

The quick win doesn't have to involve a lot of technology—the less, the better—and it should never involve a lot of work. It can be something as simple as a "mashup" with a traffic map so reps can figure out which route to drive to get to their appointments. Fortunately, SFDC's AppExchange has hundreds of free add-ons that provide features for users. Early in your project, do a survey of the AppExchange to see which freebies you can drop into the system during the implementation. Create a calendar of the "goody drops" and reschedule them as needed during the project

The project leader needs to creatively identify other opportunities for quick wins. Sometimes, just putting data in one place can create several opportunities for wins. For example, if you put all your employees' contact information into SFDC, which kind of reports could be generated? How about a mailing list for HR, or a birthday list for the administrative employees? These featurettes may take 10 minutes to implement, but each one can give you a week's worth of breathing room.

The sequence of phases can be as important as the amount of effort applied to the project, because the sequence of features determines which system benefits are visible to the users and sponsors. Unfortunately, even with SFDC some amount of effort will be required for enablers—infrastructure, integration, data cleansing, analysis, and testing—that don't deliver any specific feature (even though no feature would be possible without those functions). The resource for this infrastructure work needs to be planned first, before the visible-feature work is planned. However, always have *something* for the users. A project that devotes more than two thirds of the effort to things without visible results will have a tough time surviving in most organizations.

The project phases should start with the core of SFDC, and then add system extensions, external data, and external system integrations on top of a stable base. This order is preferred for two reasons: technical simplicity and user training. Users rarely have patience for training sessions lasting even an hour, so the amount of change you present to them during each session must be fairly small. You want users to become proficient with the core of the system that's immediately relevant to their jobs before you focus them on the fancier parts. Chapter 5 provides much more detail on training.

The early schedule for a deployment will look something like Table 1-3. Note that this schedule is **realistic only for a fairly small implementation of SFDC and a proficient**

TABLE 1-3   Schedule for Small- to Medium-Sized Company SFDC Project Phases

Phase	Description	Start Date	Completion Date	Current Status	Business Processes	Affected Departments
1	Lead capture and routing	3-Mar	17-Mar	Done	Pipeline formation	Marketing, Sales
1	Campaigns and Web site integration	3-Mar	24-Mar	Done	Pipeline formation	Marketing
1	Historic lead import, 1 year	3-Mar	1-Apr	Done	Pipeline formation	Marketing
1	Lead scoring and qualification	18-Mar	7-Apr	Done	Pipeline formation	Marketing, Sales
2	Opportunity creation	8-Apr	15-Apr	Done	Pipeline formation	Sales
2	Basic forecasting reports	15-Apr	22-Apr	Done	Pipeline management	Sales
2	Opportunity aging and backtrack alerts	15-Apr	29-Apr	Done	Pipeline management	Sales
2	Advanced forecasting	23-Apr	5-May	In progress	Pipeline management	Sales, Finance, Executives

Continued

TABLE 1-3   Schedule for Small- to Medium-Sized Company SFDC Project Phases, *Continued*

Phase	Description	Start Date	Completion Date	Current Status	Business Processes	Affected Departments
2	Order-level quoting	1-May	15-May	In progress	Quote to invoice	Sales, Finance
2	Line-item-level quoting	16-May	1-Jun	Not started	Quote to invoice	Sales, Finance
3	Historic opportunity import, 1 year	16-May	15-Jun	Not started	Quote to invoice	Sales, Finance, Support
3	Historic opportunity import, 3 years	16-Jun	16-Aug	Not started	Quote to invoice	Sales, Finance, Support
3	Contract import, 1 year	16-May	15-Jun	Not started	Support and renewals	Sales, Finance, Support
3	Contract import, 3 years	16-Jun	16-Aug	Not started	Support and renewals	Sales, Finance, Support
3	Support ticket integration	16-May	1-Aug	Not started	Support and renewals	Support
3	Advanced forecasting reports and alerts	16-May	15-Jun	Not started	Pipeline management	Sales, Finance, Executives
3	Advanced campaign reports	16-May	15-Jun	Not started	Pipeline formation	Marketing
3	Dashboards	16-May	1-Jun	Not started	Executive management	Executives

implementation team. Here are some guidelines to use as a sanity check on your schedule. Note that these recommendations are minimums, so it's fine if your schedule assumes slower progress. Many of these tasks can be carried out in parallel, so they may overlap on the calendar.

- Initial SFDC bring-up, including basic configuration of users, roles, profiles, territory assignments, security, and basic user training: **2 person-weeks per 100 users or operating country.**

- Integration with your company's Web site and Web advertising campaigns: **1 person-week for a simple static system, 3 person-weeks for a full content-management system.**

- Integration with external email blasting or marketing automation systems: **1 person-week per system,** but bugs and testing may make this much longer.

- Preparation for data import/migration: **1 person-day** on the learning curve for each data source.

- **Lead** information import, including data cleansing, deduping, reorganizing, and enrichment: **1,000–10,000 records per person-day,** depending on what kind of shape your data is in.[8]

- **Account** import, including account renaming and hierarchy creation, deduping, and enrichment: **500–5,000 records per person-day,** depending on how many sources of "accounts" you have and the shape of the data.

- **Contact** information import, including data cleansing, deduping, reorganizing, and enrichment: **500–5,000 records per person-day,** depending on what kind of shape your data is in.

- **Lead/contact** activity and campaign history, including data cleansing, deduping, reorganization, and enrichment: **500–5,000 records per person-day,** depending on what kind of shape your data is in.

- **Opportunity** history import, including creation of historical accounts, contacts, notes, and attachments as necessary, data cleansing, deduping, reorganizing, and enrichment: **40–5,000 records per person-day,** depending on what kind of shape your data is in.

- **Price list,** product structures (SKUs), and quoting rules: **50–500 line items per person-day,** depending on the complexity of your products, pricing models, business rules, and update history. Due to the nature of price lists, integrating the full price list may require several weeks of additional analysis and restructuring.

- **Contract** history import, including data cleansing, deduping, reorganizing, and enrichment: **50–500 records per person-day,** depending on the shape your data is in. Many companies actually have to scan or key in data from paper contracts, which obviously means even lower productivity than indicated here.

- Customer **asset** inventory import (such as serial numbers, license keys, and other purchase history info): **500–5,000 records per person-day,** depending on what kind of shape your data is in.

---

8. Data need to be cleaned of errors (typos, bad entries), normalized (e.g., state names changed to ISO-standard codes), and validated (e.g., checking that the postal code corresponds with the state or province name). These tasks are trivial if all relevant data reside in one system and your processes inherently clean data as those data are used. Of course, the more data you have, the more different ways it can be messed up (particularly if the data have been imported from one system to another over several years). The worst-case scenario is having to cross-check system data with paper records or unstructured files (such as email, Word, Notes, or PDFs), as often happens with contracts. In these cases, it's important to import only the essential data, and to carefully assess the business value of processing another year's worth of historical records.

- Support "ticket," `case`, or "customer incident" data import, including creation of historical accounts, contacts, notes, and attachments as necessary, data cleansing, deduping, reorganizing, and enrichment: **40–5,000 records per person-day,** depending on what kind of shape your data is in.

- Internal `reports` and `dashboards`: **1 person-week for the initial "toy" versions,** although just the meetings to decide about the reports and modify them can take that long. Note that reports and dashboards will continue to evolve, so expect this effort to require several person-weeks of work over the first year of system use.

- External `reports`, data analysis, and business intelligence: **several person-weeks,** although it may take much longer depending on the amount of data to be analyzed and the tools used.

- `Workflows`, `alerts`, and basic automation: **1 person-week for the initial set,** although making decisions about policies and business rules can often take much longer. There is often a surprising lack of clarity about sales territories, compensation plans, business rules, and other automation essentials.

- Integration with external systems: no estimate is possible without a technical analysis of the two systems. Even though several SFDC partners provide "out of the box" connectors to scores of external software packages, in most cases **significant extra work is required** after the initial connector is installed. Often, the two systems cannot be perfectly synchronized, so extensive data manipulation may be required to reconcile the two systems' data sets.

It is almost **impossible to budget too much time for data cleansing and integration** projects. Don't try to be cheap—it will only hurt the project in the long run.

Avoiding the Big Bang Project

Throughout the process of "selling" the Salesforce.com project, getting the budget, and allocating the staff, expectations are being set about all the problems that will be solved. During this process, expectations are being set about the schedule as well—and often a fixed date (usually the first day of a fiscal quarter) emerges as an important corporate milestone. Finally, management develops expectations about the nature of the deployment, usually focusing on a system cutover, where users switch from the old way of doing things to the new system. And almost always, all of these expectations will **prove to be wrong.**

This story is as old as the computer industry itself. You don't have to believe me: Fred Brooks' classic *The Mythical Man Month* described how the larger the systems project, the more likely it was to be late. Even better, the further a project was into its schedule, the more likely it was that increasing the staffing and investment would make it even later.

The classic complete-system launch, sometimes called a Big Bang project, just doesn't work for software. It can work when there is military-style command and control: the Manhattan project, Operation Desert Storm, and the Apollo program are shining examples. But in business systems, it's hard to find examples where a Big Bang was a big success. Businesses don't have tight military hierarchies, and IT has a culture of trying to accommodate new business requirements during the project. This accommodation and tendency toward scope creep—particularly in software—is a poisonous cocktail. The Standish Group, an IT consultancy, published a series of studies that extensively analyzed failed IT projects. *The Chaos Reports* concluded that overblown requirements and overzealous adherence to large, monolithic deliveries were key warning signs of failed projects.

We'll discuss this issue in detail in Chapter 4. For now, be aware that the most important thing the project team can do before any project work begins is to **avoid three things**:

- Fake, vague, or overstated requirements

- Infrequent project milestones

- Large, complex, monolithic project deliverables

AVOIDING SCOPE CREEP

Scope creep is one of the most dangerous things that can happen to a project, and the danger grows in tandem with the size and length of the effort. This problem occurs whenever a requirement is stretched, an assumption made that "we can fit that in," or an *even better idea* is proposed by executives.

The chief symptom of scope creep: the requirements list grows while the project is under way. Because items aren't removed from the priority list, the number of deliverables grows even though the budget and schedule are unchanged (or worse, are being overspent by the project).

There's a particular temptation to load up the requirements even further whenever a project needs to get a schedule or budget extension, even though it should be obvious the project is already at risk of under-delivering.

The only solution for scope creep is vigilance among everyone on the project team, regular management reviews to root out new creepy requirements, a very persuasive project leader, and consistency on the part of executives. The project leader will need to develop political skills to escalate scope-creep issues without angering the people who are proposing the additional Great Things for the project.

Even if the project has been "sold" with a lofty set of goals and tight Big Bang deadlines, it is important to quickly move to a phased approach. This isn't just because of the IT "laws of physics"; it's also human nature. Put simply, change management and confidence building take time. For even small companies, reset executive expectations by making the following arguments:

- We all know what the desired end-state is going to be, and those goals have been agreed to. But until the project is fairly far along, we can't know which problems we'll find in our data, precisely how business processes need to change, or exactly what every user will need.

- Given this inevitable uncertainty, the best way to achieve our goals is to rapidly deliver a part of the project big enough to *provide value to the business.* This first delivery will give users a chance to learn the system and provide real-world feedback that will improve later system deliveries.

- Delivery after the first phase should be incremental, with each cycle providing a new element of value to the business. Having small, frequent deliveries makes it more likely we'll have happy users and low risk while meeting budgetary and schedule goals.

In making these arguments, the trick is to find the right "cornerstone functionality" to deploy for each phase, paired with the internal constituency you want to leverage. This decision making will be profiled in detail for each phase as described in Chapter 4, but as part of selling the project you'll need to establish the constituency for the first phase's subsystem right now.

The best way to select the subsystem is to answer this question: Which system element could be deployed the soonest and deliver real value to a meaningful constituency? By producing a quick win, you earn credibility for the project as well as users for the system.

Outsourcing

Almost inevitably, you will need to use some outsource resources to assist in the project implementation, and you'll want at least budgetary placeholders for them. There are many tasks that your internal team *shouldn't want to get good at.* Even so, you cannot outsource everything—your team must be involved to define business rules, perform data extraction, review prototypes, validate data conversion, do acceptance testing, and, of course, manage the project. One thing to insist upon is a full "technology transfer" from any consultant you use, so that your team becomes self-sufficient in any area of ongoing development or maintenance.

In evaluating and choosing vendors, follow these rules of thumb:

- The product vendor's consultants will know more about the *internal* workings of their product than any partner consultant can. They will also have direct access to product engineering, and will have several "back door" tricks that can save time and make their prices a bargain. For internal extensions, customizations, scripting, rule setting, query design, and other "deep dive" projects directly related to their own products, the vendors' consultants are likely to be the best choice. However, they are less likely to be the right people for external integrations or business process design.

- A specialist system integrator with a practice dedicated to SFDC or other SaaS product is likely to know best how to do "external work" that integrates across applications. However, these individuals' level of knowledge and skill regarding business processes vary dramatically. In fact, many firms that are fully qualified at the technical level have zero capability when it comes to understanding and optimizing business processes. Check references before you make specific task allocations!

- A technical "coding shop" typically will be very good in its particular domain (for example, enhancing a CMS-driven Web site or an external order-management system), but those employees may not have experience with Web services and high-speed integration using SOAP.[9] Even though most SaaS applications use Web services for integration, every vendor uses the core technology a different way. For this reason, it's important to check the vendor's experience with SFDC's APIs and any AppExchange products you're planning to use. As always, references are more meaningful than vendor claims.

- A consultant who already works with your company has a natural advantage over outsiders. In addition to already being "connected" in your organization, the incumbent consultant is much more likely to know a lot about your technical environment and at least something about your business processes. Check with your IT organization to find out who is already under contract. If you've got only a few person-months of work to do, the incumbent's advantage may be a decisive one.

- Data cleansing and enrichment houses can be very economical (using tools and offshore resources unavailable to you), but this part of the project must be done *right and completely* to be at all meaningful. Check whether the vendor has done work on your size database in an SFDC project: most have not, and they'll experience a serious learning curve. Check references to confirm the details, because offshore data cleansing/enrichment operations tend to overstate their capabilities and are very *in*efficient at learning to do new things.

- Management consultants, sales process consultants, and organizational design specialists understand the human side of your business processes better than any other vendor type. Large organizations will typically need to use these consultants to optimize business processes, redesign sales procedures, and set policies. However, these consultants are rarely in a position to do implementation work, because they don't

---

9. Many readers won't know what SOAP is, but that's okay because it's a great litmus test for system integrators. Ask them to explain it to you: if they don't know that it stands for "Simple Object Access Protocol," or that SOAP is the way to join applications (or Web services) together in a lightweight, loosely coupled fashion, maybe you should look elsewhere. SFDC has a rich set of SOAP application programmer interfaces (APIs) that let you access and manipulate almost any system data from other applications. Ask would-be integrators which version of the APIs they've used (if they aren't up to version 14, they probably aren't up to snuff).

understand the inner workings of SFDC and other systems well enough. They also have a tendency to make recommendations that are technically very difficult or even unfeasible to implement. So absolutely include them on your team to design best practices and increase the speed of user adoption—but do not expect them to implement much in SFDC.

No matter which kinds of vendors you use, it is essential that you have a positive, cooperative relationship with them. Adversarial relationships just don't work—in terms of price, quality, or schedule. That said, it's essential that you manage each vendor relationship tightly. Although you don't manage a vendor in the same way you would an employee, vendors are every bit as important to project success and budget as any other team members. Weekly checkpoints and monthly scorecards are essential for all vendors.

Generally speaking, there are several areas that you *don't* want to outsource. It typically doesn't pay to have an outside team learn the peculiarities of your old home-grown systems. An outsourcer should not be making policy and process decisions for your company (they can make recommendations, but *you* have to own the decision).

Even if a major technology is implemented by outsiders, your internal team needs to have ongoing capability and knowledge. For example, you'll want to be able to make simple system modifications without calling in a vendor, and it's a good idea to be able to make minor changes to cope with the inevitable upgrades of external systems or minor updates to business rules. In your resource allocation, think through which of the tasks *must* be done internally, which should be done through a vendor, and which should be done jointly.

Setting Executive Expectations

Executives have been trained to see a business case that's firm and a schedule with a clear end-date. Unfortunately, large systems projects don't fit that model too often. And Agile project management, which is designed to make quality deliveries of what's really needed in the shortest amount of time, creates a frustrating uncertainty about exactly what will be delivered when. The project leader must bridge that gap.

The first step is to convince the executives that SFA/CRM systems and processes must be adaptable to evolving business needs, so they are never completed the way a building would be. The next step is to focus attention on the cutover (or "go live") date, including the absolute minimum criteria that must be met to achieve this goal. Most significant SFDC implementations are replacements for previous systems, so it should be fairly straightforward to identify the criteria for the new system to be "good enough" to support the switchover. It is important to use terms like "good enough" or "acceptance criteria" to communicate that the system will continue to evolve after the go-live date. Some functional areas need to be only at the 80% level at cutover time to support the business.

As always, perfectionism does not pay. By focusing the discussion on what is really needed to support a given business process on a day-to-day basis, you can get realistic objectives and feedback on which tradeoffs could be acceptable at the go-live date. For example, it may be okay to *manually* approve orders for the first month of operation, so as to make sure that the automatic order approval rules accurately reflect your business policies.

The executives need to know that functionality will be delivered incrementally, and that their staff will need to play active roles in assuring quality over several phases. Executives also need to know when the key business processes affecting their specific departments will be done. Consequently, we recommend organizing the presentation of the schedule in two ways: chronologically, for the overview perspective, and organizationally, for each executive. Keeping the schedule in a spreadsheet (which can be generated from your Gantt charting tool) allows rapid creation of these executives' views, as shown in Figure 1-4. In this view, many tasks are repeated so that each executive can see the impact on his or her specific organization without having to refer elsewhere.

Phase Description	Start Date	Completion Date	Current Status	Business Processes
Executives				
2 Advanced forecasting	23-Apr	5-May	In progress	Pipeline management
3 Advanced forecasting reports and alerts	16-May	15-Jun	Not started	Pipeline management
3 Dashboards	16-May	1-Jun	Not started	Executive management
Sales				
1 Lead capture and routing	3-Mar	17-Mar	Done	Pipeline formation
1 Lead scoring and qualification	18-Mar	7-Apr	Done	Pipeline formation
2 Opportunity creation	8-Apr	15-Apr	Done	Pipeline formation
2 Basic forecasting reports	15-Apr	22-Apr	Done	Pipeline management
2 Opportunity aging and backtrack alerts	15-Apr	29-Apr	Done	Pipeline management
2 Advanced forecasting	23-Apr	5-May	In progress	Pipeline management
2 Order-level quoting	1-May	15-May	In progress	Quote to invoice
2 Line-item-level quoting	16-May	1-Jun	Not started	Quote to invoice
3 Historic opportunity import, 1 year	16-May	15-Jun	Not started	Quote to invoice
3 Historic opportunity import, 3 years	16-Jun	16-Aug	Not started	Quote to invoice
3 Contract import, 1 year	16-May	15-Jun	Not started	Support and renewals
3 Contract import, 3 years	16-Jun	16-Aug	Not started	Support and renewals
3 Support ticket integration	16-May	1-Aug	Not started	Support and renewals
3 Advanced forecasting reports and alerts	16-May	15-Jun	Not started	Pipeline management
Marketing				
1 Lead capture and routing	3-Mar	17-Mar	Done	Pipeline formation
1 Campaigns and Web site integration	3-Mar	24-Mar	Done	Pipeline formation
1 Historic lead import, 1 year	3-Mar	1-Apr	Done	Pipeline formation
1 Lead scoring and qualification	18-Mar	7-Apr	Done	Pipeline formation
3 Advanced campaign reports	16-May	15-Jun	Not started	Pipeline formation
Finance				
2 Advanced forecasting	23-Apr	5-May	In progress	Pipeline management
2 Order-level quoting	1-May	15-May	In progress	Quote to invoice
2 Line-item-level quoting	16-May	1-Jun	Not started	Quote to invoice
3 Historic opportunity import, 1 year	16-May	15-Jun	Not started	Quote to invoice
3 Historic opportunity import, 3 years	16-Jun	16-Aug	Not started	Quote to invoice
3 Contract import, 1 year	16-May	15-Jun	Not started	Support and renewals
3 Contract import, 3 years	16-Jun	16-Aug	Not started	Support and renewals
3 Advanced forecasting reports and alerts	16-May	15-Jun	Not started	Pipeline management
Support				
3 Historic opportunity import, 1 year	16-May	15-Jun	Not started	Quote to invoice
3 Historic opportunity import, 3 years	16-Jun	16-Aug	Not started	Quote to invoice
3 Contract import, 1 year	16-May	15-Jun	Not started	Support and renewals
3 Contract import, 3 years	16-Jun	16-Aug	Not started	Support and renewals

Figure 1-4   Executive's overview of deployment phases

One of the biggest challenges of setting executive expectations is the iceberg phenomenon: the toughest work in the project is in infrastructure and data cleanup that has no visible feature, no immediate "win" for any department. Most executives don't have patience for these intricacies of the project, and the best way to talk about them is in terms of "laying the foundation" for the features they want to see. Foundational work typically continues throughout the project, and it's often best to depict it during all phases. Even so, every single phase needs to deliver *some* interesting feature to at least one department, so the executives don't become frustrated with the amount of effort expended on "invisible stuff."

Getting the Right Resources Committed

At some point, there will be a meeting to make the decision to move forward. Usually, these meetings focus on the immediate expenditures. In contrast, commitments for ongoing expenses and effort are assumed away or quickly forgotten—and that's dangerous.

For a truly successful large-system implementation, the following funds must be assigned to the project *at the initial go/no-go meeting:*

- Initial procurement funding for the system, add-on products, and any hardware or IT resources required.

- Ongoing funding for the recurring fees, added to the budget for at least two years.

- Fees for consultants and service providers needed to configure, extend, integrate, and deploy the system.

- Fees for training courses and user-group sessions offered by the vendors.

- Dedicated personnel, typically in the form of a time allocation *with specific measured goals or MBOs:*

  ➥ To make ongoing priority calls about requirements and schedules.

  ➥ To decide policy issues and business rules.

  ➥ To design approval cycles, exception handling, and workflows.

  ➥ To do actual work on the SFDC system, including data cleansing, record imports, and other housekeeping tasks.

  ➥ To do work on external systems such as: data modeling, data dumps, enabling external interfaces, doing testing, and other tasks.

  ➥ To assist with IT infrastructure tasks (security audits, installing wiki software, server deployments, and so forth)

  ➥ To do technical tests of the SFDC system and validation of its external integrations.

➥ To do user testing of the system.

➥ To run final acceptance tests.

- Regular (brief) intervals of executive time, to escalate issues, break logjams, reallocate resources, and do final approvals.

Surprisingly, most executives tend to focus on the top of this list. In reality, the items near the bottom tend to cause the biggest issues with projects over time.

At the meeting, you'll also need to set general expectations—preferably quantitative metrics of success and criteria for a successful deployment—for the first phase. Without these objective measurements, executives tend to remember only the date for the first phase deployment, which tends to put people in happy-ears mode. Make sure to start the project off on the right foot, with documented budgets, schedules, and success criteria.

CHAPTER 2

Reports and Data

> *"A man's judgment cannot be better than the information on which he has based it. Give him the truth and he may still go wrong, but give him no news or present him only with distorted and incomplete data . . . and you destroy his whole reasoning process."*
>
> —*Arthur Hays Sulzberger*

R EPORTS ARE, FOR MANY users, the most relevant part of an SFA/CRM system. Reports are the first way that they approach the data, the way that they measure sales activity, and the way that they monitor the business processes. Given these uses, reports need to be meaningful and based on accurate data. The first part of this chapter shows how to use report design as a way to elicit requirements from the executives who will be using the system. The rest of the chapter focuses on the underlying data itself, because no one will use the system if the data are confusing or a waste of time.

For Users, Seeing Is Believing

For many system users, the way they understand a system is through the presentation of data. They don't care about how a feature works; they care about what the screen or report looks like and tells them. To users, "data" means "visibility."

In Chapter 1, you analyzed system requirements at a general level—that is, as functionality supporting business processes. This perspective is fine for the abstract thinkers in your company, but people don't usually think in terms of business process. To understand what business users *really* need, work with them to describe the reports they need to see or the charts they'll use in meetings.

In this chapter, we describe how to scope detailed system requirements through report and screen design. This process needs to be done early, to uncover the needs for remote system access, object relationships, and data quality *before* any of the project work begins.

.ven if a specific need won't be satisfied for several months, it's important to understand the need and make provisions for the required data now, to avoid painting yourself into a corner later on.

Start with What You Have

Almost any SFDC implementation will be a replacement for some other system. If your company uses Outlook and Excel for all of its SFA/CRM needs, or even if your only tools are a blackboard and a legal pad, SFDC will be replacing what you do now. Start the process by identifying which information is currently visible and reported on. Almost invariably in the existing system, there will be some way of interacting, viewing, and reporting on the following items:

- Prospects (leads)

- Customers (accounts)

- Sales representative activity (tasks)

- Pipeline and forecast (opportunities)

- Revenue (closed opportunities)

The Executive View

Start at the top of the organization, looking for the highest-level person who reviews these data on at least a monthly basis. Typically, that person is the VP of Sales, but the actual individual who fulfills this role depends on your organization. Interview this person and find out the *one critical report* he or she needs to do the job, and the five to seven pieces of information the individual needs (whether those data are part of the current system or not) to make key decisions. Here are example questions to ask:

- How often do you look at the information?

- Why do you look there, and what are you trying to measure or control?

- Which decisions do you make on the basis of the data—which actions do you take?

- How do these data affect the things that *you* are measured on?

- Which incentives are in place for the people below you to "do well" according to the data?

- If you question the data, how would you validate that information? What would you compare it to?

- If you found an error in the data, who would you talk to about getting it fixed?

- Which other items of information would be useful for you (i.e., would *actually* change your behavior or alter a decision)?

- Which comparisons (e.g., to history, industry norms) would be meaningful for these data?

Don't spend too much time trying to figure out what the executives would also find useful in an ideal world. The hard reality is that many an executive's thoughts on extra reports and data (1) are nearly impossible to implement and (2) wouldn't be as meaningful as that manager might think (having somehow survived without having the extra information until now). Even so, it's worth investigating the executives' answers to set helpful context about the system behaviors and data requirements.

Next, ask a few questions about the usage occasions and look and feel of the data—the data *presentation*:

- For information that is ad hoc or a quick lookup:

  - How do you find this information: through a search (by name or keyword), a view (e.g., "today's leads" or "New York deals"), or a bookmark (e.g., "the things I was looking at yesterday")?

  - What is the next step that executives take (e.g., once they've found the person or account they were looking for, what do they do next)?

- For information that is for personal review or analysis:

  - Which form is most convenient for looking at this information (for example, a report, an Excel spreadsheet, or a chart)?

  - What's the occasion (is this a weekly meeting with the boss or an annual strategy review)?

  - Which decisions are being made because of reported data? What is the real business objective of the report or analysis?

- For information that is for daily or weekly "health checks":

  - Which parts of this information need to be found on a graphical dashboard or a scorecard, and which parts need to be a listing that can be easily manipulated?

  - If the senior person favors management-by-exception, which exceptions are being monitored? Which kinds of alerts would be useful (e.g., automatically page me if a quote is for more than $100,000)?

- For information that is intended for presentation to management:

  - ➡ What is the occasion, and what are the key success factors that need to be presented? Which decisions are being made?

  - ➡ Which formats are being used (e.g., spreadsheet, pie chart, time series)?

  - ➡ In the preparations for these management meetings, which kinds of data problems need to be avoided? Can political fallout occur if the data is questioned? How is the management report or presentation validated and "bullet-proofed"?

After completing this cycle with the head of the sales function, repeat the questionnaire with his or her executive peers who (should) have access to and interest in the SFA/CRM data: the head of marketing, customer support, and perhaps the CFO and CEO. Each of their sets of answers should be recorded separately, but need to be reconciled against the other responses. For example, if the CFO and VP of Sales disagree about the meaning or consequences of data, it's important to get them talking to resolve the internal contradiction before any implementation begins. This area may require some political delicacy or even escalation to the SFDC project sponsor.

The View from the Trenches

The next step is to identify the 5 to (at most) 10 system users who will be looking at and interacting with SFDC data most intently on a daily basis. These people will likely be near the bottom of the organization, but they are on the front lines of lead generation, customer capture, and transactional truth. Ask these operational people the following questions:

- Which data screens or data views do you look at most often?

- Which actions or decisions do you take on the basis of the data?

- Which of your actions are triggered by changes in system data? What portion of your decisions or actions could be part of an automatic workflow?

- Which other items of information would be useful for you (i.e., data or trend information that would actually change your decisions and actions)?

- Which kinds of alerts or exception conditions need to be in force for your job? Which kinds of system data need to be monitored on at least a daily basis?

- Which reports do you run on a daily or weekly basis? Which data are being monitored by these reports?

- Which ad hoc reports or dashboards do you run? When are the standard reports or screens insufficient, and why?

- Which kinds of reports do you run to satisfy your immediate boss? What is the boss trying to measure or assess by running these reports?

Answers from each of the people surveyed should be recorded separately and analyzed for internal contradictions and gaps. If someone needs data that are not found in the system today, you need to figure out where those data will come from and who will enter and update them.

Scoping the System via Report Mock-Ups

After completing these interviews, the business analyst should create a composite of the reports that will be needed. Using some fake data, a set of management reports should be mocked up in Excel and given to users to review. Likewise, key management dashboards[1] should be mocked up (either in Excel spreadsheets, Visio diagrams, or PowerPoint drawings). Make sure to include in the review cycle at least one highly quantitative/analytical person from both the marketing group and the finance group, to make sure that their product, promotion, pricing, program, and profitability questions can be answered from the system's data. The layout and format of these mock-ups is not important, but the *content* of the mock-ups is critical to understanding the system requirements.

Check out SFDC's internal list of pre-canned reports (there are dozens of them, in the report tab), and select the top 10 or so most relevant ones to your company. Use these templates as starting points for your mock-ups.

While preparing the report mock-ups, capture the information listed in Table 2-1 in the Comments area of Excel or in the Notes area of PowerPoint pages.

TABLE 2-1   Data Attributes

Semantics	What is the meaning of the data item, and what do changes in value signify to the rest of the business?
Data source and timeliness	The source of each data item needs to be precisely understood. If the data elements come from outside the system, the analyst needs to understand how old the data can be (e.g., daily refresh versus continuous update) and whether the data can be updated by SFDC user entry (i.e., are the data read-write or read-only).
Response/reaction time	Which information must be acted on quickly, and what's the deadline? Which data are just reference or background information?
Accuracy	How accurate or detailed do the data need to be for each data item (e.g., does the report just need total units shipped to the customer or all specific serial numbers)? It may not matter if an address is missing or erroneous, but it's usually a big deal if the company name or price is wrong.

Continued

---

1. Often, users will describe dashboards that cannot be created within SFDC. Even so, the process provides important information about the kinds of reports and underlying data that will be needed for a successful system rollout.

TABLE 2-1   Data Attributes, *Continued*

Ownership	For the data native to the system,* which department is responsible for entering the data items? Which incentives and measurements need to be in place to make sure those personnel enter data quickly and accurately enough?
Access	Which people should have access to the reports, and will there need to be more than one version of `page layouts` to hide sensitive information? Are any special controls needed on the reports for compliance reasons?
Thresholds	What is the threshold for "interesting values" for each data item? For example, transactions involving less than $1,000 may be handled according to one set of rules, those between $1,000 and $50,000 based on another set of rules, and those involving more than $50,000 by a different set of rules.
Trends	What are the trends or perspectives that need to be captured or communicated? How long does a trend need to go on before it changes a decision?
Alerts and triggers	For the fields that trigger alerts or start workflows (e.g., executive reviews or approval cycles), the analyst needs to identify the trigger value, the meaning of the trigger, the alert that should be issued, and the workflow (e.g., escalation, approval) that should be started (if any).
Supporting detail	When looking at a dashboard, which supporting "drill-down" data do users need to support investigation and understanding?
Significant relationships	What are meaningful relationships among data items? For example, if the average deal size is decreasing but the total number of deals is increasing, is that a positive indicator for the business or a negative one?
Exports	Which `data` or `report` exports are needed from the system? Which spreadsheets need to be created on a regular basis, and who gets them? Which users should be authorized to get exports? Are any special controls needed on exports for compliance reasons?

* These data are originally entered by hand into SFDC; they do not include information integrated from an external system feed or a historical import.

Once the `report` and `dashboard` needs have been captured for headquarters, it's important to get feedback from one of the international sales operations. The feedback from international staff will probably differ in important details, such as the required accuracy for the data or the meaning of specific thresholds. It's fine for them to interpret the data differently, but you want to detect and document situations where they are looking at *different* data or would make *very different decisions* than the U.S. people would, given a specific situation or set of data. As before, you're looking for contradictions or gaps that need to be resolved before the work begins.

The Crux: Semantics

Each of the international variations needs to be assessed for its impact upon the system screens, reports, and overall data design. Thanks to SFDC's sophistication, screens can be customized by user `profile` (including considerations like `role` and location), and reports can be tailored to almost any individual need. But SFDC's data model—which fields are where, what they represent, what they mean—is singular and must hold true for *all* users and situations. So the data model is a big deal, and we'll be discussing it later in this chapter.

Spend significant effort to understand the meaning and semantics of business-critical data, so that no questions arise about such issues as the following:

- What does it mean to be a qualified `lead`?

- What triggers a `lead` becoming an `opportunity`?

- What are the stages an `opportunity` needs to go through to become a closed sale?

- What are the trigger events or conditions that move a prospect from one stage of the sales cycle to another, or a customer from one support status to another?

- How can we tell that a quote has been approved by management?

- What is the definition of a customer? When is a division a separate `account`?

- When is a bundle of products a new product, and when is it just a promotional price?

- What are the vendor-specific objective evidence (VSOE) conditions that trigger revenue recognition?

- How do you reopen a `case` that was falsely closed?

- What requires special approval, and why?

- How do we know that a customer is entitled to post sales support and warranty coverage?

It's amazing how much time you can waste in a meeting when there isn't a common understanding of the words "customer" and "deal."

To avoid confusion later, spend the time up front to ensure a common understanding of the meaning and behavior of data. Be on the alert for data items where the clarity of the definitions goes *down* the more people ask about it. The ambiguities become really important when a data item is stored in two different systems and called by two different names. To get the complete meaning of these hydra-headed data items, you may have to survey a wide range of people—not only up and down the organization, but across organizations.

YOUR DATA DICTIONARY

As you collect all of the requirements for data items—both within SFDC and in other systems—you will need to document the characteristics of each piece of data. Your data dictionary should be done either as an Excel spreadsheet (if you've got a fairly simple implementation) or as a highly structured Word document (with change bars on so everyone can see the revision history). It should contain most of the items indicated in Table 2-1, plus these elements:

- Data item field name and description.
- Technical metadata: data type, number of characters/digits, allowable values, correlations/connections to other data items, rules/constraints about the data values, and so on.
- Data ownership and security: who owns the data, who is allowed to see it, who is allowed to change it, and so on.
- Provenance: What is the original source of the data? How do we know the data in this item are correct and authoritative? Where are the data stored, and which systems modify the data values? Which audit trails are (or need to be) maintained?
- Data quality: What are the known issues with the quality of data in this field? Which kinds of interactions or changes could degrade the data quality?

The data dictionary file(s) should be posted to the project's wiki.

Reports—Inside Versus Outside

SFDC has a powerful Web-based reporting system that is intuitive and useful for most initial data inquiries. Dozens of predefined reports come with the system, designed for marketing, sales, administrators, and executives. The reports can be generated quickly, are correct, are fairly intuitive, and produce charts that are at the core of dashboards.

Unfortunately, SFDC's reports cannot be made very pretty, and the large ones are hard to read. To achieve good format control and fast data scanning, even the simplest reports should be exported to Excel (either using the `export details` button or via the SFDC's `Office connector` plugin, which allows pulling down of reports from within Excel). For all executive meetings and external presentations, use Excel for report reformulation, formatting, and arranging.

More importantly for the data junkies, most SFDC reports can fully explore only one object[2] at a time. While several helpful reports join data from two objects (for example, `opportunities` with `products`), and `custom report types` provide amazing flexibility within the wizard system, it's all too common for product marketing and business analysts to need a three-way (or even more) join of objects. You are almost certain to find at least one executive asking for a report that *cannot be created* in SFDC's internal report system.

To create these more sophisticated reports, there are four options. Any of them will work, but different organizations tend to gravitate to only one of them:

- Export the raw data to Excel, and use `VLOOKUP` formulas to create the joins and `Pivot Tables` to design the views that are needed. The advantages here are intuitiveness for Excel users, the ability to rapidly create charts and exports that are easily used by the rest of the organization, and the power of VB macros. Note that this strategy will not work for data tables involving more than 64,000 rows[3] and will be quite slow for tables beyond 32,000 rows.

- Export the raw data to Access or your business's favorite desktop relational database, and use the tool's database view design and join capabilities. The advantages here are power, speed, programmability, and intuitiveness for Access users. Access can easily crunch hundreds of thousands of items, and for purely relational problems it's more straightforward than working in Excel. (Of course, Access and Excel can be used together, particularly for formatting and chart generation.)

- Export the raw data to a report generation engine, particularly for reports that need to be generated on a regular basis. These report engines are typically optimized for creating a large number of reports, but they can also be used for powerful one-time-use reports on an ad hoc basis. Several report engines are available in SFDC's AppExchange, but these engines can be expensive and require user training.

- Export the raw data to a data warehouse or business intelligence (BI) tool. The advantage here is speed and analytical power: for ad hoc "what if" and multidimensional analysis, no other option can come close to this strategy. While these tools are expensive and require user training, they can illuminate issues and make discoveries better than any other approach. They also can generate graphics that can silence any debate about the validity or relevance of the data.

---

2. Object-oriented purists can ignore this footnote. SFDC is fairly object oriented, and it organizes all data into a small number of hierarchical business objects. For example, almost all of the information about people is stored in either the `lead` or `contact` object. Information about deals is stored in `opportunity`, `assets`, and `contract` objects. SFDC's internal reports usually provide information on just one of these objects, so if you want to know about all people in the system, you have to write at least two reports (for leads and contacts).

3. Although Excel 2007 can handle more than 64,000 rows, SFDC's `Excel connector` cannot deal with any more than that. Using SFDC's `Data loader`, Excel can be filled to the rafters with data records, but the spreadsheets will take a long time to open and can be amazingly slow to manipulate. If you choose to go this direction, make sure to turn auto-calculation off in Excel before you load the spreadsheets.

> **REPORTING ON OLD DATA**
>
> *Reporting on data that are more than two years old can be tricky in SFDC—data disappear from view if you don't ask for that information in exactly the right way.[4] If you routinely need to do a lot of historical analysis, you'll probably want to dump a copy of the old data into a data warehouse or BI tool database.*

You'll notice that none of these strategies includes the idea of modifying the report data outside of SFDC. That's because it is a sublimely horrible idea. The goal is to have SFDC be the system of record for much, if not all, of the customer relationship. So while it's okay to *filter* data outside the system, actually *changing* values in the external reporting system would be—in the immortal words of Harold Ramis in *Ghostbusters*—"very bad." If you find data that mess up external reports, fix the data at their origin—whether in SFDC, or in an external system from which SFDC pulls source data, or in a business process that is causing data pollution. If instead you make data fixes in an external reporting system, you are unlikely to document what you did or to replicate those changes in the original source. As a consequence, the external reports will no longer agree with SFDC's internal reports and dashboards, undermining the credibility of the system *and* the data analyst at the same time.

All that said, external reports (particularly in a data warehouse) can rapidly expose contradictions and ambiguities in the SFDC data. Data warehouse and business intelligence tool users should be encouraged to report discrepancies in data they analyze and to notify members of the Data Architecture Review team (discussed in Chapter 3) so they can understand the problem and examine corrective measures.

Scoping the System via User Screen Design

Now that you've done a "reverse engineering" of data requirements from reports, you should use a similar tactic to capture the system's functional requirements by designing user screens. As before, create mock-ups of the key user screens in PowerPoint, Visio, or Excel. This time, however, you'll also need to create storyboards that describe the customer interactions and business situations that are the very reason the SFDC users are trying to work on the system. For example, a storyboard could describe an irate customer who is trying to get an exchange for defective merchandise. Check out www.SFDC-secrets.com for example storyboards and screen mock-ups.

---

4. Using the Excel connector or the SFDC API's AllSelect SOQL verb.

Create mock-ups and storyboards for each of the following elements:

- **SFDC screens:** For most installations, SFDC has basically one main screen for each internal object: `leads`, `campaigns`, `contacts`, `accounts`, `opportunities`, `quotes`, `orders`, `contracts`, and `cases`. Identify any screen design requests where the users are asking for things that straddle SFDC objects.[5]

- **External system screens:** Assuming that the external systems will be integrated with SFDC, the typical approach is to use `tabs` (for dedicated external screens) or `S-controls` (for external system frames embedded within an existing SFDC screen). The mock-up needs to show whether the external system has its own screen (via a new window pop-up or dedicated tab), is visible through a subwindow (via frames or mashups), or is represented as new custom data fields within an existing SFDC screen. Each of these approaches is equally valid, but each also presents a different user experience and requires a different level of effort.

- **Views and searches:** A view is a mini-report that quickly guides the user to a subset of data (for example, "deals I've edited today"); a search is a way of rapidly getting to relevant individual records. Summarizing views and searches—navigational aids—helps the implementation team see how the users think about the system, and it may uncover misunderstandings and imprecisions related to the data semantics. Each view should be mocked up as a spreadsheet, and each type of search should be described in a text document.

- **Interactions:**[6] Each class of user will use the system to complete some business process interactions (the more sophisticated the user, the more interactions he or she will have). These interactions should be documented as PERT charts, process-flow diagrams, or checklists. While almost any tool can be used for text, the diagrams are best created in Visio or similar tool.

- **Alerts and workflows:** The system will probably need to trigger automatic workflows or issue alerts for exception handling. For example, management will need to approve large discounts or unusual payment terms. These management-by-exception aids should be documented as PERT charts or process-flow diagrams, with special attention being given to the trigger criteria, escalation conditions, approval delegation, and process routing exceptions for large backlogs or "emergency" conditions.

---

5. These will be more difficult requirements to satisfy; you'll want to push back on the user pretty hard to make sure it's a real business need.

6. *Interactions* here are defined as any decisions and activities that users engage in beyond simple data reading and updating. Interactions are typically part of a larger business process. For example, it's not an interaction to update a user's phone number, but it *is* an interaction to cancel an order because of a bad payment history.

While preparing these mock-ups and story boards, the business analyst should capture the following information in the Comments area of Excel or in the Notes area of PowerPoint pages. In addition to the items listed in Table 2-1, find out about these data characteristics:

- **User resistance:** Which kinds of information will users resist updating? Which kinds of things are they trying to hide (or hide from)?

- **Clutter:** For the front-line users (telesales, sales, and customer support), determine the *absolute minimum set of data* they need to see to do their jobs. Which fields, screens, and steps can be hidden from various users to make the system easier to use?

- **Format/layout:** SFDC's default user interface supports simple two-column layouts for fields, with almost no flexibility. If some fields need special layout (e.g., quarterly financial information or other tabular data), annotate the number of columns and rows that will be needed. This will involve special `VisualForce` coding, and needs to be specified up front.

- **Required fields and default values:** What are the very few required fields? For all fields, what is the appropriate default value?

A Guided Tour of the SFDC Object Model

To understand how to map all the data requirements into the system design, you need to understand how all the data are organized within SFDC. This is not an abstract exercise: you need to develop a list of which data are a standard part of SFDC, which data need to be added as `custom fields` or `custom objects`, and which data need to be integrated from outside systems.

Business software such as SFDC includes a complex set of internal data tables that represent the business objects you work with—`opportunities`, `contracts`, `cases`, and so forth. While it is not necessary to understand the internals, you *do* need to understand some of the basics and the relationships among the largest components of the system. This knowledge is particularly important when designing reports and user screens, because much of the time standard reports or screens can interact with only one of the system's objects at a time.

So let's start with the basics: What is an "object"? The easiest way to think about this concept is as a tab in SFDC: `leads`, `contacts`, `accounts`, and `opportunities` are all examples of high-level objects. Objects are typically hierarchical, with parent–child relationships (for example, the "parent account" field in the `account` object may point from a division up to the headquarters office).

If you look at an `account` (or any of the SFDC objects that has its own tab), the top part of the page is called the `account detail`. This is the only part of the page you edit directly, and it's where the data and attributes of the `account` object are presented. Below the detail area of the page are a series of related lists—for example, `contacts`, `contact roles`, `open activities`, and `activity history`. These related lists show an overview of the children of the main object you're examining. In most cases, the parental relationship is unique: an `account`'s `contacts` aren't attached to any other `account`.

But in some cases, the items in the related list are inherited[7] from one or more children. For example, a contact may have an open activity (and if you looked at that contact's record, the activity would show up in the related list), but when you look at the contact's account you'll see the same open activity shows up there as well. This inheritance doesn't always occur for all objects, but when it would be helpful to see the "roll-ups" of things like activities, SFDC will present them.

With all these parent–child relationships, what's the "top of the family tree"? From the system's perspective, almost everything attaches one way or another to accounts,[8] as shown in Figure 2-1. But instead of explaining this concept in an abstract, top-down way, it will be more intuitive to talk about the object model in a more chronological way.

For most users, the first time they interact with the system is to look at a lead. Leads are people who have declared some level of interest in your product or service—they registered on a Web page, or attended a seminar, or stopped by your tradeshow booth. We don't know much about leads, other than basic contact information and some level of interest.

There is an amazing amount of confusion about what a lead is and how it should be treated. We'll explore the best practices for sales and marketing in Chapters 9 and 10, but here we will simply talk about what the objects are and how they are related. A person stays as a lead for as long as that individual is just curious—wanting information, but not wanting to start a sales cycle with us. A person could remain a lead for five minutes or for five years. For a number of reasons, even if a person walks up to us and immediately asks to buy, that individual should be initially entered into the system as a lead.

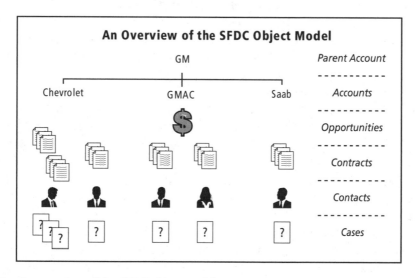

FIGURE 2-1   An overview of the SFDC object model

---

7. I know this is the reverse of the normal definition of "inherited," but these usages were invented by software engineers who, frankly, didn't get out much.

8. Of course, there are dozens of exceptions, but I'm trying to keep things simple here. For a thorough technical explanation of the SFDC object model, check out the AppExchange and DeveloperForce for presentations, white papers, and tools such as the Object explorer.

As soon as a person starts to express interest in doing business, the lead needs to be converted into a contact. Contacts are people who are attached to accounts (companies) and are considering doing a transaction with us. The possible transaction is called an opportunity. A specific contact can be attached to only one account (his or her employer), but may be involved in several opportunities. It's easiest to see a contact as a grown-up lead, but this is not quite true and causes some confusion. Think of it more like a caterpillar and a butterfly: they're the same animal, but with very different characteristics at different stages of life. Once the butterfly is born, the caterpillar is gone. When someone is a lead, we didn't know much about the person beyond his or her topic of interest and maybe the purchase timeframe. When the lead grows up to being a contact, we know more about him or her as an individual, but the information about the product interest and purchase timeframe has been stripped away. This information isn't a permanent characteristic of the person—his or her interest and purchase intentions will change over time—so in the conversion process that information is removed from the lead and put into the opportunity record.

Conversion is a one-way process: contacts can never devolve into leads.[9] The conversion process involves the transformation of a lead into a contact, the creation of an account (or the attachment of the contact to an existing account), the creation of an opportunity (the purpose of conversion is to signal the start of a sales cycle), and the creation of a follow-up task (to make sure that things move forward).

A lead and a contact are the only two objects in the system that describe a person. Every bit of contact information and personal information can only be stored either in a lead record or a contact record. All other objects in the system describe abstractions (a corporation, a contract, a purchase decision) or events (a service call, an action item, an email exchange). So a lead (a person) cannot evolve into an opportunity (a thing). Even though you'll hear people say that leads become opportunities, don't let their misunderstanding of these concepts confuse *you*.

Once the conversion has occurred, the sales rep should interact mainly with the opportunity record—that's what will become a deal, and that's where the most relevant information about the pending transaction is kept. The opportunity detail information is fairly sparse: the expected amount and close date of the deal, its current status, and maybe information about the competitors. But opportunities have a lot of related objects: the account, the contacts that are relevant to this opportunity, the roles (such as purchasing agent) of each contact, the products that are being considered, the forecasts that have been made, and the open activities that represent action items, meetings, and other next steps.

When the sale is made, the opportunity is closed out and a contract is linked to the account. The contract typically contains a small amount of unique information (such as a term, renewal date, and payment schedule), but is used to determine eligibility for support, trigger renewal marketing, and other administrative activities.

---

9. This is stated from a user's perspective. A system administrator can actually turn contacts back into leads again, but it's a very complex process that is done en masse, to correct erroneous user actions (fake conversions, usually done to game the system metrics that their bosses see).

The last major object from the user's perspective is the case, an incident reported to the customer support organization. Cases contain customer issues and resolutions, and their solutions can be summarized into knowledge bases used by customers for self-support.

If you want to understand any of these areas in more detail, SFDC has the full object model available at www.salesforce.com/us/developer/api/index.htm.

These core objects point to one another in subtle ways to make relationships. For example, a contact may be involved in multiple opportunities in different ways. Each of those contact-opportunity relationships (called a contact role) is tracked separately. By combining these objects, relationships, and states, SFDC creates its native applications. Each application shares the same data, but presents it from different perspectives, for the following purposes:

- Sales force automation

- Call center automation

- Marketing campaigns

- Support automation

SFDC makes it very easy to extend the data model, object model, and applications on your own or via plugin applications in the AppExchange (see Chapter 7 for a discussion of these free and low-cost products). Of course, the extensions you put in need to be consistent with the underlying object model because the data will be shared with other applications. Any custom fields or custom objects added into the system must reinforce the object model, which focuses the juiciest data on the opportunity and case records.

Let's take a look at some common misconceptions:

- Information about competitors may legitimately start out in leads, but competitive information learned in the course of a sales cycle needs to be added to opportunities. Competitors are situation specific, so "what's the competitive product" should not be attached to the contact, the account, or even the contract.

- Information about the customer's project team (such as the number of team members) we're working with in a deal should be attached to the opportunity, but users often ask for the data to be attached to the contact or the account. Project teams are transitory and are not the company—so they shouldn't be described in the account record. Project teams comprise more than one person. Also, even if we're dealing with the project leader, that role is transitory. The best way to describe a project team is to add its members into the contact roles area of the opportunity.

- The current state of a deal should always be stored only in the opportunity record. If a particular person is acting as our champion in the deal, that information needs to reside in the opportunity record (as a contact role), not as a field in the contact or account record.

- Phone calls and `tasks` related to an `opportunity` should be attached there, rather than to the `contact` records that are involved with the deal. The `tasks` will still indicate the name of the person involved, but it's important to attach the `task` in the most relevant, visible place.

- An `activity` indicating a casual social meeting with a purchasing agent—not tied to any specific deal, but generalities about the account management—should be attached to the `contact` record. However, if there is discussion about a new purchasing policy or an organizational budgetary cap, that information is relevant at the `account` level and should be attached there.

Of course, the worst problems with "extended fields" occur where there isn't any extension at all: users simply scribble information they want to save in random text fields such as `description`, `comments`, or `notes`. While the users may be consistent enough in this practice to make the data usable by humans, the resulting information is so unstructured and irregular that it can't be reported, summarized, or used as the basis for triggers or alerts. Although I consistently advise keeping the number of visible fields to a minimum, if you discover users adding data randomly to long text fields in SFDC pages, it's a sure sign that at least one additional field is needed in your existing data model.

What's in a Namespace?

A "namespace" is the formal way to refer to all the allowable words (or numbers) accepted when identifying or describing something. A namespace may be thought of as a naming convention.

The easiest example of a namespace is a pick list: all the allowable names (or values) are there for users, and they can select only names from the list. As only an administrator inserts new names into the list, there's no way for a user to accidentally enlarge the namespace or cause a confusing duplication.

More realistic namespaces are a lot more difficult to maintain, because no one knows in advance what the names will be—yet you have to think through at the beginning so that you'll have a paradigm to handle all possible names that your business might need.

In the case of people (`leads` and `contacts`), you don't have to come up with a namespace: society did that for you. Most of the time in SFDC, the namespace for people can just be the first name and last name. If you have a serious number of people in the system, it's best if you add the middle initial or some other identifier to distinguish John A. Smith from John B. Smith. If you don't have the middle initial, consider using a state as a placeholder (like this: John [MI] Smith for the John Smith who registered from Michigan). If you have an unbelievable number of names (millions of consumers), you may need to put a serial number or date stamp in the bracketed area.

In contrast to people's names, the names for accounts, opportunities, campaigns, contracts, products, pricelists, cases, documents, folders, reports, dashboards, and several other objects have to be very carefully designed. If you don't choose them correctly, you'll either confuse yourself, lose things, or confound SFDC processing.

Names in a namespace must be easy for a human to unambiguously understand, and be mechanically parsable by the system (for reports, filters, validation, triggers, and so forth). SFDC may have no problem with a product called 234-xy-593.23-US, but that's not likely to be very user-friendly. At the other extreme, a product called "today's special" will cause endless problems in screens, reports, and external integration—and it is so ambiguous that it's likely to frustrate the users as well.

For example, you might have an account in your system called "DOTnet Consulting" in the United States. Suppose you start to do business in Germany, and find an identically named account there. The U.S. and German companies are unrelated and need to be handled separately. So you might add a country identifier to your namespace, so that all account names are unique. In this example, "US–DOTnet Consulting" would be different from "DE–DOTnet Consulting." Naming accounts this way makes it really easy to filter by country and ensure that the two companies are never confused by humans or system reports.

To design a good namespace, think about the following issues:

- What is the range of items that the namespace will need to encompass over the next three years? For example, a product namespace might need to include new product lines, seasonal promotions, industry-specific packages, customer specials, upgrade items, and replacement parts. How will the namespace indicate this year's upgrade product versus next year's? Will the names be unique so that they can't be confused by the system?

- Will the names be easily grasped by humans?

- For the other systems that already deal with these same items, what do they currently call them? Could there already be more than one naming convention in your organization? Might one of the existing namespaces be usable in SFDC, or will you need to create a new namespace and have a correspondence between the two? If so, is there any reason why the correspondence will *not* be unique (i.e., one-for-one)?

- If you are integrating your internal systems with external systems that need to refer to your new namespace, are those external systems technically able to accommodate all of your names? For example, are the external systems able to handle uppercase letters only, with no numbers, lowercase, accents, punctuation, or other semantics? For instance, will they be able to deal with names of only 20 characters (no more, no less)?

- How will you need to use the names? Will they appear only in an SFDC record, or will they be used outside the system? Can they be easily searched for in SFDC or in your company's intranet search engine? Will users ever need to understand the name when it is read over the phone or left in a voicemail?

- How will the names look in a list or report? Can the names be sorted alphabetically and still convey meaning?

- How will the names look to people outside the United States? Can the namespace accommodate foreign character sets (for example, to handle a European company's name)? Will sorting the names using international sorting standards cause confusion?

- Do the names refer to individuals in your company? If so, can they be replaced with their function's name? For example, instead of a name like "Joe's territory," can you use "Northwest U.S. mid-market territory?" A few quarters from now, Joe is inevitably going to move on and be replaced by Sam.

- How will the names look in captions that may be automatically generated in charts and dashboards? Will people quickly get their meaning even if the names are truncated?

SFDC's Data Requirements

In the course of developing all of the mock-ups, you will almost always discover significant implications about the data that will be required. The system will need three categories of data: internal, external, and historical. As the difficulty and cost of each of these types of data vary widely, we'll discuss them separately.

Internal SFDC Data

Internal SFDC data are collected and entered directly in SFDC, involving almost no interaction with outside systems. For example, `lead` data may enter the system from the Web site and spreadsheet imports; `opportunity` data may be entered by sales reps and sales administrators. For purposes of this analysis, the internal data do *not include any historical*[10] *system data:* they consist of only the data collected from the go-live date onward.

Generally speaking, you should keep the number of fields to the absolute minimum. Resist the temptation to add lots of nice-to-have fields, because every one of them has to be entered and interpreted by someone. If a field is going to be empty 25% of the time and wrong another 25% of the time, leave it out: it will only be an irritant for the person entering the data and a detractor of system credibility for anyone trying to use it. It's very easy to add new fields at any time later—but properly *removing* spurious fields can involve a lot of data crunching.

---

10. If SFDC is a replacement for an existing SFA/CRM system, all of the current system's data is considered "historical" for the purposes of this section.

Whenever you want to modify or add a field, always create a new custom field. Leave the system-standard fields alone, as they are much less flexible than the ones you define yourself—not only in terms of the initial system setup, but in terms of the advanced functionality you'll want later. There may be a dozen system defined fields that you *must* use,[11] but I recommend that you use a custom field any time you can.

On any data entry page, a few items must be filled in before the page can be saved. Keep the number of required fields to the absolute minimum, as they irritate users. I can't remember the last time I saw a page requiring more than five items to be filled in, and even that was a debatable decision.

Special attention must be given to any user data that has legal status as "personal information." The clearest examples are credit card, Social Security, insurance policy, and financial institution account numbers: avoid these items like the plague. Storing this kind of personal information in SFDC may make the system subject to PCI, HIPAA, FERPA, or other compliance audits, and it may even incur the wrath of regulators. If your company already stores these data in other systems, **leave the data there** and specify that SFDC integrate with those systems of record via an arm's-length relationship (e.g., using a "mashup" window to view the data that are always stored in the original system).

SFDC's internal data will come almost entirely from human data entry, which is the most costly and error-prone source. To the maximum degree possible, avoid free-form typing: use pick lists ("pull-downs"), lookups, and check boxes instead (see Figure 2-2 for examples).

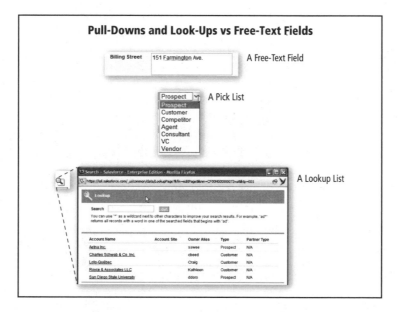

FIGURE 2-2   Pull-downs and lookups versus free-text fields

---

11. Such as opportunity stage, probability, and amount.

A pick list allows selection of allowable values. Even though pick lists must be maintained as the system evolves, they speed error-free data entry. Using pick lists means planning (oh darn . . .), but has big payoffs over the life of the system. Here are considerations for pick lists:

- A pick list should be kept to fewer than 20 items whenever possible, and longer lists should be broken into categories or hierarchies that lend themselves to dependent fields (for example, "job title" should be a dependent field of "department" to avoid presenting invalid choices to users).

- If a pick list will have only two or three items, use check boxes or radio buttons instead.

- When creating pick lists, leave out items you're not sure you need. It is very easy to add pick list values later, but removing those values involves some careful data decisions and costly data crunching.

- When a number to be entered doesn't need to be precise—for example, if it lends itself to a range or a band, such as number of employees—consider using a pick list instead of a number field. However, if the bands or ranges will not be consistent (e.g., a "midsize" company in the United Kingdom is 1,000 employees but in the United States is 5,000 employees), either define the bands vaguely (e.g., "small to medium business"), use record types, or stay with number entry.

In contrast to a pick list, a lookup field allows selection of only allowable values, but it doesn't need to be maintained as the system evolves. However, lookup fields involve a pop-up window and extra mouse clicks.

A free-text field is infinitely flexible, but it doesn't give any clues as to format or allowable values. It virtually guarantees typos and requires offline cleansing or correction. For items that must be left to free-entry fields (for example, "D-U-N-S number" or "SIC code"), think through the range of reasonable values to see if there's a way to "type"[12] the data.

- Assign data to proper types, such as date, phone number, or number. This is the first step toward trapping bad data at the source.

- If there are strong patterns in the data (such as phone numbers or ZIP codes), assign validation rules to flag bad data before they are entered (e.g., a ZIP code is 5 or 5 + 4 digits, an international postal code is 1 to 7 alphanumeric characters). SFDC

---

12. Data types are a way of structuring fields to behave in a consistent way. "Number," "currency," and "phone number" are example data types in SFDC. Typed fields are inherently easier to search, validate, and maintain than "strings" or free-text fields.

provides data-entry `validation` `rules` for numbers and text to ensure that each field's entry is within acceptable ranges.

* Data `validation` `rules` can be fairly complex formulas that ensure the correspondence of key fields. For example, validation can make sure that the state code entered is valid for the country code entered.

* Even though `data` `validation` works fine for individual data items, it can't trap "silly" entries (such as the address "123 Cherry Lane, Anytown, IL, 60609" or the email address "asdf@fubar.com"). As we'll discuss in Chapter 13, system administrators will need to create data quality reports that highlight unexpected trends in records and implement an ongoing bad-data removal process.

Long-text fields are almost always a bad idea. Over time, they will be filled with (1) nothing, (2) long narratives that are better stored as attachments or notes, or (3) weird "overloaded" data that should have been stored as one or more numerical fields. In any case, long-text fields are almost impossible to search or report on, which renders them only marginally useful. All too often, long-text fields hold "incidental information" that will be ignored by humans and systems alike. For situations where long text really is required, it's usually best to store those data as notes attached to the main record.

If certain combinations of data in a record are significant, consider creating a new field that captures the significant combination. For example, companies with more than 1,000 employees in the United Kingdom may be flagged as Major accounts, whereas as companies in the United States might require 5,000 employees to qualify for this status. Due to this ambiguity, adding a check box for "Major account" to the record can be very helpful to users looking at the screen and make it much easier to write reports. If the significant combinations are simple and routine enough, they can be automatically indicated using SFDC's `formula` fields or `workflow` `field` `updates`.

As discussed earlier, it's important to add any custom fields according to SFDC's object model, particularly with respect to `leads`, `contacts`, `opportunities`, `contracts`, `assets`, and `cases`. It's very common to put data in the wrong places, and fixing these errors can become very expensive down the road.

That said, sometimes it's helpful to denormalize data by including (partially) redundant entries in different parts of the object model to make it easier for the user to find and report on relevant data.[13] Continuing with the Major account example, the check box would normally be visible only if you're looking at the `account` object. It may be very helpful to add that check box to the `opportunity` and `contact` records as well. This can usually be accomplished with a workflow or some `APEX` code. But denormalizing always has a cost: either you

---

13. Database purists will cringe through this paragraph, but despite their rantings there are practical situations where denormalization is a valid choice. Just know the costs and risks, and engineer for automatic updating of denormalized fields.

must write some code to keep this duplicated data up-to-date, or you must have a person who updates the redundant copy of the data and cleans up others' errors.

SPLIT BRAIN

At first blush, you would expect the SFDC database to hold everything having to do with prospects and customers. But sophisticated organizations often use a split-brain approach that separates the *marketing* database from the *sales* database. Organizations take this tack for two reasons: they often have a large number of low-quality leads (really, they're little more than Names) that aren't relevant to the sales folks, and they use a marketing automation tool or service that needs to operate from its own copy of the data.

What's involved with the split-brain approach? The marketing pool of Names is managed in a separate database, and the transaction history of campaigns and responses is managed there. When a Name starts behaving more like a lead (as reflected in its internal lead score), it is promoted from the marketing pool to the sales lead area. Its data are deactivated in the marketing Names database and (semi-) automatically entered into SFDC as a hot lead.

Leads also migrate in the other direction. When a lead has been unresponsive, has lost interest, or has been demoted by sales,[14] it is deactivated in SFDC and reactivated in the marketing Names database. Neither leads nor Names should ever be deleted from either SFDC or the external database (to prevent duplication and to maintain history), but the inactive ones should carry flags marking them as such.

By keeping these databases separate, the metrics and operations of marketing can be tuned more finely without interfering with the natural way that sales works. However, the split-brain model has a side effect: sales will not be able to easily see *all* of the interactions of a large account, because some of the action will be taken by leads and some by Names. This can cause a bit of a blind spot.

If you're already using a marketing tool such as Eloqua, Vertical Response, or Exact Target, you're probably on the split-brain path. If you aren't using these kinds of tools, you have an architectural choice to make now. Do you need to have all your leads—regardless of quality—in one place, or do you want to create a category of leads that are of such low quality that they're handled externally? While there's no overwhelming cost advantage to going in either direction, changing your path after deployment will involve considerable one-time costs and changes to the workflows surrounding leads.

So, choose now. Adding the marketing Names database will add another integration point, but it will also allow for more sophisticated marketing operations over time.

---

14. Sales demotes leads either by disqualifying them or by ignoring them for so long that they go cold. You don't want to know how often the second reason is the cause of lead demotion.

Self-Healing Data

It is important to apply the principle of self-healing data: make changes to systems and processes that improve the resilience and health of SFDC data over time. Whenever system modifications are made in SFDC, its integration adapters, or surrounding systems, a portion of the implementation team's effort should go toward improving code and supporting processes that can enhance data quality and validation. Through an incremental improvement strategy, data quality can painlessly become noticeably better over time.

The most highly leveraged part of this work is making sure that new data flowing into the system will be of high quality and meaningful. Aside from human input applied directly into SFDC screens, the main sources of new data into SFDC will consist of these streams:

- Leads and contact updates from the Web site, email marketing system, and importing spreadsheets from internal and external sources

- Account and opportunity updates from order management, accounting, eCommerce, or channel management systems

- Case updates from Web and email inputs, as well as engineering's bug tracking system

We'll address each of these sources in turn.

The Web site registration pages should whittle the number of fields down to what's really essential and reduce user typing as much as possible. Use pick lists ("pull-downs") for job title, state, and country. Use JavaScript to validate the format of phone numbers and postal codes. Use mail-response loops to validate that the email address is valid and active. The Web site data feed should use deduping code, in the form of either home-brew or products such as RingLead or DemandTools. Most larger SFDC implementations will have multiple landing pages on the Web site, and it will be important to assign a unique identifier to each page (usually, a campaign code) to make it easier to troubleshoot page-specific data problems.

The email marketing system may be directly integrated into SFDC: make sure its deduping features are always on. If the email system operates as a separate silo, follow the guidance in the next paragraph.

For lead imports, most companies will use Excel spreadsheets. Beware of CSV file corruption, particularly from external sources (check out "The Joy of Regex" described in Chapter 3). Create templates for these imports, using formulas and macros that clean bad entries, validate formats, and normalize data (e.g., translating state and country names into ISO codes, fixing ill-formed phone numbers) to trap bad data before it's imported into the system. The spreadsheet imports should be done through products such as RingLead and DemandTools, with the goal being to stop duplicate records at the source.

Account and opportunity updates will occur via integration with outside systems. The single most important data pollution control measure here is prevention of duplicate accounts, opportunities, and contacts. The first line of defense is the use of unique keys and duplicate-detection code in the integration layer. Unfortunately, with outside systems such as eCommerce or channel ordering systems, it may not be possible to have a unique key that works in all situations. Develop a proxy identifier to make sure that accounts and opportunities are not double-counted. If for policy reasons a somewhat redundant account *does* need to be created in your system, make the new one be a child of the existing SFDC account. The second line of defense is to integrate as few fields as possible: the fewer the fields, the lower the chance of data corruption.

Case records are updated by web2case and email2case features in SFDC. Use the same ideas we discussed a few paragraphs ago about Web site registration pages, and configure your email2case code so that it converts ill-formatted or denormalized data at the source. Use field validation rules. The good news is that you don't have to worry about deduping cases the way you do with leads. Case records may also be updated by your bug tracking system. Make sure that the integration strategy you use (either an off-the-shelf adaptor or custom code) normalizes data and prevents duplicate creation (of either cases or contacts).

For **all data records**, but particularly in name, company, and address fields, foreign character sets must be properly handled and transferred.[15] Fix problems in this area by reconfiguring or upgrading the outside source to be Unicode compatible.

Migrating Historical SFA/CRM Data

Your company likely has some or even most of the data mentioned earlier in existing systems—for example, SFA, CRM, or Outlook—and it's important to understand how these data will be transitioned into SFDC. Here are the alternative scenarios:

- The data will be imported and expunged from the old system (or the old system will be decommissioned outright). The key issues to understand: how "dirty" is the data, how many (fuzzy) duplicate records exist, and how recently have the data been updated. Generally speaking, B2B contact information rots at a rate approaching 10% per quarter, so data more than three years old might have less information value than the cost of cleansing, deduping, and enriching the records. Check out the discussion in Chapter 3 to see how much fun this process can bring to your life. As always, the old data shouldn't be completely deleted, but rather should be archived into a relational database after import to SFDC.

- The data will be partially imported into SFDC, but some of it will continue to live in the current system. In addition to the issues outlined earlier, a key decision will be

---

15. SFDC has no problem dealing with properly encoded foreign character sets using UTF-8 Unicode. Unfortunately, some external systems simply produce the wrong codes, creating gibberish for Asian and most European languages. As we'll discuss in Chapter 10, one best practice is to create an anglicized "search-friendly" version of foreign characters in addition to the original names. The implementation team needs to implement these ISO Latin-friendly versions of fields for name, address, city, and company in the lead, contact, account, and contract objects.

synchronization.[16] Generally speaking, it's best to have either SFDC or one external system be the system of record for any particular field in a database (e.g., mailing address). In this way, all fields are unambiguously owned and there's no issue of replication or synchronization conflicts. This is a complicated topic—read the integration section in Chapter 7 before you make any firm commitments on this front.

- The old data will not be imported into SFDC at all, but rather will be kept in the original system and accessed via a mashup or other read-only mechanism.

There may be some data you've identified that must be migrated from other systems that aren't "SFA/CRM" but are nevertheless important to the customer relationship. For example, your order management system may contain important historical information that really should be reside in SFDC going forward. You have to make decisions for these data on the same issues you've just handled for the historical SFA/CRM data.

External System Data

External system data are collected, entered, and maintained in some system outside of SFDC, and will be available within the system only via integration. For example, partial-shipment data may need to be viewable from the SFDC account screen, but the system of record would be the company inventory management system. For the purposes of this section, these data do *not include any historical system data;* rather, they comprise only the data collected in other systems from the SFDC's go-live date onward.

The defining characteristic for external data is that SFDC users have no direct control over the quality or form of the data, and they may have limited control over the format and editing of the records. Most of the time, the users will have to "take what they can get" from the external system. So the task here is to itemize which data items

- Need to be seen, by whom, and under what conditions.

- Need to be edited, by whom, and with what controls.[17]

- Can be aggregated for ease of use (for example, SFDC users will care about a flag called "customer on credit hold" but shouldn't care about which specific payments are late).

The cardinal question here is "What is the minimum set of data that is required for the users to do their job?" With each request for external data comes a decision. Will it be resolved through complex and expensive integration code, or can the issue be bypassed by simplifying or restating the requirement?

---

16. Our recommendation is almost invariably to avoid the requirement for synchronization. It's a slow, error-prone step that usually adds unneeded complexity.

17. Almost always, only a small portion of the external system data will be fully editable from the SFDC screens.

AGGRESSIVELY APPLY REALITY THERAPY

The most expensive requirements an SFDC project will experience are superfluous or "gold-plated" integration requirements. At a meeting, someone who *doesn't* have to pay for it will require real-time bidirectional updates of sales activities. Don't take these requirements at face value: investigate whether there are contradictory requirements ("information security forbids real-time bidirectional updates") or practical issues that invalidate the whole ("these fields are updated only once a week").

If you haven't already done so, check out the integration section in Chapter 7. By politely but insistently drilling into the realities underlying the requirements-from-on-high, you may be able to postpone or completely avoid many months of work.

As before, the first step in analyzing the requirement is to map the external systems' data into the SFDC object model. The team needs to identify which SFDC object the field should be associated with (for example, credit holds should be part of the account object, not the opportunity or contact) and which reports the data should be included in. In some cases, there's little to map because the external system has unique data that will never be stored in SFDC. But in the cases where SFDC's data fields *do* map to an external system, you have some decisions to make:

- What will be the universal key to identify critical objects across the systems? At the very least, you'll need keys to identify account, contact, and order records; it's likely you'll need keys for product, service incident, and bug (defects or RMAs) records as well.

- How will you handle apparent duplicate or redundant entries from the external system? If there are two cases of "ABC Corporation," which one should be presented? For display purposes only, should certain parts of ABC Corporation's records actually be consolidated? If it's better to only show "half the data," what's the rule for selecting which half?

- Does the external system have a data hierarchy, such as price list bundles, bill of material (BOM) structures, or account–division–site distinctions? You will need to decide how to map these structures into SFDC.

- What's the strategy for searching through and presenting foreign character sets (particularly foreign characters or accents in people's names, company names, and addresses)?[18]

---

18. See footnote 15 on page 90.

For example, if the requirement is just a read-only view of a customer's order history, this could be presented as a few rows in SFDC's account page. But if a fully-editable view of the order history is needed, it should probably be a dedicated page (and perhaps even a tab) in SFDC's user interface. For each data item, the team needs to specify how current the data must be (for example, read-only address data may be updated only weekly, a data edit concerning a warranty claim can be delayed until a nightly refresh, and a data edit about inventory may require real-time synchronization), whether it's writable from SFDC, and the rules for data conflicts.

For any items that users will edit via the SFDC interface, it's important to inquire about the data validation that is expected by the external system of record. We need to know what SFDC is expected to do before the data is transferred, and how errors will be handled by the two systems.

Sometimes the external system represents data in a way that is counterintuitive to SFDC users, and that may not fit well with the SFDC object model. For example, SFDC has an account object and a Partner object, but no Customer object (because a customer in SFDC is just an account with a closed-won opportunity). Your accounting system probably has a Customer object, but no Partner or Prospective Customer object to match with SFDC. Because SFDC will probably have many more accounts[19] than the accounting system has Customers, some way of coordinating the two is needed (in this example, using the account's type pick list to flag customers and partners is a likely strategy).

Two areas deserve special attention, because they're so essential and so challenging to implement: customer purchase histories and price-list entries. Both of these data sets exist somewhere in your external systems, and both probably need to continue to be held in these systems of record. SFDC will probably need its own representation of these data, and synchronizing the two will be a challenge.

Customer and Account Data

Customer data—from company name to order history and payments—will almost certainly be needed by some SFDC users. The first issue is customer identification:

- What is the unique key that can be used to cross-reference customer information between SFDC and the external system(s)?

- Is every customer consistently referred to by a single key, no matter which country the customer is in or which product division the customer ordered from?

---

19. This is particularly true in a "named account model" of selling, where the sales organization may create hundreds of accounts before the company has ever done business with the customer. While this is a best practice for sales management, it causes confusion with the accounting and finance types who view these prospective accounts as bogus. See Chapter 9 for more discussion of this topic.

- If the customer is a large conglomerate, how are different divisions noted in your company's systems? For example, Japan's Mitsubishi and South Korea's Hyundai both comprise hundreds of operating divisions that make everything from transistors to cars to entire steel mills. How do your company's systems refer to Mitsubishi's television division versus its electrical machinery division? And how do those systems refer to the electrical machinery division in the United States versus the one in Canada?

It is important to clarify these company nomenclature issues early so that you don't have ridiculously complicated requests of the integration team or make unachievable promises to your users.

The next issue is, "How many external systems need to be referenced for a given SFDC object (such as account)?" Every additional system that is integrated (particularly with synchronization) brings with it a huge increase in cost and complexity.

The final issue is, "Exactly how much customer information will be required from the external systems?" Usually a customer's order history is needed for a full SFDC system, but at what level of detail? Will any SFDC user really need to know the line-item details on every order?

Price List

Price-list line items (also known as SKUs) will be needed for most advanced SFDC installations to support quoting and automate order entry. The price list may be printed in one document. In large multidivisional companies, however, it's more often implemented in several different order management systems. Finding the system of record for all the company SKUs can be a serious exercise, and you may find that the price list is partitioned across several systems. SFDC may need to be integrated with each of those systems.

Each of the external systems may have data quality issues of its own, and integrating with more than one of those systems may surface even more data quality and consistency issues. These problems must be understood early, before any promises are made about the speed and depth of external system integration.

The good news is that price lists don't change very often, even if your firm does frequent promotions. Usually, price lists can be updated with simple file imports or spreadsheets forwarded over email.

Historical External Data

Historical external data comprise any data stored in some external system of record, but presented in the SFDC user interface. For the purposes of this section, historical data are defined as anything that was collected before *SFDC's go-live date*.

THE IMPORTANCE OF UNIQUE KEYS

One of the toughest problems in IT boils down to Shakespeare's classic query, "What's in a name?" Whenever two systems or databases need to be integrated, the team must find a universal identifier that reliably and uniquely indicates "this is the record you're looking for" in both systems.

In some cases, these keys will be strings (such as "GM Corp HQ"), but usually they're unique numbers. In Web and marketing systems, the key may be the email address with which the customer registered. In accounting systems, the key may be the customer's tax ID number.

Unfortunately, almost no company has a unique, universal key that works across all systems. For each system you need to integrate with, you'll need to identify and understand its external key. You will almost certainly need to add several external keys to SFDC's records, one key for each system you need to integrate with.

Depending on the quality and breadth of the data in the system you're trying to integrate with, several viable strategies for matching keys may be available. If you're lucky, you will be able to use a reliable third-party identifier for matching records, such as a D-U-N-S number or FEIN tax ID number.

Most of the time, this strategy handles 50–80% of the historical records of a given type. For the remainder, you will need to use trickier matching strategies such as data fingerprints and matching scores (e.g., a record is deemed to match if data from seven of nine fields match). Another matching strategy is based on historical activities (i.e., if the order history is identical, it is deemed to be the same customer). The problem comes, of course, with those records where the fingerprint is blurred by typos, foreign character sets, duplicates, and other data problems. The dirtier and noisier the data, the tougher the matching will be.

What if you can't find a direct matching strategy for your SFDC records? You may have to make the correspondence through a third system that acts as a Rosetta stone for customer or order identifiers.

In the worst case, you won't have any reliable way of making the correspondence between systems. In that situation, all you can do is simply say "no history available" and record the external keys in SFDC on a going-forward basis.

While it's easy to understand how users would need last year's complete data, in most businesses users will not need to see data that are more than three years old. Use of historical data comes at a significant cost, because a three-step process must be completed. First, these data must be located. Second, they must be integrated. Third, they must be adjusted to make the historical data meaningful and comparable with today's data.

For example, if a customer ordered Promotional Package 35 three years ago, it's unlikely that this specific promotional package still exists. The records describing the package may be sketchy, and the package may have gone through several variations in different countries. In many cases, the original people who entered the data will have had context and knowledge that was "in their heads"—and they may have moved. The farther back in history you go, the more expensive this kind of reinterpretation becomes.

When specifying historical data for integration, keep the request as shallow (for a short period) and as narrow (as few fields or records) as possible. In many cases, all that's really needed is a summary field ("What's the total dollar value of orders in the last three years") that can be generated or approximated in several ways, using alternative sources. These "roll-up" fields can save significant integration work, without losing any real information.

THE DAYS OF FUTURE PASSED

Data stored in SFDC are, by default, available indefinitely into the future.

But one aspect of your system's data and report design is a data retention policy. Our recommendation is that users should *never* have the ability to delete records, and administrators should *almost never* use their privilege to do so, even if the records are erroneous or misleading. Such records should be hidden (via a change of ownership or a bad data flag) for analysis and correction, and should be stored for comparison with future error records (to identify a recurrence of an error source).

Even though data should never be deleted, it's perfectly legitimate to archive old or inactive data. The question is the time horizon. In some industries, a record that's been inactive for more than a couple of years may not seem interesting. By comparison, when you are trying to run reports and comparative analysis, it is valuable to have at least five years of data. Further, regulators in some industries may want to look back seven years—and generating reports from archived data can be amazingly difficult.

We recommend archiving attachments, as they use up SFDC's expensive storage space. Attachments can be archived on an indexed file server for ease of recovery. Unless you have hundreds of thousands of records, however, we seldom recommend archiving SFDC's parametric data before the five-year horizon. These archives should be stored as relational tables for easy analysis and recovery. See Chapter 13 for more on this topic.

There's an important caveat about SFDC data: if you don't touch a record for two years, it may be transparently moved into a kind of SFDC limbo. The old data *will* show up in all standard user screens and data exports, but they *may not* show up in reports. If you need to always see those old data, you'll have to avoid using reports. When accessing the old data via SFDC's API, you'll need to use the SELECTALL operator and filter out deleted records (when SFDC says "all," it means *all*). This is clearly a bug, but it's been there for a while.

CHAPTER 3

Preparing Your Data

*Okay kids, everybody get out your EBCDIC
decoder ring!*

—Johnny Quest

THIS CHAPTER FOCUSES ON the underlying data itself, because no one will use the system if the data are confusing or a waste of time. This chapter is intended for anyone on the original implementation team because (1) data preparation, conversion, and import are the most costly and time-consuming parts of any SFDC implementation; (2) data are the basis for all reports, which is what most people use to judge the project success; and (3) data are the basis for system credibility, which is the single biggest determinant of system usage and effectiveness.

Data Pollution

From 1936 until 1969, water pollution was so bad in Ohio's Cuyahoga River that it occasionally caught fire. Data can become every bit as polluted as that water, with equally spectacular effects.

Because the credibility of SFDC will depend on having data that are meaningful and valuable, before any implementation work begins, a "project 0" should be started to assess the health, cleanliness, and value of the data that will be flowing into the system. Fixing data quality and meaning will be much harder than programming or system configuration— so put the **best people on this task** from the beginning. If your company has experience with data warehousing and extract–transform–load (ETL) tools, try to recruit one of those people to be on your team—if nothing else to be trainers and mentors for the tasks outlined in the rest of this chapter.

As mentioned earlier, it's almost impossible to overestimate the cost and time involved with data cleansing, import, and integration. You're about to see why.

Getting the Lay of the Land

It's very easy to get lost and disoriented in a large data migration project, so it's a great idea to have a roadmap explaining which data items come from where, what they need to be reconciled against, and how data will be transformed and cleansed *before* you start the effort. Here are the overall steps to creating this roadmap.

First, understand how much of the data really needs to be migrated. To make this determination, you should look for an appropriate time horizon (Does anyone really need to know what a customer's cases were from three years ago, now that the company is not a customer any more?) and breadth/depth (Do you really need to have access to all the attachments and artifacts of a file or just a few of the columns?). Scoping the data migration down can dramatically lower both the effort and the error rate of your work.

Next, double-check that migration is the best approach: with some kinds of operational data, leaving the data in its current home and doing an integration with SFDC—rather than a migration of data into the system—will yield better results.

Take an inventory of all data fields you need, and then map them (in a diagram or a spreadsheet) to the possible sources. If there is more than one source for an item, create two lines on the chart and annotate positives and negatives about the source. Annotate technical aspects of the data sources (e.g., "FTP server, but we don't have secure access to it"). Identify *unused* items in your data sources that could be used to corroborate or otherwise validate the data you will be migrating.

This chapter assumes that you don't already have a "customer master" database that would allow a clean, single-pass import. The more common situation dealt with here is the case where you need to migrate up-to-date but flawed data from existing systems. Essentially, the goal is to find "the best of the worst" information, and make it better during the migration process.

As a first step, get the external data exported (typically into a CSV file) and stored on your migration-staging servers. For most systems, this is a straightforward task, but we have seen cases where more than 100 tables have to be painstakingly exported to build a complete SFA data set from a single ERP package.

Migrating Data from an Existing SFA/CRM System

The big task is to process the data from the existing SFA/CRM system(s) for migration into the system in preparation for cutover time. For the sake of simplicity, this section describes the situation where only one existing SFA/CRM system is being retired; if there is more than one system (whether a different brand or multiple instances of the same brand), the work in this section multiplies quickly.

Perfectionism Doesn't Pay

In importing, integrating, or migrating data, it is tempting to want a squeaky-clean system with 100% data quality—at least on day one.

This temptation must be resisted, as it can really kill your budget and your schedule. Removing impurities from data is similar to other industrial processes: it's asymptotically expensive. The first standard deviation (68%) of errors is cheap to remove, the next standard deviation (17%) costs about twice as much (even though you're only fixing one-fourth the total number of errors), the next standard deviation (4%) costs about four times as much to eliminate (even though you're fixing only one-fifteenth as many errors), and so on. Getting to Six Sigma purity (99.9998%) in data will carry an astronomical cost. Even if you found a magical way to get all of the data right, new data errors will start to creep in from the first day of system operation.

Instead of focusing on purity of the data, optimize for correctness of meaning *from the customer's perspective*. If you can save half the effort by using limiting assumptions or even outright guesswork to get the meaning of the data "close enough," that's the shrewd path to take. For example, if you don't really know which products customers paid for, assume they bought the most expensive one and have them tell you when you've assumed wrong. If you sell IT products, assuming the most expensive product means that you get to charge higher support fees—which is a major source of crocodile tears for our clients.

Unless there's something very special going on in your company, error rates of 2% are usually unnoticeable, and an error rate of 5% is often quite acceptable. Obviously, some parts of the records (e.g., customer number, amounts paid) must have a zero-tolerance policy—but does it really matter if there is a misspelling in a "comments" field?

Bottom line: data quality is both valuable and expensive. Make a sound business tradeoff here, as everywhere else in the system.

In migrating data into SFDC, it's important to understand the big picture of the data model. Figure 3-1 gives a partial overview of the standard SFDC object hierarchy. Of course, SFDC is so flexible that your system may have more objects and more relationships than are shown in the figure. It is because of these interrelationships among data items that the sequence for importing should almost always proceed as follows:

1. Accounts have few data elements, but typically have the most pointers to other records. Given that accounts appear at the top of the SFDC information pyramid, there will be relatively few of them.

2. Contacts typically have the most data elements for cleansing and enrichment, as well as a couple of pointers to other records (e.g., accounts and opportunities). Typically, contacts will be the number two population of data records in the system.

3. Opportunities have only a few data elements, but have the most interesting time sequences for update history. You'll need to process both current (open) opportunities and historical (closed) ones.

4. Products, product line items, and price lists are highly static and don't represent many records. You'll have to make sure that all of the product's attributes (such as pricing models, terms, multiple price lists, discount schedules, and revenue recognition schedules) are represented in the SFDC table.

5. Leads may have many data elements to clean and enrich, but do not have many pointers that need to be correlated with other records. Typically, the system will have more leads than any other record type.

6. Campaigns are typically a few hundred historical descriptions of marketing outreach activities. Each holds a few data items, but may have large attached files.

7. Campaign members are the history of all leads and contacts the company has touched. They account for a very small number of data items, but can consist of a very large number of records.

8. Contracts are typically a few hundred or few thousand records associated with closed opportunities. Typically there aren't many fields in these records, but they may have important attachments that need to be imported.

9. Customer assets represent the history of customer purchases. Usually, the assets are just the summary of purchases, with little or no detail about the purchase history. These asset summaries typically have to be generated from roll-up tables stored in external systems. While there is rarely a big data cleansing task here, processing of the customer purchase roll-ups needs to avoid double-counting of inventory.

10. Cases typically contain relatively few data items, but often contain pointers to other data records and attached files. You may have a lot of cases to process.

11. Solutions are "solved cases" and contain few data items, but have important long-text fields that need to survive even if they have hidden non-ASCII characters. Solutions typically also have attachments that need to be linked to the proper record in SFDC.

12. Contact roles (for accounts, opportunities, and cases) contain almost no data, as they are just pointers to other data in the system.

13. Activities, notes, and attachments typically have few data elements, but several types of corruption are possible in the fields. Clean the fields, but don't be so aggressive as to remove the text formatting (tabs and carriage returns) embedded in them.

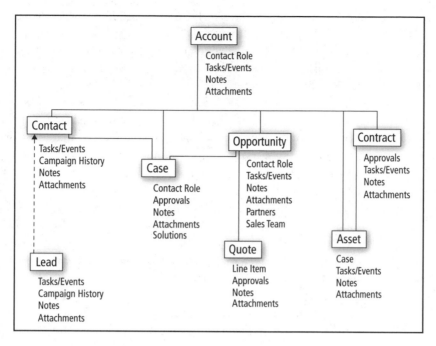

FIGURE 3-1   A partial overview of SFDC's standard object model

Now it's time to plan and do the data conversion. You'll want to follow the conversion and import cycle described below for **each of the data objects** in the preceding list. Before you even start, ask users of the existing SFA/CRM system to flag as many duplicates and bad records as possible in the current system. The best way for them to do so is to mark the records with a unique, searchable marker (such as ###dedupe### or ###junk###) in a seldom-used field. Storing the record identifiers into a spreadsheet listing duplicate or garbage records will work as well.

The first step of your process is to create a staging area in SFDC to test migration procedures and results. A free developer account will work initially, but its 2MB storage limit will soon get in your way. Ideally, you should use an SFDC sandbox,[1] which gives you an area for testing and debugging that won't interfere with the normal working[2] system. If your company can't afford a sandbox, you'll have to do frequent system backups and work very carefully in the operational system.

---

1. SFDC's sandbox is an extra-cost item that provides a complete staging system with duplicated code and data. Because it can hold all of your data records simultaneously, the sandbox gives you an area to do comprehensive development and testing.

2. The system may not be working yet, but the main area of the system will be where prototypes and mock-ups will be. You don't want to step on other teams' toes.

Next, export a subset of the data you're trying to import and look at the results in Excel. Visual inspection is important, because there's no faster way to see incomplete records, missing fields, gross data corruption (such as an email stuffed inside a phone number field), and trash data (such as a text field filled with 2,500 characters of a foreign character set). Get your mind around—and fix—these gross problems first.

The next thing to do is look at the data model of the old system and map it to SFDC's object model. If you're lucky, this task will involve a straightforward, field-by-field mapping. Of course, this task is quite likely to be a lot more complicated than that, requiring joins of disparate fields to create the SFDC objects (one memorable example from my firm involved manipulating 180 different tables to migrate the data out of the old system). Note any cases where a join with data from a third system is required, as these situations probably require special attention. At the other extreme, all of the data you're trying to work on may be in one giant table or flat files, requiring several passes through the data to synthesize the objects and events needed for SFDC. In any event, it is critically important to understand the format, meaning,[3] provenance, and acceptable range for each field. Create a checklist of steps in your mapping procedure to account for these issues.

Decide whether you will import all of the historical data into SFDC. In most cases, all of the data will come over. If you have hundreds of thousands of records that haven't been active for five years, however, you may choose to put the older data into an archive and bring over only the last few years' worth of data. If you have a million `leads`, each of which has 10 `activities`, you will quickly outgrow SFDC's storage space—and expansion is expensive.

After this "migration storyboard" has been completed (using essentially no real data), a small data set (maybe 10% of the total) should be exported from the old system to do a trial migration into an SFDC developer account. Working with the real data set, the team will discover lots of complicating factors and real-world problems that can be corrected with corrective spreadsheets, SQL queries, UNIX utilities, and other tools. The basic corrective sequence—which you may do yourself or hire a contractor specializing in data migration—is outlined here:

1. **Incompletes.** Validate that all the records you expected to migrate have, in fact, shown up in SFDC. Investigate any missing records to find out what prevented them from being imported, and fix that issue.

2. **Trash characters.** Look for nonprinting characters (which may just show up as a space) that may cause the record to not be transferred. These nonprinting characters often appear in long-text fields, where a user has cut-and-pasted text from an email or other outside source, but they can also occur because of improper foreign character

---

3. Semantics are almost certain to be misleading or misunderstood for at least one data item, no matter how small the data set you're working with. Do not assume that "phone" means "business phone" or that "amount" means "total discounted revenue amount for this transaction."

translation. To preserve the formatting of these long-text fields, the best approach is to use UNIX text utilities (such as `tr`, `sed`, `od`, or `awk`) and regular expression formulas to substitute acceptable characters in the fields. Excel formulas using the `CHAR`, `SUBSTITUTE`, and other string manipulation operators can work as well.

3. **Column swaps.** Look for rows that have swapped columns. In data sets that have been in place for a long time, any number of actions may have caused columns for certain rows to have been offset or swapped. Phone numbers may show up in country fields, street addresses in ZIP code fields, countries in state fields. Find these patterns, group the affected rows together in your data correction tool (typically Excel), and correct the columns.

4. **Foreign characters.** Foreign character sets often become corrupted (e.g., a French é showing up as e# or whatever), and they may appear in any text field. Create a list that maps the corrupted text to the original characters, and then use either UNIX text utilities or Excel `SUBSTITUTE` formulas to correct the characters. For non-European characters, you'll need someone with the foreign language skills, and someone with knowledge of Unicode, to help you set up the character correction tables.

5. **Alphas in numerics.** Numbers that include alpha characters (such as "ext" in phone numbers) need to be cleaned; this can often be done with Excel `SUBSTITUTE`, `LEFT`, `RIGHT`, and `CONCATENATE` formulas.

6. **Bogus numbers.** Numbers that are out of range should be analyzed to understand the patterns. Are the units wrong (e.g., units rather than millions)? Was the number originally a date (and corrupted to be "number of days since 1970" or "number of minutes since the beginning of the year")? Were numbers simply transposed between fields (part numbers were substituted for price)? Were numbers transformed into scientific notation (as occasionally happens with phone numbers and SFDC ID numbers)? Were leading zeroes removed? Were dates messed up by Y2K problems (yes, I saw two cases involving this issue during 2008)? You can have hours of fun understanding these error patterns and correcting them.

7. **Country codes.** Country names should be transformed into ISO-standard three-character[4] country codes. Yes, do all 246 of them—you won't save any time by leaving out country names. In case the country field is blank, you can use other information (phone number, state, and city) to synthesize the country code. In the case of `accounts`, you can use the local version of "Corporation" (e.g., "GmbH" for Germany or "Pty" for Australia) to identify the country. Leave as few country fields blank as possible, as they are needed for several SFDC rules. Note that every user in the system will need a "cheat sheet" for these codes, so make sure to create one of

---

4. Actually, most of the time you can get away with two-character codes; decide on which system to use, and be consistent from there forward.

THE JOY OF REGEX

In many cases, the tools you'll use to do data conversion, correction, and enrichment are low-level goodies you already have on your PC. While they're no-cost and familiar—which saves on the learning curve—they also have some foibles you need to be ready for.

If you're trying to clean up text, *never* use Microsoft Word. It will corrupt even the most innocent-looking text in a hurry. Use a low-level text editor (like HTML Pad or even MS-DOS's edit function) to make sure that carriage returns and other nonprinting characters are preserved. If things are really hairy, you might need to use awk, sed, tr, or other UNIX/Linux tools to keep things clean.

If you're trying to clean up a table, Microsoft Excel is the most commonly used tool—and it works well if you really know how to use it. Learn the VLOOKUP, FORMAT, CLEAN, CONCATENATE, LEFT, RIGHT, and other string-manipulation commands. Excel is usually not case sensitive, but SFDC *is* (particularly with record ID numbers), so be careful when doing searches and matches. Be really careful when using the sort function—if you don't high-light all of the columns of the table before you perform the sort, the entire data set will be corrupted.

Beware of working with the CSV file format—Excel "auto-mangles" phone numbers, SFDC ID numbers, or any other large integers by turning them into scientific notation or suppressing leading zeroes. One trick for avoiding this problem (on Windows-based systems) is to *not* double-click on the .csv files. Instead, rename them as .txt files before opening them. Then, use Excel's Open menu item, which will invoke an import wizard that allows you to assign the number columns as *text*, which (perversely) solves the problem. Then, save the workbook as an .xls file before you start working on the contents. CSV files also have interesting problems with foreign character sets and illegal character sequences that can cause columns to be out of alignment, or can cause a single field to be split into several subfields. After a while, it gets to be kind of entertaining.

Also be aware of Excel's structural limits: the individual cell size is limited, text fields can accommodate only 255 characters, and older versions of the product handle only 64,000 rows. Even with the expanded row limits in the latest version of Excel, functions such as VLOOKUP slow down dramatically beyond 32,000 rows. This warning goes double if you're using SFDC's Excel connector.

these on card-stock paper and as PDFs in the project wiki and SFDC's documents section.

8. **State codes.** State names (at least for the United States and Canada, plus Brazil, Germany, Russia, India, and China if you do business there) should be transformed into ISO-standard two-character state codes. For other countries, leave the state fields as they are—they won't do any harm and you may decide to transform them

into state codes later. As with the country codes, everyone will need a "cheat sheet" for the state codes.

9. **Postal codes.** ZIP/postal codes need to be checked for format (five or nine digits in the United States, six digits in the United Kingdom and Canada, five digits in France, and so on). They should also be checked for geographic correspondence (the postal code should match the state code, city name, or phone number's city or area code) if you can.

10. **Phone numbers.** Phone numbers need to be checked for several issues. U.S. phone numbers are completely regular, and should be in the format AAA-EEE-NNNN (where A is the three-digit area code, E is the three-digit exchange code, and N is the four-digit line number). But watch out: many North American companies have cute alpha-numeric versions of their phone numbers like 1-800-EAT-BEEF. These must be replaced with pure numeric versions prior to import. International numbers are much more variable, but should be in the format +CCC AAA NN NN NN NN (where C is the one-, two-, or three-digit country code, A is the one-, two-, or three-digit city code, and N is the six-, seven-, or eight-digit line number). Frequently users will omit the +CCC part of the number, and insert a 0 in front of the rest of the number. As the range of formatting and content problems on international numbers is fairly wide, you'll want to analyze your specific symptoms before you design corrective formulas. Part of your corrective strategy should be checking the phone numbers against the state and country codes of the address, which can help disambiguate number problems. In the United States, number portability and Voice over IP (VoIP) have dramatically decreased the efficacy of geographic/area code validation.

11. **Extensions.** Some phone numbers will include extensions or access codes. These should be split off from the phone number field and stored as a separate `custom field` in SFDC's `lead`, `contact`, and `account` records.

12. **Emails.** Email address formats should be corrected (to xxxx@yyy.com/biz/mil/edu/gov in the United States and xxx@yyy.co.cc or xxx@yyy.cc in all other countries). Watch out for the external system's "email opt-out" flags—they may not exist where you would expect them to appear. Ask about external systems (such as email vendors) where this flag may be stored. We recommend that records of people who have opted out should have their email addresses corrupted (e.g., joe.blow@abc.com.nospam) so that the addresses cannot be accidentally misused.

13. **Pick lists.** Pick-list values will need to be checked to make sure they are a verbatim (character-by-character) match to the pick-list norm. Watch out for leading and trailing spaces! Also make sure that dashes are not confused with minus signs, hyphens, or em dashes. In cases where you are transforming a free-form entry (plain-text or number field) from the outside system into an SFDC pick list, you'll

need to create a sorted list of all the free-form entries and normalize them to the pick-list values.

14. **Booleans.** Boolean values will need to be normalized to TRUE and FALSE. Remember that in some data sets manipulated by Microsoft code, –1 means TRUE. In cases where you are transforming a free-form entry (plain-text or other fields) from the outside system into an SFDC Boolean, you'll need to do a sorted list of all the free-form entries and normalize them to the Boolean values.

15. **Required and default values.** Verify that SFDC's required fields are populated in all cases. If you discover instances where a required field is empty or has an unreasonable value, go back to the original source data to make sure something in your process isn't corrupting the data. If the required field is empty in the original system, assign the default value (if applicable) to it, or see if there is a way to synthesize the real value from the available data. If there's no way to do that but the record is still valid, fill the field in with a unique value such as "DummySynthesized-031208@14:15:47" to enable the record transfer.

16. **Ownership.** Record ownership needs to be assigned to a current user[5] in the system. Each record needs to be checked against the sales rep's (or, with case data, customer support rep's) territory assignment. As representative turnover and territory definition changes occur fairly frequently, ownership for many records will be incorrectly assigned. Fixing this problem can be a simple matter when the territories are geographic and large (by state and country), but can become very complex indeed when overlays exist or territories are defined by industry, company size, or even company name. Territory definitions can be surprisingly difficult to get from sales management—just push until you get the territory descriptions or maps, and pray that they aren't too ambiguous.[6] Because of security and access control issues, setting record ownership correctly is as big a deal as it is a pain in the neck.

17. **Dates.** Record creation date should be transferred from the old system to SFDC. If the external system has more than one create date for a record, use the oldest one for SFDC's create date. A funny thing happened a few years ago—Y2K rollover—that in some cases may mean dates on old data need to be transformed. SFDC uses fully four-digit years, so look for any date kludges that may have been done in the existing system, and perform transformations on them as part of the import process. During the trial imports, you will not have historical date insertion enabled in SFDC, so the create dates you see on the first passes will always be "today."

---

5. If you have to deal with historical records whose original ownership needs to be maintained, create a hidden field in SFDC and import the original owner's name there verbatim, in addition to the standard ownership that will be used by SFDC.

6. Check out the discussion of territory management in Chapter 9 for more on this issue.

18. **Old pointers or ID numbers.** Most systems will have existing ID numbers for each data record. While these numbers are system generated and cannot be used by SFDC, they should be imported as hidden fields into the system. Further, pointers between old records (e.g., old parent–child or master–detail relationships) should be imported as well. This strategy allows the implementation team to backtrack and validate the provenance of each record during the testing cycle.

19. **Record histories/audit trails.** If your data source keeps a record (history) of changes made to fields over time, it is possible to re-create most of that information in SFDC. It is an arduous task, however, and we certainly recommend that you try to negotiate your way out of this job. Note that `stage history` for opportunities and `case history` for cases cannot be imported at all.

20. **Duplicates.** Duplicate records are a major pain, because they're deadly to both system data quality and user credibility. What makes dupes tough to eliminate is that they're almost never literal duplicate records—the matches are fuzzy, and judgment is required to do the right thing. Some of the deduplication must be performed during the importing cycle (using the email address as the unique identifier) to make sure that the process itself isn't creating duplicates (this possibility is a particularly vexing issue when data must be drawn from more than one outside system). That said, we've never come across a situation where all of the deduping *had to be done* before the data was imported into SFDC.[7] We recommend doing as much of the deduping *within* SFDC as you can (using tools from companies such as RingLead and CRMfusion), which makes it easier to see the impact of what you're doing. By contrast, if you identify a truly prodigious number of dupes, it's important to understand which system or process is creating them. Once you've identified the culprit, make the get-well project one of your highest priorities—delay causes exponential rises in correction cost.

21. **Consistency reports.** After all of the preceding steps have been completed, a series of reports should be run on the data to make sure that the record count is correct and that major statistical characteristics of the original data set have been preserved. For example, if the original data consisted of 12% of records coming from California and 0.1% from South Dakota, it would be an unpleasant surprise to find the Dakotans representing 53% of data at the end. Trust me, this kind of problem happens. The data consistency reports should scrutinize the heuristics and statistical character of every column so as to make sure that the conversion process hasn't corrupted the data set.

---

7. If you face this situation, tools that plug into Excel and Access are available. In addition, extract–transform–load (ETL) tools used for data warehousing and business intelligence may be used for deduping purposes. We discuss the deduping procedures later in this chapter.

DATA ENRICHMENT

The art of adding value to data by merging it with outside sources should almost never be done as part of the data migration cycle. While such a merger could be done at this stage, I've not seen a case where it would yield any better results than doing the merge later, after the import has been validated and all of the data have been stabilized. The data migration cycle is stressful enough on its own—there's no reason to add the risk and hassle of more tasks to this process.

Once you've completed the trial migration, you'll need to do a full pilot migration. For this operation, you'll need access to an SFDC Enterprise edition account. Talk to your SFDC sales rep; he or she can probably get you temporary access for testing purposes, even if you haven't purchased the system yet. During the complete pilot migration, you will almost certainly discover problems that occur only when you are working with the entire data set. As mentioned earlier, if you're using Excel, you'll probably need to break up big data sets into manageable chunks. Make sure the partitioning and reaggregation of the data are done correctly—it's easy to make procedural errors because of the complexity of this issue alone. To check the validity of the results, do extensive comparative reporting and analyze the data set for unexpected changes to the statistical "shape of the data"[8]—staying cognizant that you can afford to spot-check only a few hundred records in detail.

All of these corrective steps need to be carefully documented, put into a script, or configured as an ETL program workflow, as it may be several weeks before the final data migration occurs. When that happens—usually in the first wave of implementation—there won't be any time for discovery or refinement.

Migrating Data from Other Systems

You may have to migrate data from other systems that aren't "SFA/CRM" but still hold important customer data. For example, your order management system may have important information that really should reside in SFDC going forward.

The first step in this process is to make sure that the data *should* be moved—that the system of record should be SFDC from now on. Moving data out of an established system—rather than leaving it there and integrating SFDC with the existing system—can mean important improvements in performance, existing code, and user access.[9]

---

8. The heuristics should include such items as record count, mean, median, range, and modality.
9. Once the data is moved into SFDC, it will only be directly accessible by SFDC users. Some existing users of the external system may feel disenfranchised—in this case, create a report that delivers an Excel spreadsheet of the data they are currently used to.

Once the decision to move the data is made, go through the data cleansing sequence outlined in the previous section. Although the general strategies will be similar for every system from which you migrate data, the checklist and procedures will be different every time.

Your Big Weekend: Doing the Import

Up to now, you've been doing test import cycles into developer accounts, the sandbox, or temporary SFDC instances. Now it's time to import data directly into the main system, which may already be in use. Ideally, all of the discoveries and practice cycles and checklists presented earlier will pay off in a smooth data import.

The data import session should occur at a time when there are very few users on the system, and when the exporting systems can be taken offline or put in read-only mode. Almost without exception, this operation should be scheduled as a weekend session that begins on Friday evening at 7 P.M. or so in the company headquarters' time zone (or whichever time zone contains the most SFDC users).

BE PREPARED: THAT'S THE BOY SCOUT'S MARCHING SONG . . .

At least one week before your Big Weekend, open a case in SFDC's support system requesting historical date insertion—the ability to create records with create dates *other than "today" (the system default). Once your support request for a "data migration history" is logged as an SFDC support system case, call your SFDC sales rep and have that case escalated. There is no way to do your Big Weekend tasks unless this feature is enabled. Typically, SFDC will leave this feature enabled for a week or two, but ask for even more time so you can rework the portion of the import that didn't make into SFDC the first time.*

Before you actually start your migration cycle, perform a *complete* backup of SFDC. While SFDC does provide automatic backup of all your data for free, data recovery is time-consuming and expensive. *Any time you plan to muck with SFDC data in bulk,* it is vital that you *do a complete backup to a local hard drive.* Leverage the system's weekly export service—it's free with the Enterprise and Unlimited editions, and it's the fastest way to perform a complete backup. Unfortunately, you can use this strategy only once (because your import cycle will take a lot less time than a week). You will need to do a subsequent full-system backup, but complete that task using SFDC's Data loader or another bulk export tool.

If you're lucky, all your Big Weekend tasks can be done in one pass and one day. Of course, matters rarely go that smoothly, particularly if you have to import or migrate data from more than one external system. Consequently, it's important to have a disciplined, repeatable process and take careful notes with each pass. If a large or distributed group is doing the import tasks, you'll need to carefully coordinate the group members' activities, even to the point of having a coxswain for the team. Otherwise, you might do a complete system import, only to discover later that the data do not behave properly or that you did one of the steps out of order. You may then have to use SFDC's Data loader tool (or even heavier-duty tools, as discussed in Chapter 7) to erase a bad import—and you may discover you have to erase more than you wanted to because of data dependencies and pointers. Rinse. Lather. Repeat. It's okay: you get faster and better at it with each pass.

The Morning After: Deduping Records

Once data have been successfully migrated into SFDC, the very first thing you should do is a complete system backup (yes, including attachments). Once the system is backed up, it's essential to deduplicate records before users start working with the system. Duplicate records are irritating to users, who will be tempted to engage in these dangerous behaviors:

- Deleting records

- Incorrectly performing record merges, which delete or corrupt data

- Scattering data across duplicates, which results in data being lost[10]

- Lowering data standards because "It's a mess anyway"

At the time the system is brought up, there should be a zero-tolerance policy for duplicate records. Identify and remove as many of these buggers as you can, because users will notice them from the first moment.

Duplicate records can appear in any SFDC object, but occur most frequently in leads and contacts. While fixing these redundancies is important to system credibility and usability, duplicate opportunities and accounts are more likely to cause the most problems.

Accounts

Duplicate accounts occur for two reasons: (1) some system users just won't follow the best practices you taught them[11] and (2) an imported or integrated data set generates the

---

10. In fact, the data are not lost—but finding the information can be so irritating that impatient sales reps and executives simply give up. This is *not* their problem: it's the system's problem, and the team needs to prevent it from occurring.

11. Some people might say they're lazy, but we'd never put *that* in print.

duplicates as a result of faulty code or suboptimal business policies. Let's look at user-created account dupes first.

Users are supposed to search for accounts before creating them, and they should be looking for existing account names before they convert leads. In most SFDC installations, a few bogus accounts are created each week by sloppy users. The tell-tale signs of these bogus accounts are (1) the account was created by the account owner, (2) there is some relevant manually entered data in the account fields, and (3) there may be an open opportunity or a follow-up activity associated with the new account. When you first look at the SFDC system, run a report (or use APEX before-insert triggers) to identify these human-created dupes, and merge or subordinate them with the master account as described later in this chapter.

You'll want to do this kind of housekeeping on an ongoing basis, once every week or so. Wait for a system "quiet time" when users won't be updating records. That would be nights and weekends, with Friday from 8 P.M. Pacific time to Sunday 2 P.M. being primo hours. This is why data administrators do not go out on dates much.

USER ACCOUNTS FOR EXTERNAL INTEGRATION CODE

SFDC is quite good at tracking who created and updated records, and it can be configured to keep detailed audit trails for important data changes. Any code external to SFDC, including integration, data migration, and hosted functionality, must "log in" to the system before it is permitted to interact with the data. For a number of reasons, it's a best practice to have an SFDC user account dedicated to each major external subsystem (the user name is usually the "friendly name" of the IT system it runs in), so that updates are marked as having been performed by code, rather than people.

If your system has more than one complex bit of code outside of SFDC, consider having each program run under a different user account. While each of these "platform" accounts will cost about $80 per month, you'll save much more than that whenever you're trying to debug a data corruption problem. Plus, you'll get some extra storage from SFDC, which you can always allocate to real users.

More interesting is the case of accounts that have been generated by code, which almost always result from a data migration or integration gone awry. What code should do is compare existing accounts in SFDC with the new accounts being migrated or integrated in. Unfortunately, the errant code (or import procedure) simply creates a new account with nearly identical information to what's already in SFDC. The first step in this situation is to stop the bogus account generation by using a universal key or by using a search method to find the best match in the existing SFDC accounts. Once this problem has been fixed, you'll probably find that the duplicate accounts in SFDC can't be simply deleted: they have to be merged with the good data.

Deduping involves designating a master copy of the record and merging all of the updated data from other copies into that master. Once the master record contains all of the best data, the related lists (e.g., `tasks`, `contacts`, and `opportunities`) and attachments are disconnected from the duplicate record and attached to the master copy. Only when the duplicate records are emptied of good data are they deleted. This process can be highly automated using products from RingLead, CRMfusion, and others. Even so, the effectiveness of the automation depends on *reliably and consistently* identifying which is the master record.

In the case of `accounts`, this task won't be a simple one. Using "first created" or "last updated" rules will yield inconsistent results, which can be disastrous because there's no ability to "undo" a record merge.[12] You'll need to run a report on the `accounts` that appear to be duplicates, showing the `create date`, `modified date`, `created by`, and `modified by` fields. Also look at patterns in the `account` data and related lists to indicate which record should be the master. If your integration code is smart enough to put the universal key (which identifies `accounts` across all your IT systems) into the record, any record holding a universal key is automatically defined as the master.

Once you've identified the rules that consistently identify the master, change the ownership of the master records to be one of SFDC's system administrators. (If you have access security set up correctly, this action will protect the records from being accidentally updated by others, and will update the "last modified date.") Now that the masters are clearly identified, you can use the "last updated" rule as the default for the merge/deduping tool. If the tool has an option to have "filled" fields in an old record trump empty fields in the newer record, use it. Unfortunately, the deduping tools seem to delete the duplicate `accounts` automatically,[13] rather than marking them as obsolete. Once this process is complete, reassign the ownership of the master back to the proper account owner, as discussed earlier.[14]

Opportunities

`Opportunities` aren't as thorny as `accounts`. Because `opportunities` exist both in SFDC and in your company's order management and accounting system, however, they need to be handled carefully. Because a closed `opportunity` means revenue, it's important not to have double-counting here.

The secret here is proper naming and identification of `opportunities`. An external key is needed to keep SFDC's data properly synchronized with the order management system. Typically, the systems will share a quote number, which will be transformed into an order number when the transaction closes. SFDC should be configured to hold the external

---

12. This is why the *first thing you do* after the system goes live is a complete backup.
13. While this is not the right thing to do from a purist's perspective, these tools save so much time and effort that it's worth the risk of losing the data associated with "depleted" duplicate records. That said, the duplicate records will appear in your backup files.
14. The account owner for the master record may not have been correct, particularly if that record was generated from migration or integration code. Double-check record assignment using territory definitions.

INSTEAD OF DEDUPING ACCOUNTS . . .

While other system data really *have* to be deduped, there is another option for near-duplicate accounts: create parent–child relationships. While this topic is covered in detail in Chapter 9, the basic strategy is to leave the multiple accounts in place and make them children of the master account, as shown in Figure 3-2.

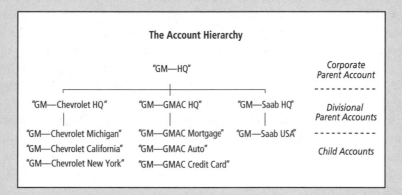

FIGURE 3-2   Example account hierarchy

In this way, none of the child account information is lost, and the people who are searching for the right division of ABC Company can quickly find the relevant information.

system's quote and order numbers, and the integration software should keep the data synchronized on a near-real-time basis.

I know of no tools for deduping opportunities in SFDC; instead, this task must be done manually. The master opportunity is the one in which the quote and order numbers are stored in the record; all duplicate opportunities will have to be compared (either in a spreadsheet or visually using two Web browsers), and any unique data in the duplicates should be manually copied into the master record. All contact roles, tasks, activity history, attachments, and other related items need to be transferred from the duplicate opportunities to the master opportunity—and all of these transfers are usually done manually. Even after a duplicate opportunity is emptied of all unique data, it should not be deleted.[15] Instead, it should have its status changed to "duplicate opportunity" and its probability percentage changed to zero.

---

15. Deletion just isn't the right thing to do. Both for Sarbanes-Oxley Act compliance and for general data hygiene, records should never be deleted because all audit trails are deleted with the record. Keeping duplicate opportunities will use an infinitesimal amount of storage, yet will provide evidence for any forensic or business process analyses in the future.

Any opportunity for new business that has not been the subject of any updates for a year should also have its probability changed to zero. (Note that renewal opportunities may be valid in the system for as long as three years, depending on your business practice.)

Contacts and Leads

The nice thing about duplicate contacts and leads is that there are so many ways they can occur, and there are such dramatic ways to collapse them. But in collapsing these items, it's important not to lose important historical data. While the data deduping tools will automatically append most of the history from underlying leads (e.g., activities), they may not faithfully consolidate the entire audit trail of changes (field history) and by themselves they can't do the right thing with the lead source. You have to take some steps first.

Most of the audit trails will be properly concatenated by the deduping tools or the SFDC merge function, but there will be cases where some subtleties will get lost, perhaps because of overlapping or contradictory updates in the multiple lead and contact records. If you really need to have a complete audit trail for forensic reporting, the best course of action is to dump the history data for all leads and contacts into an archival CSV file prior to performing any deduping.

With the lead source, the problem is that this standard field can have only one value at a time, but reality is sometimes better reflected by a series of values (e.g., Web site registration, download, Webinar). The right approach is to create a series of well-structured campaigns that mirror each lead source value. Each lead should then become a member of its appropriate campaign *before* the deduping process, so that the tools you use can properly append and transfer the campaign memberships during the deduping cycle. It's really important to get this right, even though it may take some serious time. Check out Chapter 10 for a deeper discussion of campaigns.

> ### DON'T LEAVE FOR HOME WITHOUT MAKING ANOTHER BACKUP
>
> *Do another complete system backup of any data you have deduped. Save each backup under a different name, and archive the old ones so you can backtrack if necessary.*
>
> *Even after you think the project is finished, keep these files around. You may discover a subtle corruption weeks later, and these interim files will provide forensic data to reconstruct the crime . . . and, one hopes, reconstruct the data.*

The Morning After the Morning After: Enriching Data

This section could have been called *The Poseidon Adventure II,* but that would have been too obscure a reference. So I didn't do that, and we'll just move on to the next step.

Now that the initial deduplication has been done, it is time to perform data enrichment: adding outside data into SFDC to provide more complete information about leads, contacts, and accounts. The enrichment process uses the data already in SFDC to match up with the external data, and then imports these "fatter" records back into the system.

For example, with leads the one part of the record that can be validated as correct is the user's email address. Everything else in the record may be bogus or have typos, but with the right systems in place,[16] the email address will be correct. Using a reverse lookup, enrichment vendors can provide such information as the person's name, company name, title, phone, and address. Some of this information will be unreliable, but it's almost always better quality than what's already in your SFDC data. This process typically costs about $1 per record, and takes a day or two to complete. Depending on your specific audience, these enrichment services may get a "hit rate" as high as a 50%—but don't be surprised if 20% or less of the records match (particularly for international contacts).

Contact records typically have better data quality, because someone has communicated with those people to qualify them for contact status (see Chapters 9 and 10 for more on this topic). Of course, you can use the email address enrichment strategy as you did with leads, but you can also buy business databases on CD-ROM or from online services. These databases can provide a range of information about the contact, including title, professional certification, and other information. The advantage of the databases on CD is automation: the user doesn't have to take any action. When using a CD-ROM database, it is essential to *not* dump its entire contents into SFDC (this is the most wanton kind of data pollution), but instead to perform a JOIN that simply expands the data into the records you already have in the system. The online services (such as Hoover's, ZoomInfo, and others) usually have a Web integration feature ("mashup") that allows you to add their information to your records. Unfortunately, most of these interfaces require the user to perform at least one explicit action (several mouse clicks) to add these data to the contact record. These corporate databases can be expensive, so most SFDC installations restrict the user count to keep costs under control.

The final area for enrichment is accounts. In SFDC, accounts are at the top of the information hierarchy, so enriching this information can prove quite valuable. Account enrichment is particularly appropriate with the Named Account model of selling (see Chapter 9), which tries to penetrate a small number of high-value customers without relying on lead generation. A Named Account sales rep is always hungry for more information about new account prospects. As with contacts, two data-enrichment alternatives exist: databases on CD-ROM and online services. Each source can have valuable data about the account's business, organizational structure, vertical industry, purchasing patterns, and other useful

---

16. When users register at your Web site, the site should not grant access to the requested documents or resources without sending an email to the user's address; the email should contain a link that directs the user to the requested resource(s). By clicking the link, the user is uniquely identified and the email address validated. Of course, some people will use "single-use" email addresses, but they will usually represent an extremely small percentage of the total number of visitors. See Chapter 10 for further discussion on this topic.

information. As before, it is essential *not* to indiscriminately import large amounts of data into SFDC. In the Named Account model, it is reasonable to import as many as 250 accounts' worth of data, but almost never more. As always, make sure that you're not creating duplicate account names when you perform this data enrichment. See Chapter 10 for a fuller discussion on best practices for this process.

The Ultimate Job Security

You may be old enough to remember the TV ads that proclaimed, "There will always be a future in computer maintenance." It didn't quite work out that way, but I'm here to tell you that there *will* always be a future in data maintenance.

Because system credibility depends on the volume and value of the data in SFDC more than any other factor, data quality is the lifeblood of ongoing SFDC operations. There are three levels of data maintenance—architectural, manipulative, and administrative—and they'll need to be staffed as ongoing processes.

Architectural

The SFDC data model is clean and well organized, and it is important that additions to it (custom fields and custom objects) do not introduce chaos. As discussed in Chapter 4, if your company is doing any significant degree of customization and integration, you will need to have an architectural review board to review all changes. The review board needs to set system policies, procedures, standards, and training requirements for everyone—from administrators to end users.

The following areas are the most dangerous to data quality:

- Wanton and sloppy data imports

- Lack of control over new-record creation (tons of duplicates)

- Redundant or under-utilized data fields

- Creation of custom fields "attached" to the wrong point in the data hierarchy (e.g., "competitors" attached to the account or contact object)

- Too-lax field access rules

- Missing validation rules

- Improper ownership of records, or mass transfers to the wrong owner

- Uploading of huge attachments (wasting space), which are then attached to the wrong objects

- Failure to remove the `delete` and `merge` buttons from user accounts

- Sloppy or uninformed usage of administrator tools such as the `Data loader`, `Excel connector`, or deduping products

- Mass conversion of `leads` to `contacts`, or entering `leads` as `contacts`

- Integration of external data sources without the proper deduping logic

- Creation of phantom records to deal with uncontrolled external systems (particularly from partners or the channel)

- Uncontrolled use of the Outlook connector

- Sloppy or untrained administrators

- Too many people with administrator privileges, even if those individuals are well trained

- Uncoordinated development and administrative effort (change control tools exist for a reason!)

As the first line of defense for data quality, the architectural review board should review business process changes, administrator training levels, and all proposals for significant system change. Initially, meetings will need to occur frequently, but over time a monthly cycle should be sufficient.

Manipulative

Marketing users, sales operations personnel, and support managers typically have some special access privileges in SFDC. They can see more data, and they can manipulate it in special ways. These users need to be trained to use their privileges properly to avoid data damage.

The most notable areas in terms of data quality reside in the marketing arena, because marketing users often perform bulk operations that can go wrong in a hurry. `Lead` imports, creation of `campaign` lists, and interaction with email blasters or marketing automation tools (such as Vertical Response or Eloqua) are everyday tasks that must be done correctly. Training, templates, and very thorough cheat sheets are absolutely essential for these users. We also recommend specific incentives (both spot bonuses for consistent good work and somewhat public embarrassment for errors) to ensure as few defects in this area as possible.

Another area also deserves some attention: survey design. When marketers or support people design a survey with the intent of putting the survey results into SFDC records, it is essential that the survey answer-values map verbatim to SFDC records (particularly to picklist values). If the survey is designed or executed incorrectly, some of the data will have to be thrown out—and in some cases an entire "column" of data (all the answers to a question) may have to be excluded.

Administrative

Each SFDC administrator has a lot of power to enforce the right behaviors and to provide insurance against Big Messes. In an operation of any size, the administrator's main duty is to say "no" to requests that don't fit with best practices and haven't been approved by the architectural review board.

In the course of an administrator's day-to-day duties, he or she does a lot to preserve and improve data quality. For example, on a weekly basis the administrator should perform these tasks:

- Run deduping tools

- Run administrative reports on data quality

- Update record ownership to reflect sales staff and territory changes

- Run a full system backup (although it's usually not practical to back up attachments more often than once a month, or even once a quarter)

- Undo erroneous imports

- Undelete records (using the system's recycle bin)

Check out Chapter 13 for a broader discussion of administrative duties.

Creating a Cost Model for Clean Data

Given the amount of effort that goes into data cleansing, correction, enrichment, and deduping, it's a good idea to create a model of the *cost of a good record* in SFDC. Even if the lead or contact never produces any revenue, there is a cost—and a value—in creating and maintaining it. In the model, you should estimate the business value of a fully qualified lead (a few hundreds of dollars), an unqualified lead (a few dollars), and a "name" (zip). With this cost and value model, you can make rational choices about the next marketing campaign that will generate 100,000 new (but essentially worthless) "leads" or the wisdom of importing that CD promising 13 million email addresses.

Because the perceived value of SFDC will largely depend on the cleanliness, timeliness, and relevance of the data in the system, it's a good idea to put data quality and maintenance on several individuals' MBOs.

CHAPTER 4

Implementation Strategy

Official Project Stages:
1, Uncritical Acceptance
2. Wild Enthusiasm
3. Dejected Disillusionment
4. Total Confusion
5. Search for the Guilty
6. Punishment of the Innocent
7. Promotion of the Nonparticipants

—Anonymous

T HIS CHAPTER IS FOR all implementation team participants, technical or not. Team members need to understand the project from the "top down," even though their day-to-day perspectives will be detail-oriented (seeing the project from the "bottom up"). Readers will understand how they fit in, who depends on them, and the rules of the road.

Before You Begin

Companies tend to treat SFA/CRM implementations like they do other projects: they obsess about budgetary variances and the go-live date. One of the lessons learned from a decade of SFA/CRM projects is that the technology improvements *by themselves* will be meaning-less unless users adopt the system. Without interesting, relevant data, the SFA tool is just a toy. So the go-live date really doesn't have much meaning. It's the *start* of the process of creating business value—not the conclusion. The key metric of success is user adoption of more than 50%, not the go-live date.

Further, while budgetary variances are important, they are not decisive factors. An over-spend rate of 20% (a significant amount) will be dwarfed by the productivity increases you're trying to achieve in sales. If you come in on budget but sales still loses deals due to sloppy execution and measurement, you haven't made the right business decision. The focus needs to be on revenue achievement, rather than budgetary containment.

Before you begin the project, make sure that your executive champion and the leaders in the Sales and Marketing departments not only are supportive of SFDC, but are explicitly targeting organizational improvement to accompany the new system. The automation and capabilities of SFDC are most powerful when they become the foundation of better business processes. The executives should identify the process changes for each of their organizations. Check out Chapters 6, 8, and 13 if you haven't done so already.

Big Bangs and Waterfalls

If you've ever done a "knock-down" remodel of a house, you can believe the statistic that 38% of these "Big Bang" projects blow up, causing a divorce among the homeowners.[1] Why does this occur?

As discussed in Chapter 1, Big Bang projects—which tend to feature major chunks of functionality delivered all at once—are more likely to suffer budget overruns and schedule slips than smaller, more incremental projects. While this phenomenon was first documented in the 1960s, the evidence continues to the present day:

> Technology projects bear a striking resemblance to home renovations. Both are surrounded by wildly high hopes at the start and often end up causing financial and emotional heartache. Even now 50% of projects suffer budget overruns and 62% have experienced delays, according to a new report by Tata Consultancy Services.
>
> —Elizabeth Bennett, May 2008 *Baseline Magazine*

There are many reasons for this tendency. Like a home remodeling project, big IT projects involve solving problems whose scope cannot be truly known until the project is under way. It's only as you rip away the veneer of patches in presentation logic that you discover the dry rot of bad data structures underneath. It's only when you actually try to install the new fixtures of user interface that you understand the incompatible data pipes that were hidden before. With each new problem comes the recommendation to "fix the architecture," which can only add to short-term cost and delay. As was said so eloquently in CRMSolutions' 2008 executive guide for avoiding SFA implementation pitfalls, "A majority of businesses embarking on an SFA solution make the fatal mistake of implementing too many features too quickly."

As the go-live date for a Big Bang project starts to slip, it's common to justify and "resell" the project by adding more features. This leads to scope creep, the expansion of project deliverables with little regard for budgetary, scheduling, or logistical realities. Decision makers often miss the logical folly of statements like "We promised to give you x in 90 days

---

1. The American Architects Association is too embarrassed to have ever published these numbers but the Construction, Restoration, and Planning organization conducted a survey and published it on its Web site, www.crap.com. (Okay, it's true, I made this number up.)

and weren't able to do that—but now we've found a way to give you $1.5x$ in 120 days!" Of course, the net result is that the project delivers $1.1x$ in 180 days, if you're lucky.

Big Bangs backfire because of long timelines, uncertainty, poor project sizing, false expectations, and wandering executive attention. The executives approving the project want a fixed price, a fixed schedule, and a guaranteed set of features. Meeting these criteria would be a snap with perfect command-and-control, but even in the Defense Department project overruns are legendary.

Most Big Bang projects use a waterfall model of project management. Symbolized by Gantt charts, the waterfall theory starts with requirements being thoroughly documented at the beginning and then delivered through a linear process of design, coding, testing, and deployment. There are three problems with this theory: (1) it doesn't work in software, (2) it ignores the reality of requirements discovery and business change during the project, and (3) it doesn't work in software. What really happens is that users give engineers a big spec and a budget, and then are told to go away for 11 months. After the coding work is done, the project is presented in test mode to users, who are often shocked with the developer's lack of quality control, taste, and ESP.

A clear antidote is to change the constraints and assumptions to reflect software reality, and to improve the performance and flexibility of software teams:

- Remove one of the constraints: keep the schedule and budget fixed, but allow variation in the requirements delivered.

- Focus on the end-state, rather than the delivery style: instead of delivering "everything" as a package at the end, allow the team to deliver functionality in small chunks, over several rapid iterations.

While these choices may seem scary, when properly managed they provide less risk, less trauma, and a higher likelihood of delivering what *actually matters to the users and the business* without breaking the bank.

The Agile Manifesto

In 2001, some of the industry's most innovative and productive software development organizations met to propose a new method of managing and delivering software. They knew from experience that the waterfall model and Big Bang projects—which virtually mandated long meetings, bureaucratic behavior, and long, boring specifications—simply didn't pay off. Their proposal, argued by gurus such as Martin Fowler, Kent Beck, and Roy Singham, was to turn software project management on its head. The Agile Manifesto argued for an iterative style of thinking and delivery: peeling off the layers of the onion. Requirements couldn't really be set in stone at the beginning—even if they were, during the 18 months of the project, economic or internal business changes would invalidate many parts of the "stone tablets." Fifty years of software experience has shown that users and executives alike *don't really know what they want until they see an example of it*. So why not set requirements dynamically, as the project goes along? Why not start with a prototype (or storyboard) with a business test ("Don't ship to customers while they're on credit hold") rather than some abstract document of features?

If the requirements could be set incrementally, why shouldn't testing be done at every stage? Instead of keeping everyone in the dark about quality issues until the very end—where problems are most costly to fix—why not expose as many quality problems as possible early on? At the extreme, you might even use a test first style, where you don't allow software to be developed until you've created the test it must satisfy.

If satisfying the users is the end goal, why shouldn't they be involved in the prototyping and testing processes? They know more about what's important to the business and natural for the business process than an engineer ever could. This idea took user-centered design to the next level.

The Agile Manifesto and follow-on writings argued for an adaptive style of software development and project management that molded itself to the business need:

- Projects should be optimized for frequent delivery of value to the business.

- Projects should make decisions as late as possible, because it's not really clear what's *truly* important—or the degree of difficulty involved—until you're in the midst of the project.

- Project teams should focus on being as responsive as possible, thereby ensuring they deliver working software that provides a competitive advantage.

- Projects will be more efficient and effective if they avoid large bureaucratic meetings, heavy documentation, and static waterfall scheduling.

- Projects should have predictable time cycles and budgetary impact, but allow freedom regarding the feature set delivered.

- Projects should include frequent testing, with the twin goals being to expose unforeseen design issues and to lower the cost of defect correction.

- Projects should work with rapid prototyping and frequent user feedback, to make sure that *only the essential features are being worked on.*

The user organization should perceive an Agile IT project as being like a subway system: everyone knows how much the journey will cost and how long it will take, but they don't know (or really care) which specific train they're going to be on. As members of the organization become more confident that "the next train" will arrive very soon, they'll be less upset if their favorite feature didn't happen to make *this* particular train. Executives will resist the temptation to pull political strings to accelerate their pet feature at the expense of others, or push for scope creep.

As outgrowths of the original Agile Alliance, software development shops such as ThoughtWorks, product management consultants such as Enthiosys, and software houses such as Rally and Atlassian created tools and methodologies to make Agile development more accessible to IT teams and more reliable for management. Like the Japanese auto industry, which focuses on flexible manufacturing and repeatable processes to gain speed and profitability, the Agile methodology focuses on trying to "get lean"—changing the rules to improve quality and deliver better value to the customers. Unlike the Japanese auto industry, however, software didn't have the statistical or procedural rigor of the Deming methods.

You Really Have to Plan:
Agile Development Is Not Enough

While in theory Agile methods allow for very rapid productivity, in the real world Agile works only when developers are serious wizards and users are highly motivated and engaged. The engineers will frequently ask the project leader and user representatives detailed questions and tricky priority calls, and they'll typically need to get their answer in a few hours or risk losing development time. Agile development demands a lot from the team members, and most projects don't have the luxury of perfect human resources.

Other issues have also emerged since the Agile Manifesto was published: Agile methods are highly focused on the needs and behaviors of engineers. Nontechnical managers don't get the tomes of documents and project plans with which they're familiar, so they find it tough to figure out the real status of the project. The pointy-haired bosses (PHBs) of *Dilbert* lore want to see project milestones that are fixed, are measurable, and have deliverables defined well in advance—and Agile development won't provide them. The bean counters get nervous about the chaos and uncertainty about costs.

Agile projects can appear to be very chaotic, with tasks and resources seeming to "jump around" on a weekly basis. For the participant as well as the observer, the flexibility that is the hallmark of Agile projects can also prove very stressful.

Further, Agile projects can become defocused when the teams work items off the backlog in the order they appear on the list, rather than in the order that is needed to satisfy all the dependencies and prerequisites of a complex feature.

Finally, the Agile methodology is really appropriate only for development-intensive work. SFDC projects don't involve much development—they're about sequencing the rollout of features, manipulation, integration, and importing of existing data.

Even with these sometimes thorny issues, the economic, quality, and productivity advantages of Agile development are hard to deny. The technologies of SOA and SaaS cry out for an incremental, prototype-oriented style of development. Even SFDC itself uses Agile methods in developing the system. Because SFDC is delivered as a set of modules and components, why not run the project in the way that leverages the technical foundation? What if there were a way to impose a little more structure on top of Agile development?

Wave Deployment

In small organizations, it's easy to get everyone around a table and come to agreement on which features need to be developed and which users will transition into the system at each deployment stage. In some cases, deployment can all be done at one step, and the system can remain in a steady state for six months or more. Done.

But in larger organizations, there's no way to get all the users productive at the same time, even if the functionality could be delivered all at once. With larger, more complex SFDC systems, it's important to deploy the functionality in phases, to waves of users—groups who will value the functionality that is being released in each phase. The trick is to identify the prioritized features and the most appropriate group of users at the same time.

It's traditional in SFA/CRM to have users adopt features in an iterative style, as illustrated in Figure 4-1. But our experience with SFDC is that users in one department will want to absorb features at a different time—or even in a different order—than other departments. Building on these lessons, my firm[2] has developed the Wave Deployment methodology for SFDC implementations. Thanks to the modularity and "instant" provisioning of SFDC features and the varying needs of users in different functional groups, waves provide a natural way to evolve the features and the user base at the same time.

The downside of Agile project management is that you can't predict at the outset precisely when any individual feature will be delivered. With waves, you can predict both the *order* and the groups to which features will be delivered, so that you'll have a logical story to tell even before the work has begun.

A *wave* refers both to the features—the *business deliverable* for a deployment cycle or increment—and to the group of users it's intended for. Each wave starts out as a loosely defined set of features scheduled for delivery (typically fitting on a single page). In a small company, the wave description would be something as simple as, "telesales will get call-center-lite automation by May 15." The functional description must be kept deliberately vague because the specific feature list will change throughout the course of the wave.[3] While the wave may actually include a bunch of other features for other users, the description focuses on the *main theme of value* that will be delivered to the business. Appendix B of this book provides an initial high-level wave description.

Waves should typically occur twice per business quarter.[4] No single user group should be the focal point of two waves in a row. When the features (and the required training requirements) are distributed in this kind of "round-robin" fashion, no one group has to

---

2. Sales*Logistix*, a specialist SFDC consultancy.
3. Remember that the innovation of the Agile methodology keeps deadlines and budgets fixed, but the actual deliverables variable. This counter-intuitive method is what makes for flexibility, productivity, and quality.
4. If the teams are good, waves could happen every couple of weeks. But users won't be happy dealing with that much change: they need time to get used to the technology, see how it affects the way they do business, and gain experience before they give feedback. There's nothing wrong with delivering a new report or improving some feature overnight in response to user requests—but the plan for rolling out big chunks of functionality should be more measured.

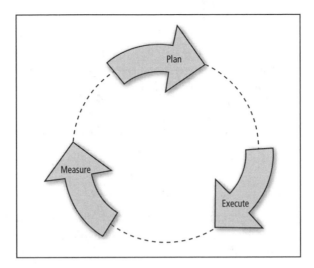

FIGURE 4-1   The SFA cycle

deal with the disruption of a new learning curve more often than once per quarter. Generally speaking, waves should not be delivered during the first week or the last two weeks of the quarter, to minimize the disruption on sales, order entry, and accounting. If a piece of functionality must be "turned on" at the first day of a new quarter, training sessions should be done before week 12 of the previous quarter.

What's in a Wave?

The trick in planning, of course, is to define "what's in the wave" and "which groups will be part of the wave" at the same time. Sometimes it's easier to start with the features that are "do-able" and define the target users; at other times it's easier to start with the affected user groups and figure out which features they'll value most.

DEPLOYMENT: PUSH VERSUS PULL

To get the highest-quality (and, in the end, the fastest) adoption of the system, avoid overselling SFDC or overzealously pushing people into using it before they are motivated to do so.

The ultimate deployment situation occurs when the next group of users is asking, even begging to be let on the system. In an ideal situation, you want to create a sense of exclusivity where "the chosen few users" are allowed to get on the system early. Use your early adopters—technophile cowboys—to create an aura of coolness around the system. Have an early access program where users have to be nominated to get in on the latest features. Remember what Gmail did with its "by invitation only" user group? Try to get some of that same energy going with your users. Check out Chapter 6 for more discussion of this topic.

In defining waves, it's important to keep these seeming contradictions in mind:

- All users need to feel some value is being delivered to them whenever you ask something new of them, *but* no user can absorb a really big chunk of new functionality more than once every nine months or so.

- The project has to be able to show delivery of value to some part of the business at least once (and preferably twice) per quarter, *but* the most significant features will take longer than six weeks to implement.

- Few significant features can be completed without some infrastructure, integration, or data scrubbing, *but* no user values infrastructure, integration, or data scrubbing per se.

- The most aggressive early adopter users may have the most to gain from deploying a new feature, *but* the most conservative, technophobic users must be cooperative if new features are to be deployed successfully (even though the latter user may perceive that they receive little immediate, personal gain for their extra effort).

Planning the Sequence of Waves: WaveMaps

In Chapter 1, we discussed development of a pro forma schedule and roadmap that can be used to "sell" the project to upper management. Like all convenient fictions, this one needs to be reworked to expunge hidden diabolical minutiae.[5] It's time now to create a schedule that is based on better information and real details.

Many companies will want to see an overview of the project deliverables for a year or more, because managers have set aside portions of the budget for the project. The job of the project champion and team leader is to set reasonable expectations for the end-state of the system, and try to give themselves enough "wiggle room" to succeed. In an Agile world, things move around.

Things get a little thornier when an executive wants to know in which quarter his or her pet feature will be deployed. Maneuver the conversation to focus on the end-state, and try to avoid committing to specific delivery dates: at the beginning of the project you simply don't know how long it will take to make that pet feature a successful reality, because you don't yet know how hard it really is.

All that said, you do need to have a roadmap and a sequence of feature sets. A WaveMap is a roadmap with a "third-dimensional" overlay showing the user groups deploying the functionality of each wave. One of the best ways to visualize this third dimension is to have the background of the WaveMap be your company's department-level organization chart.

---

5. The devil's in the details.

On top of this background, overlay the "local version" of the Wave timeline. (See Figure 4-2 for an example.) If your org chart is "flat" and this approach doesn't work, try using a geographic map (U.S. or globe) as the background instead. As you can imagine, WaveMaps tend to be fairly large, and they work nicely when displayed on a wall (with feature time-lines pinned up on the map, so they can be easily read and updated).

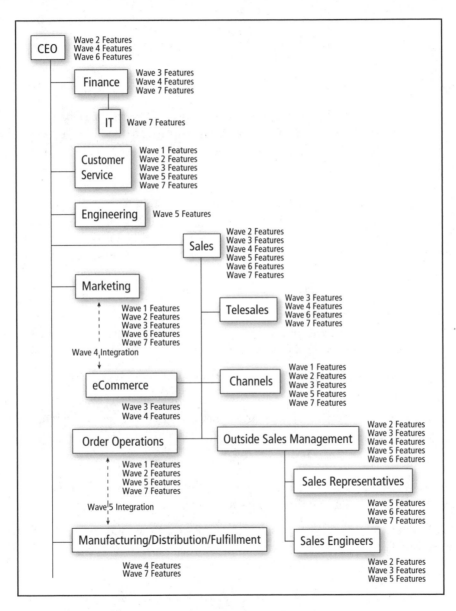

FIGURE 4-2   A WaveMap overlaid on an organizational chart

Assume that during the year you will complete seven waves,[6] and allocate the requirements priority list you developed in Chapter 1 across them. It is critical that you communicate in writing and in person that these are *not* promises or commitments—rather, the WaveMap is a logical sequence of features that *could* be deployed. The details will inevitably change as the timeline unfolds, to fit most efficiently and logically with the facts and resources that become real during the project timeline.

Of course, the highest-priority, lowest-effort items should come first, right? Not quite. Three "big picture" issues need to be considered in sequencing the features across waves.

Technical Dependency

The first issue is technical dependency: some SFDC and add-on features have a significant number of dependencies and prerequisites. As a consequence, some SFDC functions have to be delivered in a specific order. The evolution of SFDC functions will almost always follow this sequence:

1. Cleaning, deduping, normalizing, and enriching existing data is the first step for any significant SFDC deployment. It's hard to know which is worse: deploying a feature with no legacy data at all, or deploying it with crummy data that will be cleaned up "later." Either approach undermines system credibility and makes the system harder to use. If you didn't read it already, check out Chapter 3 for guidance on the best way to handle the data preparation and migration.

2. Do not attempt to integrate everything at once. It is best to delay integration as long as possible and do it incrementally so that you introduce potential destabilizing elements on top of a solid base of data and system functionality.

3. Contacts and accounts have to be in place before any other SFDC features can be sensibly used.

4. Activities (mainly tasks) need to be populated for at least a month before any activity monitoring reports are used.

5. Opportunities have to be solid before forecasting makes sense.

6. Leads and campaigns should have at least six months of good, deduped data before any marketing effectiveness dashboards are deployed.

7. The products and price list have to be in place before quoting or contracts make sense.

---

6. Generally, we recommend unleashing two waves per quarter. Usually, the team has trouble delivering one of the waves, either during the Christmas season or at the fiscal year-end. If you plan for completing only seven waves and then complete the eighth, you'll be guilty only of under-promising and over-delivering. Pray for such problems.

8. The `products` and `assets` have to be enabled in SFDC before the new system is integrated with an outside license management, inventory management, or distribution system.

9. The `sandbox` needs to be in place before serious work begins on integration or multi-currency operation.

OUR INTERNATIONAL FRIENDS

A great example of Wave Deployment is the delivery of features to international users, as it clearly shows the interrelationships among users and functionality. International users may have differences in the following areas:

- On-screen language
- Data-entry character sets and keyboard layout
- Mobile device support
- Currency
- Address and phone number formats
- Pick-list values and defaults
- `Sales processes, page layouts, and record types`
- Time zones
- Business hours and days (particularly for the Middle East)
- Business rules
- Business processes
- Legal requirements, compliance issues, and customer-privacy regulations
- Training and documentation

Make sure to put extra time into the schedule to accommodate significant international requirements, as collecting and understanding them, as well as testing the features, is guaranteed to take longer than the corresponding efforts for domestic users. While SFDC is *very* international friendly, third-party products and externally integrated systems may not be. Further, you may find that international rules and business processes may be quite opaque—even hidden from the local workers.

Multiple-currency operation requires special attention, owing to its effects on the system. If you have doubts about the need for multi-currency in SFDC, keep your system all in one currency as long as you can. You can never go back once you've turned the multi-currency function on. But if you know for certain that you must have reports and forecasts in local currencies, you might as well activate these capabilities sooner rather than later (as the transition may break reports, dashboards, custom code, and workflows that you set up).

There are too many detailed prerequisites to capture all possible permutations here. As you investigate a feature set in SFDC and add-on products, keep close tabs on the dependencies so you can analyze their effects on the feature-deployment order. *Do not* fall into the trap of leaving the uncertain (or least known) things until the end of your agenda. Do just the opposite: put the riskiest items at the beginning, where you have room to "discover."[7] We'll be keeping a list of dependencies at www.SFDC-secrets.com, so check it out as a starting point for your project.

Legal Approvals/Review Committees

As discussed further in Chapter 6, large companies have a lot of moving parts with abstruse functions and interlinkages. SFDC is an information system that may touch on internal policies, business processes, and regulatory stipulations. Be realistic about how required review and approval cycles will affect the deployment schedule. It's a good idea for the project manager to take a quick inventory of *all* the company's internal review committees and figure out which ones might want to review part of the SFDC plan. Contact the committee chair, and if he or she seems uninterested, ask that individual to write an email to the effect that this SFDC project does not need to go through that committee's review process. These emails may prove to be invaluable later on in your project.

User Readiness

The third issue that helps determine the ordering of feature sets is the users themselves. Some groups of users are much more likely to love and leverage SFDC early on, and will naturally take to using the system. Having close working relationships between your implementation team and end users is a key success factor for any SFDC implementation. In using the system, those individuals will populate SFDC with valuable data that make it a more attractive asset for other users. For example, customer support personnel are always on the phone with customers, and they naturally come across information that would be valuable to the salesforce. Having members of the customer support team store their notes about happy or unhappy customers, upcoming renewals, and possible upsell opportunities in SFDC—something that's relatively painless for them to do—will make the system more interesting to the sales reps (who are always hungry for information about their accounts).

Figure 4-3 illustrates the sequence in which user groups typically adopt SFDC. Almost always, the people manning the phones are the first users: the contact management and reminder features of SFDC make their jobs immediately easier, and they're no-brainers to learn. The inside sales reps (ISRs)[8] work naturally with the system, and the team manager

---

7. Fail.
8. This group does initial lead prospecting and qualifying. "Inside sales" is a bit of a misnomer because these representatives don't actually close any deals; instead, their job is to cultivate and prep the prospects to the point that they want to take a meeting with the company's sales reps. At different companies, this group may be called telemarketing, telesales, inside sales, sales development, or lead cultivation.

quickly figures out how to get the metrics he or she needs on reports and dashboards. Tactical marketing personnel (particularly the people who do lead generation programs) also tend to adopt the system very early. These two groups provide a bedrock of `leads`, `contacts`, and `opportunities` that are useful to others. Typically, the next group to switch to the system comprises the sales operations people, who must work with reps to push deals through. The sales operations group is typically a centralized function that doesn't ever "touch" customers, but its members do expedite quotes, orders, and paperwork through the bureaucracy. Because they are involved with deals as they progress through the sales cycle, it's natural for these employees to use SFDC to keep tabs on deals and provide reminders for follow-up.

The next likely user group consists of the pre-sales engineers and post-sales consultants or service people who "touch" the customer. Because SFDC already contains the `account`, `contact`, and `deal` information, these groups will constantly be looking up data in the system and making notes on their specific projects. The ability to attach documents to `deals` (closed `opportunities`) and to put in auto-reminders for tasks and action items makes SFDC a natural way for these teams to collaborate. Even though these employees may have used email and their personal calendars as collaborative tools for years, the shared access and visibility inherent in SFDC makes the system a better way to work as a team.

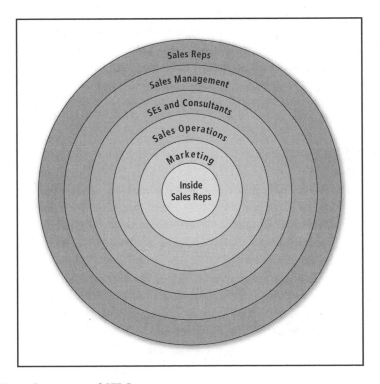

FIGURE 4-3   Typical sequence of SFDC users

At this point, sales management will have been using the system for a while, albeit usually for simple monitoring and reporting on pipelines and activities. Only as the system grows to include a significant amount of customer data do sales managers start to use the system as a personal resource. For example, if the CEO wants to know what's going wrong with a deal and the sales rep doesn't answer his phone, the sales manager can look in the SFDC system to see the "state of play" at the account. Eventually, sales managers will do mini account reviews based on SFDC data, and they will start running their regular forecast review meetings through the system. These changes in management behavior send a signal to the individual reps that it's time to get serious about using the system.

Perhaps surprisingly, the last users to whole-heartedly endorse the SFA/CRM system—which is supposed to improve a sales rep's efficiency—will be the sales reps themselves. Generally speaking, the more senior the rep, the longer it will take for that person to really leverage the system. Of course, these senior reps are often the rainmakers in the organization, so it's not a great idea to push them too soon.

As the sequence of waves starts to take shape in your requirements spreadsheet, you should identify a **theme** for each wave's features as well as the principal user group that will benefit from it. Although waves frequently include flotsam features that happened to "make the cut," discussing each wave in terms of the theme and the target users will make it much easier to sell across the organization. When you have an initial complete draft WaveMap, review it with your main project sponsors. They may have forcing functions or other real business issues that change some of your assumptions and accelerate or delay the need for a feature set. The larger the company, the more likely the roadmap of waves will resemble a patchwork quilt: there will be rationality to every decision, but there won't be a simple checklist with one department's needs being clearly fulfilled in a given quarter. This scattershot effect is almost unavoidable, and SFDC's inherent flexibility and responsiveness should be sold as a benefit.

> ### SWEETEN THE POT
>
> *When looking at the contents of a wave, make sure to cast the features in terms that the user can understand. Don't be abstract—avoid "featuritis." Instead, talk about the ways that a set of features will save users 5 minutes a day, every day.*

It's important that management not perceive WaveMaps as being cast in stone: they are a forecast of the best use of company resources given *current* information. As you'll see, the WaveMap's overview will be adjusted to reality (e.g., shifts in priorities, staffing changes) at the beginning of every quarter. This tinkering can save your company substantial engineering and staff resources, and it gets extra mileage from your budget.

WHAT IF MANAGEMENT JUST SAYS NO TO AGILE DEVELOPMENT?

Some organizations just don't believe that they have the intensity or talent to use Agile project styles. Some organizations even mandate use of more conventional development methods.

If your organization fits this description, apply as many of the principles outlined in this chapter as you can to your approved project management methods. For the configuration of SFDC features, involve the users and do frequent prototyping and review sessions. For the installation of third-party modules, use the vendor's suggested implementation cycle. In the case of integration—the most complicated part of any SFDC project—keep the requirements as minimal as you can and test frequently to make sure no data are being corrupted.

If your company advocates a waterfall management style, have as many small, independent deliverables as you can to minimize the risk of Big Bangs and scope creep.

No matter which project management and deployment technique you use, optimize the results for the users: give them features that really matter, that really work, and that increase the credibility of the data in the system.

Collecting Resources for a Wave

Waves have an interesting characteristic: you always know when they'll start and how long they are. As a consequence, resources can be scheduled with tight end-dates, which is a good thing for getting commitments. Of course, resources also have to be scheduled with firm commitments on start-date and level of effort—a sometimes challenging feat to achieve.

Every wave will require technical people to configure, develop, integrate, and deploy functionality. Usually, the overall technical team will be in place over several waves, but the individual task assignments (and subgroups) may change with each cycle.[9] On the technical side, it's a matter of allocating available talent to the specific needs of the wave.

Most waves will require a business analyst to think through process and business-rule issues. While business analysts are rarely "in the trenches" and seldom know the details of individual customer situations, they bring valuable perspective to requirements definition, acceptance criteria, political issues, and final testing. Depending on the area of specialization and overall organizational size, the business analyst may change from wave to wave.

---

9. The IT people need to read up on SFDC's API as well as the project wiki content. They also need the right tools: a free SFDC developer account for prototyping and testing, the SFDC developer tools (Object explorer, Data loader, and Eclipse plugin), and (if possible) access to an SFDC sandbox.

STAFFING: CONSULTANTS OR EMPLOYEES?

While the decision whether to use in-house personnel or external resources for carrying out an SFDC project will depend entirely on the specific needs and availability of talent at your company, there are clear best practices for staffing waves.

Generally speaking, internal staff should do 80–90% of the work in the overall implementation. Even if your staff is extremely constrained, no part of the work should be done entirely by outsiders because your organization will need internal capabilities to manage the system going forward. SFDC will continue to evolve every six months or so after the "completion" of your WaveMap—either needing expansion or readjustment of the system to meet changing business realities—so you'll need to have internal competence.

That said, it's not a great idea to have major parts of the project done without *any* outside input. There are certain parts of the project that you don't really want to get good at: technologies that provide you no particular leverage, or processes (such as data cleansing) that are incredibly boring or time-consuming. Consultants also bring valuable lessons from other implementations, and they can help you develop best practices in areas such as sales processes or Agile project management. If you haven't already done so, read the sidebar in Chapter 1 dealing with consultant selection.

Nevertheless, maintaining continuity of business analysts over several waves will cut down on learning curves.[10]

Every wave will also require dedicated time from one or more users representing the target audience for the wave's "main theme" feature set. The next step is to identify the best team participants to represent the users. Choosing the right users—those with a keen business sense and high energy level—will be a key factor in your Agile team's success. People who are too high in the organizational hierarchy have neither the time nor the day-to-day knowledge needed for this phase of deployment; people who are too low in the organizational structure do have the time and the day-to-day knowledge, but they don't understand the reason for the business process or the changes that management may have in store. Most wave development teams can work well with one user from each affected user department, but more complex (or politically charged) areas of functionality may require more users. These users will typically be involved in the project for an hour every few days during much of the wave, plus several hours per day at the beginning[11] (for requirements translation) and at the end (for testing and validation) of their project area.

---

10. The business analyst needs to know the basics of SFDC and should read up on materials in the project wiki. He or she will also need to understand the basics of any external system relevant to the business processes being targeted. The business analyst will use Word, Excel, PowerPoint, and perhaps Visio or Project to do his or her job.

11. The user representatives will need to learn the basics of SFDC, in addition to the systems that they already know. They should read up on the project wiki, and should have access to the same Microsoft Office tools used by the rest of the project team.

Every wave will also need an assigned champion—that is, an executive to whom issues and controversies can be escalated. The assigned champion should come from the department that represents the target audience of the main-theme feature set. In an ideal wave, the champion should not be needed to break logjams—but in the real world, escalations may happen every few weeks.

EVERYBODY ON THE SAME PAGE

Everyone on the wave development team—and particularly the sponsor/executive champion—should clearly understand the implications of Agile projects and time boxing. They need to agree that making the deadline is more important than delivering any particular detail in this wave.

Team members need to not only stop the tendency toward scope creep in other members of the team, but resist the temptation themselves. They need to avoid making specific promises about features because the project needs freedom in the feature list so that it can meet its binding promises related to schedule, quality, and budget.

Maintaining these behaviors can be hard, particularly for old-guard IT people. But the benefits of going Agile—particularly for an SFDC implementation—are just too important to ignore.

Every wave will need some IT resources: system access, lab access, data, review committees, and so forth. In small companies, the necessary resources may simply amount to a developer's PC or access to a database. By contrast, in complex environments, SFDC is integrated with other hosted solutions, databases, servers, and on-premises applications. Even though SFDC is an externally hosted solution, its integration interfaces may need to be reviewed for conformance with company architecture, standardized products, network security, data access policies, and even Sarbanes-Oxley Act compliance. In large companies, these IT review resources may need to be scheduled well in advance of the start of the wave and, in some cases, will change the ordering of projects on the WaveMap. If you have not already done so, at least skim Chapter 13 to understand how and when to engage your firm's IT team.

Most waves will need special resources for testing. In most cases, these resources will consist of copies of databases (or an SFDC sandbox), staging servers, test code, and test personnel. Although these test resources are used most intensively at the end of the wave, they are useful early on as well. Particularly if large amounts of data must be cloned for a test database, make sure to request these resources early enough so any delay in obtaining them doesn't impinge on the wave schedule.

Documentation—a consideration that seems to be omitted from every project schedule—needs to be the responsibility of every team member. SFDC encourages you to annotate many of the changes you make with its internal "help bubbles," but that doesn't obviate the need for documenting the following items in the project wiki:

- Rationales for decisions

- Assumptions made

- Rationales and "owners" for business rules

- Business processes

- Data cleansing and conversion procedures

- Technical approaches to integration

- Code comments

- Test setups and sequences

- User checklists and cheat sheets

- Administrative checklists.

Finally, deployment and training resources need to be scheduled. Mostly, these personnel will consist of internal resources who are already on the project, but in large organizations dedicated "train the trainers" may be required. In any case, the trainees and users form a critical path resource as well: it's important to work out the training venues and nail down the training time early so as to prevent stress as the deadline approaches. Check out the discussion on this topic in Chapter 5.

The final resource is optional only in small projects. Every project needs an incentive or a way to celebrate completion of the task, particularly when you're trying to engage users in the system development process. Each wave needs to have a *tchochke* for the team participants, though these items don't need to be expensive to be effective. T-shirts are the classic give-away, but they work only if people will wear them to help spread the word about the project. Coffee mugs and baseball caps work as well. Talk to the marketing people who do events at your company; they'll be able to come up with dozens of inexpensive ideas, from cell-phone "skins" to mouse pads to henna tattoos—the choice depends on your company culture.

Starting the Wave

Once the roadmap has been negotiated and stabilized, the detailed requirements for the current wave need to be scoped. In the Agile methodology, we don't really dig into the details of any requirement until the work begins: essentially, the details of the requirements are developed in tandem with the functionality itself.

WAVE DEPLOYMENT PERIODS

In larger organizations, there's no way to get all users productive at the same time, even if the wave's technical deployment is straightforward. People and energy levels are the throttles of effective deployment speed. In large companies, a wave may hit during any or all of the following circumstances:

- Different departments with different agendas and priorities
- Departments in the midst of organizational or political turmoil
- A range of user types, from early adopters to technophobes
- A range of locations, including users who are on the road all the time
- A range of languages, currencies, and business practices.

Because many significant waves involve installation of a bit of software[12] on the user's PC, just the wave's deployment and training cycle may take several weeks to complete in larger organizations. Some groups may even defer using a new SFDC feature for several months, in an effort to accommodate external issues.

The first step of the detailed requirements cycle entails validating that the business still values the requirement and is willing to spend the resources to satisfy it. This validation becomes increasingly important in later waves, as business priorities may shift over the months following the start of the implementation.

The next step is to scope the detailed requirements, so that they can become tasks for the wave development personnel. In the context of a wave, the first step of scoping is setting the business's acceptance criteria for the requirement (usually in the form of a test, a transaction, or a trained group of users). Next, the teams need to transform each requirement from a business requirement (completing a measurement, event, or step in a business process) into a technical one. Work with the user representatives to make sure that each business requirement is stated in the best way, and then ask questions about different ways to satisfy the requirement. For example, sales personnel may have stated that they need to see current order status for all customers, which implies a technical requirement for real-time integration between SFDC and your company's order management system. On investigation, however, you may discover that order status doesn't change more often than twice a week, and the sales people won't really mind if the data are updated only weekly. Instead of a real-time update system for SFDC, then, a weekly batch update via Excel spreadsheets will serve the business requirement. Simplifications such as this one can save the project staff weeks of time and avoid unnecessary purchases, which means analyzing each business

---

12. While the core system of SFDC is totally hosted and doesn't require so much as a browser plugin, several popular third-party features require libraries, plugins, and applications to be installed at the user's PC. As a result, beyond the initial stages of SFDC usage, there is often software to be deployed (at least on the power users' systems).

> ## THE IMPORTANCE OF NONGOALS
>
> Goals and requirements, everyone understands.
>
> I'm here to extol the virtues of nongoals. They are the things that you not only won't get done, but have no intention of even starting.
>
> In any wave, having nongoals helps manage expectations by setting the boundaries of the things that you do intend to work on. Publishing nongoals during a wave is a great way to counteract scope creep and happy ears.
>
> In stating your nongoals, it's important to not come across as whining. Don't complain about lack of resources, time, organizational support, data quality, or anything else. Nongoals should simply be bullets that briefly and simply state what *won't* be worked on.

requirement for technical alternatives can pay for itself quickly. Check out Chapter 7's discussion of integration before you try to implement any integration feature.

For any interesting functionality, one key attribute is access control—that is, who should be able to see the data or use the feature. SFDC allows very fine-grained access control, but every security element added to the system makes it more difficult for people to access and share information they may need. Start with an assumption of minimal controls and maximum access, and employ more restrictive measures only in the situations where there is a clear and specific reason to do so.

Strive for simplicity and minimalism in any feature. SFDC makes it very easy to incrementally add complexity and elegance *after* you've got the basics in place.[13] By focusing on the essentials, you simultaneously reduce workload, technical risk, and training requirements. Once the users start working with the system, if they *beg* you to add more complexity and clutter, give it to them—but not before some serious pleading takes place.

Once the technical feature requirements have been written down, the next step is to identify the steps required to implement the functionality. From this list of tasks, the level of complexity, resources, and level of effort can be estimated.

Each business requirement and its associated technical implementation tasks should be summarized in a spreadsheet for the wave development team. This spreadsheet doesn't need to be continuously updated, but an initial pass geared toward filling out its content needs to be completed early in the wave. The spreadsheet should be posted in the wiki area describing the wave, but it needs to include boldfaced warning messages indicating that these are the goals and *initial intention* of the wave development team, not the current work plan.[14]

---

13. Interestingly, it can be a bigger pain to remove features and data items from SFDC than it was to create them in the first place. In a few cases, it is impossible to remove SFDC complexity once you've used it for the first time. For this reason, you should start with a streamlined list of features, and build out from there only as needed.

14. To the frustration of linear thinkers everywhere, in an Agile project the current work plan is almost invisible—it tends to live in the minds of the team members, on blackboards, on 3 × 5 notecards, and in indecipherable spreadsheets. Resist the temptation of over-documenting, as it wastes time. If management, finance, or IT types insist on using a project management tool, avoid Microsoft Project or equivalent tools—instead, choose a tool like Atlassian's JIRA or ThoughtWorks' Mingle, which are designed to be a natural fit with the way Agile teams work.

The final step before initiating tasks is to prioritize the tasks within the wave. Even though you have already prioritized the requirements at a macro level *across* the WaveMap, the tasks now need to be prioritized in a different context. *Within* a wave, priority is generally given to those tasks that have a higher probability of success, require less effort, or have fewer dependencies (i.e., prerequisites for success or repercussions of failure). At the same time, the killer "macro priority" tasks are given priority because they're the theme of the wave. This prioritization will be reevaluated several times during the course of a wave, particularly if a task is completed earlier than expected, or runs into a technical problem or logistical delay.

WHEN A REQUIREMENT IS TOO BIG FOR A WAVE

Most functional requirements can be implemented quite quickly in SFDC: it's a matter of configuring a feature, adding some `custom fields`, using `record-types`, installing a plugin, creating an `S-control` or a `custom object`, or quickly writing a VisualForce page.

Other requirements require deep work: integrating the system with a new external database, cleaning and enriching data, developing code. These tasks just won't fit in a six-week cycle, particularly if the requirement itself needs some business analysis and restatement. What to do?

These longer projects need to be decomposed into smaller components of less than six weeks' duration. Each component is treated separately (but in proper order) on the WaveMap, with expected deliverables for each wave those components reside in. For example, integrating a data warehouse into an SFDC installation might involve the following sequence of components:

1. Analyze data flow requirements to and from SFDC; specify frequency and size of ETL cycles.
2. Identify data cleansing, transformation, and remapping required for each data extraction; identify and evaluate appropriate ETL tools.
3. Do a proof-of-concept with ETL tools, validate that they can complete the data warehouse load operation in the desired time window.
4. Purchase and install ETL tool(s), write control programs, scripts, and procedures for users.
5. Write initial reports for the data warehouse.

Each of these five component projects can be done during the six weeks allocated to a wave, though not all of them can be finished in a single wave. But there's another issue at work here: the teams aren't delivering much value to the business until the last component is completed. As with infrastructure projects, keeping the business users happy and engaged means interleaving the early "nothing in it for me" components with quick wins and other projects that do deliver business value as part of the wave.

As a Wave Takes Shape

Once the wave is under way, the team starts to work on the requirements—refining them while trying to implement them—and they make discoveries. The small discoveries about technical or business details are briefly documented in the wave development wiki. The bigger discoveries relate to the way users actually work, or the characteristics of the data the team is trying to import into the system. These discoveries may influence the overall wave plan.

Earlier in this chapter, one potential wave was initially described as "telesales gets call-center-lite automation." Let's explore what that means, including how it might evolve during a wave as discoveries are made.

The business requirement might be stated as follows: "The 15 telesales reps need to be able to complete 60 outbound dials per day including 15 live conversations. Each of these contact attempts needs to be facilitated and documented (with some fields automatically filled out). Email activity needs to be recorded for each of the contacted prospects. The telesales manager needs to be able to monitor and analyze activity and call-success rates for each individual, and to summarize the results by sales region on a daily basis with weekly summaries."

"I THINK YOU SHOULD BE MORE EXPLICIT HERE IN STEP TWO."

The initial list of technical features might be as shown in Table 4-1. During the wave, the team discovers several things:

- The real-time lead flow from the Web site may not be ready at the time it's needed for this wave. As a consequence, this feature is bumped down the priority list; later, it is pushed off to the next wave when the Web site changes are further delayed.

- The auto-data-fill function using Skype is a cool feature that could save a lot of time, but it requires a complicated setup that might be incompatible with other features that have already been deployed. As a consequence, this requirement is transformed into a research project for one of the team members. When she reports back to the team about compatibility and work-arounds, this feature will be rescheduled (either in this wave or the next one).

- It is discovered that a lightweight Skype dialer that takes almost no effort to install is available. This item is added to the list as a substitute for the more meaty Skype features that were postponed. The lightweight Skype dialer will be helpful to every user, not just the telesales people.

- The auto-dial using the PBX is another time saver. It's discovered early in the phase that this feature is fully compatible with the company's existing phone system. Even though this one feature is hard to complete, it's pulled up in the priority list.

- The automatic upsell reminders and automatic scripting are cool features that could fit in the wave, but marketing can't decide exactly what the customer segments are or what the rules for detecting them or selecting appropriate messages are. Also, customer support has some political arguments and wants to send out these reminders themselves. Because no automation can be built for renewals or the scripts until these issues are resolved, this task is pushed off to a later phase of the project.

TABLE 4-1   Initial Feature List Example

Description	User	Difficulty	Dependency	Priority
Custom screens for reps	Telesales	Easy	None	High
Real-time lead flow from Web site	Telesales	Easy	Web site	Medium
Deduped lead flow from programs	Telesales	Easy	Install tool	Medium
Auto-dial and data fill via Skype	Telesales	Medium	Install tool	Medium
Outbound email recorded	Telesales	Medium	Install tool	Medium
Inbound email recorded	Telesales	Hard	Install tool	Low

Continued

TABLE 4-1 Initial Feature List Example, *Continued*

Description	User	Difficulty	Dependency	Priority
Custom screens for managers	Manager	Medium	None	High
Automatic renewal reminders	Telesales	Medium	Renewal data	Medium
Auto-dial using PBX	Telesales	Hard	Buy plugin	Medium
Automatic upsell reminders	Telesales	Hard	Rules and scripts	Medium
Automatic scripts and cues	Telesales	Hard	Scripts	Low

In a similar manner, the team may discover that some target groups defined for a wave may not really be ready to adopt the features making up the wave. For example, a business process may not have been defined, or a reorganization may not have been completed, or other business priorities may be taking precedence.

The list of features, target groups, and priorities needs to "roll with the punches" as the project progresses. The priority list—including current status and staff assigned—should be updated (typically weekly) and posted as a new file in the project wiki. By continuously publishing the current status of items and showing the change from the previous week, the project will earn confidence in the user community. Transparency pays off in credibility.

THE U PATTERN OF CHANGE

The amount of change in a priority list seems to follow a "U" pattern as the SFDC wave evolves: high degree of change at the start, lower in the middle, and rising again toward the end. This kind of change in priority lists in the course of a phase may seem chaotic, but it's what makes for the flexibility and opportunistic productivity that are hallmarks of Agile project management.

Dirty Little Secret: The Data Are Everything

Okay, I admit it: I've buried the most important concept in the middle of the book. Bully for the careful reader—and for skimmers, tough!

Like any SFA/CRM system, the value of SFDC depends on the amount and value of the data it holds. The system credibility and usage levels depend on good data being presented to users.

Data quality is a shared responsibility that starts with the implementation team, who should do their duty in the following areas: design, import, reports, and data ownership. In designing and configuring SFDC, the team will make dozens of choices in the way data are entered and organized. Refer back to Chapter 3 during the implementation, and take its lessons to heart!

In the course of testing and early system operations, it's important to assign someone to own data quality. This person is tasked with (1) making sure the current data don't become corrupted and (2) detecting new sources of data problems and rectifying them before the wave development features are deployed. The data quality owner should turn on `history tracking` for all SFDC objects[15] from the first day, to help identify and troubleshoot data problems. He or she should also create reports that help identify flaky data entries (exporting the report details to Excel and using pivot tables is one of the fastest ways to find subtle problem data). This individual should periodically run data quality reports and use SFDC's data quality dashboard to measure the number of duplicate records, nonconforming data, and outright corruption. The data quality owner should also designate an area for corralling bad or questionable data: it's never a good idea to delete records, but it's always a good idea to analyze and rectify what went wrong with the data. Further, the data quality owner needs to establish a unique key (using a combination of data points) that acts as a fingerprint for identifying duplicates when they occur across multiple systems.

During the Wave: Real-Time Scheduling

The wave development project manager[16] cannot be flexible on several aspects of the wave. The wave needs to leverage the time, people, and dollars budgeted, but not more. The team needs to deliver on time, repeatedly. The features delivered have to work, can't corrupt data, and must include user input.

Where there is flexibility is "exactly which features are delivered." Instead of delivering a complete feature list late, the Agile methodology focuses on delivering a scaled-back feature list on time and with the desired quality. Further, Agile teams test throughout the development cycle: both with users (for feedback) and with test code (to assure that the acceptance criteria are being met). Whether the immediate task is designing a screen or integrating with an outside system, some level of testing should be done every week. Although the daily or weekly tests may be brief, it's important to reserve the time and external resources for testing so test results are available almost on demand.

The art of wave development project management is the practice of *time boxing*: breaking down the project into tasks with fixed, short deadlines. The task team does a sprint to its

---

15. `History tracking` can provide a nice audit trail for as many as 20 data items for each object (where that kind of audit trail is available). In large systems, 20 data items isn't enough—but that's all there are, so you have to choose the 20 highest-priority items to track for a given object.

16. In small projects, there is only one project manager. In larger projects, there may be a program manager overseeing managers for individual tasks. For simplicity's sake, in this chapter, I refer to the project manager as if he or she were a single person, even though the role may take the talents of several individuals. See the www.SFDC-secrets.com Web site for an example project manager job description.

deadline, delivering the most useful core features first and adding refinements and extras only if time permits. In some business quarters, the time boxes can be defined arbitrarily by the project manager. In other quarters, key dates on the calendar create forcing functions for time boxes. For example, the calendar might include a holiday, or a user group meeting, or an internal training session whose date is known well in advance. The time-boxing deadlines should simply be organized around these fixed dates, thereby ensuring that the team gets the most productive days out of the calendar.

BUILDING TRUST WITH USERS BUILDS SYSTEM CREDIBILITY

An SFA/CRM system is just a shell unless the users use it. Persuading users to adopt the system is a critical success factor for increasing sales productivity and business results. For this reason, building credibility of the system (and the data in it) is job one for everyone on the implementation team.

The wave development methodology starts this process before the system is even delivered. By delivering something of business value on a regular basis, waves foster trust with users. Even if a particular feature is missing from this wave, users trust that the next wave will deliver something even better.

In the early waves of a project, the team needs to work like crazy to deliver a component of business value and then showcase it. This approach is particularly effective when a feature solves a high-profile problem, or just makes a highly visible irritant go away. To create a buzz for system credibility, encourage important or highly connected people to send out emails about how they use the new feature. Check out Chapter 6 for more on this topic.

What makes time boxing work is short tasks with frequent (typically weekly) milestones. The project manager wants to know about any task that is in trouble as early as possible, so that adjustments can be made. The manager can make the following adjustments to bring a task back on schedule:

- Add an extra resource or buy a tool, component, or service

- Pare down the expected feature by simply leaving off refinements or "nice to have" attributes

- Implement a feature in a radically simplified way (thereby delivering a "temporary hack" that will be upgraded the next wave)

- Pushing the feature out of the wave (see "Kicked Out of a Wave" later in this chapter).

In some cases, a feature will go off schedule because of business issues such as undecided business rules, political arguments, less-than-committed team members, resource hoarding, or delayed approvals. The project manager needs to wield the scalpel of escalation with skill—using the political pull of the wave sponsor early enough to make a real difference, but infrequently enough to avoid becoming an irritant.

Inherently, waves and time boxes discourage scope creep. In an Agile project, resources do not remain slack for long—in fact, they're supposed to be 100% utilized at all times. Even so, everyone needs to be vigilant, particularly if a feature has been kicked out of a wave and the teams implementing surviving features in a wave ask for "a few more resources." Reassigning resources is never a friction-free process, so it should be avoided unless a specific reason exists to do so. If a feature is on the borderline of missing its milestone, it makes sense to redirect slack resources to it. In contrast, if the feature is basically on schedule, devoting more resources to it is practically an invitation to expand the feature's scope. Given the short intervals of waves, any expansion in scope—even with the extra resources— is almost guaranteed to cause schedule slippage.

SCOPE CREEP: WARNING SIGNS

Scope creep comes in many forms, and some of the most dangerous ones come from inside the project itself. The blatant request from an outsider is easy to detect. But watch out for these subtle internal appeals:

- "Since we're in there anyway . . ."
- "This code is not maintainable; I need to rearchitect . . ."
- "Let's refactor this . . ."
- "It'll work even better if . . ."
- "I figured out how to do _____ a better way"
- "In the long run . . ."
- "The way it really should work is . . ."
- "We should upgrade to a new version of . . ."

These phrases aren't always indicative of scope creep. But no matter how well intentioned, they can lead to perfectionism and make-work projects that add risk and delay the overall plan.

The ultimate scope-creep weapon is the WaveMap—specifically, those requirements that have survived several rounds of prioritizing. When someone asks to expand one of the requirements or features, the project manager needs to ask, "Which of the things on this priority list should be pushed out of this wave to accommodate your new request? I'll reshuffle everything if you get the project champion for the requirement you propose deferring to agree." That will usually stop the discussion dead, unless something important really has changed in the business.

MANAGING THE FEATURETTES

In old movie houses, in between the feature movie showings, the projectionist would throw in a "featurette"—a 10-minute, short-subject film about some "interesting" topic. The audience never knew which featurettes would be shown each week, but they would be disappointed if they weren't there, thrown in as fillers. Essentially the same management technique is used here: the project manager throws in an appropriate featurette or two in each wave.

Throughout the book, the terms "quick wins," "eye candy," and "user toys" are used. These are all pretty much the same thing—simple additions to the system that make it more easy and fun to use, but don't really cost the project anything. They're too small to explicitly schedule, and the whole point of having them is to "sweeten the pot" of a wave in an effort to make it more appealing to users.

Thanks to the size of SFDC's user community, more than 800 plugins and add-ons for the system have been developed, and many of them are available for free. In addition, SFDC's newsgroups and user forums have lots of hints about simple links and mashups that can provide a lot of "raw material" for featurettes.

At the start of the project, one task should be to survey all the freeware that's available in the AppExchange and elsewhere on the Web. Make sure to download and save everything you can about the featurette when you discover it, as these mini-apps tend to change URLs over time and become very hard to find. Create a spreadsheet summarizing the basic feature, the URL discussing it, the estimated implementation time (typically a couple of hours), and a best guess about which departments would value the featurette.

As the wave progresses, the project leader should identify a few featurettes to be thrown in. Typically, the three featurette audiences warranting the most attention are (1) the target users for the main theme of the wave, (2) the "squeakiest wheel" group (particularly if they aren't getting much that's interesting in this wave), and (3) any group that is likely to feel put upon or upset because of a change or delay.

Kicked Out of a Wave

Due to unforeseen problems, items may need to be pushed out of a wave. Perhaps the requirement is ill defined (e.g., no one can agree on what the acceptance criteria are), or the requirement depends on a purchase that isn't budgeted, or the implementation has failed testing. One of the benefits of Agile management is its bias toward a "fail fast" attitude—problems are identified sooner, so waste is decreased.

Of course, every attempt will be made to keep the highest-priority components of a wave going—but in the face of resource diversion intended to complete that high-priority component, something will have to go. Once the project manager makes the decision to push an item out of the wave, he or she also has to determine whether that item's team members should be reassigned to another task in the wave. If they can't contribute effectively to another task, the team can continue working on their task, even though it will not be delivered until the next wave cycle. If, however, the team members can be effectively reassigned within the wave, the project team should stop its original task. Because no one knows when they'll restart that task, members of this team need to carefully document where they left off and then put the work in mothballs. They'll need to estimate the remaining work and dependencies, and insert their task into the prioritization cycle for the next wave.

Wave Endgame

Even though every team has been doing component-level testing throughout the wave, the wave itself concludes with a final test cycle that works at two levels: technical and business.

The technical tests entail fairly straightforward validation of functionality and data manipulation. For features that are built and configured entirely within SFDC's environment, testing can be fairly light because there's seldom a risk of data corruption. For features that are written in APEX, S-controls that leverage Ajax, or connectors that integrate with outside systems and hosted services, testing is needed for the following issues:

- Functionality

- Security and access control

- Crashes, lock-ups, and race conditions

- Performance and timeouts

- Data corruption

If a feature fails the technical tests, it should be disabled in the system until it is fixed.

Given that some of these tests may require a significant amount of data, it's important to allocate lab system time for creating and analyzing the test data sets. If the data sets are not properly set up, resetting them to rerun a test may take longer than conducting the test itself. Use of APEX code requires that initial tests be developed and executed in the sandbox before the code can be brought into the product system. This is a very good thing, but this test code is just the beginning—plenty more real-world tests will be required on the running system, and their completion will take time out of the schedule.

The business tests don't require as much in the way of resources, but they often take longer to carry out than the technical tests. The good news is that the business tests can often be run in parallel with the technical tests. The first part of the business test is usability. This issue should have been addressed throughout the wave development, with an increasingly wider range of users looking at the system as work on the feature progressed. The second part of business testing is validating the business acceptance criteria. In other words, does the transaction clear, can the business process proceed, can the users do their jobs with the new feature? Usually, the business test passes at *some* level, though it might not be complete, or it might involve a few too many mouse clicks. Even so, armed with a cheat sheet and some training, the users can usually work around business-level defects until the next wave.

Conversely, if the function doesn't work at all or actually does the wrong thing (e.g., falsely approving an erroneous bid), the feature must be disabled in the system until it is fixed. If the fixes cannot be completed and retested by the deadline, that feature will have to be kicked out of the wave.

The final step of the wave is user training. As discussed in Chapter 5, best practice consists of short, task-oriented, "day-in-the-life" training that involves the user "driving the mouse" during the training session. Training sessions should be an hour or less in duration, and at least one of the live sessions should be captured either as video or as a WebEx session for subsequent replay when users try to use the feature and have forgotten their training. Podcasts are also a very effective on-demand way of getting training to the users. For most users, it's also very helpful to create a laminated cheat sheet with annotated screenshots explaining the procedures for their most common tasks. Given that each department will need a different set of cheat sheets, it's best to post the entire library of these aids on the project wiki, organized by user department.

Deployment

No matter how small the feature, it needs to be put into the operational system. And the act of deployment is never complete without communicating to the users in advance:

- What's new
- What's in it for them[17]
- When it's coming
- Where to find their cheat sheet
- What to do if the new feature gives them trouble

SFDC is a hosted solution, so the deployment of native features and system configurations is almost a non-issue: the system simply starts behaving differently once you've put

---

17. Why they should give a damn.

the customizations in. During a wave, however, there may be so many changes that it's best to keep the new customizations hidden (using screen layouts, record types, the sandbox, and other techniques) until they are done. At the end of the wave, the veil is removed and in a few minutes the new features become available to everyone.

More complex features and integrations do need to be formally deployed. In many cases, add-ons or products may need to be installed on the user's PC. Servers will need new connector modules installed. Implementation of these features will require a more deliberate deployment strategy, particularly if their full development spans more than one wave.

In the case where the new feature set simply provides access to something new or does read-only operations, the deployment is a matter of software logistics. Somehow, the new software modules will need to be packaged and sent with instructions on how to install the various components. Because prepackaged installers from several vendors are often involved, the installation cycle can't be fully automated and users will need to have really foolproof instructions. The foolproof instructions *must* include an uninstall procedure and a phone number to dial in case of problems. Make sure to test those foolproof instructions with an executive or other appropriate personnel during the wave's main test cycle. Usually, the software is small enough that it can be sent out as download link or a compressed email attachment, but even if it's large enough to require a download from a server, put a copy of the software and instructions on the project's wiki (typically in the "What's New" section) and mention it in the project newsletter or podcast.

THE VIRTUAL HELP DESK

For really significant deployments and large organizations, it's a good idea to have a user support "war room." Of course, you should have an FAQ and troubleshooting guide on the wiki. But you have to be ready for people who don't read these documents or who are clever enough to discover problems you didn't anticipate.

The war room is not really staffed, and it's not really a room. Instead, it's an email address and a voicemail box that are checked very frequently. Ideally, these support duties will be handled by one person who really has time; if no one has time in their schedule, the task should be handled as a rotating duty shared by several team members. At any one time, one person should responsible for talking with the user and another person should stand ready to handle escalations. The duty roster should pass hands once or twice a day at predictable times. It is simply amazing how much better the users react to a confusing or buggy system when you are *really* responsive on the phone and email.

The most difficult deployment case is when a system is already in place and is being replaced by a new SFDC-based capability. These deployments are so tough because the chances for data corruption are higher, users may get confused or even rebel against using the new features, and the waste involved in a failed deployment can make it highly visible. In these situations, it pays to have a set of cutover criteria (covering technology readiness, business readiness, and user readiness), with a formal go/no-go meeting to make sure there's management buy-in.

Transition Type: Slash Cut Versus Parallel Play

In a slash-cut transition, the old system is turned off forever (typically on a Friday night) and the new system is used first thing the next business day. Slash cuts involve some logistical complexity—all the moving parts have to line up—and a significant amount of time pressure. The implementation team may be pulling 18-hour days over the weekend to get all the data in shape and imported into the new system. If there's a problem on Sunday night, the new system may not be ready for business on Monday morning. However, users have a quick, decisive transition and they don't have to do duplicate data entry (the way they do in parallel play). Further, reports, alerts, and dashboards are more likely to be correct with this strategy.

In contrast, the parallel-play strategy keeps both old and new systems up for a transition period (usually from a week to a month). Users must enter data into both systems (almost always in different ways, with different error patterns). While it's painful, this strategy allows for deeper testing and debugging with less risk (only the old system contains real, live data during the parallel play period). Further, if major problems are found, the new system deployment can be postponed (temporarily ending the extra effort of parallel play), lowering business risk. During the parallel-play period, many reports, alerts, and dashboards in SFDC are likely to contain bogus data, but they are invaluable debugging aids and provide visible indications of system progress during the parallel-play interval.

Generally speaking, SFDC projects go with slash-cut transitions. But the larger, the more complex, and the more revenue-critical the business system, the more appropriate parallel play may be.

Go/No-Go Criteria

In theory, go/no-go decisions are simple: the criteria are met or they aren't. In real-world, high-stakes decisions, however, there is room for gray area and interpretation. It's a matter of assessing and trading off business risks. Some risks really should be dealt with on a zero-tolerance basis:

- Data corruption
- Lost revenue transactions

- Severe compliance or security problems

- Unplanned business interruption (for longer than a coffee break during the day)

Other risks are more subjective, calling up the question of "acceptable levels":

- Transactions requiring manual work-arounds

- Misleading reports

- Data that seem to be lost, but are actually just hard to find

- Incomplete user training

- Calculations having to be done in outboard spreadsheets

My rule of thumb for assessing deployment readiness is to judge business impact: if the new functionality is deployed, can the errors be corrected and problems be recovered from later on? As long as the rework is not prohibitively expensive, *correctable* short-term issues should not stand in the way of a feature deployment.

Getting Ready for the Next Wave

Once the deployment is done, the team needs to engage in two important but brief meetings.

The first meeting checks the WaveMap for the upcoming wave. Have things changed? Does the map need to be readjusted? Some tasks may have been kicked out of the just-finished wave, or priorities may have changed. While it's never mandatory to change the WaveMap, it is important that the map reflect reality at the beginning of every quarter (every other wave).

The second meeting is a postmortem gathering to capture learnings about the following topics:

- What were the budgetary and schedule variances? What were the root causes of the three to five worst offenders? What were the positive surprises?

- What worked technologically? What didn't work technologically, and why?

- Which resources will need to be in place to make things even better in the next wave?

- Which means of communication with the users worked, and which didn't?

- Which means of team communications worked, and which didn't?

- Which organizational/political issues came up, and how might they have been avoided or circumvented?

- Which team interactions were effective, and where was the team operating ineffectively?

- What (specifically) do we need to do differently in the next wave?

The postmortem meeting *must* include a member of the user community (someone who wasn't part of the wave implementation team) and should include the wave's executive sponsor, as well as a quorum of the actual "worker bees." The postmortem minutes and resolutions for future waves should be put in the project wiki, particularly for the benefit of future team members.[18]

Post-Implementation Implementation

Due to the flexibility of SFDC and its plugin products, expect that there will be modifications and extensions to the system every quarter or so. Even if business requirements do not evolve, organizational roles will likely change over time. Further, the more third-party products plugged in to the SFDC system, the more frequently upgrades will be needed and will require slight modifications to the system.

All this activity will occur if the system is only a moderate success. If the system is a real hit, there will be a flood of change requests that must be managed. Most of these minor changes—extra fields, reconfigurations, and so forth—will be so small that they can be done without starting up a wave team. You should just log them into a spreadsheet, which should be posted on the project wiki. An even better technique is to log requests for changes, improvements, and extensions into a simple change management system that includes approval steps. There's a free version of such a system for SFDC in the AppExchange—look for the ChangeControl plugin.

After an initial review of the proposed change to make sure it won't break anything or contradict any company policy, the task can be assigned to the technical people for quick implementation. ChangeControl has two approval cycles—one to authorize the work, and another to track acceptance of the result, so that the team can see the state of play for each request.

If we achieve our real goal—broad user adoption and optimization of business processes—there will be calls for expanding the system beyond the areas originally desired. For example, quoting may be expanded to full order operations. For these significant expansions, reestablishment of a wave team is required, giving the reader a wonderful excuse to reread this chapter months from now.

---

18. While the project team's composition will remain largely stable over several waves, typically 20% of the team members will be new with each wave. This is particularly true for the business analysts and user representatives, who will benefit greatly by learning from previous waves' experiences.

ARCHITECTURAL REVIEW

For a system of any size or complexity, sometimes the most innocent-sounding changes can have huge negative repercussions. We recommend that your system have a three-member architectural review board to evaluate proposed changes in the system and surrounding processes. The job of the board members is to make sure that the business and the users experience only progress, avoiding anything that will undermine system credibility or cause costly rework.

The board should have fairly stable membership, with each architect having at least a one-year term and not allowing more than one change in board membership per nine months. The three members of the board should fit the following criteria:

- **Application/process architect:** typically an engineer or a business analyst who understands all the moving parts of SFDC, its plugins, and your custom code. This person's area of specialization focuses on understanding the interaction among these software elements as well as the system's impact on business processes and corporate compliance standards.

- **Data/integration architect:** typically an engineer or a business analyst who understands all of the external data sources with which SFDC interacts. This person's purview is understanding the potential for data corruption and the amount of "data massaging" work that would be involved in changing the data model.

- **System administration/user architect:** typically an SFDC system administrator or power user who understands how the system is used on a day-to-day basis. This person's bailiwick is understanding the potential for user disruption or interference implied by a proposed change.

The architectural review board should examine almost any system change and should vote on the changes before they are slated for implementation. The initial vote can be conducted by email (with the conclusion posted to the project wiki). If the vote is unanimous, no further action is required. If there is a dissenting vote, the dissenter needs to write a brief opinion about why he or she objects to the change, including a rough estimate of the potential for disruption or rework.

Sometimes there is an executive mandate to make a system change: if the members of the architectural review board object to this dictate, they should email the sponsoring executive about the potential for problems and the budgetary impact if things go awry. Of course, the executive can still enforce the mandate—but at least he or she will have been properly apprised of the risks.

See the discussion in Chapter 3 for more about the architectural review board.

CHAPTER 5

People and Organizational Readiness

Automation doesn't eliminate human error, it merely replaces operator errors with design errors.

—IBM

THIS CHAPTER SHOULD BE read by the executive sponsors to set the right high-level goals, but is actually intended for everyone on the SFDC implementation team; it will help team members gauge the state of user readiness. While users in small organizations can skim this chapter, members of larger, more complex organizations will need to understand it in detail for a successful deployment across multiple divisions.

Before starting the implementation, project leaders need to understand their organization's SFA maturity and state of readiness, so as to better appreciate which benefits are within reach for their organization. During the implementation and adoption phases, users need to appreciate what other departments need from them to make the overall organization successful. Everyone needs to appreciate cultural issues that can form barriers to adoption.

Adoption Is Everything

Salesforce.com is a fine product that can be configured as an excellent sales, marketing, and support system. It can be integrated with accounting, licensing, and inventory systems to provide a full 360-degree view of your customers.

But only if people will use it.

People will rapidly adopt new technologies and methods if there's something in it for them: functionality that actually makes their job easier, improves their productivity, or eliminates waste and duplication. SFDC *can* do this for anyone in sales, marketing, support, and the executive suite, but people on those teams may not perceive it that way—and perceptions drive adoption and usage.

Getting utilization rates up–not only overcoming user resistance and learning curves, but also making the users highly motivated to use the system–is *the* challenge for any SFA/CRM system deployment. SFDC's ease of use, as well as the incremental deployment style recommended in this book, make it easier to achieve this goal. But a successful launch of an SFDC system is not just a matter of product and features: it's a matter of getting the interactions with people right.

You need to understand the perceptions of the user community to get the most out of your interactions with them during the project. These interactions will come at various phases of the project:

- Interviews and surveys at the start of the project

- Validation of screen designs and data in the middle

- Testing and business validation near the end

- Training sessions at deployment time

If communications with the users fail during any of these key interactions, the breakdown can cause significant schedule and credibility problems for the SFDC project.

Using the SFA Maturity Model

There's almost always a gap between where the organization really is–how it really does business–and where it needs to be to make optimal use of SFDC. My firm developed the SFA Maturity Model to measure where client practices and processes really are, so that we can guide companies and design projects with a high probability of success and user adoption.

The SFA Maturity Model assesses an organization's needs, sophistication, and state of readiness for SFDC features and business processes. The first part of the model helps identify the level of SFDC functionality that fits the organization's "top-down" goal. The second part of the model scores users to indicate which level of SFDC functionality each department is currently ready for.

The SFA Maturity Model needs to be used before the project begins as well as whenever a deployment phase will include a department that has not been involved with SFDC before. For example, if you're extending an SFDC implementation to include a new division, subsidiary, or foreign operation, you'll need to survey the new business unit and score it with the Maturity Model. Only by doing so can you ensure that your goals are realistic and achievable with minimum friction.

The output of this model is a set of scores that indicate the current state of readiness for each department evaluated. In most cases, the level of SFDC usage should be targeted at slightly above the median[1] score of participating departments so that users see value but are not overwhelmed by complexity and change.

The SFA Maturity Model is meant to provide guidance about the scope of the project and *general* readiness, but it doesn't take into account organizational politics or specific user adoption issues. As you'll see later in this chapter, before making deployment decisions about any specific group, it's important to do a detailed survey of its users that goes beyond the model.

Part I: What Is Management Trying to Achieve, and How Hard Will It Be?

SFDC needs to be thought of as more than just a tool. SFDC will have its most positive impact when it changes the way people allocate their time, complete processes, and make money.

That said, having too-ambitious goals for an SFDC implementation will not pay off. Overshooting an organization's readiness—requiring actions that have limited business value, relying on data that cannot be easily collected, or requiring big changes in behavior—can be quite counterproductive.

While SFDC could simply be mandated in the organization—the way organizations sometimes do with a sales process or marketing vendor—best results happen when the system capabilities are a good match for the organization's people, and those employees are intrinsically motivated to use the new system.

In using the model, it's important to *not* reach premature conclusions about deployment timing or sequence. Indeed, for many organizations it's best to do some of the levels "out of order." As you'll see later in this chapter, before making deployment decisions about any specific group, it's important to perform a detailed survey of its users that goes beyond the model's boundaries.

The SFA Model's Five Levels[2]

Although small companies can happily use SFDC in a fairly simplistic way, the demands of larger companies mean they must use the system at more sophisticated operational levels. This part of the SFA Maturity Model defines the levels (or modes) in which organizations use SFDC, as illustrated in Figure 5-1. In an ironic twist, smaller companies can implement

---

1. The median is the *middle score,* which is different from the average score. Because of the small number of user scores in a typical SFDC survey, the median is usually more reflective of organizational readiness than the average. You'll be targeting SFDC functionality that is near the median score for each department to which the system will be deployed.

2. The SFA Maturity Model is stated in terms of the needs of a multichannel sales organization. Later in the chapter, we'll discuss the needs of SFDC users that aren't sales organizations at all (e.g., venture capitalists, fundraising organizations).

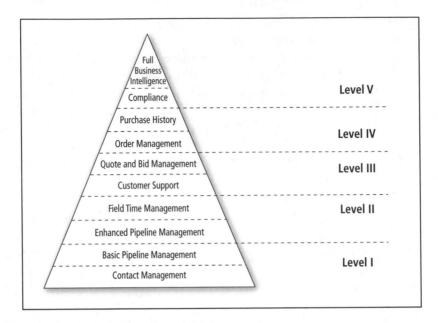

FIGURE 5-1 SFA Maturity Model levels

the highest levels of the model more easily than larger companies can, and some of the tightest SFDC implementations are at firms with only a few dozen users.

Let's take a look at the five levels within the SFA Maturity Model:

I. Contact Management and Basic Pipeline Development

This level entails using SFDC as if it were ACT, Goldmine, SalesLogix, or even Excel. All Web leads are automatically entered into the system. Leads and contacts are put in the system only by marketing, are refined by a sales development group,[3] and are passed to the sales reps for action.

Once a sales rep receives a lead or contact, he or she qualifies the prospect. An unqualified lead is rejected (but never deleted!) from the system. A good prospect is converted into an opportunity, but from that point forward there aren't many updates. Often, the rep won't put meaningful updates into the opportunity until the deal closes.

There are basic marketing and telesales reports, but they aren't consistently used (or believed). At this level, forecasting and account reviews are done entirely outside

---

3. These groups qualify and cultivate leads to ready them for the sales reps. In some cases, they may set appointments for the reps, or they may do low-level pitches and demonstrations themselves. These groups are sometimes called telemarketing, telesales, inside sales, sales development, or lead qualification—and part of the function may be outsourced.

the system, typically in monthly phone conferences. Level I of the SFA Maturity Model is achieved by companies with 10 reps or so.

II.   **Enhanced Management of Activities, Pipeline Development, and Forecasting/ Quotas**

By using tasks, campaigns, AdWords integration, Outlook integration, and PBX/VoIP adaptors, sales and marketing users gain enough trust in the system and its information to use it to track their action items, prioritize their work, and manage their schedule.

At this level, there are enough credible updates to the data to permit real pipeline management, forecasting, and quota management. Leads, contacts, and opportunities are never deleted from the system, and the reps are more diligent about updating opportunity information to signal the rest of the organization about what's needed to close the deal. All reps' quotas are in the system; territories, overlays, and splits are defined; and dashboards or reports compare the state of achievement with the sales reps' goals. Reports and dashboards show key workflow metrics in lead generation, lead cultivation, appointment setting, opportunity development, and close ratios.

At Level II of the SFA Maturity Model, all forecasting and most account reviews are based entirely on SFDC. The data in the system is accurate on a weekly basis, and reports are used consistently. Sales and marketing VPs use the SFDC data to drive their teams. This is the level that companies need to achieve when they have more than 20 reps.

III. **Quoting, Deal Management, and Customer Support**

This level makes it possible to develop and manage all quotes in the system. SFDC's Products module has been turned on, price lists have been populated, and approval workflows have been implemented to handle unusual deals. Quoting has been integrated with order management. An outside commission management system— whether a series of spreadsheets or a product (such as Centive, QCommission, or Xactly)—may have been integrated, and sales policy now states that commissions will not be paid unless a deal is in the system for at least 2 weeks prior to closing. At this level, all employees who take outside phone calls have the SFDC screen up before they even think of answering the phone.

Although pre-sales engineers may have been using the system for a long while, Level III adds post-sales customer support to the SFDC user base. Post-sales support (which may span the customer care, warranty, technical support, training, certification, and consulting functions) is a key point of customer contact that should be visible to everyone who interacts with prospects (particularly the sales reps). Within SFDC, the Knowledge Base has been turned on and populated with solutions, and the Customer Access Portal has been turned on. The company's Web site CMS, survey, and email blasting systems have been integrated into SFDC so that a history of all customer communications is visible to all users. Reports and dashboards are in place to monitor customer support responsiveness in real time.

Management now has a 360-degree view of *the sales and marketing team*. Level III is the level that companies with more than 30 reps need to achieve.

IV. **Order Management and Purchase History**

This level integrates access to the accounting/ERP system for order entry, tracking, and management purposes. Within SFDC, quotes can be converted to orders and invoices as soon as they have completed the approval cycle. If the company uses eCommerce, that order flow has been integrated and is visible to SFDC users. All quotes, orders, contracts, invoices, and supporting documents (such as RFI and RFQ responses) are stored and available from the SFDC user screens. SFDC's Partner Management Portal is available to users and allows for effective management of leads and deals that are being handled through the channel. At this stage, all bookings can be seen in real time, and even members of the Finance department can use SFDC as an authoritative source.

In addition, the history of customer transactions is available to authorized users. Within SFDC, the Contracts module is being populated with Terms and Conditions and periods of service. Through integration with ERP, license management, and other systems, a customer's purchase history (including specific line items, serial numbers, license keys, shipment manifests, and returns) is presented on the SFDC screens. Through integration with accounting, a customer's payment history, current credit status, and discount eligibility are available for the sales reps. Level IV is the level companies need to achieve when they have more than 50 reps and have established a multichannel organization. At this level, users have a 360-degree view of *customers*.

V. **Compliance, Controls, and Business Intelligence**

Through SFDC's fine-grained security mechanisms, audit trails, workflow system, and real-time integration, this level adds the ability to apply controls on critical user activities—even those that may be initiated from systems outside of SFDC. Workflows and alerts are extended from the first moment a quote is generated, through the closing of the order and issuance of the invoice. Revenue recognition triggers are put in place, and true revenue forecasts are shown on SFDC screens. Opportunity data, bookings, and revenue forecasts are "locked down" in the system to promote Sarbanes-Oxley Act compliance.

In addition, SFDC (in conjunction with other enterprise systems) is used as a key driver of analysis at every level of management and planning. By adding BI tools or a data warehouse, analysts can examine customer profitability, the cost of customer acquisition analysis, product release planning, and other strategic issues. Companies should achieve this level of visibility and integrated operations before they go public. At Level V, members of the executive staff are using SFDC information to drive the business on a daily basis, and it is a foundation for a 360-degree view of *the business.*

What Is Your Overall Goal?

Different types of organizations need to achieve different levels of SFDC functionality. Not everyone needs to achieve Level V, and some organizations can do just fine operating only at Level III.

In this section, we'll explore the different kinds of SFDC user organizations and consider which level of the model each will likely need to reach.

Direct Sales Complexity Categories

Companies have different levels of sales and channel complexity. Generally speaking, the longer the sales cycle, the more complex the organization must be to handle it, and the greater the leverage that can be provided by SFDC.

For the purposes of SFDC implementation and adoption, it's important to understand where the company is positioned along the complexity continuum, from a single geographic direct sales organization to a highly complex multichannel organization. Typically, the amount of time it takes to implement and adopt the system will be a multiple of the Sales Organization Category. For example, a typical Category 2 organization will take twice as long to get to Level V as a typical Category 1 organization will. And make no mistake about it, large direct-sales organizations *will* need to achieve Level V.

Category 1 sales organizations have the following characteristics:

- A single type of sales organization with few (if any) overlays

- Only one type of representative who can take an order (e.g., only outside reps—an inside rep's main role is to facilitate outside reps' productivity)

- Geographic or vertical exclusive sales territories

- Limited eCommerce, original equipment manufacturer (OEM), or indirect business (less than 10% of the company's total dollar volume)

- Repeat business, upsells, and long-term contracts that represent approximately 33% of total company volume

- A single business unit (product lines are closely related; every sales rep is able to sell all the company's products and services)

Typically, a Category 1 sales organization can get away with Level I SFA usage.

Category 2 sales organizations are slightly more complex:

- The organization has a mix of geographic, vertical, and named-account territories, and there are some overlays.

- Both inside and outside reps can take orders; there are thresholds and criteria for who takes different kinds of orders.

- Most territories are exclusive, but the basis of exclusivity can be complicated and cause for argument.

- Revenues from eCommerce, OEM, and indirect business are becoming important (representing as much as 40% of the company's total dollar volume) and managing customer relationships across channels is becoming a bigger issue.

- Repeat business, upsells, and long-term contracts may represent 50% of overall company volume.

- There are multiple business units and product-line specialists; many reps do not sell all of the company's products.

Typically, a Category 2 sales organization is operating at Level I of SFA usage, but it will need to achieve Level III as it grows.

Category 3 sales organizations need to coordinate their complexity to fully service customer accounts:

- The organization has a complex array of geographic, vertical, and named-account territories; the company also has some global account managers for its top accounts.

- All channels can take orders, and there are complicated rules of engagement regarding how to hand off orders and accounts across sales teams and out to the channel.

- Few territories are exclusive, except for global strategic accounts; most exclusives are temporary (a year or two) and account transition is a key success factor for ongoing revenues.

- The eCommerce, OEM, and indirect channels handle more than 50% of the company's transactions, and they may produce 50% of total company revenues.

- Repeat business, upsells, and long-term contracts may represent 66% of overall company volume.

- The company may have multiple salesforces, each focused on a different product or service line.

Almost always, a Category 3 sales organization must be operating at Level III or IV of SFA usage, but there is frequent backsliding. When the system is replaced, the team will typically have to start over at Level I.

Category 4 sales organizations are fully integrated, multichannel, multinational operations:

- The organization has a complex array of geographic, vertical, and named-account territories in each major selling country; the company also has a department of global account managers for its top 250 accounts.

- All channels can take orders, and there are complicated rules of engagement regarding how to hand off orders and accounts across sales teams and out to the channel. International channel conflicts must be managed.

- Few territories are exclusive, except for global strategic accounts; most exclusives are temporary (a year or two) and account transition is a key success factor for ongoing revenues.

- The eCommerce, OEM, and indirect channels handle 70% of the transactions, and they may produce 60% of total company revenues.

- Repeat business, upsells, and long-term contracts may represent 75% of overall company volume.

- The company has dedicated salesforces for different business units.

Category 4 sales organizations need to be operating at Level IV or V of SFA usage. As with Category 3 organizations, these companies experience frequent backsliding as SFA systems fail or are not properly maintained. Due to the complexity and depth of interactions, cleaning up a Category 4 organization and restarting the SFA system can take several painful quarters.

SFDC Sales Teams That Aren't Pure Direct

What if your team isn't a direct sales organization? It's important to understand what kind of an organization your users are in,[4] because different organizations look for different things in SFDC, measure themselves along different lines, and optimize their operations differently.

Indirect Sales. Indirect sales teams work through channels, distributors, dealers, resellers, or partners to make business happen, but they do not sell directly to customers. Indirect teams are typically much smaller than direct teams, and they focus on managing the health

---

4. In a small company, there's no question which kind of an organization the user is in. But in a large multinational company—let's say, General Electric—different divisions will have employees who fit each of the profiles listed here.

of their partner accounts. Leads generated by the marketing group are typically handed over to channel partners to pursue. Indirect selling organizations are trying to get the largest *number of deals* out of their channel. These channel management teams will typically need to reach Level II of the SFA Maturity Model, and they almost always need to add SFDC's Partner module.

Outbound Call Center. Call center teams tend to work a large number of lower-price deals for small to medium-size business or consumer customers. They emphasize the number of calls made, the number of transactions, and tight activity management. Call center operations typically have weekly or even daily metrics, so they typically use SFDC to more tightly manage their teams for the highest short-term productivity. These teams will typically need to achieve Level III or IV in the SFA Maturity Model, although they won't need a lot of functional depth because their sales cycles are so short and the average deal size is fairly small.

eCommerce. Vendors that are able to complete the majority of their transactions via the Web have a very different sales focus. Because their customers use an automated system, the overall number of transactions is higher even than for a call center, and the average selling price may be less than $100. Typically, the sales personnel for eCommerce operations are inside reps who assist customers with transactions that don't work in the "Web store" or that comprise repeat, renewal, or upsell business. eCommerce-driven users of SFDC tend to have a very real time focus because the customer will be in the store for only a few minutes. These organizations need to operate up to Level IV of the Maturity Model, but have light needs in Levels I and II.

Inbound Call Center. Inbound call center teams focus on customer support, from troubleshooting eCommerce problems to expediting shipments, returns, and refunds. Their emphasis is on the number of calls handled, the speed and expense of problem resolution, and tight activity management. Such call center operations typically have weekly or even daily call-handling metrics, and they will use longer-term customer-satisfaction metrics based on surveys. Organizations that fall within this category will typically need to achieve *only* Level III or IV in the model.

Venture Capitalist, Private Equity, and Investment Banker. In this kind of organization, the user is not a sales person at all, but rather an investment professional who is trying to prospect, evaluate, and monitor high-value investment opportunities. Even though such organizations may only do a few deals a quarter, their personnel need to cull through thousands of candidate companies each year and track entrepreneurs long after the initial meeting. These kinds of organizations use SFDC as a collaboration and tracking tool, rather than as a selling system. The emphasis here is on achieving the easiest data entry and gathering the most valuable information about potential clients in the system. Typically, these organizations need to operate at Level I of the SFA Maturity Model.

Fundraising/Not-for-Profit Organization. This kind of organization is a cross between a venture capitalist and a call center user: The employees are not trying to sell, but rather trying to track and contact a large number of people. These personnel work extensively over the phone to cultivate relationships and motivate donors. This kind of team uses SFDC as a prospect database and activity management tool to make sure that all persons on the phone bank are meeting their "dials per hour" objective. Typically, these organizations need to operate at Level I of the Maturity Model.

Part II: Is Your Organization Ready for Its Target Level?

It's important to understand where your users are today, because different levels of SFA/CRM readiness require different kinds of SFDC deployments. Without an analytical framework to assess the readiness of key user departments, the project will be lost in a sea of opinions and the project team members will likely misjudge the deployment requirements.

Organizations with lots of users who have used SFDC before in previous jobs will have a series of expectations from their previous experiences. They will immediately ask for bells and whistles that the more junior members of the organization won't even recognize.

> ### FIND THE EARLY ADOPTERS, BUT DON'T FALL IN LOVE WITH THEM
>
> No matter which kind of organization you work in, people will vary in their willingness to adopt new technologies and processes. You need to identify the risk takers—the early adopters—because their willingness to put in a little extra effort to adopt new technologies will be very helpful in your prototyping, testing, and deployment stages.
>
> While you need to leverage their enthusiasm, energy, and domain expertise, don't rely on the early adopters too much for providing "typical" feedback. They're usually so far ahead of the pack that their input will be misleading. In your surveys, review sessions, and testing, include a representative sample of users that includes several "average" users and even the occasional hardened "Luddite."

At the other extreme, organizations with little experience with any SFA/CRM system will need to have a much slower rollout of the system, allowing time to acclimate to SFA/CRM concepts, metrics, and practices. These organizations will tend to be far more resistant to SFDC adoption (particularly if they like to keep secrets) and their employees may complain for months that the system is getting in their way.

My firm has developed a 300-question survey to measure the state of readiness for each of the major groups in an SFA/CRM organization. In our interview process, we try to capture as many subtleties as we can, with the goal being to avoid surprises later in the project.

Of course, you don't have to perform this kind of detailed survey to get a feel for your own organization's readiness for an SFDC system. The goal is to understand the gap between the target level and the organization's current operations. Briefly interview two or three people in each of the organizations discussed in the remainder of this section, asking the 20 questions that are relevant to their role. Each "yes" answer represents ¼ point toward achieving the levels described earlier (e.g., if a person answers yes to 14 of the questions below, his or her department is currently operating at about Level III of the SFA Maturity Model). The Web site www.SFDC-secrets.com provides some example score sheets for an organization.

Sales Organizational Readiness

The following questions are intended for members of the sales organization, assuming your company uses a direct sales model at least to some extent.

1. Are all leads and contact information stored natively in the existing SFA system? Have all employees stopped using their "little black books" to manage their sales contacts?

2. Are all leads routed automatically, and are queues in use? Do sales reps know where to find their new leads, and do they know the difference between a lead and a contact?

3. Do the telesales/telemarketing/ISRs/sales development reps use the SFA system on "every" call?

4. Is there a clear delineation of responsibility for all phases of lead handling (e.g., marketing does lead generation and imports, sales development does lead cultivation/qualification/appointment setting, and sales does lead conversion and pipeline development)?

5. Are there clear phases or stages that define the sales cycle through which "every" deal progresses, and does the SFA system reflects these stages?

6. Is every deal in progress stored as an opportunity in the SFA system?

7. Does everyone in the sales organization know how to enter a deal and see its current status?

8. Are qualification criteria "baked in" to SFA screens and usage patterns?

9. Are leads, contacts, accounts, or opportunities *never* from the SFA system?

10. Are all forecasts based only on data in the SFA system?

11. Do reps use contact roles to show the customer politics involved in a deal?

12. Does the SFA system accurately reflect territories, overlays, quotas, splits, and sales teams?

13. Is the company's sales methodology incorporated into SFA screens and workflows?

14. Do sales executives and sales administrators see the SFA system as their key information resource?

15. Does sales management see the SFA system as the first point of inquiry when trying to find out about a customer situation?

16. Are all orders either placed via the SFA system or visible from it?

17. Are all quotes and orders seeking exceptions subject to automatic approval cycles?

18. Do reps use the SFA system as *the* way to organize their time and do their account planning?

19. Are customers' order history and current credit status visible from within the SFA screens?

20. Are commission calculations based "only" on SFA data; if the deal isn't properly in the system, no commission gets paid?

Marketing Organizational Readiness

The following questions are used to score your marketing processes—and it doesn't matter whether those processes are performed by employees or contractors. Again, the questions assume that your company sells at least partially via a direct sales model.

1. Are market segments and target customers defined and prioritized in a fairly stable way?

2. Do marketing and sales personnel jointly design and select outbound activities for each quarter?

3. Have marketing personnel implemented automatic lead input for Web-generated leads? Do they perform all lead importing for the company, including deduping, enriching, and correcting lead information before it is imported into the SFA system?

4. Are leads automatically "aged out" so that untouched leads more than 60 days old are pulled back from sales and maintained in the marketing database?

5. Are all outbound activities handled and tracked as campaigns? Are all email blasts done in conjunction with, and measured by, the SFA campaign system?

6. Do marketing personnel work in conjunction with the sales staff to define qualification criteria, conversion criteria, and telesales scripts? Is lead qualification "baked in" to the SFA system?

7. Does each major campaign have its own landing page on the Web site?

8. Are leads scored or prioritized based on data and systematic rules?

9. Are marketing tactics "tuned" using data from previous campaigns?

10. Do marketing personnel run deduping tools on the SFA database on at least a monthly basis to counteract human error?

11. Has the Marketing department deployed a follow-up ("drip email") system to make sure that each and every new lead is automatically contacted?

12. Are search engine marketing (e.g., Google AdWords) campaigns highly targeted, with each campaign having its own landing page on the Web site and separate measurements for conversion ratio and cost per conversion?

13. Do marketing and sales personnel use the same metrics and terminology for lead development, lead qualification, and pipeline development?

14. Are telemarketing/lead cultivation operations (i.e., phone people whose effectiveness is measured on numbers of appointments made) managed separately from inside sales (i.e., reps who have revenue targets)?

15. Is the effectiveness of marketing campaigns measured by the number of sales cycles those campaigns have directly affected?

16. Has the Marketing department developed campaign influence reports and dashboards that link marketing tactics to the pipeline?

17. Does the Marketing department have a model for the lead waterfall showing the expected time in stage and the conversion ratios at every stage?

18. Have marketing personnel put all customer reference information into the SFA system?

19. Have product marketing personnel put all customer survey data into the SFA system, and do they use the SFA data for product planning and feature prioritization?

20. Does the Marketing department evaluate itself by measuring the cost of customer acquisition and the profitability of running campaigns?

Services Organizational Readiness

The following questions score the technical support and professional services organization for the company. The "customer support" people who expedite orders or handle credit card refunds should not answer these questions.

1. Does the customer support/customer care team use a database for tracking customer calls, cases, incidents, and customer interactions?

2. Does the customer support/customer care team use a database for tracking bugs, product defects, and product returns (RMAs)?

3. Does the professional services group use the SFA system for storing basic customer information?

4. Does the professional services group use the SFA system for storing basic project information (e.g., bids/quotes, SOW/WBS documents, specifications)?

5. Does the professional services group use an automatic tool for time cards, measurement of progress against milestones, and project invoicing?

6. Does the company send automatic reminders that notify sales reps when a support contract is about to expire?

7. Does the company automatically remind customers when their support contract is about to expire or their professional services contract is about to run out of time or money?

8. Has the customer support/customer care team established response times that it measures itself against?

9. Does the customer support/customer care team have automatic escalation rules to ensure that the company lives up to contractual stipulations or service level agreements (SLAs)?

10. Does the customer support/customer care team measure itself on SLA compliance?

11. Does the customer support/customer care team measure itself on support profitability?

12. Does the professional services team measure itself on profitability?

13. Is the professional services team viewed as a collaborator in the sales cycle?

14. Is the SFA system viewed as a key resource for understanding customer satisfaction?

15. Is the SFA system viewed as a key resource for understanding customers' total purchase history, customer assets, and other characteristics?

16. Is the SFA system the core of a customer-facing knowledge base, showing common questions and solutions?

17. Does the support team view the SFA system as a key resource for understanding those customers who have bought through indirect channels or partners?

18. Does the SFA system have alerts and workflows that enforce approval of unusual consulting projects?

19. Is the SFA system viewed as a key resource for understanding customers' total consulting, training, and certification history?

20. Are SFA system reports and dashboards used for planning consulting and professional services offerings?

Finance and Legal Organizational Readiness

In most cases, members of the Finance and Legal departments are very far away from adopting SFDC; in many cases, they may still run everything on Outlook and Excel. Even so, you need to understand where their processes are today, and how amenable they are to integration with SFDC.

1. Are all legal documents scanned and stored in electronic form?

2. Are all legal documents stored with naming conventions and access controls so that any lawyer can quickly find needed documents without having to call another person?

3. Does the accounting system(s) used by finance have external interfaces that can "talk" to other software packages?

4. Are commissions calculated in an automated way that is driven by accounting system data (invoices)?

5. Has the Finance department's customer list and contact information been correlated to account information in the SFA system so that the two could be synchronized in the future?

6. Has the Legal department reviewed the Web site, SFA, and email blasting system for CAN-SPAM compliance?

7. Has the Finance department set up revenue recognition rules and VSOE thresholds that could be triggered by automated means?

8. Has the Finance department set up approval cycles that include delegation (in case of absence) that could be handled by automated means?

9. Does the Legal department store the sales-related documents (e.g., SLAs, licenses, contracts, letters) either in the SFA system or in a system that is integrated with the SFA interface?

10. Does the Finance department "own" the revenue forecast, but expect the Sales department to own bookings forecasts? Do finance personnel use the bookings forecast only as a reality check for the revenue forecast?

11. Is the Finance department's customer contact information fully synchronized with the account information in the SFA system?

12. Have finance/legal personnel set up contractual approval and "paperwork generation" (e.g., licenses, signature pages) in such a way that those tasks could be

handled by automated means? Has the Legal department developed a set of "need to know" rules for financial information access?

13. Does the Finance department pay commissions only if the deal is in the SFA system prior to quoting?

14. Has order entry been integrated between the accounting and SFA system? Are data "locked down" once a deal has been closed?

15. Are approvals for bids, quotes, and orders handled through automatic workflows?

16. Is the customer's order history fully synchronized between the accounting and SFA systems?

17. Do Legal department personnel use SFA reports to forecast the amount of contractual work that will be required during a given month?

18. Is the Finance department's revenue forecast based on data derived from the SFA system?

19. Have the Finance and Legal departments survived a Sarbanes-Oxley Act audit thanks to SFA controls and workflows?

20. Do finance personnel use SFA data as the basis for marketing/sales budgeting and customer profitability analysis?

IT and Web Team Organizational Readiness

For the IT organization and the Web site team, a checklist doesn't make as much sense as a discussion about the skills, prerequisites, and training these personnel will need to succeed. Essentially, any IT or Web team can achieve any of the SFA/CRM levels—the higher levels simply mean more effort (or more contractors). But it's good idea to let them know what you'll need, and ask them to quantify what it will take them to be ready for adoption of the SFDC system.

There are two basic questions that—believe it or not—have to be asked:

- Is the user hardware there? Every SFDC user will need access to a PC. If you're dealing with a mobile workforce, every user will need either a laptop or a smartphone. Don't start an SFDC implementation without these items being in place.

- Is the culture there? If your company is fundamentally uncomfortable leveraging technology (for example, everyone really uses paper daytimers), moving overnight from nothing to a highly integrated SFA system is not a realistic goal.

SFDC and other SaaS products are almost invisible to the internal IT team: the software is hosted externally and places few requirements on IT infrastructure. Even so, it's a good idea to invite a member of the IT team to the early planning meetings for your project. The IT team needs to identify corporate issues (such as security, external access, information protection, password policies, and user access controls) and make SFDC consistent with the rest of company policies. Achieving this goal may mean a full-scale review of SFDC—although the SFDC product has been so widely deployed that it should be able to quickly pass any internal review. If the IT team has never worked with a large-scale SaaS product, the architecture and deployment/operations groups will have a small learning curve (as discussed in Chapter 13).

The internal IT organization will also need to be involved with integration between SFDC and internal applications using a service-oriented architecture (SOA). The IT team probably has the generic skills needed to handle this responsibility, but will need to learn SFDC's specific APIs and data structures. To smooth the way, SFDC has developed solid documentation, some great self-training tools, and a vibrant self-help community for developers—all for free.

Sophisticated customers will need to go beyond SFDC to round out the functionality, so the IT team will need to deploy those new products (which may involve on-premises hardware and software) and integrate them with existing systems. Deploying these packaged products won't require any specialized skills, but it still takes time on the IT calendar.

The internal help desk will need to know enough about SFDC to respond to basic user questions and administrative requests. For example, these personnel need to know how to let users back into the system when they forget their passwords. SFDC offers a wide range of classes, but most help desks use a "train the trainer" model that means only one person will need to attend the full course. SFDC systems administrators (who typically work in IT, sales operations, and marketing) end up answering a fair number of user questions themselves.

The Web site team will have interactions with SFDC at several levels. Web site registration pages will need some new HTML and JavaScript. If the Web site is based on a content management system, the content downloading pages and SFDC will need to interact to some extent. Also, if the Web site is tightly linked to email blasting systems (for "vertical email campaigns" or "drip marketing sequences"), the sequencing and opt-out triggers will need to be integrated with SFDC. All of these tasks can be handled via a server-side scripting language or .NET/Java to invoke Web service APIs, but often the Web site teams don't have the technical depth needs to write these "SOAP" calls. In contrast, members of the central IT will. Fortunately, these skills are needed only temporarily, so the Web site team can get by with using contractors.

®TfL. The logo with "Mind the Gap" is reproduced with kind permission of Transport for London

Part III: How Big Is the Gap?

How do you know whether the gap between the users' current level and the desired levels of SFA/CRM execution can be realistically crossed? How do you tell if the goals have been set too high?

As mentioned earlier, a good rule of thumb is to target the expected SFA/CRM level at slightly above the median score of the affected department. But this criterion really applies only with a fairly large user population that will go through several cycles of capability improvement. In smaller organizations, you'll have to make the judgment on an intuitive–rather than a quantitative–level.

If users are anxious about the level of change, or scared about learning the new system, a more incremental goal is highly advised. For example, if the current user population uses no SFA/CRM system at all or is going through a "crash program," the users will be required to make significant jumps in sophistication and changes in their behavior. Expect this to require some effort:

- Incentives and personal measurements that give users unambiguous signals about how and what they need to change

- A deeply committed upper management champion (who almost always has to be a Sales VP or COO)

- Several cycles of user training, with scoring and "certification"

- Extensive documentation, cheat sheets, and other content on the project wiki

- An identified group of early adopters who are tasked with using the system from the first day of deployment and identifying system areas for streamlining[5]

- A long-running program of internal marketing

---

5. This "advance group" can become the basis for some positive internal competition in the organization. As membership in the advance group is by invitation only and connotes more sophisticated users, users may be enticed by the "extra toys" that members of the advance group get to use in their jobs. If this happens, do not expand the advance group too quickly: users who really aren't ready will become frustrated and waste time on unproductive system usage. Even worse, because of their lack of knowledge, they may corrupt or destroy data in the system.

As with any change management project, measuring progress frequently, managing expectations, and listening to users will be key determinants of success.

Understanding the Next Wave of Users

As discussed in Chapter 4, in a large multidivisional organization, each wave of features may involve new users with different organizational affiliations, work habits, and functional interactions. Prior to each implementation cycle, you need to understand enough about the new user groups to avoid adoption and internal-politics problems. Check out Chapter 6 for further details on adoption.

Who Are the Users?

In Chapter 1, you created personas that are archetypes of users. Now it's time to understand the specifics of *real* users—their state of mind, their goals, and their readiness.

First, assess the users' initial beliefs about the system. Have they had good experiences in the past with *any* SFA/CRM system? Do they believe that a good system can make their jobs easier, either saving them time or earning them more commissions? Can they see how putting more information into SFDC would cut down on emails and phone calls? Do they perceive the goals of the project to be reasonable, or is there disagreement about what the problem *really* is?[6] Are they suspicious that SFDC is a "Big Brother" monitoring system to put the squeeze on people? If the users have strong preconceptions, it can make deployment very tough.

HOW WELL DO YOU HAVE TO KNOW THE USERS?

In a small organization at a single location, you can probably answer all the questions in this section yourself.

But in larger organizations with many departments and locations, you need to have a feel for the people you'll be working with. For each major constituency, make contact with at least three people who are representative of the organization. After you've met them initially, keep track of their contact information (as you may need to communicate with these individuals more than once during the project).

---

6. If there is widespread suspicion that the *real* reason the project is being done is to satisfy "the bozos in marketing" or "the bad reps" or "the execs doing CYA maneuvers," you need to escalate this issue immediately. Your executive champions need to make other members of the organization believe that the goals of the SFDC project are to make everyone more successful, lower stress levels, and improve customer satisfaction.

Next, find out about the users' level of organizational trust. Do they make decisions individually or in groups? Do they share information with other departments, or do they tend to carefully manage the flow of information (and even keep secrets)? Do people tend to trust the information they get from management (taking it literally), or do they tend to interpret (and even second-guess) it?

Next, understand the users' work habits. Are they "locked in" to their computer screens all day long? Do they carry their laptops with them to internal meetings? Do users tend to use paper printouts in analyzing problems or reconciling data, or are they more comfortable working online? Do they use Excel spreadsheets, or are they comfortable with an Access database or even a business intelligence tool?

It's particularly important to understand how users in the Sales department currently handle their tasks now. Are they using paper (note pads, daytimers, or sticky notes) for callback management? Do they carry their laptops with them on sales calls, and do they have wireless access? Do they use a spreadsheet for forecasting, or are a series of spread-sheets passed around by email? Do these users prefer Outlook for tasks, reminders, and action items? Do they use a file server for document storage, do they file stuff in their own folders, or do they just leave documents attached to email messages?

The good news is that SFDC can be easily configured to work well in any of these user environments. But you can't know how to optimize (or which potholes to avoid) until you've interviewed the users.

Why Should Users Change?

When you implement SFDC, you will ask groups of users to change the way they do their daily tasks. You will also ask them to attend training, deal with a new user interface, and, in many cases, add an extra step to something they have to do already. Some people may be willing to perform new steps purely for the sake of achieving a better process or a more efficient organization—but this is rare. Most people—and particularly those in sales and marketing—are *not* process people.

So, what's in it for them?

When planning each major deployment phase, you must figure out which groups of users will be the most significantly affected by the changes, and then you should survey them so you can anticipate and counteract issues that could cause user resistance.

You'll need to identify benefits that can offset the costs of change *from the individual's perspective.* Make sure to identify and highlight situations where the *current* way of doing things could cause problems *for that individual.* For example, if employees will get into trouble if they divulge confidential information, but they regularly email a spreadsheet containing confidential data, it's only a matter of time before the "address auto-complete" feature in Outlook accidentally sends the spreadsheet to someone—inside or outside the company—who isn't supposed to see it. In another example, if a key document is stored only as an attachment in an individual's Outlook file, it's only a matter of time before a file corruption causes the permanent loss of that document. Because no one wants more exposure to risk or more manual steps, highlight cases where the new ways of working through SFDC will benefit the users directly.

There are three categories of "benefits" for individual users:

- *Making the boss happy by complying with a mandate.* For mandates to be effective, they must be genuine. It's important that the people at the top of the organization be vocal and consistent supporters of the system and show that *they* will be using the system to manage the organization. Even if penalties are proscribed for not following the mandate, if upper managers hint that they won't be using the system at all or that they won't be paying attention to SFA/CRM reports for guiding the business, their attitude will set user adoption back by several months.

- *Getting new features that will make the user's job easier or better right away.* Sometimes, these features are small things. It's important to clearly promote these direct benefits without overselling the system.

- *Providing things that will make the user's job easier at some point in the future.* The problem with deferred benefits is that users have to wait for the system to become more powerful, for the data to be more comprehensive, or for other users to change their behaviors to realize these rewards. These are the most tenuous benefits because the user has to pay the taxes *now* without getting any personal result until some vague point in the future. While some people will make changes simply because it's the right thing to do, that group will almost never amount to a critical mass of users.

CARROTS, STICKS, AND TOYS

Whenever you're asking someone to change his or her behavior, it's a good idea to clearly illustrate the benefits that the user will experience. The more personal and direct, the better. Managers already know how to use both "carrots" and "sticks" to motivate behavior. Now it's time to add "toys" to the arsenal.

Each major functional expansion of the system will typically involve some new complexity and some incremental behavioral changes. Best practice is to *give* users something new—even if it's just minor eye candy—any time you're asking them to *do* something new. As discussed in Chapter 1, "featurettes" and "quick wins" are one key way to do this.

To the degree you can, time the deployment of a featurette to match the appearance of a new "tax item" you're asking the user to do. Giving users a quid pro quo reduces user resistance and makes them feel that they aren't being taken for granted. You'll want to plan a series of these user toys, clustering the most attractive ones around the more annoying (but inevitable) "tax items."

Communicating with the Users

Throughout the project, you'll need to communicate with the user community—surveying them for input, notifying them of upcoming changes, describing new policies or procedures, and alerting them about training sessions and other events. To do so, you need to figure out the most effective and pain-free way of communicating with users.

Will users actually want a paper version of a system newsletter? Most people will want a paper-based (even laminated) "cheat sheet" for their specific user screens, but will they also want an entire user guide in paper form as well? Will users read blogs for internal Q&A? Do people pay more attention to unofficial emails and IMs from colleagues, or do they sit up when they receive official emails from corporate headquarters? Are they ready for wikis? Survey the user base, and tailor the medium and style of your communications to match their preferences.

THE MEDIUM IS THE MESSAGE

Part of the deployment cycle will be the "broadcast" of good-news stories that illustrate how much better life is becoming thanks to the SFA/CRM project. To be effective, these broadcasts need to be put through the channel(s) that will be most frequently seen and readily believed. Putting a notice up on the wiki or sending out a lame internal newsletter won't cut it. All too often, an email that starts with a person low in the organization and spreads outward is taken more seriously than official propaganda. Think about using guerrilla marketing techniques for getting the word out . . . and believed.

For more on this, see Chapter 6 and check out www.SFDC-secrets.com.

User Training

As it gets to be time to deploy each major area of new functionality, you'll need to engage affected users in training or even indoctrination. Generally speaking, classroom-style training is not effective for most business users. Typically, too much information is delivered all at once, and the information isn't very relevant to the audience at the time it's delivered. By the time the situation comes up in the real world and the users actually *need* the information, they will have forgotten it. Even if they have been given a full user's manual, they are likely to forget that they ever received any training on the topic.

You need to assess your users before deciding which kind of training to provide. Do they like classroom settings, or can they be effectively trained with self-paced, Web-based courses? Does your company use videoconferencing for training? Does the company already use podcasts for training and internal "newscasts"?

Generally speaking, the shorter and more task-oriented ("day in the life") the training, the better. In my own work, I try to keep training sessions to less than an hour, and to do training in stages (with sessions separated by a couple of weeks and extending as long as they are needed) to make sure that users have *really* learned the basics before giving them more advanced material. It's best to have the training include real examples from the users' daily tasks, and to have users "drive the mouse" during the session.

No matter which kind of training sessions you hold, record them! This step is particularly important for worldwide implementations of SFDC systems and for organizations that experience frequent turnover. Don't bother using a videocam: they're not good enough to capture any detail, they make boring sessions ever duller, and they record in a format that won't be usable outside of North America. Instead, the preferred recording medium should include both video and audio—use a good microphone and screen-capture software, or record the session via WebEx. Make the recordings available to all as files on the project wiki.

Podcasts are also a very effective way of getting training to users on demand. In some cases, you can just strip the audio track from some of your longer sessions—but you'll almost certainly need to edit each session down so the listener doesn't fall asleep.

It's also very helpful to create a laminated "cheat sheet" with annotated screenshots explaining the most common tasks for each user type. These cheat sheets should also be stored in PDF in the project wiki and in SFDC's documents area.

CLASS . . . CLASS . . . CLA-AAAA-ASS . . . WAKE UP!

Training is always tricky—everyone says that employees haven't had enough training, but nobody wants to sit through another class. To make the most of the training time that you can get, here are three formulas that work well for effective, memorable training:

- A classroom setting where every student (or pair of students) has a computer with full network access and can run through exercises relevant to their jobs during the class. These sessions are the most expensive to do (particularly in a company with many locations), but this approach is the best way to ensure uniformity and depth of training.

- A meeting-room setting where students bring their laptops, using WiFi connections to run through the exercises on SFDC and internal systems. These sessions are easier to schedule and set up (because they are closer to the users' workspace), but they are also more vulnerable to interruptions and delays as people drift back to their desks during breaks.

- A "live" Webinar training session, where users take the "class" while sitting at their desks and using their own computers. These sessions are logistically the easiest and can save considerable travel costs, but it's impossible to know how much the students are paying attention. If Webinars or other computer-based training is used, students must be tested before they have completed the training requirement—and they must know that they will be tested *before* they start the session.

See www.SFDC-secrets.com for an example training syllabus.

What User Readiness Means for Deployment

Not all departments in a large organization will be equally ready to make the move to SFDC. The Marketing department might be urgently waiting, Sales somewhat ready, and Finance/ Legal nearing Luddite levels of resistance. So the deployment of each wave of functionality should proceed at a pace that's matched to the individual department's needs. Don't mistake naive enthusiasm for readiness, particularly in Luddite groups. Those employees may have a positive attitude about using the new features, but they may have a vacuum of skills and ingrained habits that will get in the way of achieving optimal productivity with SFDC.

For organizations that are truly eager to adopt SFDC systems, deploy features quickly with user tips for maximum productivity. Make training about standards, practices, and nuance, and consider making it self-paced. You don't have to worry about confusing or intimidating users, so the more "toys" for power users you can offer, the more they'll like it.

For organizations that are only somewhat ready to make the switch, features should be deployed at a slower pace and training sessions should be more deliberate. Make sure that some kind of "user toy" (e.g., eye candy) becomes available every release or so, but don't overdo it.

Organizations that are populated with Luddites need to have the technology deployed more carefully, with full training and assurances before users actually have the freedom to do anything life-threatening. These folks can take two to three times as long to truly absorb new technology, let alone be truly productive with it. In such organizations, it's important to release cheat sheets and good-news stories (look how SFDC helped avoid this potential disaster!) on a monthly basis. New toys and eye-candy features may merely serve to confuse these users with screen clutter, so use SFDC record types and page layouts to keep the screen simple for them.

Post-Deployment User Frustration

Aside from training issues and forgetfulness, there are a couple of things to watch out for when working with any new group of SFDC users. Every security feature in SFDC is there to protect your data from being seen by the wrong eyes and to keep the Bad Guys out. But this mandate translates into ongoing issues for users, so system operations needs to have a range of strategies to handle the inevitable issues. Check out Chapter 13 if you want to know more about the technical details.

Users often forget their passwords and lock themselves out. The system has password-strength screening, which is a good thing. Unfortunately, stronger passwords are harder to remember. Plus, most organizations will configure the system so that the password "ages out" every 60 to 90 days, requiring the user to come up with a different hard-to-remember password. Best of all, most security-conscious clients turn on the system lockout feature that temporarily disables an account that has been subject to repeated failed login attempts.

The first thing you need to do is to place a detailed explanation of this behavior and its rationale—along with your company's corrective policies and contact information—on the project wiki. The second thing you need to do is to set up a special phone number and voicemail box to assist people who've been locked out. **This voicemail needs to be checked at least hourly,** and it's even better if the account (or an email address) automatically **pages the on-duty SFDC administrator.** For global companies with mission-critical usage, the SFDC administrator role needs to be covered on a 7 × 24 basis.

Users may log in from a different location or from a different PC. SFDC has a feature that authorizes not only the user, but also the computer and network he or she is working on. The first time a user tries to log in from home, or on a different computer, or even from a different network while on the road, the system will not let the user in. The remote access point needs to be authorized. This authorization takes only a couple of minutes, but it's a necessary evil.

As always, the first line of defense is information and solution checklists on the project wiki. Once users have gone through an authorization cycle, they'll need to click a link on the login screen, and then click a link in the email that SFDC sends to them. The problem comes when users can't get to their normal email accounts from the current location. This issue can be resolved by having someone else log in to the user's email account, and forward the mail (without clicking on its link) to an email account readable by the user's current computer. This solution creates a small security hole, but it can be contained. An even more interesting problem occurs when users are trying to access the system from an Internet kiosk, where clicking the email link won't work. The only approach to resolving this problem involves opening up an even bigger security hole. Both of these situations can be managed, but require careful attention by the administrator even if the company's security policy allows for their resolution.

Users may not be able to see or modify a record. SFDC has very fine-grained controls for user access to records. The essential rule is that a user can see only those records that he or she owns or that the user's subordinates own. When there's a change of territories, transfer of `accounts` or `opportunities`, or reorganization, users may suddenly not be able to change records, or even see the records at all. The main remedy here is to have very well-thought-out and communicated access hierarchies, and to let users know they'll be losing some access before the change is made (the wiki makes for a wonderful CYA resource in these situations). In cases where a sales rep needs to see or manipulate records that are not part of the rep's hierarchy (this happens frequently when there are overlay territories such as partner managers or global account managers), use SFDC's `sales team` feature to give the users access to the specific `accounts`, `contacts`, and `opportunities` that they need to see. Of course, there are numerous solutions to this problem, but all of the other strategies involve lowering security levels.

How Many Administrators Does It Take to Screw in a Light Bulb?

A classic question in SFDC deployments is "How many administrators do we need for the system?" SFDC's software and data are professionally managed by the Salesforce.com staff, and they have an exemplary record for system uptime and (with one exception) security.

Every SFDC installation will need to have one administrator, whose routine tasks include user management, data import, and system backup, among others. The administrator role is usually a part-time job, and the person who fills it usually works in marketing, sales administration, finance, or IT. It is **strongly** advised that your system administrator take SFDC's administrator course and become certified. Although this course will cost five days of time and $3,000 plus expenses, it will save significant wasted time and hassle for your users.

For any serious SFDC installation, however, there should be one administrator per continent (really, North America, EMEA, and Asia/Pacific) so that the administrative duties can "follow the sun" for 7 × 24 support. For industrial-strength SFDC installations, it is fully justified to have six administrators, with a range of talents (e.g., IT, familiarity with external systems, reporting, or political acumen). But each of these administrators needs to have an *explicit* reason for being, and duties must be assigned using consistent rules. Further, their job roles and process hand-offs must be fully documented to pass Sarbanes-Oxley Section 404 and 409 audits. Check out the discussion in Chapter 13 to learn more about the duties and desirable profiles for administrators.

If the organization has more than two administrators, a change management tool such as ChangeControl (a free tool written by my firm, and available at the AppExchange) is required to coordinate requests and work-in-progress.

Almost inevitably, there will be a power user somewhere in the Sales department (usually a first- or second-level manager) who has worked extensively with SFDC in the past. Such users will ask for full administrative powers so that they can "do their jobs better." While they may have genuine issues, *beware of these requests and almost always deny them*. There is *always* another way to solve these power users' problems, and their issues are usually a pretext designed to get them access they don't actually require. All too often, the requester is trying to get power beyond what's needed for his or her position, or is otherwise trying to game the system to the requester's advantage. In addition to causing morale and data quality issues (for example, deleting records that show weak performance), these spurious administrators are bound to cause security and compliance issues.

Just say no.

CHAPTER 6

Working the Politics

Practical politics consists of ignoring facts.
—Henry Adams

T HIS CHAPTER IS FOR all SFDC users, because they need to understand the political environment surrounding SFDC. As budgets and system adoption are creatures of company politics, "working the system" is a key success factor during and after the implementation.

Technology Is Not the Problem

According to a recent report[1] by industry analyst Forrester Research, the problems of "aligning business strategy" and "managing change" were each twice as important as "technology" and "integration" in SFA/CRM projects. Even the problem of "executive commitment" was more important than any of the technology or product issues.

In other words, getting the technology right isn't enough.

In other other words, succeeding with politics is a real part of any SFA/CRM project.

From the very beginning, you'll need to work politics to get the proper budget and get executive authority to proceed. Even when the project is firmly under way, you'll need to be working politics at every level to achieve the adoption that's required to make the system truly effective.

It's Not Just Big Organizations

Let's face it: the larger and older the organization you work for, the more politics enters into nearly every decision the organization makes. But even small organizations can have their share of friction.

---

1. *How to Get Business and IT Executives to Agree on CRM Priorities,* William Band, Forrester Research's Principal Analyst for CRM strategy.

And when it comes to the topic of sales productivity, political strife can get pretty thick no matter how young the organization is. The whole job of a sales rep is to manage information and to leverage emotions to his or her advantage—so sales organizations are going to be pretty adept at framing and managing political issues. Because sales folks are very sensitive about quotas, commissions, territories, leads—well, practically everything that's going to be held in the SFA system—expect them to engage in a sometimes fractious debate when it comes to SFDC tradeoffs and priorities.

But it's not just the sales personnel who may be worried. A lot of people have job security and bonus payments at stake:

- Marketing personnel will be concerned about the cost-effectiveness of their campaigns, the quality of leads, and the marketing metrics that will determine their bonuses.

- Customer support personnel will be anxious about how many cases will be filed, how quickly they'll be handled, and how frequently they need to be escalated.

- IT personnel will be concerned about the development work they probably won't be doing and the budget they'll probably be losing (SaaS lowers centralized procurement budgets). They'll also be concerned about the integration work they will need to do as part of the SFDC implementation.

- Manufacturing personnel will want to make sure that all orders are shippable configurations, and they won't want an inventory squeeze at the end of the quarter.

- Finance personnel will want to ensure that unapproved quotes never reach the customer, and that orders and forecasts fully comply with SEC and industry regulations.

You can't ignore these realities, which inevitably affect SFDC projects from their first inception to their ongoing management and upgrades. Politics will drive budgets, priorities, schedules, and staffing—it can't be assumed away.

Who's the Champion?

The champion is the person who drives the SFDC decisions and creates the consensus in the organization to buy a system and modify sales processes. The initial champion typically has to get the budget for the initial procurement (as described in Chapter 1), and will probably have to bear the brunt of ongoing fees.

But the champion also has to be the arbiter of priorities and the creator of deadline pressure to get something done. The champion will almost certainly be an executive with the political clout to remove obstacles and give orders. For the initial system, the champion can be any one of the roles described in the following subsections. Notice that if the champion *isn't* in the sales organization, he or she will need to have some very special characteristics.

Chief Financial Officer

The finance organization is usually quite interested in getting the most leverage out of corporate assets, and its denizens are often surprised by how much sales, marketing, and channel (partner) efforts cost. The financial gurus are typically tightly focused on sales productivity and improving measurements (because usually the sales folks are trying to obfuscate these very numbers).

It's possible for the finance organization to be the initial champion of the SFDC system, particularly if this department owns the group that handles order processing and commissions payments. The CFO may even be able to succeed if he or she is a trusted advisor to the CEO, and if the company's board of directors is concerned about sales costs and effective yield.

The problem with having the CFO lead the charge toward SFDC is that it virtually guarantees an adversarial relationship with sales management. Even if the VP of Sales is supportive, everyone on the sales team will know that the initiative is really coming from the bean counters. The individual sales reps will assume that the main purpose of the system is to give upper management a way to spy on their activities, micromanage them, and punish them for weak productivity. *Consequently, almost no members of the sales organization would see SFDC as being in their personal interests.*

In most situations, this structure virtually guarantees low system utilization, empty records, low system credibility, and very limited leverage. The individual reps will not view SFDC as a tool to help *them* manage their time or accelerate deals. Upper management will get "visibility," but the numbers they receive won't be very meaningful.

The CFO will make his or her decisions based on purely financial data. As SFDC has several benefits that are invisible in the numbers—less friction, better collaboration, happier customers—the CFO will tend to miss important values of the system. Consequently, the company will tend to invest less in the SFDC system, and it will miss opportunities to make the sales team even more effective.

Bottom line: having the CFO as the initial champion for the system is very unlikely to succeed. It's far better to have the CFO coax someone else to take the reins.

Chief Marketing Officer

The VP of Marketing or CMO is usually quite interested in making an SFA system happen because it fits his or her analytical nature.[2] The marketing folks are responsible for

---

2. Generally speaking, the difference between marketing and sales people is their relative strength of IQ versus EQ. Marketers love to think (about selling) for a living. Sales people love to sell for a living.

producing leads, and they're curious about why many campaigns produce leads that go into a black hole and are never seen again. Yet sales personnel keep closing deals, and the people they're working with *had* to hear about the company and its products somehow. Everyone in the Marketing department privately wonders what the Sales department is actually doing, and whether the reps are changing the records to make themselves look good—and the marketing staff look like a bunch of bozos.

The VP of Marketing may be the most competent person in the whole organization to run the system, but there's a problem. In most companies, there's a distant relationship between the Sales and Marketing organizations. They don't really trust each other, and they don't spend a lot of time together. At an emotional level, they're competing organizations—and marketing almost never wins this game. Even if the VP of Sales is supportive, everyone on the sales team will know that the initiative is really coming from marketing. The individual sales reps will assume that the system will be used to glorify marketing, spy on sales reps, and hold them accountable for a bunch of metrics that don't mean anything to the business. The members of the sales organization won't see what all the urgency for the SFDC system is about, and they are unlikely to see it as helping *them*.

And there's another problematic issue: most marketing organizations just don't have a sense of urgency about revenue.[3] They don't have the end-of-quarter panic *in their bones,* and everyone in sales knows it. Even if the marketing folks work long hours, they are rarely perceived as being responsive to field needs. They don't know what it takes to drive a deal home.

Even worse, most marketers just *love* data. They'll ask for lots of it. They'll churn out tons of reports and PowerPoint presentations. And most of this output is just meaningless to the sales representatives in the field. Marketers will generally fill up the SFDC system with dozens of fields that won't be filled and reports that will never be used. These data-junkie behaviors won't be viewed with suspicion the way they might be if they originated from the Finance department, but they'll still be a low-grade irritant.

In most organizations, having someone from the Marketing department champion the SFDC system is a harbinger of marginal system utilization, empty records, low system credibility, and limited leverage. The individual sales reps will not view SFDC as a tool to help them manage their time or accelerate deals. Marketing will get its analytics, upper management will get "visibility," but sales productivity—the whole point of the system—will likely remain elusive.

One way to successfully have the Marketing department own the system from the beginning is if the marketing team reports to the head of the Sales department (or the other way around). In this situation, the marketing folks are viewed as being on (almost) the same team, and the head of marketing has a close relationship with the head of sales.

---

3. Even though my background includes 20 years as a card-carrying member of marketing, this section has to be as candid as the rest of the book.

Chief Operating Officer

The Sales VP or COO is *the* natural champion for an SFDC system—after all, it's called Salesforce.com. The VP of Sales has his or her neck on the line to make the numbers, so this executive needs to be able to manage the sales managers and see what the individual reps are doing.

The VP of Sales won't be the person who actually owns the system over time—sometimes, no one in the organization really wants that role—but it certainly makes sense for the VP to be the champion. When SFDC comes out of his or her budget and is on the agenda at sales staff meetings, it subtly reinforces the message that the SFDC system is a genuinely important initiative. Even if the reps and managers don't like the system, they'll know the boss cares—and that's a powerful motivator. They may not agree with the metrics or policies being put in place for the new system, but they cannot ignore them.

But there's another issue: if the Sales VP is the driving force behind the adoption of SFDC, reps will actually try to use the system and talk about how the tool helped them close deals. Their ultimate goal may be to butter up the boss, but their open discussion of SFDC will stimulate other reps to get on the bandwagon. It might all be baloney, but it can be effective baloney.

The only time it *doesn't work* to have the VP of Sales champion the system is when that person is on his or her way out of the organization. Sponsorship by a loser VP or a lame duck is never the way to inspire confidence in an SFA system. In this situation, the system start should be delayed until a new Sales VP comes in, or sponsorship should be kicked upstairs.

The Chief Executive Officer or the Board of Directors

Most of the time, an SFA system is too small an issue for a CEO or board committee to care about or sponsor. Those executives have bigger fish to fry, and they won't spend enough quality time to make the judgment calls or push the action items.

But it *does* make sense for the highest levels of management to drive the system if (1) as mentioned earlier, the Sales VP is a lame duck, or (2) there's been a significant "blowup" of the forecast, and the company missed its numbers due to limited visibility.

The second situation will make for system priorities that are very different from those associated with the normal SFDC project. In this case, the issue won't be marketing effectiveness or even sales effectiveness—it will be making sure that the forecast is reliable and bullet-proof, and that *closing*[4] the sales cycle is streamlined.

Having the CEO or the board champion the SFA system is fine for securing the budgets, making priority calls, and having clear deadlines (almost always, the next board meeting).

---

4. Most SFA implementations focus more on the *beginning* of sales cycles and on keeping reps busier with more prospects. In contrast, board-level, forecast-driven implementations tend to focus on the *end* of the sales cycle—that is, on revenue achievement and accurate forecasts.

Once the budgetary allocation is made, however, the sponsorship needs to be deputized down at least one level so that it can be executed. Almost without exception, the Sales department is the organization that should be deputized for making the system happen.

SPONSORSHIP AND CHAMPIONING LATER PHASES

One of the characteristics of SFA systems is that they continue to evolve long after they are installed. Either they are expanded to cover the needs of more organizations, or they are modified to more completely address new business needs.

Once an SFDC system is in place and being used by sales reps, upgrades can be successfully achieved when they are sponsored by nearly any part of the organization. They key indicator of success is the answer to the question, "How ardently do the reps use the system?" If there's any wavering or grumbling from a group of users, the upgrade is better championed by the head of that organization.[5]

As the system matures and touches more parts of the business, it will be more likely for operations or finance personnel to become champions of expansions. The key, no matter who serve as the champion, is to make sure that the users of the new functionality have an inherent reason to use SFDC as part of their normal way of doing business. If new users don't care from the first day that the new feature is put in place, your investment in technology will be undermined by user reality.

Who Pays for the System?

By its nature, SFDC spans many departmental budgets. And many groups will benefit: if the system really does its job, every stockholder wins.

Of course, somebody has to pay for the implementation, the ongoing fees, and the expansion of the system. In almost any company, the overall costs of SFDC will be in the hundreds of thousands or even millions of dollars. Budgets have to be put in place indefinitely, as most SFDC costs are recurring expenses. Even though budgeting processes are highly political and vary by company, a few generalities apply:

- All the fees paid to SFDC (licenses, consulting, and training) come from the Sales budget. This approach is recommended because it reflects reality—SFDC begins with "Sales"—but also because it brings ongoing attention from sales executives that this is *their* system and they should be getting the most out of it.

---

5. Most of the time, the grumbling will come from sales personnel. But not always! Listen carefully and act accordingly.

While users may be in several other departments, typically 75% of the total user count comes from sales, channels, order management, and other sales roles. If the non-sales user count is very high or if customer support uses a large number of Mobile edition licenses (an extra cost), set up a chargeback through the finance group.

- Any add-on item or project (including associated consulting fees) is paid for by the department that asked for it or that benefits the most from it. For example, if corporate finance personnel want a fancy reporting engine or a data warehouse, let those users put their money where their mouth is. If it turns out they don't need that feature after a year, this system add-on should be turned off unless someone else needs it enough to pay for it. This practice not only conserves budget, but also keeps system complexity under control.[6]

- Infrastructure and incidental costs are paid out of IT, G&A, or other overhead budgets. Many different items fit into this category, and it's important to not neglect them because they're often the motor oil that keeps the car from blowing up:

  ➡ System administrator, developer, and business analyst training fees

  ➡ Record deduplication tools

  ➡ Lead enrichment tools

  ➡ Mobile phone "data plan" fees (sometimes required for use of SFDC's Mobile edition)

  ➡ Sandbox fees

  ➡ AppExchange tool/product fees (unless the product was specifically requested by a single department)

  ➡ Cost of disk drives/servers for storing documents, system backup snapshots, wikis, and so forth

- Headcount costs are paid out of the budgets for those employees' departments. Typically, the only people who are really devoted to the system are working on a part-time basis as part of their other roles: sales system administrator, marketing system administrator, and IT administrator/data architect. Even if a person is devoted full-time to SFDC, that individual's salary should be paid for out of his or her management chain's budget. The good news is that it's rare that any incremental headcount is involved, once SFDC is up and running.

---

6. One of the biggest lessons in conventional IT is that all too often functionality really isn't required. "Nice to have" subsystems become institutional albatrosses. SaaS tamps down this problem.

Who Will Own the System?

While the best practices for championing, sponsoring, and paying for SFDC development are pretty clear, ownership and ongoing operations of the system are a bit more ambiguous. The decision is complicated by the fact that the owner of the system will need to develop budgets and practices that shouldn't change very often. Ideally, the system owner shouldn't change more often than every three years.[7]

That said, a successful SFDC system will evolve every six months or so as a result of the following factors:

- Incremental additions of new users

- Changes to the company's products and services (such as new product lines, prices, or promotions)

- Incremental business rule or organization changes (e.g., accommodating a reorganization, new policy, or new business unit)

- Changes in the systems to which SFDC connects (such as ERP version upgrades, external system expansions, or a new data warehouse)

- The need to leverage new features that have come in subsequent SFDC releases[8]

- Expansion of SFDC to new user groups (e.g., telesales, a new product division, or overseas operations) or business functions (e.g., field support or legal/contracts)

- Integration of SFDC with a wider range of systems (e.g., ERP, distribution, or a call center)

The system owner acts as the ultimate gatekeeper, having to balance the needs of ongoing operations against these new system developments. System ownership is also important because "ownership is nine-tenths of the law": the owner is in the position to set and enforce system policies that will affect everyone. In this section, we discuss who should own the system in the first year, and who should own and run the system in the subsequent years.

Chief Financial Officer

Although the finance organization should almost never be the champion for SFDC, it *is* a good owner/operator of the system. The CFO and the operations people have the right

---

7. In a perfect world, no unplanned personnel turnover would occur. Whenever a key person in the SFDC operations team moves on, it's a natural time to review who should own and run the system going forward.

8. In the world of SaaS applications, the product will be upgraded on the vendor's schedule, whether you ask for it or not. You don't have to *use* the new features, and they won't interfere with what you already use, but there's no such thing as a "system lockdown" as there was for on-premises enterprise software. See Chapter 13 for further discussion of this topic.

attitude to invest in process and data quality, and they have to touch the system to do their jobs.

The issue with having the CFO, sales operations, or other numbers-oriented groups running SFDC is the risk that they will be overbearing or micromanagers. Either of these tendencies will put off end users of the system, which means system utilization can suffer somewhat. If this problem occurs, the amount, credibility, and relevance of the data in the system will decline. Given that these are all key success factors for a good SFDC system, it's important to monitor for these possibilities and head off these issues before they grow into real problems.

Chief Marketing Officer

The VP of Marketing or CMO has people on the team who need to touch SFDC on a daily basis. These personnel understand metrics and may be comfortable with report writing and spreadsheets. And they can relate—at some level—to people in the sales organization.

Unfortunately, marketing talent is often very thinly stretched (the people with real skills are pulled a dozen directions), and some of the ongoing obligations of running SFDC would represent a problem for them. Further, the *individuals* in marketing who need to touch the system on a daily basis—such as the folks who do events and campaigns—tend to be weak on consistency and process (at least when it comes to running SFDC).

Although in theory the Marketing department could be a great place for running SFDC, in practice it often represents a burden for the organization.

Chief Operating Officer

Most of the members of the sales organization have neither the interest nor the skills to run SFDC. Even having a contractor to manage SFDC under most sales managers would be ill advised.

That said, people in order operations, sales support, or sales operations do have the right attitudes and aptitudes to run an SFA system. They already deal with process, numbers, reports, and spreadsheets. The real question is, Do these people have the time or interest to take on another complex, stressful task?[9]

The CEO or the Board of Directors

I have yet to find a situation where the CEO, members of the board of directors, or any similar senior executive should be charged with running the SFDC system. Anything's possible, but assignment of SFDC ownership in this area seems misplaced in any organization I can think of.

---

9. In actuality, running SFDC should be neither complex nor stressful. But at the end of the quarter, when everyone is trying to get those last orders in, even the smallest incremental work will appear to be a burden. As long as the sales group has some spare capacity, consider it as a viable candidate for SFDC ownership.

Chief Information Officer

Even though the IT department should never be the champion of SFDC—and I have yet to find a situation where it was—having IT personnel handle ongoing operations of the system would not be a bad plan. IT people have the skills and attitudes to do the operational and maintenance work.

Larger companies are typically structured to include a centralized IT group as well as some IT people within business units. The IT people in business units can be a good choice for owning and operating SFDC, if they have the time available. The other option—the centralized IT department—is usually disconnected from the user community, and SFDC users tend to be an opinionated and impatient lot. If a centralized IT department will own and operate the SFDC system, it will need to have correspondents in the Sales and Marketing departments to keep the IT personnel responsive and aligned with ongoing user needs.

Smaller companies typically don't have a real IT department—just a system administrator or contractor who handles IT responsibilities. Thus IT ownership of the SFDC system won't be a viable choice.

Mixed Team

Our recommended approach is to separate who holds the ongoing SFDC operational budget (almost always the Sales or Finance department) from the management responsibilities of running the system (a departmental IT or a Sales/Marketing team). The governance team can be very small—one person each from Sales, Marketing, and Operations—and quite lightweight—emails and IMs for most issues, with short monthly meetings for tricky problems or policy changes.

By default, the SFDC administrators fit this governance role quite well. They are very familiar with how the system actually works, they already deal with users and SFDC issues in the normal course of their jobs, and they don't have any political agenda. However, these individuals are often politically disconnected, so they will need to have a management person (typically at the director level) to escalate issues to. The specific choice of "escalation manager" depends entirely on the company and the personalities and interests of the individual, but the key is that the manager must be able to effectively drive decisions to resolution. Waffling or inability to get needed resources just makes the entire SFDC team look bad.

Who Owns the Data Now?

This is a deceptively simple question, which is naively answered with "IT" or "everybody." Almost never does that answer suffice for real-world SFDC projects.

In smaller companies, everyone has access to any data they can see on the network, and there are few, if any, onerous process controls. But in most small and medium-size businesses (SMB) and all larger companies, information is kept in silos that are protected (technically and politically) from uncoordinated or unauthorized use. All publicly traded companies and firms working with the defense industry face legal sanctions if they don't keep their data from prying eyes. As you see, data access can be a big deal.

The real issues here are these:

- Who enters, handles, or controls the data?

- Who dictates policies about the data, such as access, ability to modify, ability to delete, ability to copy, and ability to report/summarize?

- Which controls and audit trails must be enforced?

- Which integration methods or approaches are acceptable or encouraged?

- What are the semantics of the data? Who knows what it's supposed to mean? What are the naming standards and pick list values?

- What is the provenance of the data? Who knows which parts of it are authoritative (system of record) versus informational (replicated or transferred from some original source)?

- Who controls or invests in the quality of the data?

Each of these issues can add significant bureaucratic inertia to an SFDC project—either initial implementation or subsequent integration/extension—so they must be well understood *before schedule commitments are made.*

The first area to explore is the current and historical SFA system data that will be migrated to SFDC. Ownership of these data must be "taken over" by the new SFDC champion and owner organizations. This data stewardship usually entails a fairly light responsibility, along the lines of the Hippocratic oath ("At least, do no harm"). But if the existing SFA/CRM system holds significant corporate history, there can be some interesting obligations. For example, many companies need to keep order history available for as long as three years, and in financial services there may be requirements for a full seven years' access. The data do not necessarily need to be available online, but they do need to be readable and consistently reportable without requiring ridiculous effort. As always, several ways of satisfying the basic requirement exist, but the point of this paragraph is the system owner needs to *know* what the requirements are before taking over the data.[10]

---

10. In the inevitable game of bureaucratic "hot potato," two weeks after an organization relinquishes control of data, its members will have no recollection of where anything came from, or how to access, use, or interpret the data—and the new owner will be left high and dry. When dealing with historical data, pay careful attention to the task of getting knowledge transfer *prior to* responsibility transfer.

The other areas to explore are the data sources with which the SFDC system will need to be integrated. Each of these information sources will have its own characteristics in the previously given bulleted list, and there will sometimes be significant sensitivity regarding information sharing. Don't be surprised to hear the information-owning organizations present all kinds of fabulous and complicated issues—if you're lucky, these stories will have the telltale odor of bureaucratic origins.

While each of the following examples has good motivations behind it, these objections are usually off-point and easily dealt with.

The auditors say that nobody can have access to this data.

On the face of it, this assertion is at least an exaggeration. Even in government classified projects, *somebody* with the right qualification can have access to sensitive data. Of course, some data do need to be protected and must not be altered after the fact. These mandates are part of all accounting disciplines and the Sarbanes-Oxley Sections 404 and 409—but they are intended to prevent alteration or deletion of legitimate records, or creation of bogus ones. In most cases, SFDC integrations will require read-only access. Further, SFDC provides very fine-grained access controls, allowing administrators to manage exactly who can see exactly what. Get the person who throws this objection to specify which auditor made this stipulation. Then talk to that person (or company), and have the auditor identify who can see which data and for which purposes. From this discussion, you can develop an access control plan that meets the specific needs of the auditors.

SEC regulations say this data can be made available only to specific individuals on a need-to-know basis.

SEC and other agency regulations are specific about who should be able to read data that will affect stock prices—privileged "insider information" about sales, revenues, collections, and profitability *in the aggregate*. Visibility into the bookings or revenues for the whole company is, indeed, highly restricted. In contrast, SFDC users typically need to have access to this information only for a few customers, not in the aggregate. By integrating the external data into the system at the individual record level and linking it into custom SFDC fields, the external system's aggregate reports would be hidden from all SFDC users. Further, SFDC's internal access control facilities can ensure that only the right people have access to each customer record, and that the aggregate views and roll-up reports are made available only to executives with the need to know.

Our legal policy is that this customer data must be kept private and cannot be shared with any other division that didn't originally collect those data.

While the legal requirements may have been interpreted this way, it is a fairly inane contortion of privacy policy. (But I'm just a businessman.) The way to work through this objection is to describe the actual business process that involves sharing these data. For example, if the purpose of sharing the data is to prevent the creation of duplicate records (i.e., "Don't create a new `account` record in SFDC if that company is already a customer of another division"), the only way that SFDC would be accessing the foreign system's data is when the customer already exists in both systems. In other words, the customer has already given consent twice, and by implication the sharing of the personal data is authorized.

Of course, there may be some cases where sharing the data would be a violation of the customer's privacy. In particular, watch out for wanton email blast requests from sales, marketing, or customer support sources.

European privacy laws say that we have to store and process these data only in Europe.

There is indeed an EC Directive (95/46/EC Chapter IV) that effectively requires European citizens' personal information to be processed and stored within the European Union.[11] Like all laws, it is open to interpretation—and the most rabid interpretation would make much of electronic commerce and even email nearly impossible. The good news is that there are several strategies to comply with the law's requirements.

The first strategy is to store only the "insensitive" parts[12] of personal data within the SFDC system (as SFDC at this point doesn't have a hosting center in the EU). The sensitive portions of personal data (e.g., email address, postal address, Social Security or other tax identification number, or phone number) would be stored within your company's European offices (for example, in an Exchange contact folder, an LDAP directory, or RDBMS). The first step in this approach—which isn't a bad idea in any case—is to document which customers' information needs to be viewed and manipulated by which specific users. While this approach would cause some annoyance for internal users and add a bit of complexity, it would allow your company to use a single, U.S. instance of SFDC. This strategy would involve the use of `S-controls`, `mash-ups`, and `VisualForce` to allow viewing and updating the European data from within the SFDC user interface.

The second strategy is to file waivers ("safe harbor policy statements") via your internal legal counsel. This process can be quite involved, but is done regularly by global companies. Because other systems inside your company will have already dealt with this issue in the past, extending your company's existing waivers to SFDC should be a relatively minor procedural matter.

The third strategy is to have your lawyers include specific verbiage that confers user permission to process personal information outside the EU as part of all your European

---

11. Strictly speaking, the EC Directive requires that personal data be transferred, processed, and stored only within countries that have the data security and privacy regulations that comply with EC laws. In fact, EC member states such as Germany have implemented national laws that are even more restrictive than the EC laws. These variations are a lawyer's dream and a practical nightmare.

12. These data elements would consist of just a person's name and a cross-reference number to other company records.

contracts and nondisclosure agreements. If your company is a pure business-to-business marketing and selling organization, your lawyers should also argue that it isn't collecting personal information for "a natural person." The information being collected in this case isn't personal information such as home phone and private email, but rather *business* contact information (e.g., business phone numbers and email addresses). In this context, your lawyers may be able to argue that the regulation is moot.

The fourth strategy—and it can't hurt to apply this one in any case—is to specifically ask European users for permission to process and store their personal information outside the EU. If you get the person's "unambiguous permission," either before the individual provides his or her personal information or as part of subsequent email/reregistration cycles (analogous to opt-in sequences), you should be able to avoid almost all of the burden imposed by this regulation. In using this strategy, you'll want to store more than one level of "opt-in" and "opt-out" information in SFDC. Even if your company has a content management system or email blaster that manages individuals' subscriptions and preferences, the key check box data need to be integrated into SFDC so that the system enforces users' preferences before you attempt to communicate with them.

A final strategy that may become available in the future will be to store all of the EU customer data within SFDC's future European data centers. This could be done in one of two ways: (1) by running the whole company's system on an SFDC[13] European instance or (2) by partitioning the customer base and using two SFDC instances (the EU one for use by European employees and customers, and the main one in the United States for use by everyone else in the world). Neither of these approaches will cost any more in terms of SFDC licenses, but both will involve some interesting complexities in implementation and operations. You'll definitely want to use the `Salesforce to Salesforce` feature if you choose this approach. This strategy isn't available yet, but stay tuned.

> **Corporate network administrators have put limits on the bandwidth requirements for replicating the data. You can have only 1,000 records per day.**

Bandwidth constraints are almost unheard of in the United States. In international markets, however, data links may be very slow and expensive—so this objection is not completely ridiculous. But it's close. From a business perspective, does it make sense to force users to be less productive and limit sales effectiveness by saving $10 on data fees?

Even from a technological perspective, this argument makes little sense. In a SaaS application, every SFDC keystroke and screen refresh comes over the Web, using some of the most verbose mechanisms available (HTTPS, XML, and SOAP). If it makes sense for the business to use network traffic to support end users, why not devote another 0.1% of network traffic to keeping the data current and relevant?

---

13. This approach requires that any add-on products or integrated systems within the company follow the same geographic partitioning strategy for any data deemed "personal." The larger the company, the more logistically complicated it becomes to use this approach.

Finally, if the point of integration is between two outside sources (e.g., SFDC and another SaaS application or SFDC and your Web site), the integration traffic will not need to go through your company's network at all. Thanks to integration adaptors from companies such as Boomi and Pervasive, integration can be handled entirely "in the cloud" of the Internet, so that SFDC traffic will not count as company network traffic at all.

> **IT security mandates forbid software elements inside the company's firewall from communicating directly with SaaS applications on the open Internet.**

This objection is more profound and reasonable than the previous ones. SFDC, as a SaaS application, stores and processes all its data in highly secure data centers in the Web. Communication between SFDC and users occurs over the encrypted Secure Sockets Layer (SSL, as denoted by the use of "https:" in the URLs). On the user's desktop, SFDC in the browser passes muster with security departments around the world.

Communication with user applications (such deduping tools) and with plugins (such as Microsoft Outlook or Excel) takes place over SSL and SOAP, and the security risk is rarely viewed as significant. But when it comes to integrating with your company's internal systems, the integration adaptors usually run on your servers inside the firewall, and they need to communicate with third-party services via the Web. The fact that your company's data go through the firewall, out to a third party whose security infrastructure is not well known—and then on to SFDC "out in the cloud"—can cause conservative security personnel to take notice. They will probably require a specific review of *which* data are needed, *why* they are needed, and *what kind of damage* could result from a loss of data or control. This kind of scrutiny is okay—after all, it's their job. SFDC has done an exemplary job with its security infrastructure, which has passed hundreds of tough security reviews both in the United States and overseas. Getting the third-party integration service providers approved may take a while, but it can also be accomplished without major surgery.

The best way to deal with this situation is to set up a *very* lightweight integration at the outset (read-only access, using one-way file transfer on a monthly or weekly basis), and then add more elegant, automated integration over time as the security personnel complete their review processes. This interval also provides time for user requests to build, becoming more urgent and eventually counteracting internal resistance to the SFDC implementation.

Dealing with Review Committees

In the immortal words of Clayton Christensen,[14] "Form doesn't follow function: it follows failure." Review committees usually exist because something yucky happened, and they often have the important function of keeping somebody in the company out of hot water in the boardroom—or the courtroom.

---

14. In *The Innovator's Dilemma,* but he may have been paraphrasing Petroski's 1994 book *The Evolution of Useful Things.*

Early on in the SFDC project, the project manager goes through the exercise of inventorying *all* of your company's review committees and figuring out which ones might conceivably be interested in approving the SFDC work. The most likely candidates include the following committees:

- IT Security

- Network Security, Architecture, or Identity

- IT Architecture or Applications

- Compliance and Audit

- Financial Controls

- Customer Privacy

- Marketing or Web Site Systems

On each of these review boards, the project manager should befriend at least the committee chairperson, so as to get this individual's cooperation in ensuring a speedy, lightweight review process. If committee members view your project manager as an annoyance, they can slow down SFDC implementation progress significantly. All they have to do is withhold a little bit of information, or not open a loophole, or postpone the discussion when the meeting runs out of time.

Everyone has to maintain the right frame of mind about these review committees and processes. They exist to protect you and others from pain and damage, and they will save you time—no matter what the people pestering you to "skip that" tell you. In talking with the committee chairperson, ask for examples where other projects have run into trouble by doing the wrong thing or a list of common mistakes to avoid. You'll find that this level of question will often get the chairperson in the mood to suggest things you can do—ways of presenting the information, safeguards to enquire about—that will help your project sail through the review cycle.

Identifying and Dealing with Opposition to the Project

Most of the direct opposition you will encounter during the decision-making process was described earlier in this book, in Chapter 1. However, even after the system is deployed, you may run into opposition when the company is making a significant decision to expand SFDC. The opponents will be focused on derailing the choice of SFDC, or limiting its scope, or simply trying to stop a new job requirement.

The easiest opponents to spot are those who simply don't want to spend the money. Whether they work in finance or sales (which will have to bear most of the budgetary brunt), the argument will usually take the form of "We're going to be spending $X00,000 per year *forever,* and for what? To do something that Outlook and Excel already take care of!" These rhetorical arguments need to be silenced by the members of upper management—the VP of Sales and the CEO—who are the SFDC champions. The issue isn't the size of checks the company will write, but rather the size and number of checks the company will *receive from its customers.* The crux of the counterargument is "Give sales personnel the tools they need to do their jobs better, the tools that every one of our competitors already has."

The next opponent group will be those people who don't want an SFA system at all, or who dislike change in general. They are usually fairly vocal, and their main issue is typically that the new system will bring them more work, yet yield little in the way of benefits. The crux of their objection is that there's nothing in it *for them.* The prospect of a new SFDC system is about as attractive as a tax increase for these folks. The best way to deal with this group is to find something that *will be* in it for them. Whether it's a process that can be automated, a new report, or a new CYA mechanism that shows who is (and isn't) accountable, discover or create something that will be in their interests—and put it in a highly visible spot on the feature list.

The next opponents are those organizational members who do want an SFA system, but want a different one. In some cases, they'll be quite straightforward about what they're advocating. When you see a competitor's "slam sheet,"[15] you'll know what you're dealing with. The way to handle this objection is to keep the comparison a realistic one, and to keep the comparison criteria as simple and easy to understand as possible. Keep the discussion focused on the *business objectives* rather than on some abstract set of requirements. As most businesses prefer fast time to value, ease of use, low entry cost, and extensive customer references, SFDC will win nearly all the time.

The most sophisticated strain of opponents to SFDC adoption will not mention a competitor's product at all. Instead, their tactic is to broaden the system requirements to cover an impossibly wide spectrum. By extending requirements into the "boil the ocean" range, the opponents hope to bog down the entire process. If they can cause the entire decision process to start over from scratch, all decisions that have been made in the process will be invalidated. The way to handle this situation is to handle it as a giant case of scope creep. Highlight the new "requirements" that are dealing with problems that don't really exist yet, and focus attention on the wastefulness of proposals that smell of pork-barrel politics. Bring the conversation back to the business basics—keeping things simple, quick to deploy, and easy for users to adopt. Promote the idea of incrementalism, where *extensive features shouldn't be added* until users are actively using the system and the data asset is growing in value.

---

15. Slam sheets are talking points that highlight the problems with one product and the comparative benefits of a competitor's. While often shrouded in "white paper" format, the telltale sign of slam sheets is their exclusive emphasis on the negative points of the competitor's product and their over-focusing on marginal or obscure issues that no real customer would ever notice.

The Politics of System Adoption

Success rates of SFA systems are quite low: most industry analyst surveys show that less than 50% of SFA projects are deemed a success by management. A key reason for this poor rating is that any SFA system—even if perfectly implemented—is a tool with little intrinsic value. The business value of any SFA system is the improved effectiveness for sales and other teams thanks to the following changes in the way the company operates:

- Better collaboration

- More complete customer information

- Fewer dropped action items or missed opportunities

- Better metrics and visibility

Every one of these factors depends entirely on data entered by users as part of their touching customers. If the data aren't there, none of the business benefits can happen. Clearly, getting users happily on board—and developing the value of the information asset—is more important than installing any particular set of SFA product features.

Once the system project has been approved, getting users interested in using the system will be job one for the implementation team. From the first user reviews of prototypes and storyboards through to deployment and training, *the* key SFA success factor is getting users to actively use the system. Accompanying this increase in usage must be a proactive "good news" campaign touting the system almost from day one.

Unfortunately, some people will inevitably look for any excuse to not use the system. They will jump at the chance to criticize it, and will point to others' criticism as the basis for not bothering to log in. To counter their objections, the project team needs to leverage every avenue for support: top down, bottom up, and inside out.

Top Down: Champions

The champions of the system are the single most important stimulants for system usage, because it is their will—and budget—that makes the system happen in the first place. It's their organizational prestige and personal enthusiasm that will drive fast adoption of SFDC.

It is incredibly important for the champions to act consistently about SFDC, and to show people through their behavior that they will be depending on the system for their own success. These advocates need to say how often they plan to use the SFDC data and reports to run management meetings. They need to have a dashboard named after them, and have that dashboard on the home screen of their organization. See Chapters 9 through 13 for more best practices in this area.

The champion should create milestones for a sequence of meetings that will depend on SFDC data and reports. For example, if the system will initially go live in January, the champion should ask that all `lead` reports at executive staff be based on the system by March, that all `opportunity` lists be driven off the system by April, and that all forecasting and pipeline reports be based only on SFDC data by May. As the year unfolds, this individual should continue to issue emails stipulating that no deal will be discussed at any level of management review unless it is in the system first. Later, the champion should send an email clarifying the requirement that deals won't be reviewed unless their SFDC data have been updated within the last two weeks. By incrementally and repeatedly emphasizing the importance of the system to every level of management, the champion cements the right kind of thinking and behavior about SFDC.

As the VP of Sales is usually the SFDC champion, it's incredibly important for this person to not break the illusion of the importance of system usage. It takes only a few negative or ambivalent words from the champion to neutralize the system's positive momentum. Rumors fly fast, and any frustration expressed by the champion will get around the company overnight. When misinformation shows up in a report or dashboard, the champion must have the discipline to say, "This information is no good—I rely on my team to keep the data in SFDC accurate and timely, and I don't want to see this happen again." If in a moment of frustration the champion says something like "This system is no damn good—I can't use this garbage," he or she will be setting back user adoption of the SFDC system by months.

Top Down: Sticks

Upper management—whether the SFDC champion or not—always has the power to mandate things. Of course, it is reasonable to make requirements, do indoctrination, train, and enforce standards. But it is easy to issue overly grandiose management commands or to use sticks too early, only to have them be dismissed by workers as "another thing they'll forget about next month." This is something the SFDC team members need to avoid.

Because the system will be delivered incrementally, the use of commands and requirements should also be rolled out gradually. Early on, the system will not be functionally complete and—worse—it won't contain much interesting data. The trick is to get users on the system doing something that will add to the system data asset as a *natural part of their job*. The user representatives on the implementation team need to find a part of the business process to serve as the beachhead for SFDC users. Ideally, it won't require duplicate data entry even though it inevitably will involve some change for users. Once this step in the business process is identified, management should mandate that the users change their behavior by a specific date. After a few weeks of data entry this way, more user steps should be transitioned into SFDC activity.

Only after SFDC has the required functionality, information value, and data quality to be a reliable asset should the big sticks come out. For example, any penalties (such as "no commission on deals will be paid unless . . .") should not be even hinted at for the first six months of system usage. See Chapters 9 through 13 for organization-specific best practices in this area.

Inside Out: Heroes and Mavens

In sales and marketing organizations, what the boss is saying about SFDC is always a little suspect. Users think the system is at least partly there to spy on their activity, monitor them, and be the basis for endless pestering and measurement.

Consequently, some of SFDC's credibility will depend on the experience of users: word needs to get around about how the system helped Sally close a deal faster or prevented Joe from forgetting a customer request. These stories are an important part of system folklore, and they need to be encouraged.

As discussed in Chapter 4, the implementation team will seek out early adopters to provide input into the system design. Exactly who they choose for this role should depend in part on the individual's maven quality—his or her connectedness throughout the organization. No matter where this person appears on the organizational chart, a maven has an informal following and a very large Rolodex.[16] Ideally, the maven should also be a blabbermouth. During the system rollout stages, it's important to coddle mavens and make sure they have great experiences with the system. By making them happy, the word will spread that the system is easy to use and saves time.

Heroes are a bit different from mavens, in that they're manufactured. A hero is someone who does something great as a consequence of using SFDC and who will be "promoted" by indirect means. For example, if a customer support rep is able to convert an irate customer into a happy one thanks to SFDC, a congratulatory email may be sent across the organization highlighting the "win." These emails need to be written subtly, though, to avoid sounding like crass boosterism or a bad newsletter.

Within the sales organization, the hero emails or verbal announcements need to be even more subtle because, well, sales reps know a bad pitch when they hear it. The sales hero is a rep who closed a bigger deal or did a better upsell—people expect to hear about that kind of news overtly. But the sales hero also has to have a "secret to success" that most reps don't know about. News of this special technique (involving, of course, SFDC) needs to come directly from that rep—*not* from management or the SFDC team—almost in the form of bragging. All of this subterfuge may seem contrived and childish, but sales reps only listen to other sales reps (particularly the ones who are more successful than they are).

---

16. Of course, it's not a Rolodex—it's probably an Outlook contact list. Mavens have contacts by the thousands, so their name is widely recognized across organizational lines.

Bottom Up: Technogeeks

At the bottom of the organizational chart are the worker bees who actually get stuff done. And in most organizations, this is the level where many technogeeks live. Whether they are sales engineers or customer support reps, marketing analysts or product managers, accounting specialists or order expediters, they have great PC skills and are known for tricks, techniques, and toys that others haven't mastered.

Having a few technogeeks on your side helps drive adoption of the SFDC system because it shows that there's a cool side to the system, some tricks that save time and may have an element of fun. Technogeeks spread the positive word though IMs, water-cooler talk, and after-work beers—the informal channels that can really count.

It's largely for the technogeek that the implementation team will put in toys and eye candy, the featurettes that might otherwise seem trivial. These things give people something to talk about, so a system that could be as dull as a spreadsheet has an element of fun. In geek-speak, plant Easter eggs.

In addition to deploying the featurettes, you can encourage "geekthusiasm" through postings on the project wiki, little contests with T-shirt giveaways, and similarly nerdy exercises. Sounds dumb, works great.

System Out: Carrots

Carrots are positive incentives for people to use the system, and they can be more powerful and reliable than many of the mechanisms described in the preceding subsections. Three types of carrots exist, and all should be used as soon as they are available.

The first carrots are the featurettes: little things that make life a bit easier, but are unavailable elsewhere. For example, you can implement a tool to automatically draw an organizational chart of the customer account, or an SFDC button to automatically dial Skype on your phone system. These convenience and gee-whiz features can be positive reasons to use the system almost from day one.

The second set of carrots takes the form of organizational incentives: procedures or activities that are more easily done through the system. For example, your sales team may have loaner equipment for use in sales cycles. If management make it easier for these personnel to get loaner equipment, or give preference to the loaner applications that are made through SFDC, you will provide a positive reason for people to use the system. In another example, if management makes it clear that action items presented as SFDC `tasks` will be handled sooner and more predictably than requests presented by email or voicemail, users will rapidly acquire new habits. After the first few weeks, you can add contests with rewards and recognition for the users with the best data, the most frequent logins, and the most complete `opportunity` records. Make these contests and incentives as relevant to the business objective as possible—awards for meaningless metrics are about as lame as the ones for "tidiest office cube" or "most recycled coffee cups."

The last bunch of carrots comprises the ones that are intrinsic to system usage: by doing things through the system, the user saves time or streamlines an onerous task. These carrots take the form of `workflows`, `alerts`, or business process aids in SFDC. This bunch of carrots becomes more important as the system becomes more functionally complete and has workflows, integrations, and data that make it *the* optimal way to do a task.

Identifying and Dealing with Adoption Problems

Adoption of the SFDC system is so critical that it needs to be measured and managed during the first several quarters of the system's life. Some adoption problems arise because of technical issues, or lack of time for training, or organizational stresses unrelated to SFDC. These issues aren't a major worry. Instead, you need to be on the lookout for adoption problems that are caused by interorganizational politics and systemic people issues, as they really stymie overall success.

Active Versus Passive Resistance

Overcoming active, overt user resistance is relatively straightforward. These critics self-announce their objections, and they will make overt arguments.

Things are a little more difficult with passive resistance, because it's more difficult to identify the individuals who are dragging their heels on SFDC adoption and pinpoint their issues. The first way to identify problem organizations is to hook into your company's rumor mill. If your company has administrative assistants, start there. Also talk with worker bees in the order operations or sales administration area. You're trying to find out both what the issues are and who is raising them.

If you hear an issue that's just plain wrong, you need to publicize the correct information quickly. Putting "the right answer" up on the wiki is not enough. Outreach strategies—at least an email plus an internal podcast—are essential to overcoming the subterranean grumblers.

When the issue isn't completely erroneous, you need to highlight the good things that will be coming to users of the SFDC system. The passive resisters will be much more likely to listen to heroes, mavens, and technogeeks, so make sure there's a constant stream of emails and hallway conversations from these informal sources.

Dealing with Luddites

Luddites are people who just don't want to participate at all. They want to keep all their sales information on paper, trusting a daytimer more than a laptop. They also tend to hide information from everyone[17] and may be quite worried about being micromanaged. They

---

17. Their customers, their subordinates, and, most of all, their bosses.

WHAT WE'VE GOT HERE IS A FAILURE TO COMMUNICATE

In many cases, the root of active or passive resistance is hard to find because people don't *want* to communicate about the real issue. They'll invent a never-ending series of problems to slow things down, looking for ways to undermine progress.

Many of the objections will be smoke bombs that are set off to misdirect attention. If totally false arguments are being raised, you can deal with those issues head on. But as soon as you get rid of one objection, another will be raised because the emotional energy—the *real* reason for the objection—hasn't been dealt with. Try to figure out what the real issue is and why the nay-sayer doesn't want to talk about it. The underlying worries typically focus on the following issues:

- SFDC will cause too much change (having to learn new complexity; having to change the way the job is done; losing one's job to automation).
- SFDC means being monitored closely (overmeasured, micromanaged).
- SFDC means being exposed (making errors; shown as being incompetent, useless, or boring).
- SFDC means extra work, with no real payoff.
- SFDC will make the critic's part of the organization look bad or unprofitable . . . because it *is*.
- SFDC will make it harder to get the real job done.
- SFDC represents a step backward in functionality or integration (particularly when it is replacing a system that was highly customized to the needs of a few pet organizations).
- SFDC represents a significant new learning curve, particularly for people who need to write, modify, and interpret reports.

Most of these issues will be temporary, so you can counteract them with discussions about future enhancements and temporary work-arounds. Sometimes, just talking through the issue dissipates a lot of its power. You may not be able to do anything about these troublemakers directly, but at least you can talk with their managers so they can work on the negative individuals offline.

can view the tiniest request for data entry with outright hatred, and they seem to enjoy getting the entire sales team riled up as a mob to oppose something that actually is there to *help* them. These guys (and it usually is the male of the species) eat nails for breakfast, listen to talk radio, and make their living by emotional persuasion and dogged negotiation. They can be tough.

But at least they're easy to identify: even if they're not openly vocal, you can spot Luddites as the people who never log in to the system. SFDC has a couple of simple ways to report on users' login history, and the telltale sign of a Luddite is two or fewer logins per month.

The cardinal rule of sales management is, "If you're making your numbers, you're golden." So don't try to force the issue with a successful Luddite. But the moment he *doesn't* make quota, bring the situation to the attention of the Luddite's boss and make sure SFDC usage is part of the rep's "plan."

Aside from using sticks, the only real solution to this problem is for Luddites to become aware of what a real SFA system can do for them. If they can see the results in their pocketbooks, very little conversation will be required.

Indoctrination

Indoctrination isn't training. Training—we covered that in Chapter 4.

Indoctrination is about religious fervor and application of best practices. Chapters 9 through 13 provide dozens of recommendations about best practices, but many of them involve—surprise!—some extra work. So it's important that users be indoctrinated about *why* they need to take on these new and different ways of doing their job.

The easiest indoctrination comes from memories of pain. Associate best practices with ways to avoid repetition of painful grunt-work experiences in previous systems. This approach can quickly galvanize worker bees in marketing, order operations, and even telesales as they scurry to avoid revisiting a painful past. Even at the executive level, an embarrassment in front of the board or an investor's meeting can be a powerful motivator.

The toughest people to indoctrinate are the individual sales reps. They aren't personally exposed to the negatives of "worst practices"—the after effects are somebody else's problem (and the "somebody else" isn't their boss). The only way to inspire religious fervor in these workers is for them to see results: faster, bigger sales that mean commission checks and membership in the President's Club. The only thing that will really get them going is hero stories from other sales reps. The internal email chatter about bigger commission checks is the ultimate motivator.

The Politics of Restriction

SFDC is a very powerful system. If it is integrated effectively with other systems, it can give users access to virtually any customer or product information within seconds. For this reason, its use must be properly restricted, to keep users from seeing or modifying things that must be controlled for legal and financial reasons. If the users aren't very sophisticated, they typically don't know what they're missing and won't notice the restrictions that have been properly put in place.

Oddly enough, the more sophisticated the user, the more you may need to restrict his or her freedom. Power users will know what they're missing, and they are likely to object to limits on their behavior in a fairly vocal manner. They will try to convince their bosses they need administrative privileges, or should have access to records that are outside of their purview.

As discussed in Chapter 5, it is important to keep the number of SFDC administrators to a bare minimum (typically three people). When obstreperous users ask for this level of access, the conversation quickly degenerates. Your best weapon is the CFO, who wants to keep things controlled and has solid, specific business reasons why access must be regulated. Your second best weapon is the corporate attorney, who will be able to invent dozens of reasons why the user access should be limited. I just knew attorneys were good for something.

CHAPTER 7

Products You Will Need

*If you have built castles in the air, your work need
not be lost; that is where they should be. Now put
the foundations under them.*

—Henry David Thoreau

T HIS CHAPTER IS FOR decision makers and project managers, who need to know
about the third-party tools and products that can really help with an SFDC
implementation. While specific products won't be reviewed here, the categories of
important products (and their selection criteria) will be discussed in depth.

SFDC Is a Platform, Not Just a Product

As mentioned in Chapter 1, SFDC is a fine SFA system out of the box—but its real advantage
is the platform that allows it to be easily extended from the boundaries of SFA to CRM and
beyond. Three core applications are delivered in SFDC's Enterprise edition:

- Sales and Telesales
- Marketing Automation
- Customer Support

The range of functionality you need may actually go far beyond these essentials, as
shown in Figure 1-3. SFDC's Force.com AppExchange currently has more than 800 plugins
that provide feature-level improvements ("point functionality") as well as full applications
(functional extensions). For example, the applications and templates listed on the next page
are available—mostly for free—in the AppExchange.[1]

---

1. I've organized these plugins in a different way than the way SFDC does it in the AppExchange, to make it easier
   to spot relevant applications.

- **Education/Training:** Recruiting/Admissions, Enrollment, Administration, Student Scheduling, Digital Media Management, School Management

- **Finance:** VC Deal Tracking, M&A Tracking, Asset Management, Banking/Capital Markets, Insurance, Mortgage, Accounting Packages, Expense Tracking, Fleet Management, Sarbanes-Oxley Compliance

- **Government:** Local Government Permits, Code Enforcement, Law Enforcement, Mass Transit, Grants Management

- **Human Resources:** Payroll, Recruiting, Vacation Tracking

- **Manufacturing:** Semiconductor CRM, Textile CRM, Warehouse Management, Service/Call Center Management, TPM, Configuration Management, Inventory Management

- **Marketing:** Lead Generation, Lead Cultivation, Email Blasting, Marketing Automation, Document/Content Management, PR/Analyst Relations, CPG Marketing, Product Management, Conference/Speaker/Event Management, Surveys, Web Site Integration, Landing-Page Generation, Social Networking, Deduping/Data Cleansing, Search Marketing, Report Engines, Marketing Analytics

- **Medical:** Clinic Management, Treatment Monitor, Physicians' CRM, Pharmaceutical CRM

- **Media:** Advertising Management, Google AdWords Management

- **Nonprofits:** Fundraising, Volunteer Management, Donation/Grant Management, Program Management, Political Campaign Management

- **Professional Services:** Time Tracking, Project Management, PSA, Recruiting

- **Real Estate:** Real Estate Broker Management, Property Management, Portfolio Management, Mortgage Origination, Hospitality Property Scheduling

- **Sales Management:** Sales Rep Productivity/Scorecards, Forecasting, Sales Methodology Enablement/Enforcement, Account Profiling/Enrichment, Incentive/Commission Management, Mobile Sales/Field Force Tools, eCommerce, Channel Management, Program Management, Quote, Order, and Contract Management, Web Conferencing, Sales Operations, Telesales Scripting, Sales Analytics

- **Service and Support:** Agent Productivity, Community Management, eLearning, Field Service, Mobile Enablement, Help Desk/Knowledge Base Management, Quality Assurance, Surveys

- **Software:** Bug Tracking, Agile Tools, Developer Tools, Integration Tools

- **System Administration:** Integration, Data Cleansing, Mashups, Issue Management, Change Control, Project Management, Systems Development, Single Sign On, Security Management, Knowledge Bases, Forums, Telephony Integration, Developer Tools

The majority of the AppExchange packages are free, so there is an embarrassment of riches here.[2] Here's the irony: most SFDC customers don't use more than a handful of these add-ons, and many use no extensions at all. This means that neither the customers nor the authors of these plugins are benefiting as much as they could.

Don't Overdo It

Even though hundreds of plugins are available, you should go easy on the add-ons, for a number of business reasons, human factors, and technical reasons. *Initially, deploy fewer than five plugins. Even as the system grows, try to keep the number to fewer than a dozen or so.*

The first issue is business value: do not add things to SFDC that don't add obvious business value. This book is full of warnings and advice about removing unnecessary complexity, and add-ons may undo the streamlining you achieved elsewhere. Add-ons typically put more items on the screen—tabs, reports, fields, buttons—which can lead to confusion and clutter. Also, most add-ons are unsupported, so you'll have to figure out how to use many of them and train your users. Of course, if the add-on stops working the way you expected, there may be no recourse with an unsupported application other than to uninstall the plugin. In the end, the free plugin may cost you more than the value it brings.

The second issue is complexity and uncertainty. Although every plugin goes through an architectural review and unit testing, there is no process that tests for all possible interactions among all the plugins. With 800 of them available, there are more than 10^{725} different combinations possible. Even though these plugins are generally of high quality and have little potential for harm, understanding the interactions among the software features—even when they work as intended—can make for a delightful learning experience. Having a lot of plugins means more moving parts, which means bugs.

The third issue is dependency and the data "roach-motel"[3] effect: once you start using the plugins, they will typically store some extra data in SFDC `custom fields` or `objects`. If you stop using the plugins, the special data they stored may be nearly inaccessible or useless to you, even though that information is safely in the system. If you want to uninstall a plugin, the system may ask, "What do you want to do with the data?"—and there may not be a good answer other than exporting it to a spreadsheet. If the data aren't worth dumping into a spreadsheet, you might want to question why you used the plugin in the first place.

The fourth issue is system limits on the number of `custom objects`, `tabs`, and `applications`. Even in SFDC's Unlimited edition there are limits, and large organizations will bump into limits in the Enterprise edition if they install too many add-ons.

---

2. Look for add-ons created by Salesforce Labs—they're all free, and they have solved some real customer problems.
3. Also known as the Hotel California effect: you can check in anytime you want, but you can never leave.

Finally, there's the issue of timing. In Chapters 1 and 4, I admonished you to take advantage of featurettes to obtain quick wins and to motivate users. These are important tricks, but you want to use them in a *timed sequence* for maximal effect. Even if you know of 10 plugins that your users will love, don't install them wantonly: dole the new features out gradually, on an as-needed basis to overcome user agitation, impatience, or frustration.

First, Seek to Understand

It's important to understand plugins before you use them, because the range of software in the AppExchange is remarkable. Some of the plugins consist of five lines of scripting that present no danger to your data or users. Others are huge hosted software applications that cost a bundle and can rock your world if used incorrectly. You should understand several aspects of add-ons before you start evaluating and using them.

Differences Between Add-On Technologies

SFDC has gone out of its way to make its system easy to extend with very different technical approaches. The solid platform and rich API explains why so many add-ons have been created in such a short time (none of SFDC's competitors comes even close on this front).

The smallest and lightest-weight add-ons are called native plugins, because they do their magic entirely within the Salesforce application. All the buttons, tabs, and interactions feel as if they're seamlessly part of SFDC because, well, they are. In some cases, native plugins don't even contain any code: they're just configurations of objects, fields, and reports that provide useful new functionality. If you're curious, you can look under the covers to see how these plugins work, and create additions and extensions to them to suit your specific needs. You can also modify things like formulas, thresholds, and workflows of the add-ons (although you'd better know what you're doing on that front). Native plugins are always installed from packages that are stored in public or private areas of the AppExchange. They can be installed or uninstalled in a matter of minutes, particularly if they don't store any special data. Many of the freebies in the AppExchange are native plugins, and these items are what you'll be using for most of featurettes.

SFDC recently added the ability to write APEX code that executes natively (entirely within your instance of SFDC) but provides low-level access to system and database functionality. APEX code allows for the creation of serious magic, in a high-performance and safe environment that is seamlessly part of the SFDC user experience.[4] You can create your own APEX code right in the system, but be aware that APEX is a development language, requiring skills similar to those used in Java programming, knowledge of databases, and expertise in object orientation. Developers will need to use Eclipse, and be ready to write test code along with the functionality they create (your code cannot be deployed until test coverage is better than

---

4. APEX functionality is available only in the Enterprise, Unlimited, and Developer editions of SFDC.

80%). APEX plugins can be quite small and easy to install (delivered in packages, just like other native applications), and a few of them are free in the AppExchange.

SFDC can work with external applications and services, and the AppExchange is full of examples of these add-on products. Although these products don't plug directly into SFDC, there is tight and secure interaction among them. The first type of external add-on product is one that runs on a user's (often, the SFDC administrator's) PC.[5] These add-ons are often geared toward data management functionality:

- Data exchange with Microsoft Word or Excel

- Bulk-data loading tools

- Data cleansing and deduping tools

- Data analysis tools

The second type of external add-on product runs on one of your servers (almost always the server run by an SFDC administrator). These add-ons are almost never free, and they are likely to provide high-value data-driven functionality:

- Report engines

- Data warehousing

- Data integration with other applications (such as accounting or ERP)

This last item requires some clear thinking when it comes to your internal security group, as these personnel need to understand exactly where the data flow to and from if they are to make the correct decisions about the plugin's implementation. If you have a data integration adaptor that runs on your server, and the adaptor connects SFDC (via HTTPS or SSL) directly to your internal application on the same server, your network security team ought to feel relatively good about the technical risk. The alternative approach will be discussed in just a bit.

The next type of add-on is a hosted service that runs on a third-party set of servers, but interacts with the SFDC screens in an interesting way. The external hosted service typically has a direct connection with SFDC (for things like Single Sign On and data transfer), and it always has some level of integration with the SFDC screen that runs in the user's browser. In the loosest integration, there's just a link or a button in an SFDC screen that starts up a new browser tab (or even a new instance of the browser). This level of integration is not very useful because users may have to reenter data or handle interactions that aren't natural or coherent with the way they work with the rest of SFDC. Such half-baked integration is often offered by vendors who are trying to worm their way into the SFDC customer base without investing much in technology or support. These add-ons may be valuable, but are not preferred.

---

5. Almost none of the external add-on products are available for Macintosh or Linux-based computers.

Another form of hosted service is fully integrated with SFDC's user interface, but provides functionality beyond what's possible in SFDC alone. The vendors that offer such plugins take one of two approaches: `S-controls` that make the add-on application behave in a coherent and natural way with the rest of SFDC, or deep integration using `custom objects`, APEX, and AJAX code. While achieving this level of integration takes more effort (i.e., more time to write) and will be a bit more expensive, it will pay off with lower training costs and happier, more productive users.

Business Models for Add-On Products

Given that SFDC now has more than 1 million users, it is not surprising that software vendors are looking for ways to leverage the AppExchange for their own growth. In the software business, getting customers in the "midmarket" (SMB/SME companies with revenues of $100 million to $1 billion or so) has always been a challenge, so the SFDC customer base is a hugely desirable target. Indeed, its size and composition have been the magnet that lures software vendors and systems integrators alike into the SFDC fold.

Why do you care about these machinations? First, you want to know how the vendor plans to charge you for its products and services. Pricing models are often obscure, and it's good to know exactly what the pricing scheme is before you commit yourself to a product. Second, you want to be able to spot the "flash in the pan" vendors that won't be around for long to support your product. If you depend on an add-on that is later orphaned, everybody loses.

The first business model to examine is open source. Although there are more than 150,000 open-source projects in the world, commercial open-source products are a fairly tricky area (you can read up on the issues in the article I wrote in Wikipedia[6]). An SFDC plugin that adheres to the open-source model is an almost unqualified good: the code is available for all users to see and modify as they see fit, so even if the sponsoring vendor abandons the effort, the plugin will live on and be maintainable. Open-source products are free by definition, but vendors frequently offer just a basic version as an open-source product, with the more feature-filled (and desirable) version being available only as standard, chargeable software. Read the product description carefully to determine whether you can live with just the open-source version's narrowly proscribed features.

Similar to open-source software is freeware or shareware—that is, software that doesn't carry any charge, but whose code is inaccessible to you. Freeware and shareware products are often created by individuals, and the risk for businesses that depend on them is that their creators will lose interest in maintaining or developing the products over time. Even if they are interested in moving the freeware product forward, they may be too busy doing their "day jobs" to effectively support users (it is, after all, a labor of love). Freeware and shareware are, therefore, a bit riskier than open-source products over the long term because

---

6. http://en.wikipedia.org/wiki/Commercial_open_source_applications

you never have access to the code. Of course, freeware and shareware strategies are often pursued by large, reliable vendors that give away a free version of a feature-stripped product, in the hopes of upselling users to more feature-rich, paid versions. These free plugins should be viewed as if they were commercial products, except that no support is available without the upgrade.

The AppExchange contains hundreds of examples of both open-source and freeware/shareware products. Virtually all of the plugins written by SFDC itself fall into this category. The plugins that my firm has published through the AppExchange[7] are this type. Of course, the commercial purpose of the AppExchange is to make it easy for small vendors to make money by charging for their products or services.

Vendors that have fully chargeable products in the AppExchange have to go through design reviews and compatibility testing, and they have to pay fees to SFDC for participating in this system. Consequently, they need a certain level of sales just to break even on the AppExchange investment. Some vendors also sell products that are *not* offered via the AppExchange, as a way of circumventing these fees. These products should be scrutinized very seriously, if not avoided altogether, because the AppExchange's compatibility and architectural reviews provide important protections for you, the customer.

Different Pricing Models in the AppExchange

As mentioned earlier, most of the add-ons found in the AppExchange are available for free. But you'll notice in the product description area a field for pricing—and in most cases, that information will tell you to contact the vendor's friendly sales rep.

SFDC customers are accustomed to a monthly per-seat fee, as part of a recurring revenue model where payments continue as long as the company uses the system. Many of the chargeable products in the AppExchange follow this same model, with a price that is typically less than $50 per month per user.

But some products don't deliver value to all users, and the benefit is really sensed only by a single person. For example, system administrator products are priced either based on the number of active system administrator licenses or as a single annual fee per site (irrespective of the number of users).

Other products deliver value to all users, but the value is sensed only when the product is being actively used. For example, email blasters, printing engines, proposal generators, and contract management systems may be priced on a per-usage basis, with the customer prepurchasing a block of usage "chits" for the year. Customers that go over their prepurchased block may be charged heavy premiums, creating an incentive for purchasing more usage units than the company actually needs (analogous to cell-phone usage plans).

---

7. Currently, Sales*Logistix* has published an administrative change control manager (ChangeControl) and a marketing lead-cleaning plugin (JunQue) designed to attract consulting customers.

A few products use a mixture of these pricing models, but the vendors try to keep matters as simple as possible to close sales more quickly. In evaluating alternative pricing, use a spreadsheet to keep all the details straight—but remember it's more important to have the product that really works for you, rather than a marginal version that saves a few bucks per month. Changing out add-on products such as email blasting or commission systems is an amazingly painful experience—and don't let the vendors' sales reps persuade you otherwise.

There aren't many "gotchas" in the AppExchange products, other than annual commitments and automatic renewals of contracts. Try to negotiate those provisions away—though unless you're a really big customer, you won't have too much luck. Make sure that you've thought through the storage implications of your add-ons: if a prodigious amount of data will be stored in SFDC records, SFDC surcharges can really pile up.

Calibrate the Level of Effort and Reward

Some plugins are trivial and involve virtually no risk or effort—and no real reward. Others require a substantial amount of cash and time to really pay off. For the really big stuff, a behavioral and business-process change will be required on your part. If your organization is not up to that task, you can rapidly disqualify several of the heavier-weight add-ons as possible extensions to your SFDC system.

Figure 7-1 shows an analysis (done by Salesforce.com) of add-on product categories for the sales and sales support functions. Although SFDC hasn't published corresponding analyses for marketing, support, or other business process areas, products in those domains lend themselves to similar kinds of categorization.

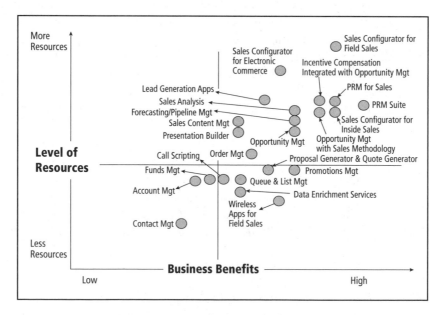

FIGURE 7-1   AppExchange product matrix *(Copyright ©2008 Salesforce.com, Inc. Used with permission.)*

Next, Weigh Your Options

With trivial plugins such as featurettes, there really isn't much thinking to do. You'll find two or maybe three plugins with roughly the same functionality: choose the one that offers the best mix of features and ease of use. With the weightier add-ons—such as data warehousing, marketing automation, commissions, accounting, or order management—you need to think a bit more deeply.

Integrate, Rather Than Extend

First think about whether the add-on functionality should be part of SFDC at all. Will it really kill you to have a second browser or application up on the user's screen? If the application is used only by a small percentage of the user base (and for the heavy-weight plugins, that's usually the way it works out), why burden all the users with another SFDC tab and set of features to ignore? Even though most of the unusual stuff can be hidden from the user base with `page layouts` and hidden `tabs`, each substantial add-on will make for some added complexity somewhere.

Using the two-window approach can actually have benefits, particularly if the other application has busy periods that make its response time unpredictable. Some third-party applications may even freeze the browser under some conditions, so having a separate window means the user can be productive with SFDC even if the other app is "busied out." Further, not every user of the external application will need to use SFDC, so you can avoid adding some SFDC user licenses if you take the two-window approach.

Of course, even though you'll have two "systems," you'll need to have a *single-system view* of the data they operate on. In this scenario, you would almost certainly need to have two-way integration of the underlying data even though the user interfaces of SFDC and the other system remain separate entities. This integration cost can be substantial—perhaps even higher than the cost of using the SFDC add-on. Using the two-window approach requires some careful thinking about how users need to interact with the systems, so don't skimp on that analysis.

Here are the alternatives for integration, in order of increasing risk:

- Read-only "pop-up" window[8]
- Read-write "pop-up" window"
- Read-only, with batch file import
- Read-only, with batch file import and export
- Read-only, with continuous one-way data flow
- Read-only, with continuous two-way data flows

---

8. This window may be a browser pop-up, or it may be implemented as an SFDC `tab` or an S-control mashup.

- Read-write, with continuous one-way data flow

- Read-write, with continuous two-way data flows

- Real-time replication/synchronization of fields

Of course, integration brings some important architectural issues to the fore:

- **Depth of integration:** Does the user really need real-time, two-way synchronization of records? Much of the time, read-only integration or periodic update is all that's actually needed. The risks and costs go up dramatically with deeper integration.

- **Tightness of integration:** Does the user need to have continuous access to the external system data, with transaction locking? This is rarely a hard requirement, and inexpensive work-arounds (such as logging in to an external system via a pop-up window) may be feasible. Tight integration must take into account timeouts (usually caused by a noisy network rather than SFDC), planned SFDC downtime (typically a couple of hours twice per business quarter), and incompatibility windows (caused by patches to external systems that have unintended consequences). You may need to use a message-buffer architecture to queue up transactions during the downtime intervals; this architecture can make debugging and audit-trail logs much easier, so it is recommended for all large SFDC installations.

- **Federating the system of record:** If systems are integrated, what is the system of record for each object? In many cases, the system of record needs to be identified at the field level, as SFDC will be the authoritative source for parts of an object, whereas the accounting system may be a more authoritative source for other parts.

Integration is a nearly universal requirement in sophisticated SFDC systems, but it's not well understood. With off-the-shelf packages (such as accounting software), you should be using an *off-the-shelf integration adaptor*. There are two main types: (1) software modules or integration appliances that run inside your own server complex (connecting directly to SFDC via SSL and SOAP), and (2) hosted services that connect to SFDC in "the cloud" and the third-party applications via SSL and SOAP. Each of these approaches has advantages, but the good news is that integration adaptors for SFDC are less expensive than the services offered by the Enterprise Application Integration (EAI) vendors of the last century. Expect to see the hosted-integration model become more popular over time.

Carefully evaluate the adaptors for three things: security, freedom from duplicate creation,[9] and complexity of required external integration code. Do *not* believe vendor

---

9. By its very nature, application integration without the right design can cause the prodigious creation of spurious or duplicate records (particularly accounts, opportunities, and quotes, but also contracts, contacts, and assets).

claims on any of these decision points without verifying them: talk with references, and test the behavior of the adaptors in a pilot project.

INTEGRATION TODAY, INTEGRATION TOMORROW, INTEGRATION FOREVER

The alternative to migrating data from external systems is to leave the data in place and use data integration to access and update the required records. Indeed, in many cases this is the only viable approach.

SFDC's APIs, workflow, outbound messaging, and APEX capabilities support very flexible integration strategies for outside systems, including closed-loop and real-time integration. With the addition of third-party integration adaptors, SFDC can be integrated with almost anything.

The business benefits of integration can be astounding. Integration is what lets an SFDC user look at inventories, available-to-promise dates, and payment history. It forms the backbone of business process automation, and it enables your company to streamline operations and improve compliance. It's where the 360-degree view of the customer comes from.

Unfortunately, integration is not without its costs. If the system being targeted for integration is old or poorly documented, the SFDC team will spend a surprising number of hours just learning how the data behave and which types of integration are possible. You may have to develop code within both the SFDC system and the external system. And, of course, anything you develop must be documented, tested, internationalized, and maintained over time. **In most SFA/CRM systems, integration is second only to data cleansing in terms of its overall cost and schedule impact.**

Finally, AppExchange tools and language libraries let you develop your own code to perform the lowest level of system integration. This strategy provides the highest degree of control and flexibility, but it requires serious in-house development skills and should be considered only if you're trying to integrate an existing home-brew application (such as order operations) with SFDC.

Build—Don't Buy—Your Add-Ons

If you have specialized needs—driven either by your organization's business model, corporate structure, regulations, or other reasons—none of the off-the-shelf plugins may really pass muster. SFDC's technology platform is robust, well documented, and rich enough to build almost any business application either natively or with some outboard code running on your company's servers. If you have a strong IT department or a specialist integrator who really understands the guts of SFDC, this approach can get you exactly the functionality you need with no unnecessary clutter or complexity.

Of course, with this approach comes engineering costs, both now and in the future. Its effectiveness depends on how savvy the software development at your company is. For example, companies such as Google, Microsoft, and Sun virtually forbid the purchase of software from the outside. If your company's technology culture belongs to the DIY or Only Best-of-Breed camp, building your own plugin is a sound choice.

THE COSTS OF BUILDING IT YOURSELF

There's nothing like a home-brew application to get you exactly the features you want. Good implementers can make features that are easy to use, fast, and exactly fitted to your business environment.

Developing something initially may also be cheaper than buying, at least in the short term. But the long-term costs can bring some big surprises in the following areas:

- Testing
- Internationalization and local-language support
- Performance tuning
- Documentation
- Self-support (Some vendors will no longer support the "main system" if your add-on is running.)
- Upgrading and retesting with each change of the main system. (Even if your organization's needs don't evolve, the technological changes can still require rework of your code.)

Take this route with your eyes open!

Before you commit resources to building in-house software products, check the SFDC product roadmap and SFDC's *Ideas* area to make sure that you aren't working on an area in which SFDC itself will implement a solution. Even if you built a highly tailored, fully customized application, it would be really frustrating (and expensive) to deploy your own nonstandard version of a feature, only to find it in the standard platform three months later.

If you do pursue in-house development of SFDC add-ons, in your prototyping stage (you should be following the Agile development style described in Chapter 4), use the free applications in the AppExchange as starting points for storyboards and UI examples. After all, there's no point in reinventing the wheel entirely.

If you are going to build functionality, make sure to use a language that has solid libraries supporting the SSL, XML, and SOAP protocols. No matter which language you use, you will almost certainly use the Eclipse developer toolset. The free SFDC plugin to `Eclipse` makes code deployment a snap, and facilitates import and export of metadata and setup configurations.

To develop functionality that actually runs on SFDC's servers, you'll use the `VisualForce`, APEX, JavaScript, and CSS languages. For functionality to run on your own servers, most developers use PERL, PHP, Python, Visual Basic, Ruby, or another scripting language. For the more adventurous, it's C# or Java. While every vendor will claim that its products are fully compatible with SFDC, the ease of working with Web service protocols varies widely. Further, even Web-savvy technologies can run into trouble with international character sets, network timeouts, and other error conditions. For the latest information, have your developers check out the DeveloperForce (www.salesforce.com/developer) bulletin boards and SFDC user groups.

Use AppExchange Add-Ons

Using AppExchange add-ons is the path that most companies take, and in many instances it's the only sensible option. Because of the user training and technical implications of add-ons, we recommend that the SFDC system be brought online with only one or two of them enabled, and that subsequent add-ons be introduced incrementally (as part of waves).

To counteract the testing and compatibility risks, we recommend that system administrators who want to try new add-ons do so only in their `sandbox` area. With this approach, normal system operations will not be affected by errors related to the add-on products.

Essential Toys: Featurettes

The featurettes mentioned in Chapters 4 and 6 are an important mechanism for wooing users to adopt the system. Several valuable but simple additions to the system don't even rate as plugins in the AppExchange: they're just special links, `formulas`, `rules`, `S-controls`, and mashups that do cute little things that are valuable to users. For example:

- A button on the `lead` or `contact` pages that automatically dials the phone number on the page, via Skype

- Maps showing the location of a `contact`, `lead`, or `account`, along with local restaurants in the area

- Data `validation` `rules` that trap bad entries before the record is saved

- An organizational-chart drawing tool that creates a graphic from the `accounts` and `contacts` in the system, at the click of a button

- A report link that creates a `campaign` `members` report for each campaign

- Maps that show all your customers and `leads` in a city

These tiny features do not count in the recommended number of plugins because almost all of them are just clever uses of HTML that don't consume constrained SFDC resources.

WHERE DOES ALL THIS FREE STUFF COME FROM?

If you look in the AppExchange, you'll discover an amazing array of free stuff. More than half of the modules you can download are available for free, and most of them were written by SFDC engineers.

Of course, because almost all of the free stuff is completely unsupported, you might wonder about the quality and origins of the add-ons. Most of the free stuff that isn't from SFDC comes from companies like mine, which are in business to deliver products and services to the SFDC user base. Companies that put modules in the AppExchange worry about their reputations, so they will not risk putting junk out there. If they did, user ratings of the product would rapidly demote garbage products to near-oblivion.

Further, all the products added to the AppExchange over the last couple of years have been required to go through a formal review of their security and architecture, and an informal review of their usefulness.

In contrast, lots of goodies available in the developer forums have not undergone any type of review whatsoever. Although I've never seen any malicious or risky code posted, there's no explicit mechanism to stop it—so be a little more wary of these unofficial goodies.

Fortunately, developers rarely post junk in any forum, and when they do community dynamics (peer reviews) rapidly push the garbage and the contributor to the sidelines. The bottom line is there's not much risk of truly bad things happening with this freeware. If you want to be extra careful, just don't use any `S-controls` or `APEX` code without thorough code reviews and `sandbox` testing.

The best way to find out about these things is to go to SFDC's developer blog and discussion boards, searching for features you might like (sometimes, it's more effective to just Google "Salesforce <feature>"). Joining your local SFDC user group can unearth a wealth of current information on these tricks. You'll also find a list of our favorites on this book's Web site, www.SFDC-secrets.com, and we encourage readers to make additions and comments to that list of goodies.

Some featurettes have real power, and should be introduced into your SFDC instance as users start to push against the edges of the system:

- Connectors to Microsoft Outlook or IBM Notes mail client, to synchronize emails, contacts, and calendar entries

- Connectors to Microsoft Office to facilitate mail merges, spreadsheet updates, and other Office–SFDC data interchange

- Google Applications, which fosters easy collaboration with employees and interaction with customers

- Business Object's SFDC Widgets, which provide a nice task manager and new-lead alert system even when you're not logged in to your browser (über-Web 2.0)

- Appirio's CRM dashboards, which are able to push SFDC dashboards to iGoogle, so people without SFDC licenses can see the highlights of your business activity (a great way to wow execs, but don't let them show these toys to the board of directors)[10]

A large number of AppExchange plugins add nice little features to the system. As there are too many to mention here, the fastest way to find these add-ons is to go to the AppExchange, look in the left-hand navigation area for your domain (say, "Marketing"), and then look in the subcategory "Free Components."

Essential System Administrator Tools

Because system administrators have to try out and install every add-on that will ever be put into their systems, we thought it fitting to talk about the tools they'll need for themselves.

Most of the administrator's tools will consist of desktop applications that run outside of SFDC, but communicate with the database via SOAP. Probably the first tools they'll need will facilitate data import, export, and maintenance. SFDC's `Data loader` is a free plugin that allows (relatively) high-speed data loads and dumps, with solid features and a good user interface. It also has a command-line interface that supports batch mode operations. Unfortunately, `Data loader` doesn't work on any edition lower than the Enterprise version. In that case, you may have to use the slower and clumsier `Excel connector` (which is also free). Watch out, because the `Excel connector` comes in two (incompatible) versions: one for the SFDC Professional edition and the other for the Enterprise edition. Although the `Excel connector` has some nice behaviors (particularly when you're just learning about the system), Enterprise and Unlimited edition administrators will rapidly move to the `Data loader` for its speed and reliability.

Informatica has released a free data loader *service* that goes far beyond the capabilities of SFDC's desktop `Data loader` tool. This service can connect SFDC to Excel and popular relational databases, has some very fancy functions and filters, and supports scheduled and repetitive uploads or downloads of data. If you are serious about integration or setting up a data warehouse around SFDC's data, this freebie is definitely for you.

Another helpful tool for learning about the SFDC system is the APEX Explorer, which easily browses the SFDC object model, showing object relationships and metadata.

---

10. To do so is to instantly expose the business to an unpleasant level of scrutiny, particularly when the sales people aren't making their numbers.

Finally, administrators with a developer bent will want to download Eclipse and install SFDC's plugin to that development environment. Although Eclipse is a fairly complex application, it has tools and features that the more sophisticated administrator won't want to live without.

A bunch of other free plugins for administrative housekeeping can be found in the AppExchange's application category "Components" and subcategory "Admin Tools." For example, ChangeControl, CronKit, PingAudit's Security Dashboard, Print Anything, and the User Adoption dashboard are plugins that my firm uses all the time.

But with real value will come real pricing. The SFDC administrator should expect to budget some money for more comprehensive tools:

- **Deduping tools.** Duplicate `accounts`, `contacts`, and particularly `leads` are a significant issue from the first day of real system usage. If you're migrating data from other systems, you'll need tools to handle the potential for duplicates even before you bring the system up. You'll need tools (or hosted services) that dedupe data in place, data imports, and data coming from Web site registration pages (via replacement for SFDC's standard `web2lead` feature). The best tools will let you dedupe `leads` against `contacts`, as well as `leads-leads`, `contacts-contacts`, and `accounts-accounts`. The tools should provide a range of matching fields and algorithms, including "fuzzy" matches and character reversals. The most advanced tools will include phonetic matches or spell-check algorithms to find the tricky "almost dupes" (think "Cold Jim" versus "Gold's Gym"). Using these tools is something of an art form, so make sure to check out the discussion of their use in Chapter 13.

- **Data cleansing/quality/enrichment.** A hosted service typically goes through the SFDC `leads`, `contacts`, and `accounts` to improve data quality or enrich it with more fields. These services can correct phone numbers, fix addresses, and add parametric data about people (e.g., title) and companies (e.g., D-U-N-S number) that can be derived from public sources or proprietary databases. Several of these services are good at populating and enriching `account` data, but only a few of them are very good at improving the data for individuals below the vice president level. The best services use data derived from both proprietary and public sources (specifically, the Web), but the services rarely enrich data associated with people who have only a commodity email address (such as an MSN or Gmail address). Use of these services should be coordinated closely with the Marketing department, so skim Chapter 10 for a discussion of this topic. Data cleansing and enrichment tools can be expensive, but you must weigh their cost against how much has been spent to collect and maintain the data up to now. Worthwhile data are always more expensive than the system that stores those data.

- **Documents and content management.** SFDC provides a gigabyte of storage with every account, and this quota grows by 120MB[11] with each additional user for whom a license is purchased. While this amount of storage is more than sufficient for the underlying data in most SFDC instances, the use of attached documents can quickly consume all of this space. SFDC's additional storage is relatively expensive, so customers often look for alternatives to storing documents in SFDC. A number of alternative approaches exist (including writing your own plugin), but the key comparison point must always be "Will the users like it?" Ease of use—and particularly the addition of documents via drag and drop—is the number one issue. It's important to ensure that the documents stored externally to SFDC can be "seen" by any user, whether that user is working in the office or on the road. Do some real-world testing before you implement your document/attachment solution in SFDC, as each approach may involve storing the documents in different ways from how you do things now. In addition, check with your company's network security group to make sure they're comfortable with the technology before you buy it. Note that attached documents are *never* searchable by SFDC, so consider setting up a search engine on any file system where you store documents.

- **Draggin' Role.** This free AppExchange tool helps with one of the system administrator's major chores—namely, reorganizing the user `roles` and `forecast hierarchies`. Instead of multiple clicks per user move, the Draggin' Role tool supports the drag-and-drop of users into relevant `roles`. Although this plugin may save you only a few minutes of work each month, you'll thank me for this tip.

- **Calendar Sync.** This free AppExchange plugin does a nice job of synching SFDC's calendar with Outlook. Of course, the Outlook connector does this, too, but it's nowhere near as elegant.

- **Sandbox.** This SFDC product is one of the most useful tools for administrators and developers, as it provides a safe haven for testing integration adaptors, code, business processes, and third-party products. While the `sandbox` may seem expensive, it will save your life (and your weekends). Most customers purchase a single complete sandbox (which can be filled with all of their system's data) and an APEX-only sandbox that holds their schemas, customizations, and code. Very large customers may need a second complete `sandbox` for very intricate integration projects. These additional applications are typically needed only for a few months, so don't buy one until you know it's absolutely necessary.

---

11. This figure is for the Unlimited edition of SFDC. For the Enterprise and Professional editions, the figure is 20MB per additional user.

Finally, if the company purchases an add-on product or decides to integrate its SFDC system with an external application, the system administrator will need to investigate additional tools for managing these other applications. Almost certainly, those administrative tools will *not* be listed in the AppExchange. You'll need to Google the application name, and with luck you will find at least some postings in online forums from your compatriots. Unfortunately, outside of the AppExchange, the information won't be well organized.

HOW GOOD ARE THE VENDORS?

If you're buying—and relying on—products from the AppExchange, you want to make sure that the vendor will be around for a while. As all the strategic AppExchange products are real products—not freebies—you'll need to have a way of comparing vendors as well as products.

Here are some factors to consider beyond the product attributes (features, ease of use, ease of administration, scalability/performance, quality, and price) when considering a purchase:

- How long has the vendor been offering products in the AppExchange?
- How many customers are using the vendor's AppExchange products?
- What portion of the vendor's business comes from the AppExchange?
- Is the vendor's AppExchange product certified?
- Does the vendor have solid customer references from the AppExchange user base?

While none of these issues should, by itself, be the tipping point, all of them are indicators of vendor commitment and viability in the AppExchange. Approximately 30% of your evaluation should focus on the vendor situation and 70% on the product attributes. Put simply, if the vendor is in the market for the long haul, its product is more likely to be of long-term value to you.

Essential Add-Ons for the Marketer

Even though the Marketing department will not have the most users on the SFDC system, and those personnel will not necessarily be part of the first wave of system users, the marketing folks are going to be interacting with larger amounts of data and more intense operations than any other department.[12] For many marketing departments, SFDC is the only

---

12. If your company's IT department isn't deeply involved in SFDC, the marketing team will need to take responsibility for the "tools for the system administrator" outlined earlier.

marketing automation system they really have. So let's look at the elements that nearly every marketing department will need:

- **Deduping tools.** Duplicate `leads` are a significant issue from the first day of real system usage, and few problems will drive sales personnel crazy faster. Every time you do a `lead` import, there's a chance to create yet another almost-identical copy of a `lead` or `contact`. Read the material on deduping tools for system administrators found earlier in this chapter. Also, check out Chapter 10 for a discussion of using `campaigns` and `activities` to really solve the problem of automatically created duplicates.

- **Email blasters.** Whether it is doing mass emailings or vertical "drip marketing" campaigns, almost any marketing team will need a real email blasting service. Using Outlook or Salesforce for these purposes is just wrong for any serious organization. Probably 10 email blasters and marketing automation tools (both within and outside of the AppExchange) claim to be compatible with SFDC, but there are some interesting differences between them. The key comparison point is *not* the per-email price, because the big differences in price tags result from annual fees and consulting/configuration projects. The products with enormous fees have features that justify their purchase by the target customer—but *you* need to figure out whether *your* needs really match their offerings. The products that cost a lot have so many features that it is quite complex to set up and use them, so don't buy a bigger product than your staff is prepared to manage.[13] Assess the product based on three key points of comparison: (1) how well the email functions and statistics can be integrated with SFDC `campaigns`, (2) how realistic and flexible the `lead` scoring and internal nurturing algorithms are, and (3) how well the email blaster's model of campaigns matches with what your company actually does. One product, for example, keeps `campaign` data private so that one marketer cannot see another's campaigns. While that may make sense for some marketing organizations, for others it's impractical. Many of the products aren't tightly integrated with SFDC, so requirements such as keeping opt-out lists fully synchronized are a pain. Do not buy any email blaster until you've gone through a real-world trial for a couple of weeks; many vendors will make you pay for that trial, but this will be money well spent.

- **Bounced Email Handler.** Even if you use an external system for email blasts, some of the emails your company sends will come from SFDC. The problem is, whenever a bounce occurs (due to a bad address or other causes), the warning mails will all come back to the person who (supposedly) sent the mail. Nothing spoils your morning coffee like 350 "DSN Warning . . ." emails filling up your inbox. The Bounced

---

13. The industrial-strength products may require half of a full-time employee, if the company is doing several blasts per week.

Email Handler—a free AppExchange plugin—helps you automatically divert bounces of any kind into a special Outlook mail folder.

- **Campaigns.** For almost any business-to-business (B2B) company, SFDC's campaigns module is a must. Even though it's free in the Enterprise and Unlimited editions, this feature isn't used often enough and is the root cause of much lead and contact duplication. Even if you have to pay extra for it, the campaigns module is a must.

- **Google campaigns.** Google AdWords has become the most relevant form of advertising for most B2B firms and some business-to-consumer (B2C) companies. Salesforce for Google Adwords allows coherent management of AdWords campaigns from within Salesforce, improving the visibility and measurability of keywords and ad performance. If you are spending more than a few hundred dollars per month on AdWords, the management challenge for the ads and campaigns warrants using SFDC's module.

- **eCommerce/payments clearing.** For any B2C company and most B2B companies with a multichannel strategy, an eCommerce system is a must-have addition to the firm's Web site. Although several simple, inexpensive services are available for shopping carts and payments processing (e.g., Yahoo, Amazon, or eBay stores; Google checkout), none of their vendors appears to have created an SFDC integration product or plugin. More heavy-duty solutions (such as Digital River's Element5 store or Vindicia's Cashbox billing system) also had not created an integration or plugin as of spring 2009, although Zuora does have a billing and payments processing system integrated with SFDC. This essential element is not available in an off-the-shelf version, however, so hiring a system integrator with XML, SOAP, and SFDC expertise will be necessary to handle the necessary custom integration.

- **Public relations/analyst relations.** If your firm has a PR function, SFDC can be configured to handle reporters and analysts as "customers" of PR "campaigns." The PR/Analyst Relations module is free, but it is really useful only if the company's PR people reside in several locations (e.g., employees in different countries or an internal PR person who works with an outside agency). If you install this module, you'll need to implement some very tight naming conventions for campaigns, accounts, contact types, and a few other fields. But you can't beat the price (nothing!), and this plugin is certainly a more effective collaboration tool than emailing an Excel spreadsheet in a round-robin fashion.

- **Reporting and analytics engines.** In most organizations, the finance and marketing personnel are the ultimate number crunchers. SFDC includes a powerful, yet simple reporting engine, but the multidimensional data analyst will quickly run out of gas. SFDC reports and dashboards can now be scheduled to run regularly, and the system has added analytic snapshot capabilities. Even so, executives who want detailed, nicely formatted reports pushed to their mailboxes at 8 A.M. on Monday can quickly become frustrated. A number of reporting engines, analytical tools, and data warehouse options are available for SFDC, with prices ranging from free to very expensive—and feature variations to go with those price tags. If you missed it, check out the section in Chapter 2 entitled "Reports—Inside Versus Outside." There are four key evaluation criteria for these subsystems: (1) Will you really use the features they offer? (2) Are they missing something you actually *do* need? (3) Are they easy enough for users to comprehend? and (4) What are the long-run organizational costs of using the system? You'll notice that initial procurement costs for many of these tools are not enormous, but they can be overwhelmed by the long-run costs.

Essential Features for Sales Management

Although SFDC was designed with the sales rep and sales manager in mind, sales managers inevitably ask for lots of extras. While it's important to keep the system as streamlined as possible for the first few months, it is very natural for extra plugins and products to be integrated into the system as managers demand them.

- **Offline edition.** SFDC stores all of its data on its servers; nothing is stored in the user's laptop. Thus, when users are on a plane or out of Internet range, they are out of luck. For the road warrior, SFDC's Offline Mode is an invaluable productivity tool. The system caches selected data on the laptop prior to leaving the network, and then presents a fully interactive (but limited) version of SFDC while the user is traveling. Records can be reviewed and updated through the usual browser interface, and when the user reconnects, the updates are synchronized with SFDC's master database. With SFDC's Professional edition, this functionality is an extra-cost item that is priced per individual user, but it's very worth purchasing for your few true road warriors. If your implementation uses `custom objects`, they are unlikely to work in the Offline edition; however, the road warriors may not need access to the `custom objects` in offline mode. Do an evaluation test before you buy the Offline Mode feature.

- **Mobile edition.** In contrast to the Offline Mode, which uses special client software and replicates data on laptops, the Mobile edition is designed for real-time connected use, optimized for itty-bitty screens and keyboards. Supporting Blackberry, Palm, Microsoft Mobile, iPhone, and even iTouch devices, the Mobile edition is ideal for the CrackBerry sales rep or CEO who wants to be able to get at anything in the system no matter when or where. Make sure the mobile device has at least 10MB of free memory before installing the client application. Of course, the navigation is limited and reports can be challenging to read, but the Mobile edition has good "wow" value and fits with the lifestyles of many sales reps. This extra-cost item is priced by the individual phone, but at $50 per month per SFDC mobile user, the charges can add up.

- **Alternate user interfaces.** SFDC has gone out of its way to present all data and user interactions as part of a standard Web application. But for users who are completely enamored with Outlook, working with SFDC presents a clumsy "second app." InvisibleCRM has an SFDC add-on that communicates with the SFDC database in real time, but presents all user interactions within extra tabs of the Outlook application. Although I haven't seen the application in production use, seamless integration of the SFDC system with Outlook is an attractive idea for some users.

- **Sales Activity Dashboard.** This free plugin provides a number of dashboard elements and underlying reports that really help you understand what every member of your sales team is doing. Of course, this visibility comes at a price: it can induce paranoia among the sales representatives. For this reason, you should introduce this dashboard—and the activity management discipline that comes along with it—gradually (wait at least a quarter before you spring it on your people).

- **Call Scripting.** This free plugin from SFDC provides built-in call scripting support for telesales reps. Using this plugin not only ensures that value proposition statements and `lead` qualification are more consistent, but also automatically scores `leads` so that they can be ranked for inspection and conversion by the sales rep.

- **Videoconferencing.** While WebEx, Citrix, GoToMeeting, and other Web or videoconferencing systems are ubiquitous, a small number of these applications have nice integrations with SFDC that provide enriched data for `leads` and `contacts`. Make sure that the connector you use for videoconferencing or Web conferencing leverages the `campaigns` feature, as a `lead source` level of integration is a step backward. (If your IT group is sharp, they can set up an `APEX trigger` to overcome this limitation—but why shouldn't you buy this functionality straight from the vendor?)

- **Account enrichment tools.** SFDC customers that use the named-account model of selling want to be able to profile companies before reps make the first call. Several commercial sources of these corporate profiles exist, but most of them have no integration with SFDC. If your reps are targeting highly specialized market segments (let's say, jet engine manufacturers), the best sources of data will be industry associations, whose only real data are likely to reside on a CD. In this case, you should use the "gray-matter" strategy of SFDC integration: get a college intern to boil the data down to what sales reps really want, and cut and paste those data into the system. In terms of more general industry data, several sources have announced plugins with SFDC that allow for push-button enrichment of account and contact information. These sources can be fairly pricey, so you want to make sure that: (1) you pay only for users who really log in to the enrichment system, (2) the information provided is what you actually need (e.g., the source may provide the number of employees, but your reps need the number of servers), and (3) the individuals you're likely to target appear in the database (e.g., most sales reps need connections at the VP level and below, but some databases contain only corporate officers who don't really buy anything).

- **Sales methodology enablers.** Many large B2B salesforces use methodologies intended to make sales cycles more predictable and profitable. The core of SFDC has stayed agnostic to individual methodologies, but several third-party add-ons are available to enforce best practices of methodologies, such as Miller-Heiman, Target Account Selling, and SPIN Selling, among others. These add-ons present special screens for the `account`, `contact`, and `opportunity` objects to prompt reps about how they should move the prospect forward. These enablers can make it much easier to persuade sales reps to use the methodology consistently, but they should not be installed unless upper management is firmly committed to the methodology.[14]

- **Content and collateral enrichment.** If you are lucky enough to have a lot of quality collateral, the next complaint from your team will be "There's too much collateral; I can't find what I need." SFDC's `Content edition` provides some nifty features to help customers and sales reps alike find what they need, and vote on what's most useful. Some third-party products are also available to create or integrate wiki-like features, both for internal and external use. When used in combination with SFDC's `Customer Portal`, these tools can provide a nice environment for pre- and post-sales information browsing and exchange.

- **Partner portal.** SFDC has an add-on product that makes it easy to "flip" leads to and from partners, and to jointly manage the progress of `opportunities`. SFDC's `PRM` product has become a lot more capable over time, and is worth the time and effort required to fully leverage the portal on your company's Web site. At least one other PRM product is available, offering a different model of managing partner and value-added retailer (VAR)/distributor operations. The key issue with PRM products is making sure that the partners are able or willing to use it. Unfortunately, large partners may rarely input data into your system (you're just not important enough for them to vary their existing processes) and Asian firms are often unwilling to

---

14. If upper management is undecided about which methodology to use or is trying to put enforcement measures into SFDC in a last-ditch effort to save an unpopular mandate about using a methodology, the enablers should not be turned on. In most cases, doing so would simply doom SFDC to the same negative attitudes the reps have about the failing methodology.

share any prospect data until the deal is signed. If your partners indicate sincere willingness to use a partner portal if you set one up, these PRM products are quite worthwhile.

- **Line-item quoting.** SFDC has created a line-item quoting plugin for the system so that `quotes` are associated with specific line items, prices, and discounting mechanisms. The tool can be configured for approval processing, so that out-of-bounds discounts or unusual configurations can be routed to management for approval prior to issuing the quote.

- **Order configuration tools and proposal generators.** With very complex products, particularly in B2B markets, the sales cycle cannot proceed without a semicustom proposal and a configured product quote. Ask yourself these questions:

  - ➥ Is there enough consistency in the proposals and orders that the process can really be automated?

  - ➥ Who will own the task of creating the content and rules for automation, and modifying them over time as price lists are updated and marketing messages change?

  - ➥ Is the task complicated, yet repetitive enough to warrant automation?

  If you have good answers to these questions, evaluate the AppExchange products in this area for ease of use, flexibility, price, and references.

- **Integration with order management.** Out of the box, SFDC cannot issue a quote or start an order. In most companies, order management systems are custom-coded (either in the form of an application or as Microsoft Word and Excel macros) because this is an area where every company likes to do things its own way. Although some AppExchange plugins focus on quoting and order management, the more frequent practice is to integrate SFDC with the company's existing order management system. Several off-the-shelf connectors are available from the integration companies that will hook SFDC up to order-management packages, although these products may require significant customization to really work with your company's business processes. Once the systems are integrated, SFDC's workflow features can add a nice layer of control and approval cycles that can make your firm more compliant with accounting and SEC regulations.

- **Commission and incentive management.** As B2B sales forces get larger and more complex, managing commissions and incentive programs can become a full-time job. Some poor sales operations or finance associate will have to manage the monster spreadsheets that are fed by SFDC and accounting data. A number of commissions and incentive systems in the AppExchange have nice integrations that work with SFDC. If your compensation plan is complicated enough, these automation packages can be a good investment. Watch out, though: if the compensation plan changes frequently, has product-specific commissions, or involves a lot of recurring revenue, implementing one of these standard packages can be just as monstrous as maintaining the spreadsheets that were built internally. Check out Chapter 9 for a further discussion of this topic.

- **Forecasting and sales rep scorecards.** SFDC provides reports and dashboards to let sales managers see what's going on in the present, but the system cannot handle deep forecasting or performance analytics chores. For the sales manager who really wants to understand forecasting accuracy, regional or vertical pipeline coverage, or rep performance over time, external tools are required. Although a general data warehouse or reporting engine can be configured to produce these reports, the sales manager usually wants things that the data analyst doesn't know how to produce. In evaluating forecasting/performance analysis tools, look for the depth of domain knowledge embedded in the analytics, ease of use that ensures sales managers won't get confused, flexible configuration, and "drill-down reports" to satisfy the curious VP.

- **Sales analytics.** Sales management can really benefit from the range of pipeline and performance analytics available for the SFDC system. Check out the paragraph on this topic in the marketing section earlier in this chapter.

- **Telephony integration.** From free plugins for Skype to high-end adaptors for PBX, ACD, and IVR systems, the ability to integrate SFDC with the company's phone system is a real plus. For outbound callers, these integrations make calls faster and more efficient, and allow for their automatic measurement. For inbound call centers, these integrations make call handling much easier by prepopulating cases with basic caller information and correlating call times, number of calls per case, and other key metrics.

- **LinkedIn, Hoover's, and other links to prospect information.** For outbound callers who are trying to identify and cultivate leads, having more information at their fingertips is a key advantage. SFDC comes with a few links (to Google, Yahoo, Google News, and so forth) in the system, but they are hidden by default. After you've added these commodity links to the `lead`, `contact`, and `account` pages, look into the prospect of including links to LinkedIn, ZoomInfo, Hoover's, and Dun & Bradstreet. These links can cost several hundred dollars per year, but their use can be limited to only a few users (typically administrators or junior reps who handle the data research for the more senior reps).

Essential Tools for Support

Customer support personnel—whether their duties include expediting orders, providing field technical support, or managing returns—have needs that are distinct from those of the sales and marketing folks. SFDC contains the basics needed for call center support, but there are several areas where the user experience and power of the system can be enriched.

- **Mobility support.** If the company has a field support or service organization, the ability to stay in sync with the current customer situation is fundamental to its productivity. Hence SFDC's Mobile edition is quite valuable, particularly while a company representative is visiting the customer's site. If the company's field support personnel use laptops, achieving this kind of communication is simply a matter of getting a wireless Internet card and using the standard SFDC product.[15] If the field personnel don't want to lug laptops around, the right approach is SFDC's Mobile edition, which provides real-time connected operation optimized for BlackBerry, Palm, and Microsoft Mobile devices. Even though the device screen sizes limit SFDC navigation and reports can be challenging to read, the Mobile edition fits well with how field support people work. As mentioned earlier, this extra-cost item is priced by the individual phone. Alternatively, SFDC's Offline edition may be appropriate, but its requirement to prepopulate the laptop before the support rep leaves for a customer call may not be realistic for the organization.

- **Call Scripting.** This free plugin from SFDC provides built-in call scripting support for the company's customer support agents. Using this plugin not only ensures that the correct information is collected every time, but can also guide first-level troubleshooting and facilitate better consistency of support. Further, the Call Scripting plugin can be configured to automatically score cases so that they can be prioritized within the support team.

- **Telephony support.** Nearly any customer support operation will have a call center—whether it consists of 3 people or 300 people—that will benefit from some level of SFDC telephony integration. At the most basic (free) level, the SFDC screens can be configured to include buttons that automatically dial the phone numbers of people in the system, via Skype or the company's VoIP or PBX system. At more advanced levels, the integration automatically notes the time and duration of the call in the system, and records phone numbers and names for inbound calls. As the integration becomes fancier, you'll want to set up more reports and metrics for tight call center management. Telephony integration is almost never free, but it can yield significant payoffs in terms of productivity and team management.

---

15. SFDC's user interface works pretty well even with Edge-based communication cards that aren't much faster than a dial-up modem.

- **Knowledge Base and Customer Portal.** Although these features are available as part of SFDC, they really aren't useful without significant configuration and integration into the company's Web site. When properly set up, SFDC's features provide a nice two-way communication path with customers (such as an elegant, semi-automated FAQ and support case workflow). A number of products in the AppExchange provide more complete content management and two-way customer communication options for SFDC, such as surveys. The key points to consider when evaluating these products are: (1) the match of the feature sets to the company's real needs, (2) the ease of configuring the features to the customers' needs, (3) the amount of work required to maintain the knowledge base, and (4) the customer and information-quality metrics produced.

- **Email2Case.** When this free add-on is integrated with the system, SFDC gains the ability to automatically update cases from inbound customer emails, which eliminates a lot of copying-and-pasting of emails and other error-prone practices. While the functionality is available for free, some real work is required to configure the add-on correctly for the email system and other infrastructure. Further, you'll want to set up new `case escalation rules`, `workflows`, and reports when `Email2Case` is incorporated in the SFDC system. If the necessary IT resources aren't immediately available, you'll need to set some money aside to hire a consultant to handle this task.

- **Integration with the problem-tracking system.** SFDC manages customer issues in the context of customer complaints (`cases`) and fixes (`solutions`), which works quite well for the outward-looking perspective of a support phone person. Conversely, the inward-looking context—product defects (bugs) and upgrades (patches)—is very valuable for the support team, as it allows them to say confidently "Nobody else has seen this bug" or "The fix will be available in two weeks." A free plugin is available that provides a lightweight bug-tracking system in SFDC. For more serious defect management needs, a connector that links Jira to SFDC can be installed. As of spring 2009, the AppExchange did not contain integration plugins for any other defect-management systems. Of course, general-purpose integration adaptors are available, but these products will require a significant degree of configuration and some coding. If the company does not have the necessary IT resources on staff, you'll need to set some money aside to hire a consultant to handle this task.

- **Integration with inventory, licenses, contracts, and assets.** SFDC includes several tables that represent customer `contracts` and `assets` (historical purchases), but these tables remain empty unless they are manually filled in by order operations personnel. Even when this is done (very rarely), the process is highly error prone. As discussed in the "Integrate, Rather Than Extend" section earlier in this chapter, using a two-window strategy (where customer support reps log in to the ERP system during calls) may be a reasonable way for customer support reps to see the serial or license numbers of products bought by a customer, the purchase dates, and other historical data. However, operational or security policies may make that approach impossible to implement. In that case, SFDC can automatically pull relevant records from the order management, distribution, and ERP systems. Although general-purpose integration adaptors are available to access ERP and other systems, you will almost always need to build custom code beyond those adaptors to make the integration truly useful. If the necessary IT resources aren't available, you'll need to set some money aside to hire a consultant to handle this task.

- **Entitlement/SLA tracking.** SFDC automatically includes the `contract` object that helps store information about the commercial relationship. The system can also be extended with `custom fields` and `workflows` to track customer service, warranty entitlements, and SLA terms. This extension establishes a place in which to store data, though all of those data must be entered manually. A free plugin, however, automatically attaches SLA response times to `cases`. In addition to tracking the `entitled response time` and the `entitled resolution time`, the plugin monitors the *actual* time parameters for each case and flags SLA violations. This functionality is very useful in both real-time escalations and end-of-quarter reporting.

Essential Extensions for Finance

In many companies, the finance and accounting organizations are among the last to use SFDC. But once the system has been up and running for a year, it has enough data to be the foundation for interesting reports and analyses that the CFO's office always wanted to do.

- **Accounting/budgeting/payments processing/expense tracking.** A number of plugin products are available to help finance and accounting people do their jobs. Expense-tracking plugins provide ways to monitor and control expense requests (particularly from sales and field support people). Budgeting plugins help develop and manage budgets, particularly for the variable expenses incurred by the sales and marketing organizations. There are even full-fledged accounting systems that can create bookkeeping and financial reports for multinational businesses. While most companies already have accounting and financial systems fully in place, for small businesses moving up from QuickBooks or other entry-level systems, the SFDC add-ons are a reasonable alternative. The key points when evaluating accounting packages are: (1) the match between the vendor's features and the company's real needs, (2) the depth of multinational and multi-currency support, and (3) the flexibility of the system to accommodate future changes in the organization.[16]

---

16. Changes such as reorganizations, acquisitions, and spin-offs can be much more traumatic to the accounting system—and to SFDC in general—than simple organic growth. See Chapter 12 for further discussion of this topic.

- **Compliance.** SEC regulations such as the Sarbanes-Oxley Act require that companies pass audits and have repeatable, documented processes for several aspects of revenue and financial management. SFDC's field history tracking provides solid audit trails to help the organization's personnel understand and measure processes. SFDC's security system, in combination with workflows—a free part of the Enterprise and Unlimited editions—can be configured to enforce approval cycles and "lock down" opportunities, forecasts, and contracts once they are approved by management. There is also a free AppExchange plugin called SoxRox that can automate the compliance processes, providing real-time visibility about the state of processes and approvals. Several other AppExchange products also sport features related to this area.

- **Integration with quoting and order management.** By integrating SFDC with existing quoting and order management systems, SFDC can enforce much better sales behavior (e.g., preventing unapproved quotes from going out or locking down quotes and contracts once they are approved) and automatically pull relevant records from the order management, distribution, and ERP systems. Although general-purpose integration adaptors provide access to Oracle, SAP, and other systems, you will almost always need to build custom code beyond those adaptors to make the integration truly useful. If the necessary IT resources are not available, you'll need to set some money aside to hire a consultant to handle this task.

- **Electronic document and signature management.** For the most highly integrated operations, a paperless document and contract routing system provides the fastest and most controlled way to manage approval and signature processes. Using products from Adobe and DocuSign, SFDC's workflow system can handle nearly every stage of this process, from quote inception to contract filing, in a paperless, digitally signed way. Implementing these capabilities is a fairly significant undertaking, but if you have to manage hundreds of contracts, it can be a boon to streamlined, standardized, controlled contract management.

- **Expense tracking.** A free plugin provides expense tracking and approval cycles for the SFDC system. Given that only full SFDC users can use this plugin, most companies will continue to use other expense tracking software. However, for companies with large field forces (particularly for sales, consulting, or after-sales service), this plugin is a great way to link expenses to customer projects or sales cycles.

- **Employee manager.** The AppExchange has a free plugin that provides a lightweight employee manager database to be stored within SFDC. When used with the fine-grained security system that's part of the Enterprise edition, this tool provides a fine solution for small businesses or for division-level information at larger companies.

Essential Features for the Executive

Executives (particularly COOs and CEOs) will typically interact with the SFDC system mainly at—surprise!—an executive level. They need to see `reports`, `dashboards`, and scorecards for the organization so they can manage in real time and characterize organizational performance and the pipeline forecast for the board of directors. For these reports and analytics, SFDC reports will typically be supplemented by outboard systems:

- **Data warehouse, business intelligence, and reporting tools.** As mentioned earlier, SFDC has an easy-to-use, yet powerful reporting engine that's great for ad hoc analysis and reporting at low levels of the organization. At the executive level, however, the questions that need to be answered are much tougher and almost certainly require an external set of tools. SFDC add-ons are available for several kinds of analytics, and some of the most popular BI tools plug right into the system. For even more complex analytics, the data must be exported to a data warehouse, and several SFDC partners offer ETL tools and integration adapters to facilitate the most powerful analysis tools. When evaluating these products, make sure that there is a good match between what the SFDC team needs on a regular basis and the features offered by the vendor: some of the most powerful tools require extensive "care and feeding" that may be more expensive than the business value delivered.

- **Forecast analytics and organizational scorecarding.** As mentioned earlier, SFDC's forecasting reports and dashboards are fine for small teams, but cannot answer the important questions about forecast reliability or team comparative performance metrics. Although a general data warehouse or reporting engine can be configured to produce these `reports`, executives want easy-to-understand dashboards and metrics that capture organizational objectives. Dedicated tools that embody significant domain knowledge and "executive savvy" are much easier to use in board-level discussions. In evaluating these tools, look for the depth of domain knowledge embedded in the analytics, ease of use that ensures a clear boardroom conversation, and flexibility of configuration and "drill-down reports" to satisfy the curious VP.

Some executives are also very hands-on and want to quickly get contact information for customers. They also need the ability to rapidly look up the state of an account when an unexpected phone call comes in. For these executives, we recommend SFDC's Mobile edition: it doesn't require these managers to lug their laptops on their travels, and it gives them the level of access they need on the go. Even if your executive team doesn't ask for it, it's not a bad thing to demo the Mobile edition just for the "wow value."

CHAPTER 8

Optimizing Business Processes

*If you can't describe what you are doing as a
process, you don't know what you are doing.*

—W. Edwards Deming

T HIS IS THE SINGLE most important chapter in the book—what really sets it apart—
but it's likely to be a little abstract. Because most business users rarely think in terms
of business processes, this chapter is full of concrete examples explaining how to see
the big picture and optimize the way different departments work together via SFDC.

The Top-Down Perspective

An SFA system could be thought of as a glorified contact manager—but if that's the way
you think about the system, you'd be missing nearly all the value it can bring as a management tool. The whole point of an SFA system is its ability to improve the speed and effectiveness of the sales team. The larger and more complex the company, the more leverage a
true SFA system can bring, because it helps manage *across* business processes.

Taking this argument a step further, SFDC gives the organization the opportunity to
improve collaboration across its sales, marketing, customer service, order operations, and
other departments to improve profitability and customer satisfaction at the same time. To
realize this potential, however, requires thinking about and making changes to the details
of how you do business—modifications to business rules, procedures, and metrics.

One of the big discoveries from the business process reengineering movement of the
1990s was that simply analyzing and documenting a process can expose big opportunities
for business improvement, even if no automation is applied. In addition, by looking objec-
tively at the organization's business processes, you may discover ways to dramatically
simplify the requirements for SFDC. This is the secret of my consulting firm's success, and
it can be yours, too.

The real potential for business improvement comes from the twin foundations of SFDC
functionality and business process changes that have been "tuned" to leverage the system.

What Is a Business Process?

The term "business process" sounds pretty vague and abstract, and almost no one really understands it very well. So why use this language?

Business processes are an enormously powerful tool because they allow you to see the corporation as if it were a machine or an assembly line cranking out profits. Business process analysis helps clarify decisions and improve the way your business does business. Although abstract and sometimes cumbersome, business processes help you think about your business in a *systematic way* that avoids getting caught up in personal foibles and company politics.[1]

A business process comprises a set of interrelated tasks or activities that are done in a repeatable way to achieve a goal (typically for a customer). Business processes are supposed to be routine and predictable, but they have enough variances and exceptions that they are only partially automated. Almost always, a business process spans more than one person's job and more than one piece of software. Most of the time, performing a business process also requires crossing organizational lines—in fact, the juiciest and most interesting ones all do. A typical business process takes a few hours or days and involves both automation and human judgment.

The vast majority of business processes have never been documented as such; instead, they're informally summarized as "the way we do things around here." A business process is a bunch of practices that have grown up over time and become part of the company folklore about "how we do business." Business processes are usually embodied in habits, rules, and culture about how to get the job done. Consequently, they often include a lot of gray areas that may be misunderstood by the people who *don't* do them ("You mean, we *don't* allow customers to return defective merchandise to the store where they bought it?").

Business processes can also be nearly invisible to the people doing them, because those workers are just doing their jobs the right way. For example, the department store Nordstrom has a merchandise returns policy that allows a customer to bring back almost anything in any condition and get a store credit. How does the company handle a return when it involves merchandise Nordstrom no longer carries? There's a business process covering that situation. A business process essentially tries to describe the way the company does business as if workers were operating a machine, so that the individual workers can do an even better job.

When organizational improvements are being implemented, business process analysis helps structure arguments about resource allocation and organizational design. Business processes force members of the organization to think about disparate elements of the

---

1. Of course, like anything else that comes from consultants and business gurus, business process engineering can itself become the plaything of politics and arbitrary decision making. That's life in the big city. The goal of business process folks is to get away from that, and to be objective and fair in decision making.

business (let's say, field service and the call center) in a way that's oriented around what *customers* value. Instead of getting hung up in departmental trivia, politics, and arbitrary rules, focusing on business processes keeps the discussion honed in on the big things that are important—like how the company can make more money.

The most important reason to understand a business process is to streamline and automate it. Business process definitions can be easily transformed into validation steps, rules, routing, alerts, escalations, workflows, checklists, and special-purpose data entry screens; further, they lend themselves to monitoring via thresholds, reports, and dashboards. In other words, good business process definitions can drive about two-thirds of the SFDC system configuration.

Although incredibly useful, business process analysis can be time-consuming. It's totally self-defeating if a business process discussion lasts weeks or months, or if some knucklehead mandates documenting 300 processes before he'll[2] make a decision.

How Do Business Processes Fit Together?

A given business process should represent a "whole transaction" that is useful or meaningful from the customer's or user's perspective—for example, the process of taking an order over the phone. Business processes fit together typically in an end-to-end manner, forming a cycle. Continuing the example, shipping and invoicing an order are tasks that are done right after order entry. An obvious example of a business process from an SFDC perspective would be "schedule and conduct a product demonstration," an activity that is part of the "sales cycle."

In abstract theory, all of a company's business processes form a giant system that behaves deterministically, so it is perfectly predictable and consistent. In practice, a company that was a perfect system of business processes would be boring[3] to deal with: an inflexible robot that could never delight any customer. Real companies add the human element all the time, because that's what builds a company's reputation and customer loyalty. Think about Nordstrom or Southwest Airlines.

There's another important point to be made about business process linkages, particularly those involving the customer: you can't control 'em. The *customer* doesn't care about the company's business processes, let alone want to fit in with their prescribed order. A customer in search of a solution may zigzag across different incomplete business-process transactions—and will expect your company to deal with that random behavior. The classic frustration comes when the customer has to give the order expediter the shipping information for the fifth time today—after having jumped from the Web site, to the local store, to

---

2. Although I try to be gender-neutral in this book, knuckleheads are always male. *Ditz* is the female form, but I haven't found a situation to use that term anywhere in this book.

3. The BPM purists are sure to object to this line of discussion, but let's face it—they're boring, too.

the warehouse, and finally into order operations. Business process designs have to antici-pate and cope with this kind of possibility.

Identifying Which Business Processes You Need to Think About

You might think, "Why analyze all this—can't we just blow away the 'cruft' that has built up over the years and replace it as we roll out the new system?" And you would be wrong.

The whole point of putting SFDC in your company is to make your business processes more efficient and effective, but the changes must be well thought out and measured. A poorly conceived business process will not be saved by automation—users will merely make errors faster and more efficiently. If the SFDC team pushes through an ill-conceived busi-ness process change, the credibility of both the new business process and the SFDC system will go down in flames. Business processes are not the place to do casual prototyping and quick rollout of changes.

Since these changes take planning, let's take a top-down look at business processes. At the very highest level, your entire business could be represented by a business process called "stay in business" or "grow profitably." Fine, but not very useful. At the very lowest level, a business process would consist of a checklist of all the things required to do a tiny task, such as answering the customer-support hotline. That's not very useful either.

The whole raison d'etre for business process analysis is to understand the steps and actions that make your business work, and that make it work better than the competition. Therefore, there is no universal list of business processes. Instead, you need to develop the taxonomy of processes that best describes the way *your* company does business.[4]

A more useful way of working with business processes is to divide them into the activities that produce revenues—tasks that touch the customer somehow—and the activities that are carried out for purely internal support. SFDC adds the most value to the revenue-producing business processes. The business processes that focus only on internal infrastructure can be ignored for all but the most sophisticated and complex SFDC implementations.

Looking at the revenue-bearing business processes, the fastest way to understand them is by using the SFDC module.

Salesforce Automation

The core of the revenue process is—surprise!—focusing demand, making quotes, taking orders, delivering goods and services, and collecting funds. SFA includes three main busi-ness processes to cover these tasks: sales cycle, sales management, and channel manage-ment. Check out Chapter 9 for more on this topic.

---

4. Developing a taxonomy that gets you what you need without wasting time will sometimes require the use of an external consultant.

Sales Cycle

The sales cycle has two major components: prospecting-to-order formulation, and quote to cash. Table 8-1 shows a generic set of business processes for sales in high technology markets. As you can see, most of the business processes have an initiator—a main actor—and an assisting organization. Once a business process has been broken down to the point where it's done entirely by the main actor, it becomes less interesting because there's less interdepartmental activity involved.

Although the list format used in Table 8-1 makes it look like these business processes all follow a linear pattern, in the real world an individual customer may "jump around" from one business process to another. The larger and more important the customer, the higher the likelihood that the customer will interact with several business process activities simultaneously. As this is one of the driving reasons for having a CRM system in the first place, you need to make sure you configure and use SFDC to give all workers the visibility they need to serve the customer in real time, no matter what the circumstance.

TABLE 8-1   Sales Cycle Business Process

Activity/Description	Main Actor	Assistant
Prospecting → Order Formulation		
Prospecting	Sales	Marketing
Qualifying	Sales	Telesales
Demo/proof of concept	Sales	Sales engineering
Focusing value proposition	Sales	Sales engineering
Order formulation/configuration	Sales	Sales engineering
Quote → Cash		
Credit check	Finance	
Quote	Sales	Sales engineering
Negotiation	Sales	Legal
Approval and close	Sales	Finance
Scheduling/expediting delivery	Sales	Distribution
Delivery/fulfillment	Distribution	Field support
Invoicing	Finance	Sales operations
Collection	Finance	
Order management	Sales operations	Distribution
Returns, exchanges, credits	Customer support	Distribution
Renewals	Sales	Sales operations
Upgrades/expansions	Sales	Sales operations

The business process elements in Table 8-1 in **boldface font** are more likely to benefit from automation and monitoring (whether by SFDC or some other system) than the ones in standard font. Put another way, they are the processes and activities that an SFDC implementation team should examine first as the highest leverage points for the system. Interestingly, the base SFDC system actually has very few features that directly affect the boldface items. This is largely because many of the actual sales process can't really be automated: if they could, we'd make all our purchases via automats and online stores.

Sales Management

Sales management is the set of processes used by the company to organize its sales personnel and manage their execution of the revenue process. This business process has three major elements: setting up the organization, running it, and working with corporate headquarters. Most of the effort in sales management is in day-to-day monitoring of sales personnel to expedite sales cycles, as shown in Table 8-2.

TABLE 8-2   Sales Management Business Process

Activity/Description	Main Actor	Assistant
Setting Up the Sales Organization		
Recruiting and training	Sales manager	HR
Assigning accounts and territories	Sales manager	Sales personnel
Assigning quotas	Sales manager	Sales personnel
Designing compensation plans	Sales manager	CEO
Designing channels	Sales manager	Business development
Writing standard contract terms	Sales manager	Legal
Running the Sales Organization		
Adjusting quotas and territories	Sales manager	
Designating key accounts, account teams	Sales manager	Sales personnel
Forecasting revenue	Sales manager	Sales personnel
Monitoring sales cycles	Sales manager	Sales personnel
Account reviews	Sales manager	Sales personnel
Handling escalations	Sales manager	Sales personnel
Scheduling executive calls	Sales personnel	Sales manager
Handling splits, commissions	Sales manager	Sales personnel
Working with Corporate Headquarters		
Executive/board meetings	Sales manager	Executive team
Forecast roll-up, reconciliation	Sales manager	Finance
Budgeting and staff changes	Sales manager	Finance, HR

The boldface items in Table 8-2 make it pretty clear that the SFDC system will be a key tool for sales management on a daily basis. Most of these activities can be facilitated by SFDC's "out of the box" features, and they are made even better with add-ons and external system integrations. Although most of SFDC's users are sales reps, and their sales cycles will benefit from the greater efficiency and speed made possible by this tool, it's the sales manager who gets much more immediate help from the system. This helps explain why most sales reps are relatively resistant to SFA system implementations, and why many may view it as a tool for management spying.[5]

Channel Management

Channel management is the art of harnessing dealers, resellers, and distributors to increase the footprint and effectiveness of the selling function. Business processes surrounding the channel are made more difficult by the number of external interfaces—the channel typically doesn't *work on the company's payroll,* so your employees have little direct control over its behaviors and actions. The channel management business process has three major components: developing partners, maintaining channel infrastructure, and operations. The channel management team handles the activities shown in Table 8-3.

TABLE 8-3   Channel Management Business Process

Activity/Description	Main Actor	Assistant
Developing Partners		
Partner recruitment	Channel manager	Legal
Partner training	Channel manager	Product marketing
Channel planning	Channel manager	
Partner account management	Channel manager	
Maintaining Channel Infrastructure		
Partner communications	Channel manager	Channel marketing
Co-marketing funds	Channel manager	Channel marketing
Referral fees and splits	Channel manager	Finance
Document sharing	Channel marketing	

Continued

---

5. We put so much emphasis on "featurettes" and other incentives because they ensure that sales reps will have reasons to use the SFDC system early on, before it becomes an intrinsically helpful tool to them. See Chapters 4 and 6 for further discussion of this topic.

TABLE 8-3 Channel Management Business Process, *Continued*

Activity/Description	Main Actor	Assistant
Channel Operations		
Lead management	Channel manager	Lead generation
Deal registration	Channel manager	
Opportunity management	Channel manager	
Forecasting	Channel manager	Finance
Pricing, promotions, and discounting	Channel manager	Channel marketing
Order cycle	Order operations	Channel manager
Shipping and fulfillment	Order operations	Distribution

eCommerce Management

Strictly speaking, eCommerce management is not part of the standard sales function, and it certainly isn't part of standard SFDC. But for an increasing number of companies, the Web now represents the single largest source of transactions (maybe not the most revenues, but surely the largest number of purchases). Because the dollar value of these transactions is typically substantially less than that of transactions completed through the other channels, for profitability it is essential that as much of this business as possible be handled without human intervention. If human intervention is required, it either needs to be very short or highly likely to generate an "upsell."

Depending on the organizational structure, the eCommerce workflows will be handled by software that is "owned" by sales, the call center, or marketing. Irrespective of the ownership, the sequence of business processes looks like Table 8-4.

TABLE 8-4 eCommerce Business Process

Activity/Description	Main Actor*	Assistant
Customer registration	Customer	Automation
Registration confirmation email	Automation	
Product selection	Customer	Automation
Checkout	Customer	Automation
Special pricing/discounting	Call center	
Payment/credit card selection	Customer	Automation
Special order problems	Call center	

Activity/Description	Main Actor*	Assistant
Order confirmation + invoice	Automation	
Order status inquiry	Customer	Automation
Shipment/fulfillment	Distribution	Automation
Order cancellation	Call center	
RMA/warranty incident	Call center	
Renewal/upgrade offer	Automation	Call center

* All of the activities with "call center" as the main actor are "feeders" to dedicated business processes described in the "Call Center" section.

Marketing Automation

For the sales cycle to work, there have to be prospects whose interests and needs match what the company produces. In this section, we will ignore the vast majority of marketing functions (e.g., product management, public relations) to focus on the lead generation process that directly feeds the sales cycle. The lead generation business process has three major components, as illustrated in Table 8-5: product marketing, marketing campaigns, and Internet marketing.

TABLE 8-5   Lead Generation Business Process

Activity/Description	Main Actor	Assistant
Product Marketing		
Packaging and pricing	Product marketing	Executive team
Value proposition and messaging	Product marketing	Executive team
Customer targeting	Product marketing	Sales management
Marketing Campaigns		
Event selection	Lead generation	Sales
Event execution and management	Lead generation	
Call to action and promotions	Lead generation	Product marketing
Lead collection, filtering, and import	Lead generation	
Lead scoring and routing	Lead generation	Telemarketing
Lead deduping and demotion	Lead generation	Telemarketing
Event effectiveness assessment	Lead generation	Business analyst

Continued

TABLE 8-5   Lead Generation Business Process, *Continued*

Activity/Description	Main Actor	Assistant
Internet Marketing		
Message sequences	Product marketing	Sales
List rental and merging	Lead generation	
Email blast design/execution	Lead generation	
Internet advertising campaigns	Lead generation	
Internet marketing effectiveness assessment	Lead generation	Business analyst

The marketing processes shown in Table 8-5 are embodied in both the Sales Force Automation and Marketing Automation applications within SFDC. The large number of boldface items indicates the degree to which marketing people will need to interact with the SFDC system on a day-to-day basis. Almost without exception, marketers will need additional plugin tools (as discussed in Chapter 7) to perform their jobs according to best practices (as discussed in Chapter 10).

Call Center

The call center may perform three distinct business processes—telemarketing, inside sales, and order management—even if these processes are performed by the same individuals. Each of these business processes is fairly small, but should be treated differently in your analysis. You'll notice the common thread, though: the call center functions have nearly continuous interaction with the SFDC system, and the call center personnel should be the most avid and intense group of users. See Chapter 9 for more discussion of these processes.

Telemarketing

Table 8-6 shows the key business process in telemarketing, an almost entirely outbound process that can be run at its own pace and interrupted without affecting customer satisfaction.

TABLE 8-6   Telemarketing Business Process

Activity/Description	Main Actor	Assistant
Generating scripts for target names	Lead generation	Product marketing
Collecting and distributing lists	Lead generation	Telemarketing

Activity/Description	Main Actor	Assistant
Lead queue management	Telemarketing	Lead generation
Calling down and recalling names	Telemarketing	
Promoting interested names to leads	Telemarketing	Sales
Demoting uninterested/unresponsive names	Telemarketing	Lead generation
Monitoring list yield	Telemarketing	Lead generation
Monitoring campaign effectiveness	Lead generation	Telesales

Inside Sales

In contrast to telemarketing, inside sales comprises a range of functions that directly support the sales process, in some cases actually taking orders over the phone. Because the specific duties of inside sales personnel are highly variable, you'll need to pay attention to subtleties: the inside folks might be authorized to sell only certain products, or to sell only to a certain deal size, or to sell only to a specific customer type (e.g., SMB).

The inside sales business process is typically linked with outside sales, telemarketing, and eCommerce business processes, so watch out for tricky handoffs and exceptions in this business process. Most inside sales teams handle only a subset of the functions shown in Table 8-7, but those tasks entail a mix of outbound (paced, planned) calls and inbound (asynchronous, sporadic) activities.

TABLE 8-7   Inside Sales Business Process

Activity	Main Actor	Assistant
Lead distribution	Inside sales	
Lead cultivation and qualification	Inside sales	
Appointment setting	Inside sales	Outside sales
Lead conversion	Inside sales	
Opportunity creation	Inside sales	
Opportunity management	Outside sales	Inside sales
Initial price quotes	Outside sales	Inside sales
Order generation	Inside sales	Order operations
Close	Inside sales	Order operations
Order fulfillment	Order operations	Distribution

Order Management

In this business process, the call center typically handles inbound calls from customers who are having problems with placing or tracking an order (typically made on the Web) or with product delivery, as shown in Table 8-8. Because these calls can happen at any time, they cannot be handled in the same routine, scripted way that outbound call sequences can. It's very important for customer satisfaction that the order management rep is able to quickly understand the customer situation and get access to whatever system has the most relevant information to resolve the issue.

TABLE 8-8　Customer Order Support Business Process

Activity/Description	Main Actor	Assistant
Call routing	Phone rep	
Special quotes and discounts	Phone rep	Marketing
Order entry/modification	Phone rep	Order operations
Order management	Phone rep	Order operations
Expediting or canceling orders	Phone rep	Order operations
Credit card or other payment processing	Phone rep	Finance
Invoicing	Phone rep	Order operations
Schedule shipping/fulfillment*	Phone rep	Distribution

*　This activity is highly variable within companies, let alone across them. Spend enough time to understand the specifics for each type of product or service you deliver, as this may be an entire business process in and of itself. You might want to use a consultant to help disentangle this area.

Customer Service

Personnel in the post-sales call center (who are usually not the same people who handle order management or pre-sales issues) handle inbound calls from customers who are having problems with the product. See Chapter 11 for further information on this function. The issue covered by this business function relates to troubleshooting the problem, identifying corrective action, and scheduling either a replacement product or a service call, as shown in Table 8-9.

TABLE 8-9   Customer Service Business Process

Activity	Main Actor	Assistant
Call and email routing	Phone rep	
Create incident report	Phone rep	
Problem identification	Phone rep	
Dispense customer help	Phone rep	Order operations
Issue RMA or schedule service call	Phone rep	Reverse logistics
Credit card or other payment processing	Phone rep	
Schedule shipping/fulfillment*	Phone rep	Distribution

* This activity is highly variable within companies, let alone across them. Spend enough time to understand the specifics for each type of product or service you deliver, as this may be an entire business process in and of itself. You might want to use a consultant to help disentangle this area.

Separate from the call center that handles first-level customer questions and resolves the "easy problems" is the technical support center that is staffed by support engineers, as shown in Table 8-10. These personnel need to have access to internal case management systems, knowledge bases, bug/fault-tracking systems, and spare-parts inventory information. Because of contractual obligations and service-level agreements, the tech support business process will tend to have the most complicated workflows, with exceptions, time-outs, and automatic escalations triggered by excessive delays.

TABLE 8-10   Technical Support Business Process

Activity	Main Actor	Assistant
Call and email routing	Tech support rep	
Verify entitlement/warranty	Tech support rep	
Problem identification	Tech support rep	
Create/update case	Tech support rep	
Create/update bug or fault report	Tech support rep	
Case queue management	Tech support rep	
Case escalation/reassignment	Tech support rep	Tech support manager
Dispense customer help	Tech support rep	

Continued

TABLE 8-10   Technical Support Business Process, *Continued*

Activity	Main Actor	Assistant
Issue RMA, software patch, or other correction	Tech support rep	Engineering
Credit card or other payment processing	Tech support rep	Finance
Schedule shipping/fulfillment*	Tech support rep	Distribution
Close case/bug	Tech support rep	
Update knowledge base/FAQ	Tech support rep	
Send survey to customer	Tech support rep	

*   This activity is highly variable within companies, let alone across them. Spend enough time to understand the specifics for each type of product or service you deliver, as this may be an entire business process in and of itself. You might want to use a consultant to help disentangle this area.

Analyzing Business Processes

Business processes are a bit tricky because they are multilevel, almost fractal in nature. According to business process experts, a large corporation may use as many as 1,000 business processes. It's the details of those processes that make your company different and better than the competition. Analyzing, understanding, and documenting any one of those business processes will involve many meetings indeed. If you try to handle more than a couple of dozen at a time, you'll never get out of the woods. Instead, your goal should be to focus your attention on a few business processes that make a difference to the customer.

Selecting Candidate Processes

As you can see from Tables 8-1 through 8-10, fully analyzing your company's business processes can quickly become a mind-numbing experience. It's important to identify a few business processes that really matter, and to understand them deeply enough to really improve them.

Really, improvement or streamlining of *existing* business processes is all you should be targeting in an SFDC implementation. You don't want to boil the ocean. If you set your sights too broadly, the business process work will become a heavy-handed exercise in organizational transformation laden with politics and controversy. SFA systems are supposed to improve sales efficiency and results, not reengineer the corporation.

So how do you determine the right number and types of business processes for improvement with SFDC? Starting with the boldface items in Tables 8-1 through 8-10, look for business processes that have a lot of these characteristics:

- Labor intensive

- Error prone/unreliable

- Involve paper[6]

- Involve manual data entry

- Require (and perhaps depend on) heroic acts or frequent overtime

- Visibly, irritatingly broken

- High on the "squeaky wheel" list

- Result in lost opportunities or waste

- High business value[7]

- Span three or fewer departments

- Not riddled with political or organizational issues

- Easily measured (for improvement)

- Part of someone's agenda (somebody already has a related goal or metric)

Once you've identified a few hot prospects for business processes, you need to check what's wrong with each of them. Demote any business process where there isn't a clear idea of how the business process ought to work, or where employees have wildly differing views about the best way to fix it. Promote business processes where it's fairly clear how the process ought to work, but the precise mechanisms and specific behaviors haven't been finalized. These candidates are likely to provide the highest payoffs under SFDC.

Analytical Steps

The first step is to very clearly identify the start and the end of the process—that is, the inputs and the outputs of a "black box." For example, the start of the quote to cash business process is a salesperson's request to issue a quote, and the end of the process is a payment from the customer. Dozens of steps may occur in between these endpoints, but don't look at any of the details until you've firmly defined the inputs and outputs of the process.

---

6. Every time a piece of paper is used in a process, it costs the company something in excess of $100 in labor. While this cost may not be measured or obvious, removing the labor and delay involved with paper handling can have amazing effects on an organization's efficiency, quality, and throughput. Ironically, eliminating paper in an organization is a license to print money.

7. Business value isn't just present in items that generate big cash flows: anything that angers a customer or irritates a board member can be of high business value, even if only a few dollars are involved.

The next step is to have incredibly clear definitions of the actors and objects of a process. An actor is a person or system that carries out an action, and objects are the things or entities that are acted upon. In the quote to cash process, the actors are the sales rep, the customer, order operations personnel, legal personnel, and finance personnel; the objects are the quote, the order, the contract, the invoice, the shipment, and the payment.

These definitions need to include the semantics for possible states or stages of the objects, such as these items:

- Draft quote

- Approved quote

- Accepted quote

- Revised quote

- Draft contract

- Amended contract

- Accepted contract

- Signed contract

- Filed contract

- Pro forma invoice

- Packing slip

- Shipment bill of lading

- Shipper tracking number

- Final invoice

- Past-due invoice

- Paid invoice

You need to describe the criteria for each of the object's stages, as well as the events, actions, or inactions (e.g., past deadlines) that trigger movement of the transaction from one stage to another.

Once the analysis team agrees about the meaning of objects and the expected behavior of actors (this can take a while), you can start to diagram the business process. Most teams like to use a whiteboard for this purpose, but you can also use a computer and PowerPoint or Visio as well. There are only a few symbols you have to use, as shown in Figure 8-1. You can get fancier if you like, but the extra complexity often gets in the way of broader understanding.

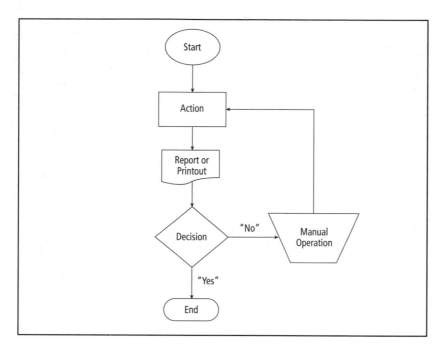

FIGURE 8-1   Essential process diagram symbols

Diagram

A few diagramming rules have to be followed: the action starts at the top and moves down the page. The flow of activity is always downward unless some sort of remedial or corrective action puts things "back in process" at an earlier step. Decisions are almost always of the "yes/no" variety—and even if they aren't, they must be incredibly unambiguous (like "route to correct person using the customer's ZIP code"). "Start" almost always is triggered by ending another business process, although a customer calling in or other exogenous event can start a business process. "End" almost always triggers the next business process, but it marks the end of your analysis.

If your business process is so complicated that it requires several pages to diagram, do one of three things: (1) find a bigger piece of paper, (2) figure out a way to draw smaller blocks, or (3) break the business process into several subprocesses. Almost always, multi-page business process diagrams are hard to follow and signify deeper problems (such as "Why have we made this so complicated?")

The most really interesting actions or decision steps will require some notes to explain them. Keep those notes, triggers, criteria, and other details off the diagram—they'll make it unreadable. Instead, put them on a separate page, either in a free-text document or in a spreadsheet.

Once the team believes that the diagrams of the business processes are an accurate reflection of how things are, create another set of diagrams for how you *want things* to be. The differences between the diagrams are what will drive your business process changes—in people, and in SFDC workflows.

Capture the diagrams and annotations in electronic form, and store the files on the project wiki. You want as many people as possible to see and comment on the workflows, as there may be things that your team didn't know about—such as "unrelated" items that ultimately affect the way the process is run. For example, an audit process may need to examine the work product of a process after the fact, and the business process may need steps or documents to support auditability. This is particularly true if the organization is a public company.

Example Business Process Analysis

Let's take a look at an example business process that's almost entirely within SFDC: the lead life cycle.

Start State and End State

The starting state of the lead life cycle is the identification of one or more large groups of people who are in the company's target market. These people may be aware of the company and its offerings, but they have no stated interest in buying. The starting action of the lead life cycle is the lead's participation in a marketing campaign (such as an email blast or tradeshow) or sales outreach (such as cold calling).

The end state of the lead life cycle is a set of fully qualified contacts who are handed off to sales personnel, so they can work on the opportunities that will form the revenue pipeline. The end of the lead life cycle is the beginning of the sales cycle.

Actors

The main actors in the lead life cycle are people in product marketing, event marketing, and marketing operations (including contractors or agencies), as well as inside sales reps, pre-sales engineers, outside sales reps, partner marketing groups, and all the prospects in the target market.

Objects and Intermediate States

Before we can have a clear discussion about the lead life cycle, we must agree on nomenclature. There's a reasonable amount of semantics-related confusion in the lead processing world. Here is the standard terminology that this book uses as part of its best-practices recommendations:

- A **Name** is the identity of someone in the target audience. You can buy Names on a list (e.g., all doctors in North America or all attendees at a tradeshow), but Names are of very little value because they neither know nor care about your company and its products or services. A Name is, at best, a receptive ear. But the probability of Names being actively interested in your company's products is so low that you should communicate with Names only via bulk Internet media. The point here is not that your firm should spam people, but rather that it should develop a sequence of interesting, relevant material to send in a low-key "drip marketing" campaign designed to make the Name more interested in engaging with your company.

- A **Lead** is someone who has specifically expressed interest in your company's product or service, typically by attending an event or registering on the Web site. We know a little bit more about Leads than we do about Names, but typically the only thing we know for certain is a valid email address at the time of registration. If the Lead has come back to your Web site or taken some other follow-up action, all of those details should be recorded in your SFA system so you can do some behavioral targeting and lead scoring. We urge everyone to be using campaigns to cover any possible activity or response that a Lead could be involved with.

- A **Qualified Lead** is someone who could reasonably participate in a sales cycle, and we know this because somebody in our company has had a highly directed conversation with that individual about his or her level of interest, requirements fit, budget, and timeline. Typically, a Qualified Lead should be converted to a Contact in a matter of hours, after a follow-up call by sales personnel. If the sales conversation doesn't go well, the Qualified Lead should be disqualified as bogus.

- A **Rejected Lead** is a lead that has been rejected by sales as being unqualified, or a contact that has been identified as uninterested or incompetent to participate in a sales cycle. Rejected Leads should still be given the best treatment by marketing, but they will be ignored by sales until they have done something new to prove their worthiness of proper attention.

- **Contacts** come in four flavors: a qualified lead that has been converted to initiate a sales cycle, a person who works for a company that is already in a sales cycle, a person who works in a company we've done business with in the past, or a person who works at a company we're targeting for future business. Unfortunately for zealous supporters of the Named Account model of selling, these definitions get very blurry. People get paid the big bucks to sort them out.

- **Dead Contacts** are contacts that have left the prospect account, have changed jobs and are no longer relevant as potential customers, or have told us to stop contacting them. Dead Contacts should not be deleted, but should simply be flagged as no longer relevant (this flagging will make them disappear from the sales rep's view, but they'll still be available for historical analysis).

The contact is the end state for the lead. Nevertheless, the contact goes through several subsequent stages as part of the sales cycle:

- **Opportunities** are indicators that a fully qualified contact should be pursued or that an existing customer is interested in some additional product. Many Opportunities will be immediately closed when the sales representative discovers that there is no current sales potential. Only after an Opportunity has been accepted by a rep as a genuine sales-cycle candidate will a dollar amount or probability be assigned to it.

- **Customers** are contacts who work for an account that has a contractual relationship with us, and who have paid us something.

- **References** are customers who are foolhardy enough to have their names bandied about in the press. References require special protections to prevent them from being overused by both sales and marketing personnel alike.

Lead Cultivation Workflow Narrative

Most of the early cultivation of Names is focused on increasing their level of interest, to the point where they really qualify to be `leads`. The workflows for Names and demoted `leads` should be nearly 100% automated, using clever combinations of email blasts, Web site materials, and recorded Webinars. Your marketing automation system should be managing this communication flow for you, and maintaining behavioral scores for each individual.

Once a `lead` is sufficiently warm to require human attention, marketing should almost never be involved in contacting that person. Representatives from inside sales (or telesales or telemarketing) should be doing the outbound phone calls, demonstrations, and qualification steps. In most organizations, the final decision on qualification is made by the sales rep, but the appointment for that call is made by the inside sales team. The processes involved with nurturing and cultivating a `lead`'s interest tend to span several weeks or months, and the specific steps usually aren't worth documenting. But at some point, the `lead` matures and expresses deep interest in your company's products.

Once a `lead` is fully qualified, it should be a matter of moments before it is `converted` into a `contact`. `Conversion` does an amazing array of things in SFDC system, and the user is given a few options at this time. At `conversion` time (and we recommend that this step also be handled by the inside sales group for consistency), best practices are to create a new `opportunity` (typically, for $0 at 0% probability, unless the `contact` is being attached to an `opportunity` already in progress) and to attach a `contact role` and a `campaign` to it (to support sales and marketing effectiveness analyses).

The `opportunity` is handed over to the direct sales team and serves as the input to their sales cycle process. `Leads` and `contacts` per se aren't handed over—they're important, but they're supporting elements of the `opportunity` that will turn into a deal.

What if the `contact` turns out to be bogus, or falsely qualified? Never, ever, ever[8] delete the `contact` or `opportunity`. Instead, set its status flag as "rejected by sales." If you are clever in your report designs, the rejected items won't mess up any operational metrics, but they will provide quantitative feedback to the Marketing and Lead Cultivation functions.

Moving to the Workflow Diagram

The preceding narrative may be good enough for the people involved, but it contains several areas of ambiguity and interpretation. It is not detailed or precise enough to guide the SFDC development team.

WHEN WORLDS COLLIDE

Unfortunately, in analyzing real-world business processes, the SFDC team may discover collisions of business processes—instances where two exclusive business processes appear to be triggered in parallel. This can happen in sales, order management, or support, particularly when handling exceptional cases.

This situation is never supposed to happen, so you need to figure out whether there's just a misunderstanding (a terminology, semantic, or procedural disagreement) or a logical conflict (a contradiction or a redundancy).

If a logical conflict exists, the team needs to identify and analyze the ambiguity that lies at the conflict's core. This is most quickly done in a meeting with a walk-through of the business process, looking for situations where an object's state is "gray" rather than "black or white." In cases where an object may have several valid states (as embodied in a pick list or calculation threshold), look for conditions where the object can have more than one state at a time.

Some logical conflicts are caused by frustrated customers who try to get answers by going down several paths at once, abandoning those that are unresponsive. These "dangling inquiries" need to be resolved either through a timeout (such as "nonresponse of customer within 48 hours closes the case with state 'resolved'") or logical cleanup (such as "if customer already has inbound request in the Web site, close that request and move any relevant data into the call center part of the system"). These logical resolutions can either be handled as checklist items (for rare, high-value situations) or as system integration improvements (for frequent, low-value situations).

The act of drawing the workflow will likely expose several ambiguous or troublesome areas, forcing the team to break the process into further subprocesses so that it can be turned into a checklist or an SFDC workflow. Ask questions "around the edges" of the narrative, to

---

8. Not ever? Nope. Deleting records obliterates forensic information that helps identify problems in business processes and systems. The larger and more complex your system, the more damage it does to delete records.

make sure that the workflow will be able to handle all situations and exceptions. For example, the narrative doesn't mention how leads are handled internationally, how they are handled for partners, how they are processed by the marketing automation system, whether different kinds of leads are distinguished for different categories of products, and other important issues. You will often find that a single narrative may require several "nearly parallel" workflows to handle variations that were missed while writing the narrative.

In developing the workflow diagram, it's almost always best to have a meeting of the subject-matter experts in a conference room with a *lot* of whiteboards. While developing and double-checking the diagram, do not eat doughnuts or drink a bunch of coffee:[9] people will get overly argumentative and focus too much on unimportant details. It is usually best to have a meeting facilitator with a big-picture perspective, a very analytical mind, patience, and legible handwriting. Business-process consultants are a special breed, but they can save you a lot of time and frustration.

Figure 8-2 shows the lead life cycle described in the earlier narrative. Due to the space constraints of this page, the figure shows just the promotion/qualification/demotion part of the narrative. Check out the book's Web site at www.SFDC-success.com to get more complete example diagrams from various business process analyses.

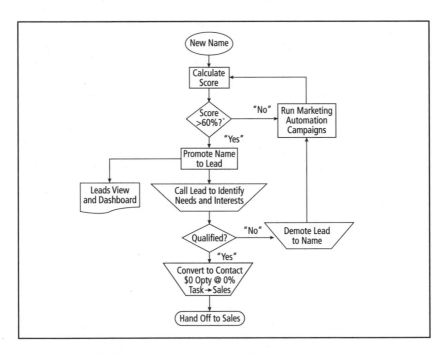

FIGURE 8-2   Example lead life-cycle business process diagram

---

9. Seriously, consuming this stuff can mess up team thinking and lead to contentiousness and nervous energy.

How Much Should Be Changed?

In analyzing business processes, it can be tempting to fundamentally improve things by really reworking a broken area of the business. However, redesigning from a blank slate is almost never a good idea—it's more pragmatic to make incremental changes in a business process that offers the biggest bang for the buck.

This recommendation is not just a consequence of the technical risk involved; rather, it reflects the reality that there can be a lot of politics involved with business process change. In some cases, you'll be changing the daily tasks of workers—or even changing their jobs entirely. This transformation can lead to a lot of questions, endless meetings, and user resistance even if the workers are given orders from on high. It is *critically important* to review the before versus after business process with affected managers at all levels. You may want to include HR personnel in the discussion, particularly if jobs will be redesigned in a big way.

Refining or streamlining an existing business process involves a lot less uncertainty than starting from scratch. Plus, if you are upgrading something that exists, it is easier to identify valid comparative metrics (e.g., 20% fewer errors or 10% decrease in labor costs).

Improving two or three clumsy business processes by the initial SFDC go-live date is probably sufficient to prove the business case for the project. As with the rest of the project, best practices call for making incremental business process changes every quarter or two after the initial go-live date.

That said, sometimes larger business process changes are required. For example, there may be new regulatory requirements (like those wrought by the Sarbanes-Oxley Act) or mandates from customers (such as Wal-Mart or Boeing) that must be implemented by a deadline. In these cases, you will have to make dramatic changes to several business processes, or design new ones from scratch.

Best Practices with Business Process Redesign

While entire books have been written on business process redesign,[10] being aware of a few generalities can help keep the project within reason.

- **Maintain appropriate simplicity.** If the diagrams are to be comprehensible, they cannot cover an entire wall. Process steps in the diagram should be at the level of a single person's (or fixed group's) unwavering task, activity, or decision. Within any of the process steps on the diagram, there may be a checklist of a dozen or more items needed to complete the tasks, but these actions should be documented as notes rather than being shown as discrete lower-level steps. There are two sure signs

---

10. The author believes that these books are too dull for you to actually read.

that a process step probably needs to be split: (1) if the activity must be handed off to another person or (2) if the checklist for the task contains a "branch."

- **Work on processes that are naturally linked.** Assuming you will reword two or three business processes, it's better that those processes be linked in some way, rather than be disparate and autonomous. The learning curve (read: surveys, discussions, and meetings) involved with really fixing a business process can represent a significant amount of the total effort, so you want to leverage your learning across teams as much as possible.

- **Focus on profitable revenue.** For an SFDC-related business process, the goal of the redesign should be streamlining the revenue generation part of the business—specifically, reducing the time and number of errors associated with that process. While cost reductions and efficiencies will almost certainly occur, don't make them the true focus of the improvement. The net result of the business process change should be happier customers and richer salespeople,[11] as these are the highest-leverage ways of improving company profitability.

- **Get executive championship.** Early on, cultivate support from a specific executive for the process change. Even the most worthwhile process improvement stands little chance of overcoming natural resistance if there isn't an executive pounding on the table about it at staff meetings.

- **Remove paper.** One of the deep ironies of computerization is that it has increased the consumption of paper in the office. I have nothing against the stockholders of Hewlett-Packard, Xerox, or Ricoh, but in business process design, paper is a sign of very poor automation. Paper is too often used as the way to transfer information from one step to another, or even from one system to another. (I can't tell you the number of times my firm has discovered people rekeying data.) While paper printouts must exist for signatures, legal documents, or reviews of really large amounts of text or data, in most cases an on-screen display of information will be faster and more accurate. Be willing to "over-invest" in removing paper from business processes,[12] as this step will remove a lot of hidden costs and wasted time. Replacing paper with on-screen forms will also make the workflows much easier to monitor, measure, and improve.

- **Increase information sharing.** While some information must be carefully partitioned and protected, the goal of redesigning the business process is to increase the

---

11. This statement assumes that the sales people are on commission. If they aren't, this sentence should be translated to "bigger and faster sales cycles," which is more accurate but won't be as exciting to the Sales VP who is probably paying for this project.

12. The investment will be in system integration, data validation, user-input screens, and SFDC approval workflows.

amount of information that can be easily shared. If both sides of a conversation have instant access to all relevant data, arguments can be resolved rapidly and fixes implemented immediately. Better collaboration also means faster identification of unintended consequences, such that problems are fixed before they have time to fester with resentment and politics. Finally, better information sharing means more meaningful measurements and a higher chance of congruent goals and behaviors.

- **Minimize manual exceptions.** While human judgment is what sets great businesses apart from the competition, exceptions need to be handled in a methodical way in your business processes. Managing by exception—spending time on the variances and unusual cases—is a best practice because it forces you to systematize and streamline how you handle 90% or more of the business process. But managing by exception should still be part of the process—the unusual actions should be handled as a branch on the business practice chart. Of course, not every step of the exception handling can be done via automation, but this activity should still be systematized and measured so that the organization doesn't spend too much time on the unusual cases. At all costs, avoid the situation where handling certain customer situations means "jumping off the chart," with a person solving the problem in a unique and undocumented way. Even if the customer is satisfied, down this path lies gross inefficiency, inability to manage, and risk of legal problems.[13]

- **Combine individual steps.** In reworking a business process, the goal is not to speed up the execution of silly steps, but rather to make the steps more sensible and systematic. As you're interviewing workers to understand precisely what they do, watch out for activities that seem clumsy, out of order, repeated (listen for red flags like "and then I have to double-check that . . ."), a patchwork, or work-arounds (listen for red flags like "I have to watch out for . . ." or "sometimes"). Spend time investigating the root causes of these unusual activities, and see if they can be made more regular by correcting problems and combining the "micro-steps."

- **Validate business rules.** When your company started out, every business process was simple and straightforward: they had to be. But over time, everything became more complicated. The most complex and broken business processes are typically the oldest ones, having become gnarled messes as layers of business rules, standards, and executive mandates were wallpapered over them as the years went by. Business rules that were set up by long-gone managers are still in place, with new rules implemented as a patchwork. The single highest-leverage goal you can accomplish in business process reengineering is to eliminate obsolete or redundant rules, policies, or standards. When you spot a convoluted mess, it usually exists to help

---

13. Manual exceptions in the forecasting, quoting, closing, or revenue recognition processes will make it very hard for a company to pass a Sarbanes-Oxley Act audit. Visits by SEC investigators are not happy occasions.

the company avoid some costly mistake of the past. On further examination, you may discover that this mistake can't happen again anyway, so all the protective cruft can simply be removed. If Clayton Christensen is correct in saying that "form doesn't follow function: form follows failure," then working to expunge artifacts of old failures is a noble quest. If you must have complex rules, make sure they provide something of beauty or value to the customer, rather than just avoiding a hypothetical negative.

- **Optimize globally.** This statement is fancy-talk for "do the right thing for the company, not just your department." In falsely "fixing" a business process, you might make it much easier and faster for one department to achieve its goals at the expense of another department. The point is to make the *entire system* (the company as a whole) work better, faster, and more pleasantly *for the customer*. Thinking globally, the "customer" is anyone who buys from the company, sells to the company, or invests in the company.

- **Keep it small.** Even though you should be considering the big-picture effects, do not attempt to boil the ocean. Work on a business process that's small enough to get your mind around and fix in a few weeks.

- **Bake in measurements and thresholds.** Any changes to a business process should try to establish new metrics that allow for follow-on analysis and improvement. If there is a clear metric that is meaningful to the customer (such as "how long it took the company to get back to the customer about a problem"), add thresholds and alerts to the new process so that management can see problem areas before they boil over. SFDC can be configured to send emails, set up `tasks`, and start `workflows` when thresholds are exceeded or minimum standards are not achieved. These metrics should not be viewed as micromanaging, but rather as freeing people to apply management by exception more broadly.

- **Accommodate market-specific requirements.** Some markets have special requirements for pricing, invoicing, and revenue-handling processes. For example, sales to government agencies may involve specific approval cycles, paperwork, and discount schedules. In some industries, powerful customers may have "most-favored nation" contractual stipulations that require specific approval cycles for particular product discounts. In the delivery and services part of the business, certain requirements and service level agreements may be enforced only for particular customers.

- **Understand and account for international variations.** Expect to find significant variations of business processes in different national operations in the company. The most obvious differences will relate to currency, tax, and legal regulations that affect many parts of the sales and revenue-handling processes. More subtly, the trade laws and commercial customs may be quite different and imply different `workflows`, `screen layouts`, and `reports` than for domestic operations. Further, marketing processes may have to be different to comply with privacy and consumer protection laws in Europe versus North America. Finally, sales management in each country is very likely to have local directives that diverge from the norm—sometimes causing significant process differences.

- **Gain approval before reimplementing the business process.** Involve as many subject-matter experts as possible while you are analyzing and modifying the business process, but don't actually implement the changes until you've gotten approval from each of the organizations affected by the business process. Make sure that the business process that triggers the start of the one you're working on, and the business processes that your business process triggers, do not depend on an activity or decision that you will be eliminating. It's a good idea to perform walk-throughs of the business process, beginning two business processes before yours and ending two business processes after yours, to make sure your change will not create a new problem. These walk-throughs should be conducted in a single meeting, if practical, to make sure you haven't missed anything. The actual change approvals can be done entirely by email, but don't skip the formality of getting a sign-off.[14]

Making the Changes

You've identified the right business processes to change, you've analyzed them and designed process improvements, you've created diagrams of the business processes (before versus after), and you've gotten explicit permission to make the changes.

Now it's time to set overall metrics to use as criteria for gauging the impact of your business process changes. These metrics need to be objective, realistic, and directly related to the business process area targeted for improvement. Make sure the metrics are achievable—at least in theory—and connected to relevant business results. Do some "devil's advocate" work to make sure they aren't easily gamed or create perverse incentives.

I can't stress enough the importance of metrics in managing change: they help justify investments, they give people meaningful goals to strive for, and they show how much better the company is doing now than it was "before." Good metrics also let you know when you've succeeded.

Within SFDC, several areas of the system are likely to require changes. Data input changes are handled through new `screen layouts`, and user-specific (or process-step-specific) input changes are implemented using `record types`. Data entries will need to be validated with new formulas and thresholds. `Triggers` will need to be established or modified, and `workflows` established. `Approval processes`—both the items being approved and the approval path—will almost certainly need to be changed.

14. After all, your changing of a business process should itself be a business process, rather than an unpredictable act.

Outside of SFDC, business process changes may require changes to system integration parameters. In some cases, code in external systems will need to be written or modified.

As the system modifications are made, support for the old business process will almost certainly degrade or even disappear. For a while, the automation support that workers are used to will not exist, so they will have to handle an increasingly manual process. Consequently, it is important to get the changes made and validated quickly.

Actually implementing the "people side" of a process change consists of developing and documenting new semantics for objects, activities, and thresholds. Users need to be trained about any new wording or naming standards, procedures, or caveats. To help them make the transition, the SFDC team should create new checklists or cheat sheets for the people involved.

After the Changes Are Made

The modified business processes need to be monitored for their performance against the metrics set up. Review sessions should initially take place on a daily basis, with corrective actions being applied as rapidly as possible to minimize rework. The frequency of these reviews should rapidly diminish as variances and unexpected consequences subside. If you discover persistent errors, validate the business process diagram and annotations, make sure the changes were implemented in SFDC and any supporting system, and take whatever corrective action is required. Do not let problems persist for more than a few weeks, as they will undermine the system credibility and irritate users if they linger for too long.

CHAPTER 9

Best Practices for Sales

Sales reps are coin-operated.

—*S. Nelson French, Sales VP*

T HIS CHAPTER IS THE centerpiece in explaining how to get the most out of your SFDC system, because the system is first and foremost intended for sales users, from individual reps and sales administrators up to the VP or COO. This chapter organizes these best practices along the business-process lines described in Chapter 8. To make them more accessible, however, they have been reordered here to fit sales personnel's job titles. That said, skim all the sections: you'll find useful tips throughout the chapter even if the section doesn't exactly match your job title.

In addition to reading this chapter, you'll definitely want to visit www.SFDC-secrets. com to see the latest checklists, recommended pick-list values, screen layouts, and other essential items as they evolve for different product/service categories and vertical industries. If all of them were included here, the book would be a half-inch thicker—and would need to be updated constantly.

"Universal" Best Practices

When it comes to sales management, there aren't too many best practices that apply across every industry and sales/channel organization. Nevertheless, there are some critical success factors that consistently hold true, even if they aren't practiced everywhere:

- Management should look at marketing and sales collectively as a single business process, with an investment (e.g., salaries, programs, travel, customer dinners) and a payoff (revenue). The goal is to reduce the cost of customer acquisition, given the company's growth objective. This goal isn't the same as "shorten sales cycles," because the point is to obtain the sales cycle with the best business yield—which isn't necessarily the shortest one. Management should be looking to maximize customer life-cycle profitability, not simply "get more sales." The trick for both of these key success factors is to balance the investments in marketing, Web sales, inside sales, indirect sales, and direct sales. The classic mistake is to invest too much in direct sales, without having enough real, profitable deals to go after. You'll definitely want to set up SFDC metrics and incentives to help bring this distribution into balance.

- The key for better sales productivity is to relieve the reps of busywork and overhead meetings so they can spend more time selling and working on the most promising accounts. The 80–20 rule[1] definitely applies here, and SFDC can do a lot to improve reps' productivity by helping them manage their time and focus on the accounts that will really pay off.

- Although growth typically comes from getting new customers, *profit* definitely comes from repeat business. The glory and sex appeal may come from hiring the most aggressive reps to break open new accounts, but that kind of selling is rarely the most profitable. Industry statistics show that upselling and expanding existing customers requires only one-third to one-tenth the cost and effort of acquiring new customers. *Of course* it is important to get new customers, but over-focusing on them just burns cash. You'll want to evaluate this area carefully with SFDC metrics (that examine both the sales and the customer support function) so you can understand the growth and health of your customer franchise. For example, SFDC reports can identify the frequency of orders from a customer, the overall upsell business (percentage of total dollars, percentage of total deals, and percentage of total profitability), and the customer support renewal percentage.

- It's critically important that marketing, inside sales, and outside sales personnel agree about the sales model for your business. This model doesn't have to be a complex sales methodology—it can simply be a description of the life cycle of the company's pipeline, the waterfall of sales stages, and the conversion rates along the way. Things tend to fall apart when disagreement arises about the metrics, responsibilities, workflow, and semantics of the sales model. If you can't agree on what a qualified lead is or what triggers creation of an opportunity, how can you optimize and streamline anything about revenue production?

- If you have three sales channels, you are likely to have three sales models—and SFDC should be integrated so it fully supports each of them.

- The marketing and sales team needs to work as a lead processing machine, characterized by both policies and systematic follow-up. Identify the optimal response patterns for new leads and repeat visitors, and enforce the right behaviors with

---

1. In most selling organizations, 80% of the revenues come from 20% of the customers. So it's important to focus everyone's effort on those one-in-five customers that will really make a difference to the business's results.

incentives and measurements. Look for the number of untouched `leads`, the time to first touch, and the conversion ratio percentages; put in `workflows` and alerts so that `leads` don't go cold.

- Leads and visibility are nice, but in and of themselves they don't put bread on the table. Focus the marketing effort on the things that start sales cycles and close deals—such as customer "referencability" and testimonial quotes—and pay less attention to arbitrary statistics that are easily gamed. Set up SFDC metrics that focus on sales-cycle starts that have directly resulted from marketing activity.

- `Opportunities` must be managed systematically, with checkpoints and alerts being put in place to make sure that deals don't go sideways or backward. A global forecast should be created on a weekly basis, and the SFDC system should contain enough information so that you could do a mini account review at a moment's notice. Look for workflows and alerts that ensure key players know the state of every deal, and set up serious pipeline metrics and sales-rep scorecards. There should be no mystery about how each territory will make its quarterly number.

- The SFDC system needs to act as a public kiosk showing the state of the deals. It also needs to be *the* place for all people working on the account to find out what's going on, and where they can post updates so everyone knows the state of play. The goal is to get away from using intramural email as the way to handle action items and updates. Let's face it: we're all overloaded with email and nobody can find *all* the relevant emails all the time. By using a kiosk model of deal and account information, all the information is available to everyone equally, and at the time they *need to know* it (which is rarely the time when the typical email would be sent). SFDC makes it easy to keep the entire sales, support, and executive team in sync and to bring new resources on board without a lot of ramp-up time.

- To leverage the SFDC system effectively, it should be configured to be more like a well-integrated CRM system than just a stand-alone SFA system. There are two things to watch out for in this regard: keep the system simple, and question the need for each external integration. There are a variety of ways to satisfy requirements, and integrations can be costly and buggy. Read the section in Chapter 7 on this topic.

- Recognize that almost any change in the SFDC system or surrounding processes will draw criticism as being "harder" or "taking more time," even if a bit of effort actually saves time for the complaining individual and adds value to the company. Pay attention to negative feedback about change only if it grows over time. Have someone (e.g., a well-connected administrator) listen for scuttlebutt, and put the signals into the project wiki.

- SFDC should be driven and owned by the sales organization. Not marketing. Not finance. Not IT. Although all of these departments can help with operations and expertise, only the sales department has the urgency and the firepower required to make an SFDC system work to optimize revenue.

- Unless the company is a very small, early-stage operation, at least SFDC's Enterprise edition is called for. It's more expensive, but it is the only way to achieve the best practices described in this chapter.

- Sales reps' behavior follows the incentives that are set out for them in the commission plan. They aren't going to follow jaw-boning instructions, particularly from marketing or finance. For the commission plan to be powerful, make sure it is tightly aligned with the financial goals of the corporation. To make it really effective, keep the plan stable and simple—if you use more than three metrics to drive behaviors, everyone is likely to become confused. Keep the SFDC system clearly aligned with reps achieving their commission plan!

For more exciting news in this area, check out newsletters like *The Taber Report* and *Sirius Decisions*.

Define and Document the Sales Model

Revenue generation is a business process, and it needs to be managed as such. Of course sales owns the number, but the business process of revenue generation spans most of marketing, all of sales, a bit of finance, and much of customer service. While some elements of the revenue business process hold true for all sales organizations, the particulars of how *your company* grows prospects into customers and customers into repeat business depends on the company and its target markets.

Before you can apply any of the recommendations in this chapter, you need to develop a model of how your company's revenue generation process works.[2] Spend a bit of time (it can be done in an afternoon if you're serious) defining and documenting your revenue model. Involve sales, marketing, and support managers in the process, and encourage argument: if the model isn't realistic or consistent across the organization, you'll be working at cross purposes. Each group will be pointing to the others as the "revenue prevention department."

It doesn't matter whether you use a drawing, a bulleted list, or a narrative to depict the model. What does matter is that your model be written down and answer these questions:

---

2. Just saying, "Go out and sell," is not a sales model. Developing a coherent, working revenue model and sales process is what the VP of Sales is paid to do.

> ### WHAT'S THE BOLDFACE FONT MEAN?
>
> *When an item below appears in boldface font, it's the best practice for most sales organizations. But your organization may not even have a functional group with that title, so adjust the idea accordingly. If there's a good reason that the answer is something else for your organization, write down the reasons why in the description of your sales model.*

- Who are the company's target customers? (brief written description needed for each product line)

- Who is responsible for lead generation? (**marketing**, inside sales, or sales[3])

- Who schedules Webinars and other broad outreach events? (**marketing**, inside sales, or sales)

- Who handles inbound inquiries? (marketing, **inside sales,** or sales)

- Who makes the first call to prospects? (marketing, **inside sales,** or sales)

- How are territories defined? How are overlays defined? What are the rules of engagement (ROE) for territory conflicts within the company?

- Which kinds of channel partners does the company leverage? What percentage of the business is brought in by each type of channel?

- What's the definition of a named account, and how many of them are there? How often are major or strategic account lists allowed to change?

- What is the organization's hierarchy for account ownership and forecast management? (SFDC really wants a clear, **unambiguous hierarchy;** dotted-line relationships and matrix organizations are a real bear to work with.)

- How are leads prequalified and routed to partners? How do partner leads get assigned within the team? (**automatic routing,** manual daily process, manual opportunistic process)

- Who does cultivation, nurturing, and qualification of leads? (marketing, **inside sales,** or sales)

- How are leads qualified? What are the criteria for conversion? Are these triggers **written down and used consistently?**

---

3. Throughout this chapter, the term "sales" is used when discussing outside sales or direct field sales representatives. "Inside sales" refers people who do sales activities entirely over the phone; these people may have job titles of telemarketing, telesales, inside sales, sales development, sales associate, or sales support.

- Who schedules customer Webinars, demonstrations, or other initial proofs of value? (marketing, **inside sales,** or sales)

- How are sales teams selected (for example, in global accounts or purchases that involve products from several divisions)?

- Who opens an opportunity, and what are the opening parameters? (marketing, **inside sales,** or sales)

- How are quotes issued?

- How are special orders, discounts, or contractual terms approved?

- Who closes opportunities (both wins and losses)? (sales, **sales operations,** finance)

- How are commissions, splits, and referral fees calculated? (case by case, **manual spreadsheet,** automatic commission system)

- What's the waterfall model for the pipeline? (Each of the following questions should to be answered for each sales channel.)

  ⇥ What's the average deal size?

  ⇥ What's the average length of the sales cycle?

  ⇥ What's the proportion of repeat/upsell deals to new customer wins?

  ⇥ How many deals does each channel need to do to make its numbers?

  ⇥ How many sales cycles have to be started to achieve that number of deals?

  ⇥ How many leads need to be collected to start that number of sales cycles?

  ⇥ How many stages are in the sales cycle? If there are fewer than four or more than eight, why?

  ⇥ What are the sales stage names, how long does each stage last, what are the required sales activities, and what are the customer actions or criteria that trigger transition from one stage to the next?

  ⇥ What is the conversion (or, alternatively, the drop-off) ratio at each stage?

  ⇥ What are the probabilities of closing the deal at each stage?

- How broadly is information shared, beyond the standard managerial roll-ups? Can all reps see all accounts and opportunities, or should they see only those in their own territory?

- How are divisions and subsidiaries handled? How are international sales handled? How are distributors and channels handled?

- How are marketing, inside sales, direct sales, and the channel measured and incented?

Once you've worked through your model, compare it to the model used in this chapter, and adjust the recommendations given here to fit your organization. As its ongoing example, this chapter uses the high-tech B2B sales model: a combination of eCommerce at the low end, inside sales in the mid-range, and direct sales at the enterprise level. Further, "inside sales" personnel are assumed to handle all lead cultivation, nurturing, and qualification, so that the direct reps can spend their time on the most highly leveraged part of their job: expanding the size of the deal while increasing the probability of winning.

Inside Sales

As mentioned previously, this team is called different things at different companies. This book uses the term "inside sales" to refer to these personnel, but they are often known as telesales, telemarketing, sales development, sales associates, or sales support. In small organizations, this team may do pretty much everything *except* outside sales. They may do cold calling, lead generation, lead cultivation/nurturing, lead qualification, appointment setting, order management, and even pre-sales customer support. In some organizations, they also make sales and assist with tricky eCommerce transactions.

No matter what the specific job title, this function needs to have *very* tight communications with outside sales reps. Almost always, best practice is to have members of this team report to the sales organization, and to have them report to the appropriate geographic territory manager (e.g., the western U.S. inside sales team should report to the VP of Western Sales). Typically, the inside sales team will be managed by an inside sales pro—not a sales rep or a marketing person. The skills, pacing, and management of inside sales are just different enough that a specialist really will get more productivity out of the team. If the company does not have enough headcount to permit this organization, many consultancies are available to provide really tight management of inside sales on a part-time basis. The data and features of SFDC make this kind of operation straightforward and effective.

The inside sales team is the "natural" audience for using SFDC. So that's the first best practice: get this team using SFDC intensively *before anyone else in sales.* Inside sales personnel spend enormous amounts of time on the phone, they already have a browser up (to hit their prospects' Web sites or find out about leads), and they're already using some sort of contact manager, organizer, or spreadsheet to keep track of their call-down lists.

Initial Setup

The lead status pick-list field needs to be modified to indicate the realistic life cycle of a lead,[4] as documented in the revenue model. Typically SFDC's lead record will need to have a few extra fields added (such as those for the lead score, sales territory, and product interest

---

4. For example, the field items might be called new, contact attempt, contact made, working, hold, qualified, bad data, no interest, lost interest, wrong person, or remarket.

pull-downs) for the company's unique products or target audience. Resist the temptation to put in a bunch of extra fields that you know, in your heart of hearts, no one will ever fill out or use. These "great idea" fields will simply lower the system's credibility.

COORDINATE WITH MARKETING ON THIS STEP, IF NOTHING ELSE

Because the inside sales team will be focused on leads, *in addition to reading this chapter they should check out the corresponding discussion on lead generation, collection, handling, and cultivation in Chapter 10.*

Some other SFDC features and add-ons will also benefit the inside sales team:

- If your company uses Skype or Cisco IP phones, put the free[5] dialer buttons on the SFDC screen next to the phone numbers of leads and contacts. Initially, the button will save the inside rep (and anyone else who uses it) a few seconds on every call, while preventing misdials. But over time, the use of the button means that users will keep the phone numbers in SFDC up-to-date not because someone told them to, but because it's in *their own best interests*. This force of gravity—using different specific "natural features" in each case—should be used at every turn to increase adoption in the field.

- Over time, the initial button can be replaced with a fancier (non-free) one that automatically logs the time of the call, creating an activity history item so that the caller doesn't have to do it manually. This saves at least 10 seconds and 4 mouse clicks for anyone who makes a call. Of course, this fancier item is a double-edged sword: now everyone will know how many times anyone has attempted to call the prospect—a good thing to prevent double-calling, but a bad thing for reps who are worried about being micromanaged.

- Make use of SFDC Consoles. These special screens can be configured to provide everything you need to see about the prospect on one screen.

Prospecting and Initial Contact

The inside sales team should point their browsers to SFDC before they even pick up the phone. Make sure that the daily lead flows, call-down sheets, and renewal reminder lists get to them *only* via SFDC pages—stop sending emails containing spreadsheets and lists to these reps. To implement this kind of structure, SFDC needs to be fully integrated with the company's Web site, content management system, marketing automation system, and import/deduping tools.

---

5. There are also similar (non-free) buttons that connect to other telephony systems and PBXs.

WHO'S DOING THE INITIAL CALLING, CULTIVATION, AND QUALIFYING?

Although this book designates the people who do the initial lead development as "inside sales," there is a counter-intuitive key success factor for this function: the people who do the initial calling, cultivation, and qualification should *not* be carrying a sales quota. The existence of a commission is distracting, and it undermines the thoroughness of the (admittedly boring) process of dialing out and reading scripts. Having both a revenue target and a lead generation goal confuses not just the individuals on the phone, but their manager as well.

Said a simpler way, don't confuse telemarketing with telesales.

This is a highly controversial topic that will generate endless debate, but even if you disagree with the recommendation, separating telemarketing from inside sales (i.e., breaking apart the function of initial qualification from selling) carries three benefits:

- You can measure each operation better.
- You remove excuses.
- You can outsource one part without affecting the other. Different kinds of firms are available for outsourcing each part, which reinforces the notion that telemarketing and telesales really are different functions.

Leads should be automatically routed into and managed in queues unless the company's sales team is very small. Queues serve as a holding tank for leads that have not been claimed or worked by someone in the queue's sales region. They provide important metrics for inside sales team management, lead quality, and conversion rates, so it's important to use them properly. Typically, a queue is seen by all the reps in the queue's territory, and any lead in a queue can be handled by anyone on the team. As soon as someone in sales wants to work on a lead in his or her team's queue, that individual needs to take ownership of the lead by clicking on SFDC's change owner link to reassign it to the sales rep. Leads should never go from individual ownership back into a queue; even if the lead owner leaves the sales team, the leads he or she is working should be explicitly reassigned to an individual, not returned to the territory's queue.

When a new lead comes in, it should be transferred to the inside sales reps in real time. It is almost impossible for sales reps to call back too soon: prospects are always impressed with prompt responses, and it says a lot about the company's customer-focused attitude. Recent studies have shown that in our fast-paced world, prospect response rates fall off dramatically within hours after the initial contact. Indeed, within 48 hours most prospects will not even remember having visited the company's Web site, let alone have a clue about its value proposition or competitive advantage. Use SFDC's auto-response rules to send an email to the lead the instant that the potential customer registers. Best practice is to make the first phone attempt—at least leaving a voice message—on the same day that the lead contacted the company. Some companies go so far as to have an inside rep on the phone to the prospect before the `lead` even leaves the company's Web site (this advice isn't for everyone, but you can see how doing so might make a powerful impression on the prospect). This kind of responsiveness is possible only with solid automation, integration, and user indoctrination, but it pays off in higher conversion rates and cold, hard cash.

Given the variety of things an inside rep needs to do, it's important to prioritize `leads` so time is spent on the most promising prospects. The default SFDC field called "rating" is just a hot/medium/cold pick list, and we advise against using it unless the company has a very small sales team. It's far better to have marketing set up a `custom field` on `leads` with a scoring system. While simplistic `lead` scoring can be done by *profiling* (giving points for location, title, company size, industry, and other properties), it is best practice to add *behavioral* scoring (anyone who does a download or attends a Webinar should pop up as a priority; anyone who has been silent for a month should drop down in terms of urgency). Behavioral and profile scoring are available as part of most marketing automation tools. By presenting only high-scoring leads to the inside sales team, marketing improves perceived lead quality and can directly affect the effectiveness of sales overall. Of course, even the best tools require time to tune the `lead` scoring—during the first few months, the scores will inevitably be misleading (because they're based on theory, rather than the behavior of your best-performing target customers). Give feedback to the marketing personnel who run the scoring system so they can steadily improve its function. We'll discuss this topic in more detail in Chapter 10.

Another tactic that dramatically improves conversion rates is to have marketing set up a "drip marketing" system (also known as sequential auto-responders or vertical campaigns). Once a prospect has registered interest, the `lead` is sent a series of *relevant informational* emails covering the topic of interest. The sequence of emails is usually along the following lines: same day, next day, three days later, one week later, two weeks later, one month later. Each email provides a new bit of information or perspective to move the prospect farther down the learning curve about the company. The emails should contain calls to action, but they should be subtle ("find out more" is way better than "buy now") and *sound* different in each email. The emails should appear to come from the relevant inside sales person, even though they are fully automated. The emails *must* have an opt-out mechanism that works, and they need to automatically stop the instant that a human conversation has happened (of course, the only way for this kind of interaction to occur is for the inside and outside sales folks to actually register their calls using SFDC's `Activity` button). Check out Chapter 10 if you want to know more about this way of doing business.

Move away from paper—get rid of binders and cheat sheets. Put documents that are useful to the inside sales people within easy reach: store them in SFDC's documents section,[6] and create custom links to rapidly turn them into call scripts that inside sales reps can read and

---

6. Only the most essential documents should actually be stored within SFDC. For storage limitation reasons, you want to store only items that are small and don't have to be individualized for every prospect or account. A few dozen pieces of sales collateral, white papers, or PowerPoint slides that everyone needs should be held in SFDC; everything else (e.g., case studies, RFP responses, quotes) should be *linked to* the relevant SFDC records, but should be stored in the company's file servers (or shared directories).

PDFs they can email to prospects. When these documents are housed in the system, there's never a risk of using an outdated version. SFDC's `Content edition` provides a great way for marketing and sales personnel to better manage collateral documents, and it's almost essential for any sales team that has to sell a wide range of products from several company divisions.

It's really important to have tight scripts for the inside reps. While the company might want to experiment to find out what works best with prospects, the *only* way to get real productivity out of an inside sales team is to have 80% of the calls made according to the approved formula. The other 20% can be experiments, but they need to be tightly controlled and measured as part of "A/B split testing."[7] Evolve the scripts that achieve the best test results on a monthly basis (more frequently if things are changing radically in your market space) and *keep a log of what the changes and results have been.* It's a good idea to involve marketing personnel in this exercise, as they tend to like tracking and crunching data. SFDC dramatically simplifies the conduct of these kinds of A/B tests, and the reporting system can provide up-to-the-minute comparisons of conversion rate results. That said, it's important to not react too quickly to preliminary test data: virtually any test you run should last for more than a week, owing to daily fluctuations in user responsiveness.

If the inside sales team has to deal with a lot of products or very different market segments, embed the script sequences and qualifying questions directly in their SFDC screen. (A free AppExchange plugin will get you there.) As the inside reps check boxes or select pull-down list items (e.g., "has budget" and "50–100 users"), the screens can change to reflect the script path being followed with the prospect. Further, automatic rules within SFDC can be set up to score the degree of the prospect's qualification according to the script answers. The system can even be set up to send notification emails to sales reps about the hot leads that deserve their immediate attention.[8]

Lead Cultivation, Nurturing, and Qualification

Moving the prospect from awareness to interest to desire to willingness to take an appointment is almost always done by someone in the sales team.

For marketing personnel to produce the right *quality* and quantity of `leads`—what's really required to fill the top of the funnel—they need to have a contract or service level agreement with inside sales covering the life cycle of `leads`. Items to be explicitly agreed

---

7. Split testing is a technique for comparing the results of using two versions of the call script, Web page, or other marketing/sales messaging. The two versions are used randomly with prospects, but the results of the A version (typically, the baseline) are tracked separately from the results of the B version (typically, the "new and improved" one). Following the scientific method, this style of testing can rapidly prove whether the B version is an improvement. As soon as a round of A/B testing is completed, the stronger version becomes the new A version, and a new B version is set up as the challenger.

8. If you really want to go nuts, have your implementer write a bit of code that automatically qualifies high-scoring leads and initiates the `lead conversion` process. This strategy is not something we recommend for the first year of SFDC system operation (because too often there is disagreement about what qualifies as "qualified" or as something warranting a sales rep's attention), but SFDC technology makes this possible.

to include how quickly `leads` get into the system, how rapidly they are contacted, how many calls or contact attempts are made, and what the "perishability date" of a `lead` is.

How long should your inside folks spend on a prospect before they give up? The answer to this question varies by company and customer base, but there's one cardinal rule: never, ever[9] delete a `lead` or a `contact`. Generally speaking, the timing of the lead processing should be along these lines:

- If a `lead`'s contact information is bogus (the email bounces and the phone number is incorrect), the inside sales folks should mark it as such (with a status of "bad data") within 24 hours of receiving the `lead`. These `leads` should be sent back over to the marketing staff so they can debug the problem (and almost certainly demote the `campaign` or source that produced the trash `lead`).

- If the prospect is a `contact`, not a `lead` (i.e., the person is a returning participant in the company's marketing activities and was already listed in the system as a `contact`), the new information about the `contact` (his or her participation/response) should be added to the *existing SFDC record*. This is best done through the `campaigns` feature, where an existing contact becomes a member of a "new" `campaign`. If the `contact`'s contact information is bogus, an inside sales rep should set its status to "bad data" within 24 hours of receiving it, and its ownership should be transferred to the marketing staff so they can investigate.

- If a `lead`'s or `contact`'s contact information is good but the prospect is not responsive to email and voice messages for 30 days (e.g., an entire drip-marketing sequence), the `lead` or `contact` should be demoted and put back into the "remarket" or "newsletter" queue handled by marketing. Note that "dead" or "disqualified" `leads` or `contacts`—when properly cultivated and nurtured over time—can represent as much as one-third of the company's business. Industry statistics indicate that dead leads will buy product from *someone* in the next 18 months—it's just a matter of which company they will purchase from.

- If a `lead` or `contact` is responsive, but is unable or unwilling to move forward in qualification, the inside rep should maintain ownership of the person, set the prospect's `status` to "on hold," and create a `task` to call the person in 60 days (or whatever).

- If a prospect is responsive and can be qualified by inside sales, the sales staff should do so within 15 days of receipt. If it takes longer than that span, you'll want to investigate and understand why. Of course, if a prospect is qualified before then, that person should be immediately `converted` and sent over to sales.

It's best to create a timeline such as Figure 9-1 showing the sequence and timing of activities leading to a `conversion` or demotion of a `lead`.

---

9. Not even if somebody dies? NOT EVER.

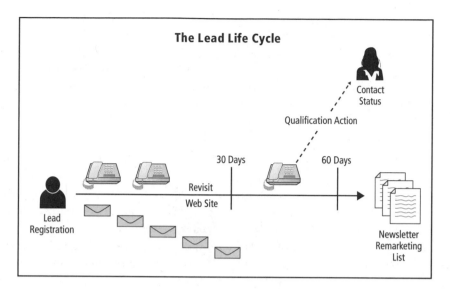

FIGURE 9-1   Timeline showing the life cycle of a lead

One of the key elements of the contract between inside sales and marketing is, "How do leads get refused or rejected by inside sales?" There should be clear criteria for this decision, and whenever an inside sales rep rejects a lead, that individual needs to set the rejection reason pull-down for the lead.[10] Once the lead is rejected by inside sales, the expectation should be that the prospect will continue to receive newsletters and other electronic marketing indefinitely—forever, unless the prospect explicitly opts out of this process.

SFDC's lead status pick-list entries should be adjusted to fit the company's contact, cultivation, and nurturing pattern. For example, the pick list could include the following items: new, contact attempted, contact made, working, hold, qualified, rejected, and bad data. It is common practice to add a few extra fields to the lead record (to capture the specifics of product interest, a promotional special, or other characteristics), but keep their number to a minimum. A lead record should be fairly brief: long lead pages are almost never filled in and just frustrate everybody.

The most interesting part of a lead record *isn't* the lead detail information at the top of the page; it's the related lists underneath. The evolution of a lead's interest and potential shows up as entries in activity history, campaign history, and custom objects such as download history. Many of these related list entries are filled in automatically by Web site, email marketing, content management, license server, and other external systems

---

10. The rejection reason pick list is a dependent field of the lead status, so it's only after a lead has been explicitly rejected by inside sales that this pick list becomes visible. Items on this pick list might include bad data, no interest, lost interest, no budget, no power, no vision, and no competitive advantage.

OUTSOURCING LEAD CULTIVATION OR NURTURING

Lead cultivation can be effectively outsourced, particularly if the company has a large sales operation and some of the workload can be clearly partitioned (for example, a special promotion, a new product offering, or an uncovered territory). However, outsourcing requires a lot of careful design and monitoring—and you need to have very tight management to make this strategy work properly.

Here are the most important rules for success: give the outsourced team the same tools that the inside folks have, and measure them just as tightly as the company measures its own people. This statement translates into "give the outsourced team full access to the SFDC system."

Most outsourced telemarketing/telesales teams will already be familiar with SFDC. If the team is small (or if you are buying the services of a dedicated team), it's a relatively straightforward matter for them to use your SFDC system directly. Of course, you'll need to pay for the licenses those team members use. You'll also want to restrict their access to the system (you'll almost certainly need Enterprise edition to handle this issue properly) so they see only what's relevant to lead processing and they can't run reports.

If the outsourcing firm is large, it will have to manage several clients and is likely to have its own internal system for managing and monitoring calls. In this case, the outsourced team is unlikely to use your company's SFDC instance. Thus one strategy in these circumstances is an export/import cycle between your system and the outsourcing firm's system. However, SFDC's new `Salesforce to Salesforce` feature makes it easy to share information across systems. If you can talk the outsourcing vendor into it, this effort is well worth the cost of setting up the feature to work as your real-time bridge.

If the outsourcing firm doesn't use SFDC, then you'll have to do things the twentieth-century way. Your company sends the `leads` to the outsourced team on a daily basis (typically as a spreadsheet), and it sends the "hot, ready-to-convert leads" back to you pretty much in real time. On a weekly basis, the team will also send the lead status information. Most of the time, you will not get any detailed call metrics from the outsourced team in the same way you would with an inside team; instead, you'll probably just receive data on the aggregate number of dials and conversations, plus the snapshot of the lead status.

While a `lead` is in process with the outsourced agency, its SFDC ownership should be changed to the `queue` or individual who's handling it. You may also want to add a `custom field` or two to the `lead` page to hold information that's relevant to the outsourcing process. For example, a `formula field` indicating "how long in this status" may provide a useful metric for monitoring the outsourcer's performance.

integrated with SFDC. The idea is that every automated outbound touch should show up as a campaign entry, and every response (whether opening of an email, an RSVP, an attendance, a download, or a registration) should show up as either a `campaign response` or a completed `activity`. When the company's phone system is integrated with the SFDC system, every outbound dial and inbound callback will also be recorded automatically. With all this information, the inside sales people can immediately see the profile of the lead and the prospect's recent level of interest. This information is particularly useful if a large sales team shares the workload for a territory, as anyone can instantly see the state of play for any lead in the territory.

This level of instrumentation also gives sales management much clearer metrics on the inside sales people, and it helps them determine whether their model of activity management is realistic.

On the lead page, make it easy for the inside reps to get supplemental information from outside sources. Smart reps will want to do a little research before they call a new lead. Use the page layout tool to install links to Google Search and Google News (for general information about a prospect company), and to Hoover's, Dun & Bradstreet, or other service (for financial and business information). For information about the individual lead, add links for LinkedIn, ZoomInfo, or your favorite lead database service.

For a wide range of reasons, the best way to improve the lead cultivation and nurturing process is for members of the SFDC team to meet frequently with the marketing team. Help them understand which changes are needed in terms of content, messaging, or lead production. When evaluating metrics, make sure the conversation focuses on achieving objectives and improving the number of first sales meetings—stay away from words that sound like a performance review, over-measurement, or the assignment of blame. Outbound marketers are the natural partners of inside sales reps, so do everything possible to foster good communications and a tight working relationship with these individuals.

Many different metrics can be implemented for inside sales. Even so, we recommend going light on these measurements at the outset of SFDC implementation. It is important that SFDC not be viewed as an enforcer or a tool of micromanagers. Adoption and usage—with quality data that makes SFDC a more valuable asset to the sales organization—are the only metrics that matter for the first nine months or so of system usage. Early on, have metrics and incentives for logging in, having complete records, and using the system's features. Leave the heavy-handed activity management for later (a point that is discussed later in this chapter).

Conversion and Hand-Off to Sales

Once a prospect has been qualified, in many cases the inside team's job is over (depending on how the company organizes its sales roles). The last thing an inside sales rep should do is to schedule a follow-up call for the outside rep, enter call notes, and convert the lead to a contact. The conversion process makes the lead disappear and be replaced by a new contact, which will be attached to an account (ideally, with a contact role) and a named opportunity. Figure 9-2 illustrates the lead conversion process.

It's a best practice to hand over ownership of opportunities to the outside sales rep because that way the inside sales rep never has to look at leads. Instead, he or she can focus on deals (where the money will be) and sees only the relevant, up-to-date contact information.

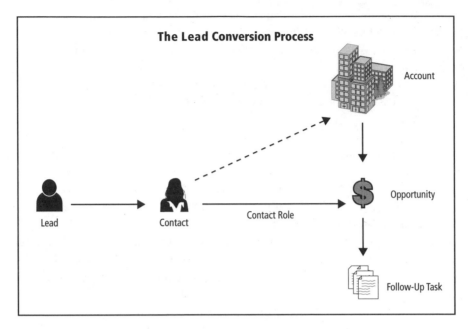

FIGURE 9-2   The lead conversion process

Note that best practices in this area vary tremendously—your company and its business practices may need to do things in a completely different way from the "vanilla" formula described here. Check out www.SFDC-secrets.com for variations and templates that make sense for different kinds of customer and pre-sales situations.

Here are default best practices for the conversion and hand-off process:

- Usually, the new `contact` (and `opportunity`) should be attached to an existing `account`. If SFDC finds more than one likely `account`, it will allow you to select among them via a pick list. If SFDC doesn't find an `account` that is a close match to the `lead`'s company field, it will automatically create the new `account` upon conversion.

- The `account` object should have the standard `Name` field filled with a "friendly" name that people will search for (for example, "Disney") and a `custom field` called "Legal Entity Name" used by the Accounting, Legal, and other departments to indi-cate the formal name of the legal entity (for example, "The Walt Disney Company"). While this may seem redundant, how many people will know to search for "The Great Atlantic and Pacific Tea Company" when they're thinking of "A&P"? The friendly name needs to be free of foreign characters, accents, apostrophes, and hyphens to make searching and report-filtering more reliable (for example, if you're searching for Conde Nast, the system won't find Condé Nast).

CREATION SCIENCE

Okay, okay: I apologize for the title. But it got your attention, right?

There really is a science to properly creating `leads`, `contacts`, `accounts`, and `opportunities` within SFDC. Do it wrong, and you end up with a bunch of duplicate records that need to be cleaned up later. Do it right, and you save a bunch of time.

The First Commandment: *thou shalt not create anything without searching for it first.*[11] Just put a short string in the "Search" box (which should always be set up on the left side of your screen) followed by an asterisk (*) wildcard to find whether a variant of the thing you're trying to create already exists in the system. If you find an existing `contact` or `lead` record, apply your new information to it. `Accounts` get a little hairier:

- If you find an existing `account` that's nearly an exact match to what you want to create, use that one but don't update its information (send an email to the system administrator with the changes you think need to be made).

- If you find an existing `account` that *isn't* an exact match, create a new `account` with your information and have its "parent" field point to the existing account.[12]

An important corollary of this commandment: *sales shall never import lists into SFDC.* This is the devil's work and must be performed by marketing or system administrators.

The Second Commandment: *thou shalt not delete things.* The system needs to keep track of bad data, falsely qualified `leads`, and bogus `opportunities`[13]—the only way your marketing and inside sales groups will ever improve is to get concrete, quantitative feedback in the form of dead records. Identify bad records, mark them as such, and save them. SFDC has lots of ways to make bad records disappear from view and reports, but if the records are actually deleted, no one can ever learn anything from the past or measure process improvements.

The "do not try this at home" corollary of this commandment is "deduping is to be done only by professionals." They have special tools and magical methods all their own.

- The account name should be more than just the friendly, short name for the company. It needs to have some descriptive data for fast searching and viewing, including items such country, segment, and year of first sale (for example, "Corporate–Disney–US–2004"). The use of double-dashes (or the em-dash character) is needed to distinguish the spacer from a standard hyphen (that will occur in company names like Lockheed-Martin). If you want to understand more about this issue, check out the "What's in a Namespace" section in Chapter 2.

---

11. You don't want to create duplicate species, do you? What kind of creation would that be?
12. System administrators may consolidate these `accounts` later, but they will follow a careful set of business rules to do so.
13. To see who's been naughty and who's been nice.

- For really big `accounts` (i.e., big companies, albeit not necessarily big sources of business for your company), create a master `parent account` that is named either "Company–Headquarters" or "Stock Symbol–HQ." Even though your company may never have an `opportunity` within this corporate entity, it's helpful to have a top level of the `account` hierarchy for *Fortune* 500 companies with dozens of divisions. See Figure 3-2 for an illustration of this practice.

- The `account` object should have a pick list for `type` that contains indicators for the different classes of companies with which your sales team must deal. For example, types might include NAM[14] `prospect`, `Strategic`, `Customer`, `Partner`, `Distributor`, `Supplier`, `Government`, `Inactive`, and `Out of Business`. The `account` object should also have roll-up fields to show key summaries of orders, such as "last 12 months order $" and "total lifetime order $."

- The `opportunity name` also needs to follow a naming convention, typically along the lines of: account Name–Department/Project–Product–QQYY. This standard may seem time-consuming to follow, but you quickly get used to it and having `opportunity` names in this format makes it much easier to see what's going on in forecasting, views, reports, bar charts, and management roll-ups. For instance, an `opportunity` named "Disney–Pixar–Film Stock–3q07" will be easy to find in a long list of `opportunities`, whereas "Disney film order" could be quickly lost.

- At the moment of conversion, the `opportunity` should be opened with a $0 amount and 0% probability, even if there are clear signs of a big deal. Until the sales rep has explicitly accepted the `opportunity` as real, it's just speculation. Inside sales reps' intuition about the size and probability of the deal should go in the `opportunity's` `description` text field.

- The last stage of conversion creates a follow-up `task`, which is usually assigned to the rep who needs to take over the `opportunity`. This type of task needs to be carefully monitored, as it represents the official hand-off to the field—and dropping the baton at this point is as important to results as it was for the U.S. 4 × 100 meter relay teams at the Beijing Olympics.

- Immediately after completing conversion, open the `opportunity` record and set a `contact role` for the person who's just been converted. Assign the role that seems most likely from the sales rep's conversations with the prospect, or at least assign a "blank" role.

---

14. See the "Named Account Model of Selling" section later in this chapter for a discussion of this issue.

Inside sales reps need to have a service level agreement (SLA) with field sales reps about hot prospects, along these lines:

- It is inside sales team's responsibility to contact the prospect, determine the products or services that the prospect is interested in purchasing, qualify the `lead` according to the criteria set up by sales, set up a follow-up discussion for outside sales, and convert the `lead` to an `opportunity` within 15 days of the initial connection. `Reports` and `workflows` should be set up to provide clear metrics and alerts to the inside sales team.

- It is outside sales team's responsibility to fully qualify the `opportunity`, determine whether there is a chance of a real sales cycle, and update the `opportunity` within 48 business hours of the prescheduled call. If there really isn't a deal here, outside sales should set its stage to "Closed: Bogus Opportunity" and reassign the `opportunity`'s ownership to the inside sales rep who generated it. It's also smart if there's a dependent pick list that the rep has to fill out, indicating the reasons for refusing the `opportunity`. These bogus `opportunities` should not count against the outside sales rep—if anything, they should be an indicator of failure for the inside sales team. `Reports` and `workflows` should be set up to provide clear metrics for both the sales reps and the inside sales team.

- Once the outside rep has accepted an `opportunity`, it is the rep's deal to win or lose (i.e., there's no one else to blame). As a consequence, reps will be hesitant to accept opportunities unless they are *real*—and that's a good thing, because it prevents them from chasing low-quality prospects, clarifies the metrics, and makes bottlenecks and shortfalls more evident.

The Sales Cycle

In some organizations, the inside sales people take orders for certain products, territories, or deal sizes. In these cases, they are passing `opportunities` to *themselves* for rapid closure.

As the customer moves through the sales cycle, inside sales should update `opportunity` records with relevant notes and other information, and the inside sales rep can rapidly step through the prescribed `stages`. SFDC should be set up with `record types` and `sales processes`[15] that streamline the `opportunity stage` sequences that are visible to inside sales users. Because the sales cycle is typically so short, the inside sales team won't need to make much use of SFDC's `task` or `forecasting` functionality.

---

15. For example, the inside sales `stages` might be `open`, `fully qualified`, `trial`, `pricing`, and `closed-won`. In contrast, the outside sales `stages` might be `open`, `first meeting`, `fully qualified`, `demo`, `trial`, `short list`, `quote`, `selection`, `negotiation`, and `closed-won`. As you'll see later in this chapter, there will also be some hidden sales `stages` for legal and accounting use.

In many cases, the orders are immediate in nature: no formal quote is required, and the business rules are set up so that the inside reps can issue only "valid" orders. Even so, the SFDC system should be set up so that order items and discount rates are validated prior to closing the quote and the opportunity. This is done through use of SFDC's free Sales Quoting tool (discussed later in this chapter).

If the reps must handle complicated product structures or sophisticated discounts that can be valid only in certain combinations, the SFDC team should consider acquiring an external configure/price/quote engine via the AppExchange. Several of these engines are available for SFDC, but often they require a lot of configuration and ongoing maintenance that undercut their cost savings. Perhaps a better solution would be to simplify and stream-line the company's price list, so that the sales and manufacturing folks don't have as many troublesome configurations to deal with in the first place.

If the inside sales team must handle eCommerce transactions that have gone awry, the rep should enter the user's shopping cart ID and store transaction ID into SFDC's opportunity record, so that auditors can reconcile order flows and overrides across the two systems.

Order Operations for Outside Sales

Inside sales teams sometimes handle the quoting and order entry tasks for outside sales teams, particularly when the company has highly distributed field operations and complex orders. Even if inside sales doesn't perform this task at your company, *somebody* has to take responsibility for order operations—and these folks need to read this section because order placement, tracking, expediting, and cancellation practices can have powerful positive effects on customer satisfaction and the speed of order flow. Through the use of approval processes, record types, and page layouts, SFDC can provide an iron-clad assurance of process compliance while actually streamlining the sales rep's duties. See www.SFDC-secrets. com for examples of how this process works.

Because quoting is an optional part of SFDC but actual order entry is not, best practices in this area can be highly variable—depending on the level at which the SFDC system is integrated with the company's order management and accounting systems. Overall, it is a good idea to integrate SFDC's opportunity object with the company's order entry system's quote, order, and contract screens,[16] so that order operations can see the customer's entire order history as well as the status of current "in flight" transactions. Check out www. SFDC-secrets.com for example workflows and alternative implementation strategies.

Quotes without controls are dangerous because they commit the company to terms and prices; if abused, this practice can trigger unpleasant customer and regulatory problems. For example, a company may have to comply with "most favorable pricing" criteria that it has committed to in contracts with very large customers or the U.S. government. In this circum-stance, generating even a provisional quote must be subject to an approval cycle. At least,

---

16. These screens may be handled by the company's accounting system, ERP, distribution/warehousing system, or a dedicated order-management system. These systems are often the home-brew variety, or rickety, or both.

OFFSHORING ORDER OPERATIONS

Offshoring or outsourcing of order operations frequently happens, particularly in highly competitive, high-volume operations with overseas manufacturing. There are a few key SFDC practices to consider when customer contact functions are carried out by offshore entities.

SFDC is fully internationalized and can easily be configured to be user friendly with order operations in several countries, languages, and time zones simultaneously. The offshore personnel will need to have full access not only to SFDC, but also to any transactional systems with which the SFDC system is integrated. This means you'll want to implement fine-grained security and Single Sign On to make sure that members of the order operations team can see everything they need, but *only* what they really need.

We recommend implementing `record types`, `sales processes`, `workflows`, `approval processes`, and `page layouts` for each major order-entry region, as the `workflows` within these regions will probably be somewhat different from those employed in their U.S. counterpart. Using this approach allows for spelling, approval cycles, and other variations to fit the sales customs in each area.

We also recommend setting the offshore order entry screen's time zone to the main time zone the offshore operation is *covering*, rather than its local time zone. This issue can become quite important at the end of the business quarter, when the last-minute order push can be quite hectic.

Although many offshore operations use VoIP phones, we discourage the use of Skype buttons in SFDC for order operations because of the marginal call quality. Skype can become quite congested, particularly during the busy hours of your local Internet service provider. This results in poor call intelligibility, which in turn produces a bad customer impression. Of course, if your offshore operations have dedicated high-capacity lines (e.g., T-3) for Internet service, then Skype is a fine solution.

SFDC should be set up so that a `quote` can't be started until an `opportunity` has reached a specified `stage`. Using SFDC to collect all the elements to generate the customer `quote`—rather than cutting and pasting fields into a Word document—can help the company streamline its quoting and approval process.

Even though SFDC does not include a quoting application in the system, it does have core functionality available as a free AppExchange add-on called `line item quoting`. Using SFDC's `pricelist` structure, `line item quoting` builds the quote from the ground up, with the correct product description, pricing, and discounting information. Several other quoting and order configuration applications for SFDC are also available, and many customers build their own quoting applications in `VisualForce`. In any case, best practice calls for structuring all of the company's offerings—even consulting and associated travel—as fixed-cost line items (e.g., "3 days on-site consulting" and "3 days U.S. travel") with flags to trigger revenue recognition schedules in the accounting system.

The quote should not be printable until it is approved, and the system should check the quote for compliance with product, term, and discounting rules. If the quote is out of bounds, it needs to be sent through an SFDC approval workflow to make sure that management has approved the variances. This automation can save hours of time and sales-rep hassle on every order. Once approved, the specifics of the quote should be locked down so that (1) it can be printed and (2) it cannot be changed without going through another rule review/approval process. Each quote sent to a customer should be saved as a PDF file and stored as an attachment to the opportunity record (as noted earlier, to save space you may want to store this attachment in one of the company's file servers and merely point to it with the SFDC URL field in the opportunity record).

Once a quote has been accepted by the customer, the order operations people should mark the opportunity as "Closed: contractual approval," which triggers a workflow. This event will lock down nearly all the fields in the opportunity so they can be changed only by finance personnel or the system administrator. (Example fields that can be changed by anyone after closure would be cross-reference numbers and comments.)

The order operations people should then open their order entry or accounting screens to properly book the order. Whether these other systems are fully integrated with SFDC or not, the SFDC opportunity number and quote number should be recorded in the accounting/order entry system (dedicated fields should be set aside for this information) and the accounting/order entry system transaction ID number should be recorded in a dedicated custom field in the SFDC opportunity record.

WHAT ABOUT DUPLICATE OPPORTUNITIES?

I know of no tools for deduping opportunities in SFDC. Instead, this work needs to be done manually and should be performed only by an administrator.

To see how this works, let's assume you have two opportunities: the master and the duplicate. For the master opportunity, the quote and order numbers are stored in the record. The duplicate opportunity must be compared to it (either by using a spreadsheet or visually inspecting two Web browser windows), and any unique data in the duplicate should be manually copied into the master. All contact roles, tasks, activity history, attachments, and other related items need to be transferred from the duplicate to the master (all of these transfers are usually done manually).

Even after a duplicate opportunity is emptied of all unique data, it should not be deleted.[17] Instead, it should have its status changed to "duplicate opportunity" and its probability percentage changed to zero.

---

17. Deletion just isn't the right thing to do. For Sarbanes-Oxley Act compliance, and for general data hygiene, records should never be deleted because all audit trails are deleted with the record. Keeping duplicate opportunities will use an infinitesimal amount of storage, yet will provide evidence for any forensic or business process analyses in the future.

Moving the opportunity status to "contractual approval" should initiate the following workflow:

1. The next stage in the approval cycle should involve the Legal or Finance department, which should have hammered out the final details of the contract earlier in the sales cycle. Even so, legal and finance personnel need to perform final review of the opportunity to make sure nothing important has changed. Once they've approved it, the status should be moved to "Closed: won," with the next approval authority set to the Accounting department. At this point, the Legal department should create an SFDC contract, and attach the file of the final text and the signature pages to that record. Order operations should also attach licenses, serial numbers, and shipping bills of lading to the contract object (usually as a pointer to the files rather than using the file attachments themselves).

2. Accounting issues the invoice, using the information from the approved quote; once this is done, the opportunity status should be moved to "Closed: invoiced" and the next approval authority set to the Finance department. A copy of (or pointer to) the invoice should be attached to the SFDC contract record.

3. If the product or service has an expiration or renewal period, at this point the order entry staff should create a new open opportunity (set to 10% probability) with a close date of one year (or whatever the period) from now, with the line items and amount reflecting the expected renewal transaction. The order entry operation should create a task for the sales rep (or whoever handles renewals) to remind that person of the coming renewal transaction, and should set up a workflow that sends out a customer reminder email about the need to renew.

4. Finance reviews the invoicing and any payments for recognizable revenue. When revenue recognition criteria have been met, the Finance department should change the opportunity status to "Closed: recognized." At this point, the workflow will permanently lock the record so that only a system administrator can make changes to it.

During this entire sequence of final status changes—which most reps don't pay much attention to, as they assume the deal is closed—the records are locked down and only the back-office people can change them. Following this best practice, the rep no longer completely closes the opportunity, but that's the only way to truly comply with requirements like those established by the Sarbanes-Oxley Act.

Sales Representatives

As mentioned earlier, this chapter assumes the company has at least a three-level sales organization: eCommerce, inside sales for small deals, and outside sales for enterprise deals.

Perhaps surprisingly, the company's outside sales reps may be among the last people to embrace the SFDC system. At the beginning, the likelihood of their being happy and productive SFDC users is pretty low. There are a dozen reasons for this reluctance, but we urge you to *not* push system usage for the reps too hard, because it will only generate greater resistance. Eventually, they'll be attracted to the system naturally, and become avid users—once they see what's in it for them.

As described earlier, the sales reps should have an SLA with the inside sales team to make sure that the field operators don't waste time pursuing low-quality `leads`. Instead, they should be spending time only on fully qualified `opportunities`.[18]

Reps who are on the road a lot should be using SFDC's Offline edition because it allows them to keep things up to date without having to be connected (sometimes a difficult task in the security-conscious corporate networks). The Mobile edition (for the rep's smartphone) has great "wow" value, but the limited screen space and keyboard make it challenging for clumsy fingers to use for anything beyond simple lookups and minor field updates. Further, if your sales reps need to have access to other systems to get their jobs done, switching back and forth on their mobile device between the native SFDC client and the WAP browser used for other applications will be hopelessly unwieldy.

The opportunity screens seen by the rep should use SFDC's `record types`, `sales processes`, and `screen layouts` to achieve streamlined `profile-specific` screens. The screens should be as brief as possible, using `collapsible sections` and other tricks to make the system less intimidating. Consider making the `collapsible sections` represent the major phases of the sales cycle (something like "develop," "quote," "negotiate," and "close") to bring the essentials into focus for the reps. See www.SFDC-secrets.com for examples of this kind of customization.

As soon as the rep gets a new `opportunity` from the inside sales team, he or she should do research on the company and collect as much context as possible before calling the prospect. Account intelligence tools from Hoover's, Dun & Bradstreet, and other sources are available as plugins to SFDC, providing account and industry information on almost any U.S. company. Executive and organizational intelligence is also available from list-building and social-networking vendors such as ZoomInfo, Jigsaw, and iProfiles, thereby providing information on the individuals and teams within the account. Even if your company doesn't want to invest in fancy tools, Google, Yahoo, LinkedIn, and other Web sites can provide an amazing amount of raw data within a few seconds.[19] No matter which tool you choose, have

---

18. While I'm a firm believer in having reps develop the business in their territories by working their networks and developing business in obvious accounts, having them "cold call" can be demoralizing and is an expensive waste of time. In high-tech companies, the sales team represents the organization's most expensive headcount. If there aren't enough high-quality `opportunities` to keep them busy, you need to build up the inside sales and telemarketing team.

19. The problem with these sources is not the amount of data they provide, but rather the organization and quality of the data. It's easy to waste an hour sifting through stuff that really isn't the right information—so it can be a false economy to "save" by using only free Web sources.

the SFDC implementation team create a magic HTML link that automatically pulls in the customer's data from the outside service.

It also helps for the outside rep to have a clear idea about the organizational politics of the customer. Although some data-mining companies publish organizational profiles (with organizational charts and solid background information) for the *Fortune* 100 companies, their products are expensive and none seem capable of being integrated with SFDC. The good news is that a couple of really nice tools are available that can quickly generate organizational charts from any data already stored in SFDC, and these plugins can be very helpful in mapping key relationships. For these tools to work well, however, it's essential to populate the `Title` and `Reports to` fields in the `contact` object, the `site` field and the `parent account` and `contact role` relationships in the `account`. With these data in place, the system can generate a very usable organizational chart diagram in just a few seconds. This output has great "wow" value for internal account reviews.

Outside sales reps have longer, more complicated sales cycles than inside reps do: the whole point is for the outside rep to expand the footprint of the deal and increase the order value. During the sales cycle, the customers being targeted by these reps are likely to require demonstrations, proofs of concept, executive calls or visits, special contractual terms, and other activities that require corporate resources. Sales reps should not be allowed to request these kinds of special resources via email or phone—over time, the company should make it a practice that such requests will be ignored. The best practice is to create request check boxes on the SFDC screens so that these requests are made entirely through the system, are evaluated only with data entered in the system, and are approved via a `workflow`. Following this path ensures that the sales rep gets something of value—the sales assistance he or she needs—in exchange for the information that the company needs to allocate expensive resources more efficiently.

Sales reps should also use email templates for the emails they send to customers on a routine basis. Although the specifics will vary for each company, reps frequently send emails for the following purposes:

- Scheduling meetings

- Setting up demonstrations and proofs of concept

- Acknowledging a question or action item

- Following up on a question or action item

- Responding to an RFI or RFQ

- Sending a quote

- Responding on contractual issues

- Reminding prospects of deadlines for quotes or discounts

- Acknowledging receipt of a contract or purchase order

Each of these types of email should be set up as an SFDC email template, with the messages actually being sent from the system. Not only does this structure save the sales rep time and effort, but it also ensures a certain level of professionalism in interactions with existing and potential customers (for example, the mail merge function always puts in the right name and salutation for the prospect). Further, these templates can be used in workflows that lend themselves to future automation that can streamline the rep's workload. Because these emails will be sent by the SFDC engine, the contents and timing of the emails will be automatically recorded for the relevant accounts or opportunities. Email templates really are a win for everybody, if you can just wrest your reps away from using Outlook and their CrackBerry phone for all their communications.

If your customer base still works via paper communications, the same techniques and benefits apply for automatically generating fax and postal mail.

Opportunity Management

In outside sales, the length of the sales cycle may be nine months or longer, so the reps need to make use of more parts of the SFDC system. Here's a priority list of things that the rep and others should keep in the system:[20]

1. The complete cast of characters (contacts and contact roles such as influencer, budget holder, champion, and economic buyer) should be included, along with their contact information.

2. Notes and files should be attached to the opportunity record.

3. Deal-specific action items and ticklers should be set up as tasks attached to the opportunity record (particularly when the rep needs to leverage someone who doesn't report to him or her).

4. Requests for corporate resources (e.g., executive visits, on-site demonstrations, proof of concepts, loaner equipment) should be attached to the opportunity record, implemented as check boxes that initiate approval processes.

5. Logged calls or emails should be recorded in the opportunity's activity history for each *significant* phone call or *any* on-site visit to the customer. There doesn't have to be much data in this history, but simply knowing how many times the company has been in touch with the prospect[21] is an important metric.

---

20. Many sales reps tend to manage information too tightly, perhaps because of their fear of being micromanaged. If you detect this attitude, you need to reread the discussion in Chapter 6.

21. This, of course, is the ultimate lightning rod for reps who are worried about being micromanaged. The only way to allay these fears is to clearly and consistently demonstrate that you're not micromanaging them.

6. Forms and `account` profiles that fit within the company's sales methodology should be attached to the `opportunity` record. These items can be created using AppExchange plugins for specific methodologies, or can be created as `custom fields` in `collapsible sections` (such as "needs assessment" or "demonstration of value") in the `opportunity` record.

STALE OPPORTUNITIES

Any opportunity *for new business that has not had any updates for 100 days should have its probability changed to zero, even if the rep says the deal is still alive. In contrast, renewal opportunities may be valid in the system for as long as three years, depending on the company's business practice.*

Forecasting and the Pipeline

Maintaining the individual `opportunity` records for deals is the first part of any forecast. In managing `opportunities`, it's particularly important for the rep that the `amount`, `stage`, `probability%`, and `close date` reflect reality; thus these items should be revisited on at least a weekly basis. Assuming that the company's forecasting has a weekly pipeline-review call on Mondays, the individual reps should update their `opportunity` records on Thursday nights (you'll see why in a few paragraphs). It is *very* common to have stale `close date` entries, but they cause just as much havoc in management as having an incorrect amount—so reps should update *all* fields regularly (if for no other reason than that their manager will bug them about this issue).

For many companies, it's important to break the overall `amount` field into its components (such as hardware, software, training, maintenance, and consulting services). Early in the sales cycle, neither the rep nor the customer may be certain about this breakdown, so `opportunities` will initially have only an overall amount attached to them. As work on the deal progresses, the rep will learn more about the underlying elements of the deal. Using SFDC's `products` functionality, the rep can enter line items that will better reflect the expected order, and the system will automatically calculate the `amount` field. If your company doesn't want to use the `products` functionality, the SFDC system can be configured with `formulas`, `workflow rules`, or APEX code to calculate the `amount` field from other system data.

Many companies will use SFDC reports and Excel spreadsheets to drive the core of their weekly forecasting cycle. And every single one of those companies would be **wrong** in doing so.

Even if your company doesn't have to comply with Sarbanes-Oxley Act requirements, forecasting needs to be an iron-clad process that is as consistent, objective, and free from prying eyes and meddling fingers. All of the information used in the corporate forecast should be stored in SFDC, where it is subject to a full audit trail, and where it can be securely stored, shared, and locked down if necessary. While exporting the opportunity list to a spreadsheet is fine, this information should never be used as the basis for any forecast. Any modification of data, adjustments to forecast parameters, managerial overrides, and roll-ups of forecast information must be done entirely within the SFDC system. Even though an individual rep's forecast may be garbage, it is essential that no one views the overall *process* of forecasting as unreliable baloney.

While the rep can adjust the probability of the opportunity to reflect his or her degree of confidence about closing the deal, this is **not the right thing to do.** Instead of fudging the data (which misleads everyone), we recommend adding a probability adjustment field (a pull-down list, actually) so that management can really understand what's going on in the current deals. Check out the sidebar entitled "Sales Stages Versus Probabilities" later in this chapter.

The second part of the forecast (the customizable forecasting feature that is usually turned on[22] in big sales organizations) allows each rep and manager to override the roll-ups of individual opportunities. The rep can exclude any deal from the committed forecast, adjust the total amount he or she believes the deal will produce, or move the expected close date. Given that these adjustments are made by every level of sales management, this approach is a great way of increasing each manager's confidence in his or her personal forecast. The net result in a large organization is several layers of adjustment that lead to better accuracy.

Quoting and Closing

If the task of generating quotes is handled directly by your company's outside sales reps, see the "Inside Sales: Order Operations for Outside Sales" section earlier in this chapter.

Reps love the close—that is, the thrill of the win. But in this Sarbanes-Oxley world, closing an opportunity consists of a series of controlled steps involving other groups. Thus the sales rep will initiate the close, but it should be executed by others.

What happens if the deal is lost? The rep closes the opportunity, but he or she needs to put in a loss reason via a pick-list selection. Many companies try to add several fields to the SFDC system to collect information about competitors and other "win/loss" criteria, but reps are not really willing to fill in these fields. Instead, keep things really simple, to increase the probability that the rep will actually fill out the form in its entirety.

---

22. Customizable forecasting is automatically turned on in SFDC versions from 2006 forward. In older versions, you'll need to make a support request to activate this feature. Once the feature is turned on, it cannot be turned off.

Named Account Model of Selling

The lead-development model discussed in the previous sections—in which deals are promoted from the inside sales team—is popular with SMB organizations. With enterprise target accounts, however, more sophisticated sales forces use a Named Account model. Sometimes these teams are called "major account managers" (MAMs), "global account managers" (GAMs), or "strategic account managers" (SAMs). Regardless of the specific name, these teams work in an entirely different way from the leads-driven geographic sales model.

MAMs, GAMs, and SAMs are not usually looking for leads to be discovered, cultivated, and elevated into opportunities by someone else. Instead, they are looking to increase business from existing customers or to target accounts that they *know* will be interested in the company's product or service. For example, if a MAM works for an avionics manufacturer, nearly all of the direct customers will be airframe manufacturers such as Boeing, Airbus, Lockheed-Martin, Fokker, and Bombardier. A MAM/GAM/SAM probably also knows the job titles and professional affiliations of all the prospects in these target companies—and the list of the prospect universe, including full contact information and profiles, can be purchased for a reasonable fee.

Consequently, the MAM/GAM/SAM won't be using lead generation from marketing or lead cultivation, nurturing, or qualification from inside sales. Instead, these account managers will identify who's a hot prospect in their own way, selecting targets from a known population.[23] These reps will use SFDC in a very different way, but their way of using the system has to be congruent with the way normal sales reps use it.

The SFDC best practices for Named Account managers include these behaviors:

- Before anything is loaded in the system related to Named Accounts, sales management must agree on the definition and number of Named Accounts, to prevent poaching and hogging of big deals. Typically, there will be somewhere between 50 and 500 Named Accounts worldwide.

- The definitions and "boundaries" of Named Accounts need to be set tightly, particularly with accounts that are large conglomerates. "Mitsubishi" probably consists of 100 companies in Japan alone, and 200 companies worldwide—ranging from retail banking to IC manufacturing to shipyards. So is Mitsubishi one Named Account, or several? Sales management needs to clearly state the rules here.

- The top-level account—which is often a holding company or conglomerate—will rarely become an ordering customer. Even so, an account should be created for it in SFDC, and separate child accounts should be established for the operating

---

23. This same type of process is used by business development people who are trying to work organizations they already know. Even though BD typically isn't working a quota the way MAM/GAM/SAMs are, they can use SFDC in a very similar way.

divisions and remote offices. For example, General Electric (GE) is unlikely to be a customer, but RCA, NBC, CNBC, GE Plastics, GE Jet Engines, GE Medical, and GE Leasing are likely to be. The top-level `account` should be owned exclusively by the NAM rep, and the `child accounts` should be owned by the NAM rep and shared with the relevant sales team for the territory where each division is located.

- Because the MAM/GAM/SAM's territory is not geographic in nature, there's almost inevitable conflict with the standard geographic territories. The difficulty comes when a small division of a big conglomerate is claimed by one of the regular territory reps, but the conglomerate is a MAM/GAM/SAM account. These internal workings can confuse the customer and lead to contentious relations inside the company's own sales organization. It is essential to have a quick escalation mechanism that resolves these kinds of issues before they have time to fester. Once the management rules are in place, use SFDC's `sales teams` feature to properly share information about cooperative deals.

- The Named Accounts should be loaded into SFDC even if you've never had a `lead converted` or an `opportunity` there. Create the `account` (assuming it isn't already there; if it is, just update it) with a `custom field` check box called "Major account" (or whichever name is appropriate for you). The `account status` field should be set to `target` unless the company is already an active customer. Depending on your `sales process`, it may also make sense to create a `record type` and `page layouts` for Named Account managers so they don't interfere with what the reps use on a day-to-day basis.

- For the people with whom your company has done business at the `account` (these are `contacts`), assign `contact Roles` and `Reports to` relationships to reflect their political standing in the organization.

- The SFDC system administrator needs to `relate leads` to `accounts`, and to show the `related list` for `leads` on the `account page layout`; this layout should be explicitly set up for the Named Account team.

- Anybody the company has ever heard of at the `account`—even if the company hasn't done business with that person—should be entered as a `contact` with ownership set to the appropriate NAM rep. The company may not know any more about these `contacts` than it would with Names (see the discussion on this in Chapter 8), but it can handle that issue by setting the `contact's score` to a low number, and setting the `type` to prospective target. These `contacts' source` field should be set to "Named Account," and the `Type` field should be set to "prospect."[24] (Always

---

24. Views and reports of `contacts` should bet set up to filter out these Named Account `contact` statuses, so that people don't get confused and metrics don't become distorted.

search for these people as either `leads` or `contacts` before you create new `leads` or `contacts`—remember the commandments given earlier in this chapter). Make sure that the `contact` is associated with the *correct* `account`, if it's part of a complex `account` `hierarchy`.

- Only after the NAM sales rep has actually talked to the individual and fully qualified that person should the `contact` have its `Type` field set to "active contact."

The hallmark of Named Account management is a strategic account plan that outlines a series of actions that will be taken to win and grow the major/global/strategic business. While MAM/GAM/SAMs should be flexible enough to help with small deals at their large accounts, the core of their value lies in the proactive work that deepens the corporate relationship. Their account plan should provide a model for orchestrating the efforts of individual sales reps across the world to achieve the corporate goal. Of course, no one is really going to appreciate those kinds of personal obligations just because a written plan exists. Using SFDC's `campaigns`, `workflows`, and `tasks`, the MAM/GAM/SAM should communicate to the rest of the sales organization the specific action items in a structured way, and improve the level of coordination and follow-through on plans and action items. Further, by putting this information in SFDC, pertinent `dashboards` and `reports` can be made available on a real-time basis. Finally, the account plan document files (Word, PowerPoint, or Excel) should be attached to the relevant `account` so that no one has an excuse for not knowing the objectives and rules of the road for each strategic account.

The other hallmark of Named Account management is knowing and leveraging the customer's organizational politics. It is essential for the MAM/GAM/SAM to know who's where in the organization, and what their current `roles` are, and where the political battle lines have been drawn. Anytime *anybody* in your company (sales, marketing, customer support, or consulting) makes a connection or has a conversation with someone in a target Named Account, they need to take the following steps:

- Make sure the person is present in the SFDC system as a `contact`, with updated contact information.

- Make sure that the `Reports to` field reflects the person's latest organizational status.

- Add or update the `contact role`[25] relationship at the `account` level, particularly for `opportunities` that are within the purview of that individual.

- Add `notes` on political issues, and attach them to the `opportunity`.

---

25. My firm usually adds entries to the `contact role` pick list to add some political context to the organizational chart that develops around each deal. Example items might include `champion`, `blocker`, `passive-aggressive`, and `bystander`.

- Keep referencability information up-to-date (see Chapter 10 for a discussion of this issue). These `custom fields` that marketing has set up are intended to help the company track and manage customer happiness as a resource, so that references don't get burned out by sales overuse or PR abuse.

By using everyone in your company as "sensors," the large-account management function can become much more effective at working customers' organizational politics and pumping out deals.

Partner Management

Most companies now must leverage several channels—direct, inside, Web, distributors, and resellers—to make revenues happen predictably and profitably. SFDC can be configured to help the indirect channel management in a big way, but most SFDC customers don't do enough in this area.

If your partner already uses SFDC, you can use a feature called `Salesforce-to-Salesforce` to share data in a systematic and continuous way. This is the über-cool solution, because it provides transparency and real-time updates.

If your partner uses a different SFA system or if it is unwilling to integrate with your company through `Salesforce-to-Salesforce`, then members of the partner organization will rarely log in to your company's SFDC instance. SFDC's `Partner Portal` is meant for these workers, as it allows casual access to your system with security controls that ensure the partner's employees see only their own prospects and deals. The SFDC `Partner Portal` is the core of its `Partner Resource Management` (PRM) functionality. Through this portal, partners can register `leads`, add information about `contacts` and `accounts`, and update `opportunities` with the latest deal and `case` information.

Beyond these SFDC features, here are best practices to keep your company's partners as productive as possible:

- Score `leads` (or at least rate them hot/warm/cold) and prequalify them *before* you send them over to the partner, to help the partner manage its `lead` flow. Sending junk `leads` is bad for productivity and doesn't build a good partnership. Make sure the `leads` are as high quality and fresh as the ones you give your own lead-cultivation/nurturing people.

- Send `leads` to individual reps, not just partner companies. This will improve their `lead`-response time by hours, if not days. Using SFDC `workflows` and APEX code, you can automatically route `leads` according to the partner's territory definitions.[26]

---

26. In simple situations, you might be able to use SFDC's `lead` assignment rules to accomplish this routing, but it is nearly impossible to get right for many partner situations.

- Route the highest-value `leads` (the ones that appear to be the biggest deals) to the best-performing partners. Of course, it takes a while before SFDC has enough data to indicate who those best-performing partners are, but this best practice leads to even higher-performing partner relationships.

- In SFDC, mark `leads` you've sent out with the partner's name (using a `custom pick list` field or, if you have a ton of partners, via a `lookup` field).

- Do not send a given `lead` to more than one partner. Let each partner know that each `lead` you send is an exclusive opportunity for that partner. Make your `lead` routing to partners flawless to avoid creating a mess.

- Monitor the progress of the partner's `lead` qualification, conversion, and opportunity development. Establish a waterfall model (with norms for conversion time and percentage) and compare the partner's performance to it. If your partner's `sales process` requires approvals from the channel manager, make sure that approvals are handled in a timely manner using `workflows` and `alerts` to escalate any delayed approvals.

- For the `leads` that a partner sends to *you*, make sure they are marked with the individual referrer's name (`custom field`) and the partner company (`custom pick list`) and make sure that they are included in the `campaign` that's been set up for each partner (ask marketing personnel to handle this task, if they haven't done so already). Do the same for `leads` that have been *converted* by a partner, and `opportunities` that have been *opened* by the partner.

- Set up SFDC's `lead` entry and `opportunity` registration system so it's available to your company's partners on a 7 × 24 basis. Make a habit of accepting `leads` and deals, even if they seem a bit dubious. Nothing angers a partner more than "instant rejections" by your company's sales reps. If they do have to reject a partner's input, make sure the reps send an explanatory email that is as polite as it is complete.

- For the `leads` or `opportunities` that the partner sends to your company, monitor *your* progress with them and keep the partner informed with reports or dashboards. Use `workflows` to make sure that progress on deals doesn't stall and to remind accounting personnel to send referral fees when deals close. You want your company's partners to feel that information access and measurement is a two-way street.

- Put the company's internal document library and collateral in the `Partner Portal`, or give the partner access to your company's intranet content management system.

- Review the partner's forecast and performance-against-goals using the SFDC data as the basis for all discussions so that the partner understands how important it is to keep the data updated and clean.

- Drive the partner's incentive fees off of SFDC data. While the calculation of incentive checks is always complicated (and is best done by the finance folks), make sure that all relevant data (including co-marketing funds) are stored within SFDC.

- After you've got a few quarters' worth of data in the system, ask the marketing staff or perhaps a finance analyst to look at the partner productivity and to create a profile of what makes a good partner and what makes a dud. Use these analyses to guide your partner recruitment efforts going forward.

To the extent possible, leverage SFDC to make the company's partners feel like equals, with the access and information they need to succeed. If they feel like they are part of your company's team, they'll be a more effective extension to its own selling efforts.

For the `leads` and `opportunities` that a partner sends to *you*:

- Use SFDC's PRM system to manage `leads`, `opportunities`, and `cases`.

- Make sure the partner `leads` are routed to the proper sales rep or product specialist on your team, using `lead assignment rules` or `triggers` (for complex situations).

- Make sure that the `leads` and `opportunities` are properly attributed to the partner that submitted them, for both tracking and reporting purposes. This means, of course, adding a partner `custom field` to those two objects.

- Using `workflows` and `email templates`, send an acknowledgment email from the receiving sales rep to the partner, thanking the partner for the referral and providing full contact information for the two sides' reps to connect with each other.

- In the `Partner Portal`, provide links to documents that describe very clearly the rules of engagement and deal qualification for the partner, so the partner knows what to expect and how to "work the system" for your company.

- Create `reports` and a `dashboard` for the partner manager to see performance on an ongoing basis. Partner referral fees or commissions should be calculated based on the SFDC data.

Business Development

The business development (BD) function varies significantly across industries and channel positions (e.g., vendor, distributor, reseller). In fact, in many companies, the BD people don't even need to log in to SFDC. Nevertheless, to the extent that BD is about identifying and cultivating future customer relationships, their efforts *should* be captured and aided by SFDC. The best practices for BD are really a combination of Named Account management (for prospects prior to contract signing) and partner management (once the deal is done).

Many times BD negotiations must be highly secretive, so appropriate security measures must be taken before the prospect information is entered into SFDC. These strategic BD people should be designated as direct reports to the CEO within the SFDC `Role` hierarchy, even if most BD people report to the VP of Sales. The reason for this structure is many operations and analyst types will have access privileges at the VP of Sales level, but they should not see the account information being developed by the BD reps. Once this `Role` hierarchy is set up, use SFDC's `sales teams` features to allow the VP of Sales—and only that person—to see the BD target accounts.

The BD function should probably have its own `record types` and `sales processes` for `opportunities`, as they are not really conventional sales cycles and shouldn't be included in the standard forecast.

Field Sales Engineers or Product Specialists

In most high-tech firms, product specialists help the sales rep win the deal. Whether they're called sales engineers (SEs), pre-sales support, sales specialists, or sales associates, these individuals are *involved* in the big deals, even though they don't close the sale or run the paperwork.

In most organizations, SEs are a shared resource: each specialist has to help three or more sales reps on deals. This can make their lives hellish, as reps fight for priority and SEs get jerked from deal to deal on a daily basis.

As a consequence of their jobs and their personalities, SEs are often great early users of SFDC because the system lets them rapidly come up to speed on the crisis du jour, update the status of action items quickly, and easily manage their backlog and workload. The best practices for SEs are outlined here:

- Set up an internal process such that requests for SEs must be made through SFDC, rather than via email or voicemail. The SE manager should make it clear that those requests made via the system, and with more complete/informative data, will be serviced sooner than requests that do not go through the SFDC system.

- The SE should turn each customer interaction into a `task` (open or completed, attached to the `opportunity`) so that the entire sales team can understand the state of action items and follow-ups.

- Any customer requests for technical information should be logged as a `task`, and the responses should be attached as either an email or a document to the `opportunity` record. For formal RFQ and RFI processes, the original requesting document and the company's response should be attached to (or at least pointed to from) the `opportunity` record.

- Any competitive information (such as knock-offs, benchmark results, or customer feature evaluations) should be attached to the `opportunity`.

- For very complicated products, the SE should be included in the quote's `approval cycle`, to make sure that the best configuration of products has been selected.

Sales Management

This section applies to all sales managers, although some of the advice applies only at the executive level. Even if a particular item doesn't apply to you, read it so you can see what the organizational direction is—and how you fit into it.

The first job of sales is to make the number. No argument here, right? In a similar way, the first and only job of the team working on SFDC is to get user adoption up[27] to 100% during the first few months of operation. And the only way to achieve that goal is to have high-quality, meaningful data in the system. Otherwise, the system is just an empty shell that won't do anybody any good.

Sales management's decisions, personal behavior, and word choices can make a big difference here. Your team knows you, and they can read what you think at a nonverbal level (i.e., through your tone of voice and facial expressions). A few of the wrong words carelessly thrown around when you're stressed out at the end of the quarter can set SFDC adoption back by months.

Setting the Example

Show the team what to expect in terms of the SFDC system through your actions. Make sure you convey these messages both verbally and nonverbally:

- SFDC is what you'll be using to drive the boat. It's how you'll implement quota decisions, commission splits, and territory plans. It's how you'll do account reviews and pre-call briefings. It's how you'll run the weekly forecast meeting.

- SFDC will be the *only place you'll look* for information about customers and prospects, so anything relevant should be available and accurate within SFDC. Reps are not to keep "little black books" containing all the real information, whether they're using paper, or Act, Excel, or Outlook. Make it clear that it's a real pain for you to look outside of the SFDC system for information about people, accounts, or deals.

- SFDC is how you expect the individual reps to manage their time more effectively. Field reps are business people who have been given an exclusive franchise to sell your company's product in a territory; as CEOs of their own businesses, they need to manage their time wisely above all else. SFDC will be optimized *for them* to increase their leverage, so they can avoid the duds and close more real deals.

- SFDC is *not* a spying machine. It's not a micromanagement tool, and you will not use it that way.

---

27. I know I've been repeating this endlessly, but it's a message that has to get to everyone who reads any chapter of this book.

- SFDC *is* a way for the reps to get more out of the resources that the company gives the sales team—people, loaner machines, travel budgets, leads, and so forth.

- SFDC is *not* an administrative burden. Through automation and better collaboration, it *is* a liberation from data reentry and forgotten action items. Tell the sales personnel to use the Outlook or Notes connector to their email system, so everyone has less to type. Consider using the InvisibleCRM product if your sales reps live in Outlook. If necessary, hire a temporary administrator (with a dedicated phone line and voicemail box) to do the reps' data entry for the first few months. *Remove all excuses for not using the system.*

THE VIRTUAL WAR ROOM

Way back during The Bubble, I worked in a sales organization that had a war room—a physical space manned 18 × 5 during the last 10 days of the quarter to coordinate every company resource to bring in the number.

I don't think that a physical room is a good investment in these times, but SFDC can become your company's virtual war room. Almost of all the information you need for the end-of-quarter chaos is already in one place in this system; it's just a matter of getting responses quickly and without any misfires.

Use `tasks`, `workflows`, `escalations`, and `alerts` to make sure every action item gets done on time. Store all the sales information—customer notes, RFIs, quotes, and contractual terms—as `notes` attached to the `opportunity`. Set aside an email box for high-priority deals (mustwin@yourco.com is my favorite), and a voicemail box (at extension 2946[28] in your phone system) for the same purpose.

During key times, designate an explicit "officer of the day" who receives all escalations (via SMS or voicemail to his or her cell phone), and put the duty schedule inside SFDC's `documents` area for everyone's reference.

- SFDC is your preferred medium for communication about prospects, opportunities, and customers, and you consider it to be much better than email for this purpose. You want to see the number of internal emails decrease by 10% or more, because the stuff that reps and others need to close deals and service customers will be available via a central, organized resource that everyone will be able see. Further, inform reps that you will give lower priority to requests made via email and voicemail than to requests that come via SFDC. Emails and voicemails are fine for *alerting* people to change, but all the substantive information should be in the deal "war room" that is provided by SFDC. If necessary, buy the reps a new phone and SFDC Mobile edition so they have what they need at their fingertips in real time.

---

28. This spells "2-WIN" on the phone pad.

- If your team is thoroughly indoctrinated with a formal sales methodology, SFDC is the most efficient way to leverage that sales model. Buy plugins or stand-alone applications that interface with SFDC to streamline the use of the company's sales methodology and reduce the amount of keyboard work for their reports and forms. This step can save hours of work for the reps every week.

- SFDC usage is so important to team efficiency that you'll put in place small reward systems for completeness of information and effective use of the system. Even small awards and contests can bring out competitive behavior in a sales team, so use them wisely (particularly with the company's inside sales teams).

- The adoption and extension of SFDC will occur in an *incremental and measured* way. You're not going to ram drastic changes down the reps' throats. More importantly, you plan to measure the improvement (or lack thereof), to make sure that the changes really are best for everyone, and adjust the system along the way. Training won't be heavy-handed full-day sessions; instead, it will be light, need-driven, tailored to the company's specific operation, self-paced, on-demand, and self-scoring.

Mandates for the Reps

To get healthy use out of the SFDC system, you need to put some mandates in place over time. Every one of the following measures is designed to steer the sales reps in the right direction, even if they want to do something that is verboten.

- Contact information for every person who is involved in any deal must be in SFDC. If you give the reps the Mobile edition, the *only* place contact information should live is SFDC. If you don't get the Mobile edition, tell the reps to have a system administrator push their Outlook (or Notes) address books into SFDC (due to data corruption issues, people must *not* attempt this feat themselves). If thousands of contacts must be synched, a couple of tricks described at www.SFDC-secrets.com can help you easily get the situation under control.

- When a sales rep first gets on the system, he or she must be forbidden from attempting wholesale uploads of address books or contact spreadsheets into SFDC. These data dumps cause data pollution that's painful to recover from. Instead, all (and that means *all*) lead or contact uploads must be done by the marketing staff or a system administrator. This is one of the few things these workers are really good at, so use them (plus, they can take the blame if they do it wrong).

- Perhaps even more important, sales reps must not create new accounts[29] without searching for them first. As accounts are the top of SFDC's information pyramid,

---

29. The same goes for opportunities, contacts, and leads, although duplication of these items has somewhat less potential for damage.

creating a duplicate `account` creates more damage and undermines credibility in more ways than just about any other action. Check out the "Creation Science" sidebar earlier in this chapter. There needs to be a very strict naming convention for accounts (if you want to know more about this issue, see the "Conversion and Hand-Off to Sales" section earlier in this chapter), and rules about `parent/child` account relationships.

The next big change for the reps—and they'll whine endlessly about it—is to stop them from using email or voicemail for assigning and updating internal action items. Email is just the wrong way to handle action items: if someone wasn't copied on that one relevant reply, that person is out of the loop and may make a wrong decision. Instead, use SFDC `tasks` to assign action items, follow-ups, and reminders across the company.[30] In this way, everyone on the sales team will know whether a task has been done, what the response was, and which follow-up action is necessary. Managers can run reports to see which deal-oriented tasks are overdue, and they can spot bottlenecks before they turn into big problems around vacation time or the end of the quarter. Of course, when a communication needs to directly include the customer, you can't use `tasks`—but the email the rep sends can be attached to the `opportunity` record (using SFDC's free Outlook or Notes connector) so that everyone can see the state of play.

A related change is to stop reps from using the `comments` area, `description` field, or `notes` button when trying to store information about the state of the deal. These free-text fields are almost useless, and relying on them leads to dropped balls. Anything transitory or sequential in nature should go into `tasks`. Notes, comments, or `description` are for information that *won't change* during the deal (e.g., "You MUST have your driver's license to get past security in this building!").

Move away from issuing quotes using stand-alone Word documents. At the very least, use the mail merge functionality in SFDC to generate quotes based on data directly from the system. Better still, move toward quotes being generated directly out of SFDC, the accounting system, or the ERP system. Doing it right will require either a bit of `VisualForce` and `APEX` code or considerable integration, but either way the decrease in manual processing will speed up quotes, increase customer satisfaction, and lower error rates.

All forecasts must be created via the SFDC system—no more external spreadsheets to manage the pipeline. The reps must understand that gaming the system screws things up for everyone and *will* be noticed by sales management.

---

30. Eighty percent of the people receiving `tasks` need to have a full SFDC license for this strategy to work properly, so make sure that key players are all working in the system. The other 20% will really be a "department" rather than an individual. The department will get an email with an SFDC link on it, and then use the departmental SFDC account to see what's coming its way. Department employees will, in turn, respond through the SFDC system, so the results are visible to all members of the sales team and attributed to the responding department. For details on how to do this, visit the Web site www.SFDC-secrets.com.

Assign "ownership" of the quality of different parts of the data to different departments. For example, the Marketing department should own `leads`, inside sales should own `contacts` and `accounts`, and outside sales should own `opportunities`.

For *everyone* in sales, all the juiciest information should be stored in or attached to `opportunities`.

Provide subtle penalties for inputting garbage data, and praise and small incentives for adding good data. It's pretty easy to determine who deleted something or who created the duplicate records that everyone hates.

Configure the SFDC system so that `merge` or `delete` buttons aren't available for the sales team. There are a lot of reasons why normal users should never delete anything from the system (see the "Creation Science" sidebar earlier in this chapter)—and there are ways to mark records so they'll disappear from view even though they are still stored in SFDC.

Configure the system so that the 15 or so pieces of data you really want to analyze in the future are recorded via `history tracking`. This feature is free and doesn't slow the system down, but it's an invaluable resource for future account and territory planning.

Keep your team out of the SFDC system's innards, even if they really do have the skills to change the system. Even if they were successful in modifying an `approval process`, or changing a `trigger`, or tweaking an `email template` without goofing up other parts of the system, this is not the way for *sales* personnel to spend their time. They're supposed to be closing deals. Head off this behavior at the pass, so your more techie-oriented reps don't waste their time.

No one on the sales team (except maybe a sales operations person) should have full SFDC system administrator access. It's just a dangerous waste of time—just say no.

Now, let's look at the best ways *you* will use SFDC in the key sales management functions.

Revenue Planning

The core of revenue planning is to ensure that you have enough accounts and deals to make your target as a manager. If the territory isn't big enough or doesn't have enough targets, there's not much SFDC can do—so fix that issue first. Implementing territory changes involves a lot of manipulation in SFDC (see the next section in this chapter), so don't put the system administrators through that stress until a really solid reason exists to do so.

To implement the revenue generation model discussed at the start of this chapter, SFDC needs to be configured with basic information: sales rep territories, inside sales territories, partner territories, named account lists, rep quotas, and so on.

When it comes to quotas, there are two schools of thought. My recommendation is to over-assign the target to your subordinates, typically by 20% or so at each level of management. This is because you want to leave margin for error, in the knowledge that on average about 40% of your reps won't make their individual numbers (if more than that *did* make the numbers, you're either setting quotas too low or being sandbagged by your reps). As a

THE DEVIL'S IN THE DETAILS

Sales management has traditionally been relatively nonquantitative. While sales personnel certainly know about *the number,* most of the day-to-day decisions are made with your gut and communicated with your emotions.

Even if the SFDC system were able to provide perfect metrics—which it really can't—it's important to use reports and analytics in a genuine and productive way. It's easy to ask for reports that you won't actually use, but it's far more dangerous to ask for reports that you *will* use to bad effect.

Before you ask sales reps to enter any more data (which they'll view as an overly taxing burden and an intrusion), figure out what you would *do* if you already had the report based on those data in front of you. Which decision would you *actually* make differently? If you're just curious or not sure what you'd do differently, **don't ask** the reps to enter anything new. This goes double for activity management.

If you ask the reps to do something new, walk a mile in their shoes first. Top-down edicts practically guarantee attempts to game the system, particularly if the edicts have clear penalties or rewards. If you're going to lay down the law, make sure that gaming the system has the biggest penalties of all. Reps' evil manipulation of the system not only undermines SFDC's credibility (and data integrity), but also insidiously undermines *your* authority—so don't open the door to it.

sales manager, there is nothing *mas macho* than raising your target in midyear—and that's possible only if you over-assigned[31] quotas in the first place.

The other school of thought is to *never* over-assign quotas, or even to slightly under-assign them. The reason: over-assigning quotas simply increases the probability that reps won't make their numbers, which increases turnover, which decreases the Sales department's effectiveness. Your whole team spends all their time in learning curves, rather than productively closing deals.

With either strategy, you have to manually put quotas into SFDC, either by the month or by the quarter. For managers, calculate the amount of over-assignment (or not) in a spreadsheet, and enter the data into the SFDC user screen. If the company has a really large sales team, have one of the system administrators import the quotas directly from your spreadsheet using the free Excel connector or Data loader.

SFDC doesn't have anything fancy when it comes to revenue planning (such as sales-rep productivity ramps, new-product introduction bookings effects, or other bells and whistles), so you'll have to perform all of those data manipulations in external spreadsheets or purpose-built tools.

---

31. Or were being severely sandbagged.

In developing your revenue plan, you'll need to create a waterfall model that takes into account the selling behavior of each of the company's major channels. This model is typically a spreadsheet, and it should include product launches, sales rep productivity ramps, quarterly timing, and the length of the sales cycle. Make sure to write these assumptions down. My experience is that faulty assumptions are the most insidious and deadly ingredients of a bad forecast, so you'll want to confirm that the model's assumptions hold up before you bet your career on them. To validate your model, ask the SFDC team to create reports that help you measure your team's performance against them on at least a quarterly basis:

- Percentage of `leads` ignored
- Time to first touch for `leads` that aren't ignored
- Percentage of `leads` qualified
- Percentage of `leads` converted
- Percentage of `opportunities` rejected by sales
- Number of `opportunities` accepted by sales
- Average time for each `sales stage`
- Percentage of `opportunities` stalled
- Percentage of `opportunities` regressing[32]
- Total length of sales cycle
- Win rates for `opportunities` accepted by sales
- Upsell/renewal rates
- Average order size

Territory Management

Along with quotas, territories can be a constant source of squabbling, even if they are supposed to be stable for the year. That goes double for the Named Account model, where the NAM reps are looking for accounts to subsume and geographic reps are looking for large company divisions to plunder.

The key to effective territory management is to have clear, documented roles and responsibilities for the reps, rules of engagement with partners, and appropriate commissions (splits

---

32. A deal is regressing when its `amount`, `stage`, or `probability` is decreasing, or when its `close date` is moving out in time. Deals regress when the client experiences a budgetary cut or political upheaval, or when a competitor throws a counteroffer to keep its chances of winning the customer's business alive.

or double commissions, depending on the situation). Territories can be really messy to manage if there are several types of overlays (e.g., new business direct, new business dealers, repeat business direct, repeat business dealers, national accounts, special situations) and a matrix-format (or rapidly changing) organizational chart. SFA systems can accommodate all of these things, but setting the systems up to do so will be painful, cost lots of money, and cause delays. Plus, when you attempt to do historical analysis of territory productivity when the territories change over time, your analysts will go crazy. In summary, make your territory system as complicated as you want—just recognize the consequences in advance.

SFDC works best with a conventional hierarchy—where the reporting relationships form a pyramidal organizational chart with a clean "inverted tree" structure. For example, in terms of territories, California reports into the Western United States, which reports into North America. Virtually all SFA systems are set up to accommodate this kind of pattern.

You will want to add `custom fields` and set up SFDC features to handle `sales teams`, overlays, overrides, and splits. If the company engages in a lot of partner business, you may want to set up the SFDC system to manage referral fees, cooperative selling, and two-level invoicing (one type of invoice for retail pricing for the end customer, and another type of invoice for wholesale pricing for the partner).

For the purpose of evaluating the size/layout of territories, reports should show the number of target customers, the number of leads, the number of sales cycles, the revenues, and the profits per region. The goal is to compare these metrics and make sound resource allocations. You may discover that the company makes a profit in only five U.S. states: maybe the company's sales reps should concentrate on those areas, and leave the rest of the geographic regions to distributors and partner sales.

When you *do* need to redesign a territory, the goal is to get the most leverage out of the sales staff by balancing their workload and their opportunity to make money. These days, you'll also want to minimize travel because it's so time-consuming and expensive. When undertaking a territory redesign, gather both the historical sales data from SFDC `opportunities` and the market sizing data from lead generation, marketing analyses, and external data sources. Most sales managers use a whiteboard or a spreadsheet to organize these data, but the key is to start with the best data you have from SFDC.

SFDC really works most easily with geographic territories that can be unambiguously defined by state lines, ZIP codes, or area codes.[33] If a more elegant way of defining territories (such as industry or customer profession) is desired, they must be defined in an unambiguous and consistent way that prevents arguments among the reps. Implementing these nongeographic territories and overlay salesforces will require APEX code in SFDC or some external programming. This doesn't come cheap, but it works well.

---

33. Due to telephone number-portability requirements in the North American Numbering Plan and VoIP, city codes and area codes are becoming less reliable markers for territory definitions in the United States. Other countries' numbering systems are evolving in different directions, so this territory-definition mechanism won't work for much longer.

When you do redesign a territory, the following parts of SFDC need to be changed—so be ready for the questions for the administrators:

- Web `autoresponse rules`, to thank clients for their interest while using the name of the correct rep in the signature/address block

- `Lead assignment rules`, to route leads to the correct part of the sales team

- Custom `assignment rules`, to route eCommerce sales to the correct rep for follow-up

- `Role` and `territory` hierarchies for roll-ups of forecasts and reports

- Names for the overall sales region (at least North America, EMEA, APAC, ROW) and specific territory (e.g., Western United States) to be used in `custom pick lists` in `opportunity`, `account`, and `contact` records to facilitate reporting and analysis

- `Data access rules` that allow you and your subordinates to see information in your territory, but not outside it

- `Case assignment rules` and `data sharing/access rules`, to help route customer issues to the correct part of the support team and sales rep

- Ownership of `accounts`, open `opportunities`, and open `tasks` needs to be changed to the new territory owner. While sometimes you can just use SFDC's `mass-transfer wizard`, in the interesting cases this needs to be done with a series of data downloads and uploads. With complex overlays, this process can take a surprising amount of effort.

- Historical analyses and commission calculations will be far easier if you don't make big changes to territories more than once per year,[34] and if you maximize the number of customers that stay with their reps when changes do occur. Maintaining some sort of stability also enhances rep productivity, so this should be an easy best practice to follow.

PERFECTIONISM STILL DOESN'T PAY

As discussed in Chapter 3, trying to have "perfect data" is incredibly expensive. But there's one area where reps are incredibly sensitive—and you need to watch out for it. If 0.1% of `accounts`*,* `opportunities`*, or* `tasks` *are reassigned incorrectly, you will hear no end of complaints about the mistake. When just a few dozen items are wrong, it will be cheaper and faster for everyone if the reps just fix it themselves using the SFDC user interface. While mass data fixes are best done using the system administrator's tools, when there are tiny changes to be made, use of these tools carries a relatively high risk of introducing new errors when fixing an old ones.*

---

34. Of course, if a rep leaves or the company goes through a reorganization or merger, unplanned change is sometimes unavoidable.

Account Planning

Account planning attempts to provide an evolving answer to these strategic questions: How can the company get more out of its existing base, how can it catch the really big fish, and how can it build its reputation to "own" the market? SFDC doesn't help that much when it comes to analyzing new markets (e.g., geographies, industries), because SFDC data are richest for *historical* analysis. Use market research or external data (such as data from Hoover's or Dun & Bradstreet, or hire interns from a local business school) to do this kind of exploratory work. This kind of forward-looking analysis is best done in conjunction with the marketing staff, who should be good at this kind of analysis.

That said, SFDC should contain incredibly valuable data about how to get more out of the company's existing customers. This is *the* strategic reason to have reps, SEs, and consultants entering information into the system, even when "the deal is already won." SFDC's most relevant data for maximizing repeat business is the sequence of `campaigns`, `events`, `activities`, and decisions that won deals in the past. When analyzing these data, you're looking for repeating patterns that lead to big deals. The key information will be the patterns of `tasks` (as collected in the `activity history`) and field/state changes (as recorded in the `field histories` for `account` and `opportunity` records). Look for patterns that lead to repeat business and opening new departments within existing customers. To identify these patterns, you may need some help here from the quantitatively oriented folks in sales operations, finance, or marketing.

Once you have spotted the patterns, try them in other account situations, and measure the results. Eventually you'll find the recipe that gives the most consistent growth results.

Account Management

Account management is the tactical, "let's bring the deal in" part of the sales cycle. Before assessing this portion of the deal, let's look first at the whole `opportunity` cycle from a management perspective here.

Before an opportunity even exists, a `lead` has to be brought in, cultivated, nurtured, qualified, and converted. It's *really* important for sales management to use consistent terminology, and to assign responsibility to the team members who own each of these steps. Sorry, but this means you're going to have to read this whole chapter, or download the cheat sheet from www.SFDC-secrets.com. When consistent semantics are used, opportunities will be easier to manage even if three layers of management separate you from the actual deal.

While an opportunity is being developed by the rep, it's particularly important to be very disciplined in the use of sales stages and probabilities. Most sales cycles consist of four to eight stages between the creation of an opportunity and the hand-off of the win to order operations; make sure that you have clear entry and exit criteria for each stage, and manage sales activities to those stages. Within the SFDC system, a best practice is to put check boxes in the `opportunity` so that the rep advances the deal stage by answering questions about specific buyer commitments or behaviors, rather than by manually changing the probability of success. While this process can be complex to implement across vertical salesforces and multiple countries, the more consistent you can make the sales stages, the better the visibility and control you will have over the sales cycle.

Account and pipeline reviews should rely on the data found in the SFDC system. Move away from external spreadsheets and PowerPoint presentations—show reps how much time they will save by abandoning these traditional tools—and just work with the facts and reports already available in the SFDC system.

Don't get too fancy with the analytics too early. These kind of metrics scare sales reps, and half the time the data aren't very good when the system is just starting up. Add a new report, dashboard, or analytic every six weeks or so, looking at things like time in stage, deals going backward (i.e., declining probability, lower amount, or later close date), the number of sales cycles in flight, and the number of customer visits required to close a deal. During `account` reviews, ask how much time reps are spending on creating forecasts, how much time on internal meetings, and how much time on selling (none of this information will be in the system, but it *will* be there in the rep's gut).

Partner Management

While most partner interactions are handled by the individual rep or partner manager, it's important for the sales executive to get a bird's-eye view of what's going on. Achieving adequate visibility into what the partner is doing—and how the partner helping the company's overall performance—is the most commonly cited problem that executives have with channel business. Once the company has a healthy number of partners—10 companies, or 10% of its overall sales—SFDC's PRM module will help you assess partner effectiveness.

Ideally, the partner will have properly restricted access to the `leads`, `contacts`, `accounts`, and `opportunities` in the SFDC system. The latest version of SFDC's PRM module is the right way to establish this access, particularly when you set up a `Partner Portal` on the company's Web site. But be realistic about how many people in the partner organization will actually use the SFDC system. A partner of significant size will have its own SFA system, so its employees will not use the PRM portal very often. It's reasonable to expect the partner's employees to log in once or twice a week to get new `leads` or update a few `opportunities`, but their day-to-day pipeline and `lead` flow management will most likely stay in the partner's SFA system.

When sending `leads` to the partner, make sure that those prospects are sent to a specific *person*, not just a corporation. As many of the partner's sales reps will not log in regularly on your company's PRM portal, it's best to send every `lead` to the appropriate individual in the partner's inside sales team. Although SFDC's `lead assignment rules` can't handle this task, the system's `workflow` rules can be configured to send lead-alert emails automatically. It is also smart to send a weekly update report to the partner's "partner management" person, so that individual can see the lead flow on its way. These reports can be generated and sent automatically as scheduled reports or dashboards from within SFDC.

An interesting issue with partner salesforces is unresponsiveness: they've got lots of things to do besides responding to your new `leads`. To counter this problem, you need to make it clear to the partner that timeliness of response is something you're going to measure: the better the partner's score, the greater the number of `leads` it will receive over time. The most primitive measures of responsiveness are (1) has the individual logged in to the PRM at all, (2) how many `leads` have they updated in any way, (3) how many `leads` have been converted, and (4) how many `leads` have been closed. It's best to give the partner specific goals for these metrics, as well as an overall revenue goal.

One of the best ways to encourage the partner to be more responsive is to *not* give the partner all of the information at once. For example, if you send 100 `leads` with all the details, the partner's employees are less likely to follow up than if you take one of these approaches:

- Send `leads` in small batches more frequently

- Initially send only profile information, and require a "lead-accepted" response before you send over the full `contact` information

- Create a dashboard that everyone can see in the PRM portal

- Send the partner managers a monthly update on performance versus goals

You should also set up `workflows` to trigger alerts and escalations when a `lead` has been left untouched too long and when a partner deal is taking too long or has actually moved backward. Even if these alerts are used only within your company, they foster a healthy management-by-exception style.

From a management perspective, most of what you want to understand is partner performance: the number of deals closed and the total revenues. Once you have that basic data, you'll then want to go deeper. SFDC's reports can easily be extended to examine the partner business, so you can understand the product mix it is selling, how quickly it is ramping up on new products, the referral fees being paid, and other details.

What you *can't* measure from any report is channel conflict. You'll have to get that information anecdotally from your company's sales reps. You want to find out when partners are viewed as competitors, stealing deals from the reps. Then, you need to drive home the idea that the partners are to be viewed as an extension of the company's own salesforce—that's why you brought them on. Achieving the desired level of synergy through these kinds of partnerships requires iron-clad territory definitions, clear rules of engagement, and a commission system that encourages the reps to use the partner as a resource.

Partnerships can work really well when the company's salesforce has a high quota, tight management ("No, you can't go after deals worth less than $20,000"), and a channel-neutral commission plan. The last point causes a lot of angst for most CEOs, because it means paying out double compensation. Even so, the only way to *really* have a rep view a partner as an ally is if the rep makes the same amount of money whether the partner takes down the deal or it's done directly through the company. Contrary to popular belief, double-comping doesn't rob the company of profits if the commission and accelerators are designed so that *the company pays more only if it earns more* overall revenues.

Forecasting

The forecast is the single most visible area of sales management, yet it's often the least well-understood part of SFA systems. Companies large and small suffer from forecasting accuracy problems, even though they may put a significant amount of effort into creating their forecasts. Forecasting is also a risky business: if company executives make public comments based on a shaky forecast, stockholder lawsuits may not be far away.

Forecasting is inherently an unreliable process. Industry averages indicate that more than 50% of the opportunities in a quarter will be forecasted wrong. SFDC can help identify *which* specific deals are most likely to be the subjects of erroneous forecasts, providing a real measure of risk mitigation for the Sales VP.

The forecast is the battle of two hockey sticks, as shown in Figure 9-3. In this figure, the top hockey-stick line is the typical trend of forecasts during the quarter, and the bottom one is the typical trend for closed business in a direct-sales organization. The gap between the two lines is the cause of a lot of stress in the executive suite.

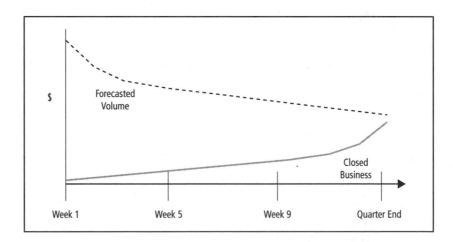

FIGURE 9-3   Forecast versus actual sales data for a typical quarter

Mechanics

While many sales managers seem addicted to exporting the `opportunity` list to their pet spreadsheet, problems arise when data are modified in that spreadsheet. Who made modifications, and why? Will those same modifications be made in next week's forecast run? How will the forecast be defended if nobody knows precisely what's in those numbers? Every time the data are modified outside of SFDC, there is increased risk of error, wasted time, and even regulatory hassle. Any modification of forecast data—adjustments to parameters, managerial overrides, roll-ups, and consolidations—must be done entirely within SFDC or subsystems that are tightly integrated with the system's security features, where the data are subject to a full audit trail and can be securely stored, shared, and locked down if necessary.

The individual rep puts the core forecasting data in at the opportunity level: `close date`, `amount`, and `stage`. Best practices state that the rep leaves the probability percentage alone: this value is set automatically by selection of the `opportunity stage`. It's an even better practice to have the sales `stage` be set by `APEX triggers` based on the status of check-box entries that reflect customer commitments.

SALES STAGES VERSUS PROBABILITIES

SFDC lets you set up multiple `sales processes` to reflect the sales cycles of differing channels and sales teams. These `sales processes` let you expose different subsets of `opportunity stages` and `probabilities` for different teams, all drawn from the master list of opportunity stages.

For any given sales process, the list of `sales stages` should be in two parts: four to eight stages that are directly under the rep's control, and two or three that are in the paperwork departments (i.e., sales operations, legal, finance). See the "Inside Sales: Order Operations for Outside Sales" section of this chapter to learn more about this issue. As discussed earlier, make sure that everyone in the sales management chain agrees on which activities need to be completed in each `stage`, and on which customer behaviors trigger the transition to the next `stage`. So far, so good.

Each `sales stage` is configured with a default probability, which can be overridden by the sales reps either in the `customizable forecast` or in the `opportunity` itself. All too often, the probabilities that companies establish are far too optimistic. The probability *ought* to mean, "What percentage of deals that make it this far in the process actually close?" For example, if you had 10 average deals, each rated at 60%, you would expect 6 of those deals to yield revenue. If you looked back at previous quarters in almost all companies, you might find that perhaps 4 of those 60%-ers really closed. Whoops. Adjust the percentages to reflect the *actual* close probability for deals that reach each `stage`. This usually means that the percentages for all `stages` between 40% and 90% need to be adjusted downward (sales staff being optimistic folks). As painful as it might be, reality is important to avoiding chronic over-forecasting and under-delivery.

Continued

Even though `stages` and probabilities will reflect "what effort the sales reps have made," they don't necessarily reflect the customer's likelihood of buying. The sales team may have done everything right, yet know that politically a competitor is on the fast track to winning the customer's business. Many reps handle this situation by adjusting the percentage up or down in the `opportunity` record, but such an approach has three problems: it's gaming the system, it doesn't convey any information to management, and the adjustment is erased the next time the `stage` value is changed.

A better strategy is to use SFDC's `customizable forecasting`, which allows the rep and each level of management to adjust the amount, `close date`, and `forecast category` of the `opportunity`. But note that while this approach is better, it still doesn't convey any information to management as to *why* the deal is being adjusted.

To overcome this shortfall, we recommend putting an additional pick list in the `opportunity` record entitled "probability adjustment," along these lines:

+++	Deal all but done
++	On inside track
+	Competitive advantage
\<none>	
-	Competitive disadvantage
--	Severe politics
---	Deal all but lost

While this field won't affect any `forecast` calculations, it provides warning signals that can be easily summarized in management reports.

With `history tracking` enabled, you'll be able to see signs of trouble much sooner than with just the standard fields.

SFDC's `customizable forecast` module and `User Roles` add important functionality on top of these base data. The customizable forecast lets the rep withhold doubtful deals from the committed forecast, and it lets every level of management override the forecast probability, close date, and category to make the forecast as realistic as possible when it reaches the CEO. Unfortunately, this system of overrides can also be abused, and it may serve only to allow reps to game the system. If you suspect this kind of nefarious data manipulation is happening, use reports on the underlying (lowest-level) forecast data to identify the level where misleading information is being entered.

For SFDC forecasting to work properly, every rep's quota must be in the system on a monthly or quarterly basis. The `profiles`, `role hierarchy`, and `forecast` hierarchy need to reflect reporting relationships, so that managers can see the right parts of the forecast while only the executives are allowed to see the entire corporate picture. Use the `sales teams` feature to provide the right level of "dotted line" access, and the `forecast delegation` feature to get the best possible deal information and account intelligence into the forecast.

If the system is set up properly, you will be able to run your weekly forecast call exclusively from the SFDC data. For most organizations, the system's forecast reports are sufficiently flexible and informative to handle internal management meetings. When it comes to board or investor presentations, the data should be exported into Excel, which makes it easier to create nice charts.

Interpreting the Numbers

SFDC's forecast categories are counterintuitive for many sales managers, but these definitions cannot be changed[35] in the system:

- `Committed`: The total of `committed` opportunities plus the total `opportunities` that have been `closed-won` in the period.

- `Best Case`: The total of `committed` opportunities plus the total of `best-case` opportunities.

- `Pipeline`: The total of all currently open `opportunities` except those that have been marked as `omitted` from the forecast. This means that `opportunities` that have been `closed-won` are *not* part of the `pipeline`.

Because of these definitions, the `pipeline` value may be lower than the `best case` value for a given forecast period (this can't be changed in the system's `forecast` views, so people will still need to be trained about interpreting the differences). In many organizations, management wants the `pipeline` to include all currently closed deals as well—if so, your external reports will need to add the `pipeline` numbers to the current `closed-won` amount.

If the company's management team and sales reps need to see the forecast along different lines, SFDC's `VisualForce` will let you create metrics that are completely customized; you can even add the probability adjustments mentioned earlier into your calculated totals. By contrast, if you want any real modifications, creating the custom code will cost several thousand dollars and will likely require rework every year or so as your territory definitions and channel overlays change.

---

35. In other words, you can't create, redefine, or delete `forecast categories`, although you can *rename* the labels to suit your terminology.

THE BLOOD COMMIT

Many sales managers feel that the categories of `committed–best case–pipeline` categorization just aren't solid enough. It seems that only 80% or so of the `committed` deals come in. For this reason, managers may want a more solid term that indicates the rep's deepest commitment. Depending on who you are, one of these terms will work for you:

- Worst case
- Blood commit
- Bet the farm
- Career commit

SFDC does not allow the addition of new `forecast categories`, so the work-around is to add a "blood commit" check box on the `opportunity` record. Checking this box is the rep's signal that this deal is a must-win, and he or she doesn't think management should override the rep's forecast of "committed" because the rep is doubling-down on that deal.

If you implement a `custom field` along these lines, you'll need to tell management about what to do when they see it. You will also need to modify forecasting reports so that they do the right thing when this box is checked.

The Forecasting Cycle

Best practices for forecasting in a large organization follow this pattern. There should be a weekly forecast for all divisions (including professional services), focused on bookings. If this weekly call happens on Mondays, the individual reps should be directed to have all `opportunity` data and individual forecast overrides correct and stable on the previous Thursday night. On Friday, first- and second-level managers should review the forecast numbers, understand them, and talk with reps about trouble spots. Managers should look at the `activity history` to see what has (or has not) changed about the `opportunity` in the last week, and they should look at reports designed to spot deals that have stalled or—worse—regressed. The managers' inputs should all be in the system and stable by Friday night.

The Sales VPs should look at the numbers on Saturday, and if there is an international roll-up of the forecast (to a COO) those discussions should happen on Sunday. The Sales VPs will make heavy use of reports or dashboards generated for them by sales operations to see the big picture of the forecast, because their biggest nightmare is a rosy pipeline based on wishful thinking. Looking below the top-line numbers, the VPs should have indicators or dashboards that examine average deal size, sales-cycle length, pipeline coverage, number of deals regressing, and number of deals disappearing from the quarter altogether. If the company's revenues follow a severe "hockey stick"[36] pattern, the Sales VPs should have graphics that illustrate how this quarter's weekly revenues match the hockey-stick curve that's normal for the company. A parallel hockey-stick pattern comparison should be done for the series of weekly forecasts, allowing managers to identify weakness or upside surprises early. SFDC's `pipeline` "as of" reports are a great place to start when conducting this assessment. The analysts should show the expected effects on revenues owing to product changes ("The company had a new product launch in week 4") and competitors' moves ("We're being attacked with a big ad campaign and discount"). Finally, the VPs should be looking at ramp effects ("We've got 10 new reps"), pipeline effects (deal-velocity metrics), and regional issues ("Five holidays in France, our number three market, during the quarter") to make sure that the forecast is believable and as solid as possible. A number of great sales scorecards and forecast analytics tools are available in SFDC's AppExchange. The good ones are more expensive, but they're worth the money because they prevent embarrassment before your boss, the board of directors, and even investors.

The Monday worldwide forecast call should be run from the SFDC system, and the focus of the conversation should be on what can be done to firm up the shaky parts of the forecast, rather than a mind-numbing account-by-account review. If the forecast for a region has shrunk or jumped, there should be discussion about why the change has occurred, and what can be done to reverse the shortfall or solidify the advance.

Any modifications or amendments to the forecast as a result of this call should be made directly to SFDC records. Any follow-up items for the forecast should be sent out as SFDC `tasks`.

When it comes to forecasting, it is important for the company to be a learning organization. Improving forecast accuracy requires providing candid (but nonthreatening) feedback to *every single quota-carrying person in sales*, including the Sales VP (he or she is the lucky recipient of input from both above and below). After six months or more of forecasting data have accumulated in the SFDC system, your team should perform analytics on a quarterly basis:

- Percentage of a quarter's deals closing within 10% of the forecasted value

- Accuracy of the forecast in each of the last four weeks of the quarter

- Individuals who chronically under- or over-forecast, and the average variance

- Characteristics of deals that regress (so the company can spot them in advance)

- Characteristics of deals that are upside surprises (so the company can identify the telling factors that cause a leap in forecasted value or probability)

---

36. Hockey-stick patterns occur when most of the deals happen in the last few weeks or days of the quarter. For software companies, it's not unusual to have 20% of the quarter's deals close on the last *day* of the quarter. These patterns make forecasting difficult and inaccurate.

The SFDC forecasting system works entirely with bookings and *cannot* by itself produce a revenue or GAAP forecast. While the SFDC system should hold information about all of your products' subscription prices, revenue recognition schedules, and other details, only the Finance department can do a true *revenue* forecast based on revenue trigger events, inventory/ shipment availability, and time. It is a best practice for the SFDC system to automatically feed the accounting system[37] on a weekly basis the product and order-level information needed for revenue calculations. However, the revenue final forecast is highly privileged information that should *not* be fed back from the accounting system into the SFDC system.

Commission/Compensation Management

While SFDC holds a lot of data that are immediately relevant to the design and implementation of a commission and compensation plan, the system offers no direct functionality to support calculation of compensation amounts. If the company uses a spreadsheet or dedicated software package to calculate commissions, make sure that it is driven directly from SFDC and accounting system data.

As discussed in Chapter 7, the choice of which spreadsheet or software package to use for figuring commissions is a tricky one. If the company has fewer than 25 reps and 5 products, a simple spreadsheet is probably the right choice. While larger sales teams or longer product lists argue for a dedicated commission software package, implementing these packages can be just as tough (or sometimes tougher) as continuing with the spreadsheet system, particularly if the compensation plan has any of the following characteristics:

- It changes frequently.
- It uses product-specific commissions.
- It incorporates lots of sales contests or incentives from suppliers.
- It involves a lot of recurring revenue.
- It has to deal with frequent territory changes.
- It has to deal with lots of temporary promotions or product changes.

Activity Management

The ability to see what people have been doing—to really see the blow-by-blow events that have shaped an account or opportunity—is something that's never been possible prior to

---

37. If your company's accounting system is separate from its ERP system, SFDC should also feed data into the ERP system on a weekly basis to assist with inventory and manufacturing planning, particularly for items with long lead times.

the advent of SFA systems. Activity management helps the company to understand what's really involved in closing business and to develop realistic models for the sales team. It can mean fairer quotas and better resource allocations for assets such as pre-sales engineers, travel budgets, and loaner systems. It can also provide early warning signals that pipeline formation isn't going fast enough, long before the problem shows up in the formal forecast numbers.

Unfortunately, too-aggressive attempts at activity management are also a major reason for user resistance, low adoption, and failed SFA implementations. People are suspicious of activity management because they're afraid of how *you,* the manager, will abuse the information. Further, most reps will simply see activity management as a tax—that is, as a burden that offers no direct benefit to them.

Clearly, before you start using activity management, you have to make people comfortable with the idea that **the information they put into the system will not be used against them.** You also have to persuade them that putting information into the system is *for their own purposes*, to make *their* job easier. That notion explains the emphasis on the "nothing falls through the cracks" message at the start of the "Sales Management" section. When everyone uses the SFDC system to hand off and track action items, provide ticklers for follow-ups, and record customer interactions, the system will be full of information that's useful to the sales team. While sales personnel will have to enter data into SFDC, they *won't* have to write anywhere near as many emails to get things done.

The core of activity management is monitoring and evaluating the sequence of `tasks` (including attached emails and phone notes) recorded in the `activity history` of `accounts` and, preferably, `opportunities`. Early on, you'll be looking only at gross measures such as "the total number of activities per rep" without paying any attention to exactly what those activities are. The first step is to get the reps tracking anything at all as activities.

Once you've gotten beyond the basics, activity management requires you to develop a model of the activities required to close a sale, and the best way to do that is with real data from successful sales cycles. Of course, you will need at least a couple of quarters' worth of data before you can really see anything valuable in terms of activity management; early on, there just won't have been enough sales cycles to make reasonable generalizations. You may discover that the average sale requires four on-site visits and six phone calls. You may figure out that pilot projects or proofs of concept are involved in 80% of sales amounting to more than $50,000, but that they indicate a 70% chance of *losing* deals worth less than $20,000. These kinds of discoveries can help you dramatically increase your forecasting accuracy or avoid low-probability deals altogether.

Generally speaking, inside sales personnel will be much more comfortable with activity management than the outside sales staff and partner management organizations, because they are more used to being closely monitored. In an ironic twist, the biggest payoff from activity management comes for the outside sales team, even though those reps are usually most wary of it. You knew the job was dangerous when you took it.

The principles for activity management should apply to everyone, though: you start with a baseline model of how workers should be optimally spending their time, you measure, and then you look for odd patterns. Sometimes the patterns mean an individual is doing the wrong things—but be wary for cases where the "variance" is the *right* behavior, and you need to adjust your model or norms. Know that the specific patterns are expected to vary significantly across groups: be willing to look at different details, and to measure and evaluate reps in different ways.

The output of activity management is guidance for all of the sales people. Your first foray into giving this guidance should be done at the group level, showing new discoveries that are good for everyone. For example, you can show that at week 4 of the quarter, successful reps (the ones who consistently make their numbers) are making 30 prospecting calls and 4 on-site visits per week. Show the correlation between certain activities and building a healthy pipeline. If you can show reps quantitatively how they *ought* to spend their time in the last month of the quarter, you'll be telling them how to invest their time to make a ton more money—a message that they'll certainly listen to.

Invite debate from the team. They may have good reasons for disagreeing with your suggestions, and their input will make the model you're developing more realistic for everyone.

After providing guidance a few times at the group level, you can start giving feedback to the individual sales reps—usually the most junior ones, or the ones who are having consistency problems. This feedback must be given in private, and it should be delivered in a collaborative environment where the rep can see you are trying to make him or her even more money. If you deliver the advice in the form of punishment or criticism, the rep will soon stop entering activities, or will put in fake information to game the system—which is actually worse.[38]

Even though this feedback must be handled with some delicacy, during the early weeks in the quarter activity management can give the company's upper management better information than the forecast does. At the very least, it will provide a context in which to interpret the forecast and the pipeline numbers.

Performance Management

SFDC records an amazing array of information that can be used as the basis for performance management of sales personnel. However, like being too assertive with activity

---

38. The fake data will corrupt the results of the real stuff, making the situation look too uniform and positive. Fake data that look real are very hard to expunge from the system.

management, this is dangerous medicine. It is imperative that sales leaders avoid two key issues in this area:

- Do *not* make SFDC the center of attention during the performance review process. To the degree that the reps believe that the system will be used as Big Brother, the ultimate spybot, they will stop using the system in the best ways. Instead, they will try to hide information from the system, undermine management visibility, and game the measurements.

- Do not measure the wrong things—and make sure to temper the measurements you do make with "reality factors" such as the quality of a territory and the loyalty level of existing accounts. Identify the right things to measure by evaluating the beliefs, behavior, and activities of the top 20% of your reps (because they probably deliver 60% or more of the company's revenue and profits). Ask *them* what makes them different and better: how they spend their time, how they evaluate which prospects have the biggest potential, and which activities and tactics help them close deals more reliably.

THE OWNERSHIP SOCIETY

No sales team wants to do housekeeping. But the Sales department needs to be the owner of SFDC, and to keep things on the right track, the department needs to have a *"data owner"* for the system.

The data owner needs to be the guardian of semantics and data quality, making sure that the sales staff enter the right things into SFDC, and keeping changes to the system to the absolute minimum—the things that will actually increase revenue. This data owner will work in conjunction with the marketing system administrator and the IT people to manage change in the system. In choosing this data owner, find someone who likes computers, wants to grow his or her job a little bit, and is good at foreseeing problems. Often, the data owner will be found in the company's sales operations group.

CHAPTER 10

Best Practices in Marketing

Half the money I spend on advertising is wasted.
The trouble is, I don't know which half.

—*John Wannamaker*

T HIS CHAPTER IS FOR every member of the marketing team, because every part of the Salesforce.com system holds data and tools that can make your job easier. The Marketing department is usually the first or second organization in a company to adopt and effectively use SFDC. But the marketing team almost always makes mistakes in how they set up and use SFDC because they haven't really looked deeply enough at their business process—what can be called "the life of a lead." Consequently, marketing looks bad—and undermines system credibility—when SFDC reports are misleading.

Marketing Organizations

Across the range of company types and industries served by SFDC, the marketing operation is organized in very different ways. Sometimes it reports to engineering, sometimes to sales, sometimes directly to the president—and sometimes sales even reports to marketing. So there's no way to organize this chapter around marketing *job titles*. Instead, it is structured around *job functions*, which may or may not report to the marketing organization.

The First Order of Business

Most of marketing's interactions with SFDC surround the early stages of pipeline formation—lead generation, processing, cultivation, nurturing, and qualification. This is the early part of the revenue generation business process, which is spearheaded by sales.

Although I'm a card-carrying marketing guy, my first bit of guidance is that the marketing group should almost never be the owner of the SFDC system. This system is called *Sales*force for a reason, and you have to admit that the sales animal is a lot different from the marketing wonk. The SFDC system should be owned by the team that owns the revenue number—almost always, that's the sales department.

That said, marketing *must* be very actively involved in the design, usage, and analytics of SFDC. The core of many marketing functions will live in SFDC records. Marketing must own `leads` and `campaigns`, and should have control over several policy areas in the system. Marketing personnel will play a critical role in creating some of the fanciest reports and spearheading several of the key integrations between SFDC and supporting systems, such as the Web site, the content management system, the license management system, and the eCommerce system.

Further, marketing will design the database characteristics that lie at the core of closed-loop marketing[1]—where every customer touch, from first mailing to customer support to PR, is logged and monitored through SFDC. Closed-loop marketing focuses on the feedback loops between the marketing message, sales activities, customer behavior, and customer response. Because SFDC will be used by marketing, external service bureaus, sales, customer support, and professional services, the system can hold *all* the data about a customer relationship, and be the touch point for all customer-facing activities. Add the elements of listening and adjusting the responses to input, and you have closed-loop marketing. Such a seamless operation means huge wins in conversion, loyalty, and profitability.

Developing a Model of Sales and Marketing Interactions

Before you can apply any of the recommendations in this chapter, you need to develop a model of how the company's revenue generation process works, and how sales and marketing need to interact. The goal is to create a service level agreement (SLA)—that is, a contract between sales and marketing about who does what to make revenue happen. Read the section "Define and Document the Sales Model" in Chapter 9, and participate with the sales team to get the details of this model nailed down and documented. This task can be achieved in an afternoon if you're serious, but it's one of the most highly leveraged things you can do to ensure that the marketing staff is on the same page with the sales team (as well as helping marketing personnel get on the same page with each other!).

Lead Generation and Collection

Before any `lead` generation starts, it's important to have a common understanding with sales about the life of a `lead`—how `leads` evolve, who handles them at various stages, and how the `workflow` triggers the conversion or demotion of `leads`. Read the discussion of this topic in Chapter 9, if you haven't already done so. Also check out the articles on www.SFDC-secrets.com for further discussion and tricks.

---

1. To find out more on this topic, check out *The CMO Strategic Agenda: Automating Closed-Loop Marketing*, published in March 2008 by the Aberdeen Group. Several wonderful consultancies will also help you implement closed-loop marketing systems for a nominal fee (nominal as long as you sell expensive stuff).

Some issues need to be argued through in detail. One of the critical decisions is "Which information should we collect at the start of the prospecting process?" Almost always, marketing wants to collect a lot of information about the customers' demographics and the competitive products they are considering. Sales typically wants to collect the customer's title, purchase timeframe, and other qualification questions. While these are all valid requests, it's not practical to collect these data at initial registration time, for three reasons:

- The collection form isn't always under your control, particularly for tradeshows and videoconferencing services that allow the collection of only their standard fields.

- In almost any collection medium (but particularly the Web), the more information you ask for, the higher the likelihood of user drop-off. Typically, having more than five fields will cause a significant reduction in the number of leads and an equal increase in bogus responses (such as emails of asdf@asdf.com).

- Many target audiences get really irritated by nosy questions about purchase intent. In market segments where prospects hate sales calls, asking these questions can dramatically lower the quantity of `leads`.

In debating which data to collect, always ask what the information will *really* be used for, who is going to take the time to enter it and validate it, and whether the information could be inferred from some other data that can be purchased or obtained in the public domain. You'll probably get to ask for only five items, so make sure they're the best five. The questions should provide the minimum information needed to route/process the next step for the inquiry. The rest of the information that people would love to have should be collected during the first step of the qualification and lead nurturing process.

The next issue that needs to be argued about is "What constitutes a lead?" Best practices are to focus more on lead *quality* than on lead *quantity*. Low-quality leads are simply a waste of everyone's time and money. Why market or try to sell to people who don't have genuine interest? The first step to lead quality is to distinguish leads from "Names":

- A Name is merely the contact information for a person believed to be part of the target audience. Names are typically purchased from lists or are obtained from outside, but have not explicitly indicated they want to know more about the company, its products, or its services. Names are the lowest-quality leads and should almost always be relegated to mailing-list status and excluded from the telesales call-down list.

- A true lead, who is a respondent to marketing efforts, has explicitly requested more information about the company or its products. These leads should immediately be scored (a topic discussed later in this chapter) and put on the telesales call-down list. Check out the discussion on this topic in Chapters 8 and 9.

Once these basics are agreed to (and documented in the project wiki), the SFDC screens and variables need to be customized to fit the company's model. Almost always, a few `custom fields` (such as a calculated field for the `sales region`) need to be added to the `lead` object, and pick list fields for `status`, `industry`, and `rating` should be replaced by custom ones. `Field history tracking` should be turned on to provide an audit trail for the 20 most interesting fields in the `lead` object.

In addition to the SFDC modifications, it's important to modify the user registration screens on the company's Web site. Use drop-down pick lists for as many fields as you can (e.g., country, state, and job title) and use multiple landing pages to obviate the need for entering certain items (e.g., product interest area or vertical industry). Don't use a `lead source`, but instead populate the relevant `campaign` for the action the user has taken (more on this topic later in this chapter). If you decide to collect phone numbers, do so after you've collected the country information (so the user doesn't need to enter the country code for the phone number) and have a field for city/area code separated from the actual number. To avoid the infinite variety of misentered phone numbers, put example formats in small font immediately under the fields in the Web page. These tricks can dramatically increase both the data quality and the form-completion rates on your Web site.

Even if your company doesn't use email for marketing, it is *imperative* that its Web page forms collect the user's email address and validate it. Email addresses are essentially the *only* universal identifier that exists on the Web (and even they aren't completely reliable), so collect this information and validate it as early as you can. The strong form of validation is to send the user an email at the address the user provided, with the mail containing a unique URL[2] that must be clicked for the user to get access to the desired information, download items, or other goodies. A weaker form of validation is to simply send the user an email including the links to the documents or other goodies they've requested. This technique has become less effective as more users learn to block HTML mail, and each new release of Outlook raises filters to higher and higher levels. Either way, you need to let the registrant know what will happen when the user clicks "submit" (typically with a splash page on the Web), so he or she knows what to do next. Inevitably, some people will employ "single-use" email addresses for their registration, but in most markets they usually constitute only a tiny percentage of the total audience, and you still know that the registrant is a human, rather than a Web bot.

If you want to get really fancy, create an "account" page on your Web site where users can select and maintain their preferences. When a user registers, your Web server software creates the account and drops a cookie on the user's system so you can track all of that person's actions on the site going forward. Every few months, when the user returns (assuming you have a highly informational site, or lots of short-term offers), you ask the user for

---

2. By making this URL unique, you can measure which individuals follow through and when their actions occur. This information can be used to trigger some detailed lead scoring, or assist in Web site redesigns.

just a bit more information. Such a request is typically couched in terms of "Our records aren't quite complete . . ." and asks for only one or two new items each time. This progressive registration technique allows you to collect quite a bit of information about visitors without irritating them. Of course, you need to make sure that all this information is completely integrated with the company's eCommerce site, so that users don't ever have to reenter any of their information. As discussed in Chapter 2, do *not* collect or store highly personal financial information (credit cards, Social Security numbers, health ID numbers, or the like) in SFDC.

Special attention needs to be given to email opt-in/opt-out preferences. For a good discussion of general principles of user privacy and email preferences, check out www.SFDC-secrets.com. The key point is that the lead-capture page should really be a *user account creation* page, so that when users come back to the site in the future, their information and personal preferences will be remembered. On the registration page, give visitors clear guidance about what registering will do, which kinds of communications they can opt in/opt out for, and how they can change their preferences later.[3] A new CAN SPAM requirement mandates that opting out must be achievable from a single Web page, so keep the design simple. What you *don't* want is to have a single opt-out check box, as offering just one choice greatly increases the probability that users will tell you to leave them completely alone—and you would then have to honor that overly broad request.

The following sections describe best practices surrounding typical lead generation activities. For all tactics, make sure to read the "Lead Capture and Insertion" section later in this chapter.

Tradeshows and Conferences

At tradeshows and conferences, you have almost no control over the data the show operator will collect. The data are usually provided in one or more spreadsheets or CSV files, and you need to watch out for and fix the following problems: states and countries that are misspelled and do not conform to ISO standards,[4] phone numbers with erratic formats (particularly with international attendees, who forget to include their country codes), and foreign character sets that become garbled (particularly for individuals' names and street addresses). Often, the data are not made available to sponsoring companies for several days after the event: get them in the system immediately thereafter!

---

3. These choices are typically implemented as short HTML links that point to help/FAQ pop-up pages.
4. When importing or entering data into SFDC, it's a good idea to *not* spell out country and state names, but instead to use ISO-standard three-character country and state codes. Using these short codes makes it much easier to develop and maintain lead routing rules, formulas, triggers, reports, and other SFDC features. You can find references to this best practice at www.SFDC-secrets.com.

Tradeshows and conferences will sometimes deliver a bunch of information you didn't ask for, and probably won't get again. For example, questionnaires may ask attendees, "By what percentage will you be expanding your office/operations in the next 12 months?"— this could be great background information, but you don't collect this kind of thing for everyone. Don't throw this information away! You can either store it verbatim as a `note` associated with the `lead`, or you can abbreviate it in some way and put it in the `lead`'s `description` field (in the preceding example, the information might be stated as "Growth in next 12 months: 8%").

Webinars

Webinars—whether recorded or live—are typically conducted through a service such as WebEx or GoToMeeting. These services collect relatively fixed types of data. The spreadsheets or CSV files they send to sponsoring companies have all the same problems as the data collected at tradeshows and conferences, but at least these services provide the data more quickly. Get these data cleaned and put into the system right away. Write a standard import template with macros in the spreadsheet that prep the data quickly and in a repeatable fashion.

Events

Seminars, meetings, dinners, and other lead generation events can deliver much better data quality for leads, particularly if attendees are required to register for the event on the company's Web site. If your registration page follows the guidance given earlier in this section, you're good to go. Plus, the leads will be entered into the system immediately, thanks to the `web2lead` automation; thus the lead response times can be very short.

Banner Ads, Site Sponsorships, and Other Internet Advertising

Banner ads and their brethren will typically generate traffic to your company's Web site, with no intrinsic lead or other tracking information. The only lead-related data that can be gleaned from this traffic is anonymous (unless users happen to have a browser cookie you're tracking) and of no real relevance to SFDC. If, however, there is a referring user ID embedded in the URL (as happens with big ad networks), store this information as part of the campaign record for each visitor.

Of course, if the site visitor is interested enough in your offerings to fill out a registration form, you have a lead to which you should attach all the "anonymous" information that HTML traffic provides. It is a best practice—although fairly complex—to correlate the lead's information with his or her page-visited history (using Web analytic software) so you can understand more about the nature of the prospect's interest. Pass this user-profile information into SFDC via `hidden fields`, so that your `lead` records are as rich as possible.

Google AdWords

Like other online ad media, Google AdWords can generate traffic for a company's Web site. Unlike more primitive online ads, AdWords traffic can be tightly correlated with SFDC campaigns and tracked through the conversion and sales-cycle process. Use the Salesforce for Google Adwords features—they really work and improve the visibility into your ads' effectiveness.

To increase lead quality[5] for AdWords' ads, follow these guidelines:

- Organize your campaigns around your product's *use cases* or *target segments*. If you create a database accelerator, create campaigns around online transactions versus data warehousing, or financial versus telecom comparisons.

- Once you've focused your messages on these use cases or segments, create coherent content for the AdWords keywords and ad text. Keep the coherence going throughout the landing page content and the call to action.

- On the landing page registration area, encode the campaign name in hidden fields that will be transferred into SFDC along with the rest of the registration details. By default, SFGA does not map Google AdWords campaigns to SFDC campaigns. You'll need to handle this chore yourself by writing some APEX code or creating a workflow.

- Tune the entire set of content (keywords, ad text, landing page text, and landing page call to action) as a whole, trying to optimize for *the total number of converted clicks*. There is no point in trying to increase just the number of clicks or the conversion ratio in isolation—those statistics aren't meaningful. First, optimize the click-through rate by matching the keywords to the ad copy. Next, optimize the conversion rate by matching the keyword/ad to the landing page content. Collect at least a week's data for each tuning cycle (shorter periods of data are misleading, due to the variable nature of Web site traffic).

- Use Google's ad-rotation feature to do A/B "split testing" of content sets; do split testing of landing pages as well. These comparisons will help you systematically analyze the effectiveness of the content and improve the results; do it right, and you can double your high-quality lead flow at no extra advertising cost.

- Review the content sets on at least a quarterly basis, and preferably biweekly. Your competitors will be making improvements to their ads when you aren't paying attention, and lead flow (measured in terms of both quality and quantity) can degrade rapidly in highly competitive situations.

---

5. Even though lead quality is king, many advertisers focus instead on the bid value for AdWords. While doing so can make your budget go farther, it's much *less effective* than most people think, and it will do nothing to improve the company's lead quality and yield. Focus on these issues—that is, on the results—rather than concentrating solely on lowering your costs.

An important caveat: each SFDC instance can only link to one AdWords account. As a consequence, if you are working for a large organization, you will need to consolidate all of your AdWords activity into a single AdWords login. This requirement has several ramifications (e.g., for budget-splitting issues, politics, and marketing organizational needs) that can make SFGA a bit impractical. There is an alternative approach, which involves splitting your SFDC instance (one for each AdWords account) and using `Salesforce to Salesforce` to bridge them. While this strategy will work, it's really not advisable.

Search Engine Marketing

Despite all the justified excitement about Google AdWords, getting results in the *left* column (the natural search results, as opposed to ads) is more effective (and far more *cost*-effective) than brute-force advertising (in the right column). A number of search engine marketing (SEM) tools and books are available, although none of them is specifically targeted at SFDC usage. Follow these guideline to get the most out of SEM techniques in conjunction with your SFDC system:

- Invest a small amount of time almost continuously (rather than doing big bursts of effort infrequently).

- Examine what the competitors are doing on their Web sites, and copy what works in their strategies. (You don't want to copy them verbatim, but learn from their results and do them one better.)

- Drop "cookies" as early as possible in the Web visit, and analyze the visitors' page-view metrics carefully.

- Start to use landing pages for visitors who fit certain profiles, and tune the landing pages for best results.

- Pass visitor profile data into the SFDC `lead` record when the user completes a registration (or information-request) page.

Email Marketing

As for SEM, AdWords, and other online marketing techniques, dozens of books have been written about email marketing. As with those other tomes, however, none focuses specifically on SFDC. There are two main methods of email marketing relevant to SFDC: the broadcast ("mass email blast") and the vertical campaign ("individual drip sequence"). No matter which of these approaches your company employs, the same key success factors apply:

- Use an email marketing tool that integrates with SFDC's `campaign`, `contact`, and `lead` objects, and that presents useful information on the system's screens. Several companies have done a great job in creating such tools, with new entrants and product upgrades happening all the time. As these products come with a wide range of features and price points, there is no universal best choice—but it is imperative that you use the email system on a trial basis for at least a month before buying, to make sure that its features and concepts fit tightly with your company's needs.

- Make sure the content the company is sending out via emails is relevant to your list. If you don't know whether the prospect would be interested, you're not ready to send the mail yet! Sloppiness here is the root of most spam complaints (which could cost you $10,000 in fines per incident).[6]

- Recognize that the best list to email to is the one you already have—the one you've been nurturing and cleaning all along. While you can certainly buy email names by the millions, those data are virtually worthless and emailing those addresses puts your company at risk of spam complaints. Leverage partners' and industry associations' lists, but do a full opt-in cycle before you add those prospects to your list of blast names.

- Depending on your audience, as many as one-third of the emails will be read on a mobile phone. For this reason, keep the emails brief, clean, and "upper-left-corner optimized" so the readers can get the point without panning or scrolling. Make the subject line compelling!

- Make sure that any links in the email point to a unique URL, or pass a hidden field into the registration process for identifying where the lead came from. Make sure all the landing pages feed data directly into SFDC.

- Don't use images for anything important in the email—they should just be decoration for those email clients who let images through. In some audiences, more than 50% of the recipients will not see any images in the email—or may never receive the email at all because the embedded images trigger spam filters.

- Don't email the entire list at once. Instead, roll out emails in phases (separated by a day or so) to catch errors in your copy and make minor improvements as you do. You don't want to burn your list out with too-frequent mailings (monthly seems to be the de facto limit unless you've *really* got fast-changing information or offers). Mail those individuals too often, and you risk a dramatic surge in unsubscribe requests and complaints.

- Use your partial-list mailing strategy to support A/B split testing of format, content, and calls to action. *You can't know* what will be effective with your audience: you will find out only through testing and tuning for better email response rates.

---

6. Even though the FTC has chosen to leave this regulation nearly unenforced, such a law actually makes good business sense. Sending email to people who don't care about the content is a *waste of your brand,* as well as your time. Just say no.

For drip marketing campaigns, there's a big twist: the recipient has declared interest in a topic, which means you can have a much more relevant and frequent email conversation with this prospect. Instead of consisting of just one generic email per month, a drip marketing sequence should be highly specific, with a series of messages that move the customer along the learning curve for the company's product.

Drip marketing entails an additional best practice (which involves an email system feature). If the individual target is contacted by anyone in the company (pre-sales, sales rep, or post-sales support) during a drip sequence,[7] the sequence should be terminated. This event is triggered by a `task` or `note` in SFDC, so the inside sales people need to be briefed on the importance of putting even an empty note into the records of the `leads` or `contacts` with whom they talk. If a human conversation has occurred, the robot-generated emails are rarely appropriate and can be quite confusing.

Drip marketing campaigns can be the core of automated `lead` cultivation and nurturing, and the fancy systems provide dynamic `lead` scoring based on recipient behavior and click-throughs to the Web site. Marketing systems such as Eloqua and Marketo are great starting points for this kind of closed-loop marketing.

Lead Generation Campaigns

The power of marketing comes from repetition—a series of prospect contacts that gets increasingly more relevant and effective over time. The whole point is to carry out a series of touches that educates the lead and moves the prospect closer to purchasing the company's offerings. SFDC provides a simple `lead source` field (a pick list) to indicate the origin of each lead. But for any serious marketing company, `lead source` is a "training wheel" that will rapidly get in the way. If you create a `lead` and use `lead source` when that person responds to a second outreach from your company, what are you supposed to do with the `lead source`? Ignoring the new `lead source` or overwriting the existing one destroys information. Conversely, creating a duplicate `lead` to hold the new `lead source` causes confusion and lowers data quality.

The solution is to not use `lead source` in the first place.[8]

The SFDC `campaigns` feature[9] allows you to capture much better information about target audiences and respondents for your marketing activities. If you've been using `lead source` until now, your data can be converted to `campaigns` with no data loss.

---

7. Typically, emails are sent out on a sequence of days after the initial registration, such as on days 1, 3, 5, 7, 10, 15, 21, and 30. Different audiences and industry preferences may make the sequence more or less frequent.

8. Actually, `lead source` is a system field that you can't delete anyway, so it's okay to store some interesting information there—but it will be a redundant field whose semantics you need to manage carefully. It's particularly important to not use `lead source` in reports unless you really know what you are doing.

9. Included in the Enterprise and Unlimited editions; an extra-cost item in the Professional edition.

Once a campaign is set up, SFDC tracks which leads and contacts are target partici-pants (for example, they are sent email invitations) and respondents (they replied via email or HTML links) and stores the sequence of all participation and response. When campaigns are configured properly, looking at lead or contact pages will reveal the entire history of every prospect touch the company has attempted or completed. Further, SFDC's new campaign influence feature lets you identify all the campaigns that had some impact on each of the opportunities in the company's pipeline. This capability makes it easier than ever before to calibrate the ROI of marketing activities.

The campaigns feature is really a management tool, not an execution tool. It is used in conjunction with third-party marketing automation tools to organize, monitor, and report on the company's outbound marketing activities. This magic requires some planning and careful execution. The good news is that after the first few weeks, working with this feature will be second nature. The bad news is that virtually every company I've ever seen does *not* use campaigns correctly—so some explanation is in order here.

Naming Campaigns

Before you start using SFDC's campaigns feature, you have to examine all the ways you collect leads, whether directly generated by marketing activities or not. All of these streams—even cold calls and customer referrals—need to be represented as campaigns. It's best to create a list of every way that customers may contact the company (and every vehicle that the company uses to find them). The list is best organized on a spreadsheet that looks like Table 10-1.

Most of the information in Table 10-1 is self-explanatory, but the campaign naming convention needs some special attention. You will want to be able look back over cam-paigns years after they were done, without getting them confused with one another (if you want to understand more about naming issues, check out "What's in a Namespace" in Chapter 2). You should think of a naming convention that is intuitive, short, and easy to

TABLE 10-1   Campaign Summary Information

Type	Name	Description	Start/End Date	Audience	Number of Leads	Expected Budget
Ad	2008-Goog-NA-Svcs	Services promo	Sep 08/Jan 09	USA execs	200	$2000
Event	2008-Dinner-NYC	Exec dinner	Oct 08/Oct 08	NYC execs	50	$5000
Show	2008-GGSymp-USA	Symposium expo	Nov 08/Nov 08	USA execs	300	$30,000
Email	2008-Email-upgrade	Upgrade promo	Dec 08/Dec 08	Customers	50	$500

identify even if you weren't involved with running the campaign. The exact parameters of this namespace will depend on your company's marketing and target markets, but generally the names should look something like this:

<year>--<event/activity abbreviation>--<geography>--<product line or message>

The year should be at the head of the name, so that you can rapidly sort campaigns by year in HTML or Excel list views. The double-dashes are needed in the name so that they can be unambiguously parsed[10] by reporting software. The overall name is long, but it ensures that humans can rapidly identify the campaigns that they're looking for in reports or long other listings.

You will need to have campaign names for every single lead source you use in the system today, and every one you can conceive of using in the next few years. Expect your list of campaigns to be somewhere between 50 and 500 lines long—even more if your company does a ton of highly variable or experimental campaigns. This amount of data sounds daunting, but summarizing this list actually goes pretty quickly once you put your mind to it. Besides, this list is simply representing an already-complex reality.

The campaigns list needs to include things that go on indefinitely, even for leads that are inbound calls. In addition to the traditional outbound activities marketing explicitly does, make sure that your campaigns list includes items for natural searches, newsletters, customer referrals, employee referrals, press articles, analyst recommendations, call-ins, word of mouth, and other data streams. These never-ending campaigns should be named with the year field as "20XX."

Setting Up Campaigns

You already do some planning before you execute a marketing campaign. It's important to extend this planning a bit and put the information into the SFDC system, as it will become the system of record for all campaign information.

First, you will probably need to add some custom fields to the campaign page to hold the following data items:

- The business unit, target market, or product line for the campaign

- The value proposition, message, or call to action

- The geographic reach

---

10. This is fancy-talk for "filtered and sorted."

- The media channel
- The Web site landing page URL or other registration vehicles
- The offer or promotional item
- Venue, timing, and logistics
- The organizations and agencies involved

You'll also almost surely want to expand the campaign response pick list to reflect the expected response workflow surrounding the campaign.

When preparing for a campaign, identify the qualitative goals and quantitative metrics for it. Summarize the costs (include internal labor allocation as well external agency/materials costs). Identify the call to action for the campaign, and think through any special handling that might be required. For example, a campaign for a local prospect dinner would need specific action to deal with the restaurant for headcount, and a reminder call-out activity for the telesales group. These special actions should be embodied as either SFDC tasks or workflows associated with the campaign.

Enter the campaign information into the SFDC system, and make sure to set up appropriate campaign sharing rules so your colleagues have visibility into the campaigns. Also set up campaign hierarchies to reflect relationships among campaigns (such as geographic, product line, or target market groupings) for easier analysis and roll-ups over time. Make sure to fill out the description field with as much relevant information as possible about the target audience, goals, and call-to-action sequence. At the time, all this information will seem completely obvious and boring—but six months after the campaign ends, no one will be able to remember any of these details that make the campaigns relevant to generating real business.

Add all of the creative pieces (whether an email or a PDF file of paper deliverables) to the campaign record as attached files. If any coupons or discount offers were made available, make sure that they include an expiry date, have been reviewed by the legal staff[11] prior to sending them out, and are attached to the SFDC campaign record.

If the campaign has experimental or innovative elements, the telesales group will need tools for follow-up to responses. Include scripts and pointers to follow-up email templates in the campaign description field. SFDC has a free AppExchange call-scripting feature that will make it easier for your phone jockeys to say the right things to campaign respondents, no matter how new the messages or offers might be.

You might also store ideas about best responses to certain situations (e.g., competitive objections, unable to travel to your event) as attachments to the campaign.

---

11. Of course, these bits of advice are not unique to SFDC. But I can't tell you the number of times I've discovered illegal or unethical elements accidentally included in marketing offers.

> ### A HISTORY LESSON
>
> Campaigns *are the way to handle the full variety of prospect interactions. But in many cases,* campaign membership *records are unwieldy for workflows or formulas. So here's a trick: create a download history as a single ASCII field (in* leads *and* contacts*) that grows indefinitely. The history field has brief codes that you can use in* filters, formulas, workflows, *and* reports. *Here's an example:*
>
> *Product download = P*
> *Subsequent product download = p*
> *Whitepaper download = W*
>
> *So your download history field might look like this:*
>
> *P12.10.08-p01.05.09-W01.07.09- . . .*
>
> *Note the use of "." rather than "/" for date separators, and "-" as an event separator. Using these characters makes it easier when doing regex and string processing in your scripts, spreadsheets,* formulas, *and* workflows. *Also note the use of leading zeroes for day and month numbers, which facilitates parsing and character counting (each download uses exactly 10 characters).*
>   *This history field can become arbitrarily long, but if its length gets unwieldy you can have a* workflow *formula that truncates the field to remove any history more than two years old.*

Running Campaigns

The first step is to make sure the system administrator has set up the campaign member report[12] as a custom link in the campaign, contact, and lead pages. This AppExchange freebie is worth its weight in gold and will make it much easier to see what's going on with the campaign in real time.

The next step is to set up a campaign-specific landing page (for registration, confirmation, or download) on the company's Web site. Add the campaign ID value (the last 15 digits of the URL for the campaign page in SFDC) as a hidden field in the appropriate Web registration page, email link, or name-import spreadsheet template for the respondents.

Make sure that you've set your campaign to active status before you do any test runs of the registration and other user interactions. Unless the campaign is activated, no data will be recorded.

---

12. Make sure your administrator sets up the special link for campaign membership reports, as shown by SFDC at
    https://www.salesforce.com/appexchange/detail_overview.jsp?NavCode__c=&tid=a0330000000j5OdAAI.

Test the `campaign` response system (typically, the Web landing pages) before you fully implement the outbound elements of the `campaign`, to make sure that all "sent" and "responded" data end up in the right bucket. The whole point of `campaigns` is to keep these data properly separated, so make sure that everything works correctly before you go live.

Before you push the `campaign` offer out, send an email to the relevant sales reps, tele-sales people, and product marketing folks so they know the `campaign` is about to begin. Include the URL for all collateral, "hot tips," objection-handling, and promotional documents (these documents should be placed on your internal wiki so that any partners' sales reps can get to them as well). Also send out the URL for SFDC's `campaign` page and the relevant drill-down reports. You'll want to train everyone to look in the SFDC system first for all the real-time information about `campaigns` because, well, that where's the information will appear first.

The larger the `campaign`, the more appropriate it is to send out the `campaign` offer in batches. Batching allows you to do tests that compare the wording of emails, layout of Web landing pages, and a dozen other details that can dramatically improve response rates. Using A/B testing on every part of a `campaign` will help you discover what works best for your target audience, so that you can improve `campaign` designs while the `campaign` is in progress. But you must track your A/B tests very carefully, and ideally you should manage each batch as a separate sub-campaign (with a common `parent`, but with all the change details recorded separately). Although this involves some effort and complexity, over time it can easily double the effectiveness of your `campaign` dollars.

Once you've reached the end date of the `campaign`, you must manually deactivate it. There's no real harm in leaving it `active` beyond the scheduled end date, but it's good housekeeping (for reporting and other analytics) to turn `campaigns` off once you don't expect any more responses.

Lead Handling

One of the areas ripe for the highest leverage by marketing people, which can help them enhance their own credibility as well as that of the SFDC system, is proper lead handling. Although managing leads properly does not involve any additional effort, it *does* require preparation and discipline—which is why lead handling is all too often done wrong.

Read the "Creation Science" sidebar in Chapter 9 right now.

First, Make Sure It's a Lead

As discussed in Chapter 8, the best operating definition of a *lead* is an individual who has asked for information or some level of contact from the company. Job one is to make sure that the data you've been handed really are for leads.

The first thing to watch for is Names purchased from industry associations, memberships, or attendee lists. Unless the list is brand new, there will be substantial information rot: typically email and phone numbers degrade between 1% and 10% per month. Because the Names have not expressed any interest in your company or its offerings, the unsubscribe (or worse, complaint) rate will be quite high when you try to contact them. Consequently, this category of Names should not be imported into SFDC at all, because the bad data will merely muck up the system and produce misleading metrics.

Instead, we recommend that Names be entered into the hopper of your email blasting system (see the "Split Brain" sidebar), where their quality can increase over time until they eventually graduate to real `leads`. Although mailing to Names is a high-risk strategy, you have to start from somewhere when you're going after a brand-new market. First, select a list that has a decent chance of being interested. For example, if your company sells a dental laser, you would look at the membership list of the American Dental Association but not the American Association of Orthodontists. You would go to a list broker and rent email addresses for a blast, and deliver information or an offer that was specifically interesting to dentists (such as a case study about how dental lasers improve the patient flow through dental offices). For the email recipients to get the offered information, they would have to go through an opt-in process so that they are legitimately part of your ongoing list. Typically, if you don't have any connection with members of a given list, very little additional yield is produced after hitting them three times (typically a month apart), and the costs of list rental can make it too expensive to go even that far.

SPLIT BRAIN

At first blush, you might expect the SFDC database to hold everything having to do with prospects and customers. In reality, sophisticated organizations often use a split-brain approach that separates the *marketing* database from the *sales* database. There are two reasons for this separation. First, the marketing database contains a large number of low-quality leads (really, they're little more than Names) that aren't relevant to the sales folks. Second, some marketing automation tools need to operate from their own copy of the data.

If you're already using a tool such as Eloqua, Vertical Response, or Exact Target, you're on the split-brain path. You don't really have a choice.

If you aren't using this kind of tool, you do have an architectural choice to make: do you need to have all of your leads—regardless of quality—in one place, or do you want to create a category of leads that are of such low quality that they're handled externally? While there's no overwhelming cost or operational advantage to going in either direction, changing the path you take after deployment will involve considerable one-time costs. So choose wisely, grasshopper.

The next thing to look out for is sales reps who have used SFDC's Outlook connector to import their entire contact lists into the system. These data are really dangerous (which is why we recommend that no one except the marketing staff ever be allowed to import leads/ contacts into the SFDC system) because the information is of unknown quality, provenance,[13] and age. Expunging these kinds of mass imports from the system isn't especially difficult (with careful use of SFDC's free `Data loader` or `Excel connector`), but it's a chore you would rather avoid and the bad data may mess up reports for a while. Most of these imported contacts will show up as "private contacts," but some may not and (through deduping) may corrupt data already in the system.

Some other messy symptoms can occur if the same contact is synched from two different reps' Outlook address books. Life becomes even more fun when different versions of Outlook are involved. Obviously, this area requires some careful thought and testing before you try to establish a federated (shared, yet distributed) contact management system.

Lead Capture and Insertion

From the moment a lead has been collected, it is already starting to go stale. Recent studies have shown that in our fast-paced world, prospect response rates fall off dramatically within hours of initial registration. Indeed, within 48 hours most prospects will not even remember having visited a company's Web site, let alone have a clue about its value proposition or competitive advantage. Use SFDC's `auto-response rules` to send an email to the lead the instant that they register.

The "freshness date" of leads is calibrated in hours! Add automation at every step to get leads over to the inside sales teams right away. But the sense of urgency should not be limited to speed: it has to be about accuracy. It is much easier to fix data before they are entered into the system than afterward, and it's worth an extra couple of hours to really get things right before importing leads.

Part of accuracy is "the lead is routed to the right person." The SFDC system provides automatic lead routing, but some lead entry points (particularly manual ones) don't automatically trigger the system's `lead assignment rules`. If a large proportion of your leads are not being routed properly, ask the SFDC development team to create an `APEX trigger` to catch the exceptions and route them in real time.

The system's `lead assignment` rules are easy to set up—and even easier to set up incorrectly. The rules are similar to the email filter rules used in Outlook: they're simple Boolean matches, with no `case` or `if` statements. The rules are evaluated one at a time, and as soon as one of the matches occurs, the now officially assigned `lead` is routed to the individual user or queue[14] in the territory. All subsequent rules are ignored for that `lead`. Most

---

13. Are these names even legal for your company to have? If the rep's list "fell off a truck," you might have a customer privacy issue on your hands, as well as some other company's confidential information.

14. See the discussion of queues in Chapter 9.

companies can live with a few dozen well-structured rules, whereas other companies might have 150 of them. Rule sets this large will almost always have bugs, and they're basically unmaintainable. If your sales organization is really *that* complicated (with lots of overlays, national accounts, special markets, and other sources of complexity), you might do better using a bit of APEX code or an external module to do the routing. This strategy would be implemented by configuring a queue that's used only as the input for all leads going through routing, and using a workflow to invoke the routing code. For more details, see www.SFDC-secrets.com.

Now, let's take a look at the various sources of leads that need to be inserted into the system.

Manual Data Entry

I know, it's hard to believe that anyone types in leads any more. But it does happen, particularly when reps collect business cards at cocktail parties. Fortunately, there are only a few things to look out for when entering such data. First, never enter a name without searching for it first. A business card name may be in the system as either a lead or a contact: if it's there as both, go to the contact record and update the data there. For the state and country fields, best practices state that these items be presented as pull-down pick lists of two-character ISO codes[15] that minimize typing. For the person's employer, search for that business name (using multiple tabs in a browser is really helpful for this kind of thing) before you enter it; don't forget to search for both the friendly name (discussed later in this chapter) and the formal one (just in case). Creating duplicate companies or accounts is even less amusing than creating duplicate leads or contacts in the system.

Leads also come in via inbound phone or email. It's particularly important to get back to these inbound touches right away, as they are more likely to have a conversation that will enable their quick qualification and conversion.

Web Leads

With leads that come in over the Web (from one of several registration pages on your company's Web site), the lead entry is automatic and nearly instantaneous. Unfortunately, the basic Web2lead functionality in SFDC is satisfactory only for very small companies. Most SFDC customers use a third-party Web entry application from companies such as RingLead or CRMfusion. These AppExchange add-ons confirm that the Web registrant isn't

---

15. These codes are found in ISO standard 3166. In most cases, a two-character code is all you need. However, if the company has a worldwide operation that does business in really obscure places, you'll need to use the three-character versions of these codes. When you make the switch, make sure you enforce it everywhere, and normalize the existing two-character codes to their three-character versions.

already in the system as a `lead` or a `contact`, and update existing records rather than creating a duplicate.

More highly sophisticated marketing operations may want to develop their own code to create multiple `campaign` memberships per registration, call a `lead` enrichment service to validate and extend data, create an `activity` for the user's download history, create a "friendly" version of the company name (see the sidebar on the next page), create `custom object` record entries for users' page-view sequences, update a "last campaign date" field in the `lead`/`contact` record, or append topic-interest strings to fields in that record. These are all best practices for preventing duplicates while ensuring full visibility into the customer's behavior, both in real-time views and in reports. Implementing these capabilities will require a bit of code in the company's content management system or Web page logic to push the data properly into SFDC, and a bit of retry and logging logic to handle the times (typically one hour per month) when SFDC is down for scheduled maintenance.

Spreadsheet Imports

Virtually all SFDC customers need to deal with external `lead` sources that are presented only via spreadsheet or CSV files. It is best practices to allow only a few individuals (all of them in the Marketing department) to perform imports because of the number of steps involved in doing an import correctly. Before the spreadsheets are imported into SFDC, the marketers need to complete the following tasks:

1. Fix the individual entries to correct spelling problems, number format problems, foreign character sets, data in the wrong fields, and other issues.

2. Normalize the data (particularly state, country, and phone numbers) so they are in the correct format and match the system's pick-list values.

3. Add columns for fields that can be inferred from the source of the spreadsheet (e.g., this spreadsheet came from WebEx, therefore the product-interest field should be filled in with the topic of our most recent Webinar), and create a friendly name for the company.

4. Remove duplicates from within the Excel list.

5. Change the column ordering to fit with SFDC's template.

Create a standardized template including Excel macros to streamline and automate as much of this process as possible. You need to get the import done in minutes, not hours or days.

FRIENDLY NAMES

The company names that appear in `leads` (and will eventually be propagated into `account` records) typically start out as "whatever the user typed on the registration page." But sometimes the user types stuff that's frustrating to search for or view in a report. A user might have typed in "GMAC," but really mean "General Motors Mortgage." With some companies, foreign or domestic, the names aren't recognizable (e.g., E. I. DuPont de Nemours) or have characters that make search difficult (e.g., Nestlé). This goes double for companies whose names are also acronyms (e.g., Badische Anilin und Soda-Fabrik [BASF] or Bayerische Motoren Werke [BMW]).

A best practice is to use the system-standard name field to hold a "friendly" name that people will easily search for and recognize. Initially, this `name` will consist of whatever the user originally typed in, but over time your lead cultivation people should change it to the form (usually an abbreviation) that is most likely to be searched for. Friendly names are *always* in the native language of the headquarters office of your company, and they need to be free of foreign characters, accents, apostrophes, and corporate suffixes (e.g., "Inc.," "Pty," "Ltd").

In addition to the friendly name, create a `custom field` called "Legal Entity Name" that is initially filled in (via automation) with the user's original entry. Over time, the Accounting, Legal, and other departments will change the legal entity name to indicate the formal legal name for the customer (for example, "Pixar Animation Studios division of The Walt Disney Company").

During the import of these spreadsheets, it is imperative to use a deduping tool such as RingLead's or CRMfusion's tool,[16] as SFDC's deduping feature for spreadsheet imports is very basic. As mentioned earlier in this chapter, using `lead source` is really for amateurs, so *don't* use that field. Instead, once you've imported or updated the `leads` with the deduping tool, you import the entire list (*without* deduping) as a set of `campaign members`, using the wizard within the `campaign` main page.[17]

The import procedure should be set up to route new `leads` to the proper `queues` or users via the standard `lead assignment` rules. But what about registrants who were already in the system as `leads` or `contacts`? The SFDC system will not send emails to the appropriate sales people to indicate that one of the people they are tracking has participated in a new

---

16. These are different products, but use the same kind of logic as the companies' `web2lead` dedupers.

17. Different deduping tools will import these `leads` in different ways, so it's not possible to describe a universal procedure here. What you are trying to achieve is (1) a set of `leads` that is truly new, (2) a set of updated `leads` and `contacts` for people already in the system, and (3) all the individuals (new or updated) added to the `campaign member` table for the marketing `campaign` in question.

campaign. However, there are a couple of steps that the marketing staff can take to provide appropriate cues to the sales people:

- Modify all `lead` and `contact views` that the sales folks use to set "recently modified" (rather than "recently created") as the filter criteria.

- Modify any reports that the sales folks use to filter on `modified date` rather than `created date`.[18]

- Create a `workflow` that automatically sends an alert email to the `owner` when one or more of that person's existing `leads` or `contacts` are `modified` by a marketing employee.[19]

- Manually create a `task` for any sales person whose individual records have been modified or who has received new `leads`. This approach is more time-consuming for marketing, but is a best practice because it sends *a single alert to each sales person*, irrespective of the number of new or modified `leads` that individual has received.

Lead Scoring and Aging

By default in SFDC, `leads` are given a `rating` of A/B/C or Hot/Medium/Cold. Unfortunately, these ratings don't hold up well in sophisticated organizations, particularly if the company uses the Named Account model of selling. Further, the SFDC system doesn't let you score `contacts` as well as `leads` to indicate their current level of interest.

Prioritizing `leads` and `contacts` (to answer the sales rep's inevitable question, "Which ones do I call first?") is better done with a sliding-scale score that is automatically recalculated with each significant update to the `lead` or `contact` record. The scores typically range from 0 to 100, with a cutoff of 60 (below which `leads` are retired or demoted to "remarket" and `contacts` are demoted to "dormant"). The score should reflect the `lead`'s readiness to hear the company's message and convert. It is used to sort and filter `leads` and `contacts` in views, reports, and dashboards.

There are three important things to look for in a `lead` scoring system:

- **Profile scoring** (or explicit scoring) assigns a static number based on the individual's demographic or descriptive information, such as job title, company name, industry, department, or product interest. Points are typically added for "more fields filled

---

18. When a record is first created in SFDC, the `created date` and the `modified date` are the same—so there won't be any apparent change to the views. But when a record is updated, only the `modified date` changes—so only the modified views will work properly.

19. Be careful in designing this `workflow`, as it can generate hundreds of annoying emails if not set up properly.

out on the page"[20] and are subtracted for data that are contradictory (the ZIP code doesn't match the state), irrelevant (the person says he or she is from a country your company doesn't sell to), or unattractive (your company doesn't think `leads` with a Yahoo email address are likely to be qualified). Profile scores should be adjusted to reflect where the company is strong (competitive superiority, more references, better track record with sales). Profile scoring is a good start, but is subject to a lot of faulty assumptions (particularly regarding attractive versus unattractive entries).

- **Behavioral scoring** (or implicit scoring) yields a dynamic number that results from the individual's choices and patterns in interacting with the company. Points are added for any action taken by the individual (e.g., responding to an email, registering for a Webinar, attending a seminar), and special points are added for desired behavioral sequences (e.g., the most-qualified prospects will view the demonstration video and request a trial download within the same week). Points are deducted for behaviors that indicate "tire kickers" or other low-yield people (such as students). In some markets, behavioral scoring is *way* more effective at predicting the most interesting `leads`. However, setting the point values and triggers requires a lot of experimentation, configuration, and even coding.

- **Decay scoring** (or time-based scoring) is a refinement of behavioral scoring that demotes the score value every week or so, thereby moving stale `leads` farther down the priority list over time. After 30 or 45 days, inactive `leads` or `contacts` should disappear from view because of these scores. This system is fairly simple to implement with `APEX` code or external marketing automation applications.

A number of free, simple, `lead` scoring tools are available from the AppExchange. In any event, SFDC's `formulas` and `validation rules` can set you fairly far down the path for pure profile scoring. If you are just starting out, begin with those features.

Fancier `lead` scoring algorithms are often embedded in advanced lead cultivation/nurturing applications such as Eloqua and Marketo. Even though using one of these packages is simpler than coding the algorithm yourself, configuring these off-the-shelf systems is relatively complicated and can cause buggy interactions with other systems. In other words, there's no free lunch.

Even the best tools require time to fine-tune the `lead` scoring. During the first few months, the scores will almost certainly be misleading because they're based on theory, rather than the behavior of your actual target customers and sales folks. Put time into understanding your target customer behaviors, working closely with the sales team to steadily improve the realism and accuracy of the scores. Expect that tuning and enhancing the `lead`

---

20. It doesn't matter where the information comes from—whether manually entered by the prospect or imported from a reference database. In the case of `contacts`, most of the information will have been entered by employees. Of course, any `contact` who is a customer receives an instant and permanent score of 100.

DIAGNOSING BAD DATA

Whenever a record is marked as bad data, someone needs to examine the patterns of data input in an effort to understand which process, system, or individual is causing the bogus records. It is all too common to have hundreds or thousands of bad records pile into the SFDC database every month, particularly when external systems are inserting data into the SFDC system.

There are two major classes of bad data: duplicate records and spurious fields. Duplicate records are dangerous because they rapidly confuse people and can be very difficult to rout out. Work on those first. Duplicate records most commonly derive from the following sources:

- Incorrect importing procedures
- Untrained or sloppy users
- Incomplete or poorly implemented external logic or integration
- Poor naming standards or semantics

The most prolific and dangerous sources of duplication are those that you cannot control, such as an eCommerce system, a partner's database, or an internal accounting system. One SFDC customer's external integrations systematically created hundreds of duplicate `accounts` every *day*, and the company couldn't turn the source system off. This way lies madness.

The only real solution for this kind of situation is to create a message buffer system that takes in the external "new record" requests, runs deduplication logic, and properly updates the existing SFDC records. This kind of message buffer is needed in any case, to handle the times when SFDC is down for planned maintenance. Nonetheless, creating this "holding pen" requires some fairly expensive custom code.

The problem of spurious fields can be interesting as well. Look for patterns: when are the fields correct, and when are they bogus? Common issues are mishandling of foreign characters, coding errors, and mishandling of spreadsheet data (particularly when somebody sorts only *some* columns of a spreadsheet).

When you've identified the needed data corrections, it's usually better to update existing records than to delete trashed ones and reinsert new records. Using updates preserves history and provides important clues for future data forensic analysis, should it be needed.

scoring system will be an ongoing responsibility of the marketing staff, and recognize that the scoring factors and thresholds will need to be updated on a quarterly basis.

In addition to sliding-scale scoring, several helpful tools do filtering to immediately eliminate garbage `leads` from view. These `lead` garbage collectors range from free standalone plugins (such as JunQue from Sales*Logistix*) to features available in more sophisticated add-on products.

When Leads and Contacts Need to Disappear

As discussed earlier, leads and contacts (like accounts and opportunities) should never be deleted from the SFDC system. But there are plenty of situations where you want individual records to disappear from view. For example, a record that holds bad data and a contact that will never go anywhere should be removed from the marketing and tele-sales lists.

The mechanisms for hiding records are ownership values of the lead or contact, in conjunction with the roles, profiles, and sharing settings for those users who should not see particular leads or contacts. By setting a lead's owner to a queue named "Remarket" or "Newsletter," the lead will disappear from view except for the Marketing department users. If the lead *doesn't* disappear, adjust the filters on users' views and reports. Using the status or type pick-list values for the leads or contacts can just as effectively cause disappearance, but of course the specifics are a little different.

What about leads and contacts that haven't been touched in years? I have to confess that I'm an information pack-rat. It is very rare for leads or contacts to cause real problems or excessive storage use in the system. At some point, of course, there's a limit: even the IRS doesn't care about information that's more than seven years old. Leads that are far too old can be archived (into a CSV file—Excel can't handle large data sets as well as other tools can). Because contacts are linked with many other records in the system, it's much more complicated to extricate them: it's probably not worth the effort to create a contacts archive.

Opt-Out

As discussed earlier, it's essential to company credibility—and common sense—to comply with CAN SPAM email requirements. You may be fairly aggressive about allowing people to opt *in* to your email campaigns, but you need to provide them *several* ways to opt *out,* including email response, Web links, personal profile editing, and even phone calls. Once the opt-out request has been made, you need to service it quickly and thoroughly.

Most email blasting systems handle this task automatically, and they should be used as the system of record for opt-outs. But these systems can only know about opt-out requests made from within their emails or opt-out pages. You'll need to import opt-out requests from your external systems and sources on a regular basis.

Further, you'll need to export the opt-out requests from the email system, and update them in SFDC. Even if the email system doesn't perform this task automatically as part of its SFDC integration, the export/import cycle can be completed in a few minutes via spreadsheets or CSV files using the Data loader or other tools in batch mode.

An additional step is needed to do things really right. SFDC maintains an email opt-in flag, and it enforces the right behavior—but only for emails that are sent from within the

SFDC system. What if a sales rep runs a report from SFDC, or exports an SFDC contact into his or her desktop version of Outlook? The opt-in flag will be ignored, and the email will go out to customers who specifically asked you to stop contacting this way.

To protect against this possibility, create a formula field in the lead and contact records that automatically corrupts email addresses. These addresses are guaranteed to bounce, yet still preserve the original email information. Check out www.SFDC-secrets.com for a checklist that explains how to create the email address auto-corrupter in your own system.[21]

Lead Enrichment

In many cases, the only thing you know for certain about a lead is an email address, which you can (should!) validate through an email-response cycle. Depending on your target audience, many of the other data entries may be empty or clearly bogus—but that doesn't mean you should throw all of the leads into the remarket bucket.

Several services are available to enrich, correct, or supplement data that have been entered into the SFDC system. Services like Hoover's and Dun & Bradstreet provide information at the account level (e.g., number of employees, headquarters address and phone number) and can be invoked when the company name is obvious from the email domain. Other services, such as iProfiles, provide account overviews and organizational charts. Finally, services such as ZoomInfo and EmailAppenders provide supplementary information about individuals.

The telesales folks typically want to know more at the *individual* level (such as job title, location, phone), but unfortunately this is where the available information becomes notably less accurate. Further, the ability to match entries based on the individual's name or email address can be quite poor (depending on the audience, far less than 25%) even for the B2B areas these data sources cover. B2C lead enrichment is even more sketchy.

Some of these lead enrichment services are nicely integrated into SFDC, and more of them will likely become integrated over the next year or so. The bottom line: the best information you can get applies to the people already in your database, and the best way to improve this information is to get it directly and voluntarily from those individuals. Use the progressive-registration techniques discussed earlier in this chapter to get "just a little more information" in exchange for providing the user with some relevant information or a small incentive (it's surprising how much information people will give you in exchange for a chance in a sweepstakes contest). Hit your entire database with progressive-registration requests at least once a year so the information is as complete and up-to-date as possible.

---

21. Yes, the address auto-corruption will undo itself if SFDC's email opt-out check box is unchecked to reflect a "re-opt-in."

Demoting a Contact

As discussed in the "Split Brain" sidebar earlier in this chapter, leads can be effectively demoted to Names, but can later be promoted back to being a lead when their behavior indicates a rekindled interest. The same logic can be applied to contacts as well. Maintaining them in the database in some fashion is worth doing because industry sources estimate that half of all leads in the "remarket" or "dead lead" area will be viable purchase candidates—you just don't know when or what will trigger them to actually buy your company's product or service. You can't afford to send these prospects all of your high-cost marketing items, but you can't afford to ignore them either.

Contacts are not so easy to demote as leads are, because the lead conversion process is a one-way street: once a lead is converted to a contact, several changes are made that cannot be undone. Even so, it makes sense to have contacts go stale if they are unresponsive for a year or more.

Demoting a contact in a way that preserves all history requires the following procedure:

1. Change the contact's type or status pick-list value, or its ownership, so that it disappears from view. Be particularly attentive to the views and filters used by your deduping tool, so that the contact is truly invisible to the deduping process.

2. Create a lead from the contact's information, with a score that's low enough that the prospect falls into the remarketing process. Record the contact's universal object identifier (UOID)[22] as a hidden field of the cloned lead.

3. Create a workflow that is triggered by leads when they reach qualified status. If a lead has a hidden UOID that's not empty, the workflow will bring the hidden contact back into view. Reverse the type, status, or ownership value changes you made in step 1 to bring the old contact back into view. During the next deduping cycle, the deduping tool will automatically merge the two contacts and all history will be preserved.

Lead Handling in the Named Account Model

Generally speaking, there is very little for marketing to do with leads in the Named Account model of selling, because this model doesn't use the traditional lead generation and

---

22. SFDC's UOID is pretty clever, in that it consists of the last 15 characters of the record's URL. If you look at your browser URL field, most of the time it will show something like this: https://na1.salesforce.com/001000054UxeyTER. The UOID is "001000054UxeyTER."

nurturing process. However, at least once a year the NAM reps will come to you and ask to add new contacts into their accounts.

Read the section in Chapter 9 entitled "Named Account Model of Selling" for the specific things you need to help the NAM reps with.

Lead Cultivation and Nurturing

While automated systems (such as Eloqua) that assist in lead cultivation are best owned and run by marketing, the manual process of lead nurturing—moving the prospect from awareness to interest to desire—is almost always done by someone outside of marketing. Even if a telemarketing group handles this duty in your company, that group usually doesn't report to the Marketing department. Because of this natural hand-off, the success criteria and service level agreement between marketing and inside sales must be clear and detailed.

If you haven't already done so, read the section on lead cultivation and nurturing in Chapter 9. Pay particular attention to the discussion of the "life of a lead" timeline.

On the lead page, make it easy for the inside reps to get supplemental information. Smart reps will want to do a little research before they call a new lead. Use the page layout tool to put links to Google Search and Google News for general information about the company, and Hoover's, Dun & Bradstreet, or some other service for financial and business information. For information about the individual lead, put in links for LinkedIn, ZoomInfo, or your favorite lead database service.

In the lead cultivation and nurturing process, marketing is responsible for creating a significant amount of content: email campaigns, special offer response Web pages, call scripts, qualification questions, objection responses, and competitive FAQs. These content elements should all be stored in SFDC, both as general documents and as attached files to campaigns. Further, call scripts and qualification questions should be baked into the SFDC screens used by inside sales. A free plugin available from the AppExchange makes it easy to set up these screens, and with clever use of dependent fields and record types the system can become a good prompting system for the reps. Even though this solution is certainly elegant, don't overdo it: if your messaging isn't stable (because it's not mature, or because the competitive environment is changing too fast), the benefits derived from perfect screen sequences may not be worth the effort.

For a wide range of reasons, the best way to improve the lead cultivation and nurturing process is to meet frequently with the inside sales team. Understand their challenges, find out what's working in the real world, and measure every part of the process. When evaluating metrics, make sure the conversation focuses on achieving objectives and improving the number of first sales meetings—stay away from words that sound like a performance review, over-measurement, or the assignment of blame. Inside sales is the natural partner of outbound marketing, so do everything to foster good communications and a tight working relationship between the two groups.

Lead Qualification and Conversion

Marketing isn't directly involved with the `lead` qualification and conversion process. Nevertheless, it should be involved with setting the criteria and the process steps involved, because these elements are the materialization of the target market description, value proposition, and messaging that are the results of your work.

Some companies talk about having a "marketing qualified `lead`," in the sense that marketing personnel think the `lead` is good enough to deserve starting the manual `lead` cultivation/nurturing process. In my professional opinion, there is no good reason to have such a label, and there are several good reasons *not* to use it. Real qualification means that the company has a communication cycle with the prospect where the inside sales folks determine the match of needs and values, and assess the prospect's readiness to buy. This conversation is *not* handled by the marketing function. What marketing *can* do is screen and score `leads`, and pass only high-scoring `leads` to the inside sales team.

The real qualification conversation should be *scripted* by senior people in marketing and sales. Typically, there will be 5–10 qualification questions with yes/no answers, and a `lead` is qualified when 80% of the answers are yes. Some companies use a sliding scale (High/Medium/Low or 1–10) and set a composite score as the qualification criterion. Even if members of the sales team actually write all of the scripted questions, the marketing guys and gals need to know what's being said about the product. The marketers also need to see where prospects are falling out of the funnel, and why, so they can quickly identify areas for improved retention and conversion.

Once the qualification criteria and scripts are stable, they should be built into the SFDC `lead` screens. SFDC offers a free AppExchange plugin to facilitate call scripting, but you may want to go beyond its baseline capabilities if your company has multiple product lines with different target markets and qualification criteria.

Once a `lead` is fully qualified, it is usually converted almost instantly. Several details of conversion need to be nailed down from the beginning:

- How will the `custom fields` be mapped from the `lead` to the `account`, `contact`, or `opportunity`?

- Who does the conversion process, and under which conditions?

- What are the naming standards for `opportunities`?

- How will duplicate `accounts` or `opportunities` be flagged or handled if discovered during the `conversion` process?

- What are the `stage` and `probability` values for the new `opportunity`?

- What is the `task` resulting from creating a new `opportunity`, and who receives it?

- Under which conditions can a sales rep reject an `opportunity`? How does inside sales learn from the rejected `opportunity`?

These details are discussed in the `lead` conversion section of Chapter 9. The SFDC system should be set up so that `field history tracking` is turned on to provide audit trails for the 20 most interesting fields in the `lead`, `contact`, `account`, and `opportunity` records. Doing so will help you see what's going on and allow the marketing staff to base improvements on data from real sales cycles instead of folklore.

Partners

The marketing team almost never develops or owns partnerships, either on the technology side or on the revenue side. Nevertheless, the company's marketing staff must interact with partner marketing folks and supply their sales teams with collateral, information, and `leads`.

As discussed in Chapter 9, the way to get the most out of partners is to treat them as much as possible as being an extension of the company's own sales team. This means giving partners access to the sales tools, testimonials, product training, and other documents that are in the company's marketing arsenal.

If the company does cooperative marketing with its partners (e.g., joint advertising, shared tradeshow booths, cooperative Webinars), make sure that each partner's information is included in the `campaign` description in the company's SFDC system. Depending on your `lead`-sharing arrangements, you will want to create a `campaign member` report with special filters for each partner.

Customer References

Customer references are the most essential ingredient of company credibility, and are required elements for many marketing deliverables. Analyst relations, PR, Web marketing, and the sales team all depend on quotes, reference customers, and testimonials. Perhaps surprisingly, most marketing departments show an amazing lack of aggressiveness and discipline in collecting and managing this key resource.

Before discussing ways to handle references in SFDC, we need to consider how the customer happiness and usage information is collected. The main problem with most reference marketing programs is that they jump too quickly to "Can we get your quote?", thereby scaring off the customer. It's far better to develop a large population of customers who have provided core information about their businesses and the way they use your company's product or service. Once these people have told you something about themselves, it's easy to extend the conversation with very specific requests based on who they are and how they benefit from your product.

To build this pool of customer information, several processes need to be tapped to collect the highest-quality reference information:

- Customer support, technical support, and consulting personnel are the most under-utilized sources of customer reference information. These people are on the phone (or even on site) with the customer base more than anyone else in your company, and they should be finding out as much as they can about how the customer is using your product. While they're helping the customer, they can be asking subtle questions that can reveal interesting information about the number of users, the business impact, and factoids about the customer's business and how it has bene-fited from using your company's product. When done correctly, this kind of data collection won't feel like prying, yet it will gather at least one "gee whiz" story each week. This information should be added to `opportunities`, as it is relevant to the project or purchase, rather than the individual `contact` or the `account` overall. Marketing should write these questions and format them as prompt screens, using the free call scripting plugin from the AppExchange.

- Product marketing personnel may conduct periodic customer surveys that collect great demographic and usage profiling information. The key is to ask the right questions and provide an incentive for the customer to respond. Use an embedded URL with a unique identifier so you automatically know who generated each response. This advice applies equally to customer satisfaction surveys sent out by the customer service department, and even to warranty registration cards.

- The company's PR team may conduct customer phone surveys to collect quotes and testimonials, and they should be designed to collect customer usage information even if customers are totally unwilling to have their names published. Set these surveys up with subtle incentives to provide information that will be kept private, as the majority of customers will be unwilling to have any contact with reporters or analysts. These survey results should be attached to the `contact` record for the individual involved.

- The company's support or account management team contacts customers at product or service renewal time (assuming the company has some sort of ongoing service element). Have the renewal cycle begin with an "application" that collects demographic and usage information. While this information will be useful for the support organization, it's pure gold for the marketing team. Attach these data to the `opportunity` that is being renewed.

- If your company runs a blog, online forum, or Web-based user community, require users to register (only with a valid email) to read the content located there. When users want to post or add to the comment trail, ask them for further registration information that gives you a better profile of who they are and how they use your company's product. This information should be attached to the person's `contact` record in SFDC.

Once you've thought through this issue, the key is to add—in a disciplined way—specific information from these sources to the relevant `contacts`, `accounts`, and `opportunities`. Of course, you can attach surveys and emails to the records, but they will not be very easy to search, manipulate, or report. Instead, the essential elements of "referencability" should be added to the records as `custom fields` or `custom objects` that answer questions such as the following:

- Which products is the customer using? How long has the customer been using the product, and which departments are using it?

- Which other products did the customer evaluate? Why did the customer decide to go with your company's offering?

- How many users are there, and how many *non*-users benefit from the product?

- What are the economic benefits of the product? How soon did the product pay for itself, and what's the long-term ROI?

- What is quotable about the customer's experience, and what are the names and titles of people who would be willing to talk about their experiences?

- How happy is the customer? Would the customer buy again?

- Would the customer be willing to take a call from a prospect? An industry analyst? A reporter?

The exact design of the reference management system will depend on how the company wants to use the references, but the guideline is to store the information as close to the user or project as possible. Use `page layouts` or `collapsible sections` to keep clutter down. To make the information easier to see from a top-down perspective, use `roll-up fields` or `workflows` to provide referencability indicators (e.g., "total potential references") at the `account` level.

All of this implies that everyone in sales, marketing, customer support, and PR has an SFDC login and uses the system to store the customer data. This is the way life should be anyway, but proper customer reference management turns SFDC usage into a requirement.

To prevent anyone at the company from burning out a reference through overuse, it's important to track every time the reference has been used. Create a `custom object` that records when references were used, who used them, and what the purpose was. Generally speaking, using a reference more than once per quarter will probably irritate the individual, and it may get the reference in trouble with his or her company's PR department.

In many organizations, it's best to use `record types` and `page layouts` to hide the customer reference information from prying eyes. Because customer references are coveted resources, sales reps try to hide the good ones. To protect the customer's trust level, it's best practice to handle customer reference requests through SFDC as an approval process, and to have the reference marketing person be the unbiased decision maker who approves and allocates usage of this precious resource.

Public Relations

Most PR departments wouldn't dream of having an SFDC login. Most PR departments are also behind the times.

In addition to the reference marketing functionality described in the preceding section, PR departments need to know how SFDC can help them in their day-to-day tasks. PR departments are in touch with reporters, editors, and industry analysts, and they need to manage their contact information. They need to track action items. They launch campaigns and want to track their results. Sounds sort of like the SFA functionality with a twist—right?

SFDC developed a free add-on for the AppExchange designed around the needs and workflow of PR teams. This add-on provides the basics for the PR function, and it can be easily extended to match the workflow of nearly any PR team. Assuming the company uses a PR agency to supplement its internal team, SFDC's Web-based functionality is a great way to coordinate all of the organization's PR efforts.

The PR Manager plugin works well if what you are really trying to do is replace shared contact and task lists in Outlook. As always, SFDC does a great job of handling shared tasks and exposing the history of tasks and conversations across a distributed user base. The integration via SFDC's Outlook connector is a bit clumsy, and the scheduling[23] of repeating events (such as conferences or meetings) is ugly, but it works.

In using the plugin, there are a couple of things to think about. First, the PR agency (or agencies) used by your organization may have its own in-house systems and may not be willing to keep the blow-by-blow details in SFDC. While this proprietary attitude is understandable for the senior partner in the agency or specialists who are not dedicated to your company's account, the account manager or the dedicated underling should be able to use your company's SFDC system without any double entry or interference with the agency's system.

The second issue is keeping the reporters, editors, and analysts separate from your customer contacts. This segregation is most easily accomplished by setting the owner of the contact to someone in the PR group and by setting the type to be "reporter," "press," "analyst," or another appropriate indicator. If you set up the filters in views and reports properly, the PR targets will be kept totally separate from your prospects and customers. In a similar way, you want to keep the companies they work for separate from your accounts,

---

23. You may find that SFDC's integration with Google Docs really helps with calendar management.

typically by having a special form of company naming (e.g., "PR–TimeWarner–DO NOT TOUCH" versus "TimeWarner Music," a real customer) and establishing an account type value with which to tag these special accounts.

Once the basics are under control, use SFDC campaigns to monitor the pitches, events, and outreach you have done to all reporters, as well as the responses they have given to your pitches. Of course, you need to keep these PR campaigns separated from the standard prospect campaigns, but doing so provides you good metrics on what works.

You'll need to adjust pick lists to reflect the status of reporters and editors, as opposed to evaluators and buyers. You'll almost certainly want to use record types and page layouts to customize the look of SFDC for the PR users.

Another consideration is the handling of press citations, blog threads, and other reporter's content. If what you *really* wanted was Vocus or a custom PR database, you'll need to adjust your expectations downward a bit. Because document attachments aren't searchable in SFDC, this kind of content is typically stored in a file server, with a pointer to it from within SFDC's reporter record. Although this structure means that content searching must be done entirely outside of SFDC, it also means that searchers don't need to have SFDC licenses.

Product Management/Product Marketing

The product manager, vertical market manager, and product marketer roles are classically held by people who love the product and have no problem writing. Typically, they are also starved for real data about customers, prospects, and markets. SFDC is an amazing resource to help these personnel ply their trade in the following areas.

Marketing Collateral and Documents

SFDC has an internal documents section that can act as a central store for all of the company's marketing collateral. If a ton of documents need to be stored, you should probably provide just a high-level guide to what's there—and when each document should be used—in SFDC's internal store. By contrast, the actual documents should probably be stored on an intranet or file server to save space in SFDC.

SFDC's Content edition provides a great way for marketing and sales personnel to better manage marketing collateral, and it's almost essential for any multidivisional sales team that has to sell a wide range of products. In addition to providing more economical storage, the Content edition provides a very intuitive way to organize large libraries of documents; it even includes a voting system that allows readers to rank which are the most relevant documents. For the product manager, this voting system provides important feedback regarding which documents should be enhanced or retired.

Analytics and Business Intelligence

SFDC is a godsend to the numbers-driven marketer, providing that the data are organized properly and support analysis and reporting.

As discussed in Chapter 2, the most advanced reporting and analytical requirements will involve an external reporting system. Of course, the data must be entered into SFDC in the first place, which is why product marketing needs to be involved early in the design process.

That said, it is imperative to keep screens simple and data entry as unintimidating as possible. Customers and sales folks alike get annoyed when they are asked to enter too much data.[24] If the product marketing folks say that they will require a bunch of data, always ask, "Who's going to type in and validate the data?" Also ask, "What's the likelihood that half of these records will be empty?" If there's a fair chance of empty records, *don't* ask people to manually fill the desired information in—get the data some other way.

This recommendation goes double for competitive information. In theory, your sales reps should know who the competitors are and what messages they are using against your company. In practice, it's rare when reps really have this knowledge base and even rarer when they are willing to fill in more than one field in the SFDC database with the relevant information. That said, it may be very easy to get system integrator, consulting, or customer support personnel to provide detailed competitive intelligence. Use `page layouts` to facilitate this data collection without annoying users with clutter.

Price Lists

The price list is the most basic marketing deliverable: every rep needs to use it, and every product manager needs to contribute to it.

Price lists don't have to reside in the SFDC system, but they should. Maintaining the price list in the system enables `line-item level` quotes, product-level `forecasting`, and integration with your order-entry and accounting systems.

SFDC's price lists are fairly simple SKU-based tables; they do not allow BOM structures for bundles. Essentially, SFDC's `Price Books` and `Product` tables contain a single level of SKU: bundled products are simply handled as new SKUs with no hierarchy or pointers.

SFDC doesn't handle discount schedules natively. Most companies simply store the discount level as a `custom field` for each SKU in the price list (perfect for per-product discounting). Other companies create a SKU called "discount" with a negative value that is applied to the entire order.

International price lists are simple, yet profound data structures. If the company's system is set up to handle only one currency, you must create foreign price lists that override the home-country price, expressed in the company's home currency. If you are running SFDC's

---

24. Too much can be as few as five fields per page. Keep it simple!

`multi-currency mode`[25] (you'll definitely want to use the advanced option), the foreign price lists are given in their own currency (£, €, $, ¥, and so on) and the home price list is given in the company's home currency. The translation across currencies occurs at quote time, using the then-current exchange rate. `Reports` and `views` of orders will show all information in the local currency of the individual who's viewing the data. Pretty fancy stuff.

Polling and Customer Feedback

Out of the box, SFDC gives you solid information on `leads` and `contacts`, but no direct interaction with *customers*. Over time, as the system is configured with more and more options, it will likely begin to include touch points for several kinds of customer interaction:

- The PRM module includes a `Partner Portal` that can provide good metrics on the company's interactions with its intermediary "customers." If the marketing group owns some of the partner relationship, add a survey link to the portal page so that marketers can get feedback from the partner on a continuous basis.

- The `Customer Self Service Portal` provides an obvious place for interaction with those customers who are actively using the company's support services or are in warranty periods. Add a survey link to this page as well. In addition, it's smart to have the Web-tracking analytics engine inspect traffic through the `Knowledge Base`; this setup enables you to quickly spot troublesome areas related to the product and its documentation.

- SFDC's `Ideas` module is an ideal way to get feedback from customers about new feature ideas and priorities. If you plan to use this module, make sure to prepopulate the `ideas` list with items that you suspect could be killer customer issues—if the customer eventually discovers them. Also, add `idea` items for product attributes that the customer might reflexively ignore: reliability, performance, fit and finish, documentation, international issues, level of support, pricing options, and features to remove. If these items are omitted from the list, all the feedback statistics will be misleading and over-focused on bells and whistles that *aren't* critical to customer satisfaction.

- As discussed in the "Customer References" section earlier in this chapter, SFDC should be configured with several `custom fields` to track and manage customer happiness and testimonials. By using these data carefully, you survey your customer base to help guide the company's product development roadmaps and strategy exercises. If you are trying to set up a customer review board, this effort should be tracked through SFDC as well.

---

25. Turning on the multi-currency feature in SFDC is a one-way street: once it's on, it can never be turned off. Turning it on will also break some of your `reports`, `calculated fields`, `S-controls`, and other customizations. For this reason, it's best to turn this feature on at the beginning if you know you will need it.

- A few of the popular survey engines have plugins that support SFDC, and you should strongly favor using them. Be willing to sacrifice a few advanced features to get the data fully integrated into the "customer system of record." The pain of trying to keep data synchronized between SFDC and an unintegrated tool will quickly overwhelm any advantage that some other "perfect" survey tool might have.

- Rally Software offers an Agile requirements collection/management tool that plugs into SFDC. If your internal product development team is focused on Agile practices, this tool can be a huge asset for both marketing and engineering personnel.

Marketing System Administrator

As discussed previously, a common mistake among SFDC customers is to give full system administrator privileges to too many people. Best practice calls for having two or three administrators, unless the company has a huge SFDC installation.

We recommend that someone in the Marketing department be one of the administrators, because marketing personnel typically are intimately involved with new-product launches and understand what's coming in the next several quarters. Marketers can make pretty good guesses about what the sales folks will need in the future—and they have the most analytical thirst for numbers.

The marketing-based SFDC administrator should coordinate his or her efforts with those of the administrators of other marketing tools (such as the email blaster, content management system, customer portal, and customer data warehouse products). As these systems become increasingly integrated over time, the administrators will need to interact fairly frequently.

THE DATA ADMINISTRATOR

Someone in marketing needs to be the God of Data. This person needs to be an SFDC system administrator (or at least be trained up to that level) so that he or she can make good decisions about data standards, new fields, expanded pick lists, and lead-handling processes.

There is no universal best practice for data management, because there are just too many market and company variances. Even so, *somebody* has to set your company's standards and enforce the rules. *Somebody* has to be the owner of data definitions. *Somebody* has to play referee in internal arguments about data ownership. The best kind of *somebody* will be involved with lead handling, cultivation, or nurturing; will know people in both sales and marketing; and will be systematic and detail oriented.

Check out the discussion of the data architecture review board in Chapters 3 and 4 to understand the duties a little better.

While this role could theoretically be outsourced, it's typically not economical to do so. The good news is that it's nowhere near a full-time job, even in the largest company.

Privilege Restriction

Some of decisions related to privilege restriction are policy issues that can have political overtones, but the following really are best practices:

- Delete and merge buttons should be hidden from all standard users.

- API and import-wizard access should be turned off for all standard users.

- Reports should be turned off for all sales reps (but not managers).

Chapter 13 describes a number of general best practices related to permissions, which should be reviewed by marketing's designated SFDC administrator.

Report and Dashboard Logistics

One of the biggest problems with SFDC's reporting capability is the huge pile of prefabricated reports found in the system. It is so easy to get lost and overwhelmed.

The first order of business is to clean out the "unfiled public reports" that come with the system and put them in folders meaningful to you. If a particular report doesn't seem especially meaningful, create a report folder called "Ignore Me" and put it there. As always, I do not recommend deleting reports from the system: you never know when one will provide a good idea for solving a future reporting problem.

Create another new folder called "<Company> Special Reports," and put this folder on the top of the list. Make this folder read-only, so users can't accidentally mess it up. For any reports that are really important, create duplicate copies and put them in a new read-only folder called "Backups."

Create yet another read-only folder called "Dashboard Reports—DO NOT TOUCH." Put the reports that feed dashboards there.

Check out the AppExchange for prebuilt reports and dashboards. Dozens of freebies can be found there, and they can save you a bunch of time when you are trying to set up your own SFDC system.

There's some good news on the report logistics front: the Force.com `Eclipse` plugin includes ways to view, archive, and upload report definitions. It's a much cooler way to get the job done and avoids the tedium of mouse driving that SFDC users have had to endure for the last eight years.

Ongoing Tasks

The marketing SFDC administrator needs to become very comfortable with the deduping tool that your company has bought. Because these tools typically need to be run on at least a weekly basis, the administrator needs to understand all of the chosen tool's detailed settings (e.g., fuzzy logic fields, thresholds) and the workflow of deduping a large batch of `leads`.

Although SFDC runs continuous backups on all system data, recovery of data is neither free nor fast (it requires a small consulting project). The marketing SFDC administrator should take a weekly system "snapshot" of the system's entire contents. This task can be carried out as an automatic scheduled event through the system itself, or the administrator can use an external batch-oriented tool from Informatica or another vendor to do the job. While the snapshots can get really large with all the attachments, it is not necessary to back up absolutely everything every week. Anyway, disk space is cheap, and the peace of mind that comes with having your own backup will more than compensate for the 10 minutes per week devoted to this chore.

Before attempting any significant amount of data manipulation in SFDC, it is always best to take an immediate "before" snapshot of the data object(s) you're working on. This is most easily done with SFDC's free `Data loader` plugin, but you need to be trained before you use this software. For more on this topic, check out the sidebar entitled "Backups and Snapshots and Replicas, Oh My!" in Chapter 13.

Marketing Executives

SFDC provides the foundation for many important improvements in the way marketing works. Its use requires behavioral changes of the marketing team, but it can mean dramatic improvements in marketing's effectiveness, relationship with sales, and overall corporate reputation.

Many of the SFDC best practices immediately translate into marketing best practices. Further, SFDC brings into focus the real cost of customer acquisition and the importance of repeat business—the most profitable revenue that any company can have. By aligning the marketing effort with the most profitable revenue sources and improving sales cycles, the marketing team will automatically align itself with the goals and objectives of the sales team and the stockholders.

After a few months of proper use, the SFDC system should be able to screen out low-quality leads, identify low-yielding sources, and help tune marketing messages so that they yield the biggest bang for the buck. It will take a few months longer to lower the cost of lead generation (or at least increase the bang for the buck) and increase the sales pipeline. Because of seasonality effects, SFDC will likely continue to reveal new opportunities for marketing improvements more than a year after it goes into production. However, the only real cost reductions that most companies will find are in eliminating "dud" marketing vehicles; do not expect the SFDC system to reduce the company's headcount.

The best practices for marketing team members have been discussed throughout this chapter. As a marketing executive, you need to reinforce marketers' behavior with incentives and pep talks:

- Don't ask for data items that you won't really use, or that won't fundamentally change the outcome of any decision.

- Add instrumentation to as many customer points of contact as you can, involving customer-facing individuals in support, service, and consulting.

- Involve the customer in as many marketing processes as you can,[26] and record the data in SFDC so that the information becomes a shared resource.

- Strive for closed-loop marketing, where you can track a single customer's interactions through every "touch" by your company. That said, don't bite off more than you can chew: work incrementally, starting with email and click-through behaviors. Test messaging and refine it with email threads for specific customer segments. Add behaviorally targeted offers as you learn more about the customer's preferences and responses.

- Integrate as many marketing systems as you can afford to with SFDC. This seamless operation will reduce errors and dramatically increase visibility into the customer's behavior.

- Use SFDC and other systems to conduct A/B split testing at every level of customer interaction. From word choice in messaging and scripts to the design of the purchase button in the company's online store, testing can significantly improve the results and power of the marketing effort. There is simply no substitute for real-world testing with the company's own prospects and customers.

- Use `workflows` and `alerts` to support management by exception. SFDC can streamline the majority of marketing processes, while giving you better data for more solid decisions.

Read the last few pages of the Executive Summary in this book to find out about the general behavior changes and mandates you personally need to make—they're all quite pleasant, actually, but it's important for the troops to hear and see coherent behaviors directly from you.

---

26. If you haven't already done so, read *The Cluetrain Manifesto* by Christopher Locke (Basic Books, 2000). You can also read it online for free at www.cluetrain.com/book/index.html.

Marketing Best Practices

When it comes to marketing in general, several critical success factors seem to be ignored all the time—often because of internal politics, board-level beliefs, and company culture. Here are the things I find *missing* most often in marketing management:

- Lead quality is *much* more important than lead quantity. It is very easy to generate tons of low-quality leads that will waste a lot of everyone's time. What's the point of handing over to sales a stack of leads a foot high if there's an infinitesimal chance of those leads being converted to a sale? Focus on *reducing* the total number of leads while increasing the number that convert and start sales cycles! You'll definitely want to set up SFDC metrics and incentives to bring this issue into focus.

- Lead response time is *much* more important than branding, persistence, and lead scoring. It is almost impossible to be too quick in responding to a lead, and recent studies by Professor James Oldroyd of MIT indicate that lead response rates drop dramatically within *minutes* of a Web registration. Providing a professional response to a lead in near real time *really* sets companies apart. Statistics show that a prospect's attention moves on to other things very soon, and the vast majority of Web site visitors will have no recollection of a company within 48 hours of visiting its site. Make sure that leads get into SFDC very fast, and that a drip marketing sequence starts the same day. Set up SFDC metrics, escalations, and incentives to optimize "first touch" response times.

- Generally speaking, field sales reps should not touch `leads`. Marketing and inside sales should be converting the `leads` before they are ever handed over to the field. The field reps should be focused on `opportunities`, and any `contacts` and `tasks` associated with them.

- Although leads are quite perishable, paradoxically they don't have a real "expiration date." Generally speaking, leads that are unresponsive or uninteresting should be moved from the active-working list into the "remarket" list within 30 or 45 days. But with the right kind of newsletter marketing, a lead that first signed up with the company two years ago may come to life and be immediately ready to purchase.[27] You can never know which specific lead will prompt this reaction, or when the prospect will be ready to make a purchase. So the only time you should give up on a lead is when (1) all of the contact information is no longer valid or (2) the lead has explicitly asked you to go away and die.[28]

---

27. One of my favorite customers came to me after three years, saying "Taber and his incessant marketing have finally worn me down."

28. Okay, so they rarely ask for this exactly. But unsubscribe requests and opt-outs *must* be immediately and permanently honored.

- The match of your marketing message to the target audience is much more important than the inherent power or uniqueness of that message. *Of course* you want to have a unique, powerful, and eloquent message, but if it really isn't all that relevant to the target audience, why should they care? Properly segmenting your target audience is job one, and it's almost exclusively a marketing responsibility. SFDC's data will be the foundation for that segmentation, and as a marketing executive you should demand that any target market analysis be based on customer and prospect data in the system.

- Related to the previous point is the importance of the design of the company's Web site: the first page a visitor lands on will qualify or disqualify the company from consideration. Web visitors will rarely get to the proof points and the company's value proposition if they weren't motivated by the home page or the landing page they first saw. Keep the word count down and the call to action straightforward on these critical pages—and that goes double for B2C companies.

- Marketing doesn't focus enough on customer loyalty and upselling. Marketing to customers really is like shooting fish in a barrel: although these `campaigns` will never generate a single lead, they'll generate plenty of revenue. It is sublimely important to set up metrics and standards for marketing to the installed base, because this is an area where the marketing department can truly shine. It also is the most profitable kind of revenue your company can have.

- Customer reference information is the highest-value data the SFDC system can possibly hold. Marketing should spearhead the collection, updating, and management of customer references so that: (1) the company gets the highest marketing impact from them and (2) the references are not burned out from overuse.

- It's critically important that marketing, inside sales, and outside sales agree about the company's sales model. Get the following things right: the leads-to-opportunity workflow, the division of labor, the number of contact attempts to be made, the stages of lead development, the criteria for qualifying and converting leads, and the semantics of the SFDC data fields. If you can't agree on what a qualified `lead` is or what triggers the creation of an `opportunity`, how can you optimize or streamline anything?

- SFDC can become an important point of collaboration between marketing and sales. Improving the quantity, quality, and usability of the customer information in the system is one of the critical ways marketing can show how it's adding value to the sales process.

- The Sales department clearly runs on a monthly or quarterly cycle—that's the rhythm of their work. Be keenly aware of this schedule (there's no point in generating a ton of leads in weeks 11–13 of the quarter), and make sure that the sales personnel aware of *your* rhythm—that is, planned marketing campaigns and product launches. It's a best practice to establish a wiki for marketing that publishes exactly what marketing will be doing for sales on a month-by-month basis, and to supplement that with a weekly (or biweekly) email[29] highlighting the things the marketing team is doing.

For more exciting news in this area, check out newsletters like the free *Taber Report* (www.taberconsulting.com/download/archives.htm).

Metrics and Analytics

I've worked at the VP level in marketing for more than 10 years, and a lot of things have changed over the years. But in high-tech marketing, some bad habits seem to be evergreen. Much of the time, marketing is measured (or measures itself) by metrics that aren't very meaningful to the business. SFDC, when properly configured and used, can move companies to much better behaviors.

Here are some measurements that are simple to ask for, quick to measure, easy to fake or game, and almost pointless:

- Number of activities

- Number of mailings

- Number of new collateral/creative pieces

- Number of attendees and size of lists

- Visibility, buzz, and attitude indicators about your company

- Number of press releases

- Number and reach of ads

- Number of click-throughs and Web site visits

- Number of registrations or downloads

- Number of leads

- Cost per lead

The last two items on the list are sacred cows in many companies, but unless you measure something about the *quality* of the lead, its convertibility, and it's readiness to be qualified— well, these aren't sacred cows, they're just a bunch of bull.

---

29. Do not expect the sales reps to read your wiki—give them tidbits in the email to motivate them.

WATCH OUT FOR MULTIPLE REPORTS AND DASHBOARDS

It is very common for organizations to inadvertently create several versions of a report or dashboard. This is almost always dangerous, because SFDC reports are easy to create, and even easier to create incorrectly. There are too many ways to filter and sort data incorrectly, and too many assumptions that can differ. Contradictory reports become a big source of politics when sales, marketing, and the executives are looking at "the same metric" with very different numbers.

The only antidote is to use one official set of reports that are designed and implemented by a single team. Using the requests from sales, marketing, and the executives, a business analyst (typically in the Marketing or Finance department, but perhaps on loan from IT) should create the company's official management reports for lead generation, pipeline, and forecasting metrics. All other report versions should be disparaged and hidden from users.

Instead, match your measurements to the prospect's evolution in the pipeline/funnel—visibility and awareness are relevant only at the start of the relationship between customer and company. Use your revenue model (described at the beginning of this chapter) as your guide about what to measure, and when. Here are example metrics that can be quite meaningful:

- Time to first touch

- Number of converted leads

- Average time to convert

- Accuracy of lead scores

- Ability to segment customers and predict behavior

- Conversion ratio

- Number of fully qualified leads accepted by sales

- Number of sales cycles started due to marketing efforts

- Proportion of leads rejected by, and neglected by, sales

- Marketing cost of acquiring a new customer

- Value of sales pipeline started due to marketing efforts

- Value of sales pipeline influenced by one or more campaigns (SFDC's new `campaign influence` feature makes this much easier to measure.)

- Profitability of new customers due to marketing efforts

- Loyalty of new customers

- Percentage of repeat business

Each of these metrics can be analyzed on a per-campaign basis, so you can identify which activities really drive the business. The same items can also be analyzed by region, vertically, and by product line so you can determine which parts of the marketing message are working in different geographies. There are usually some great surprises on this front.

Most of these reports can be generated entirely within SFDC's reporting system, although some will likely require some external help. For example, a "time to first touch" report requires either clever use of SFDC's `custom report types`, exporting of SFDC data to a spreadsheet with a bunch of `VLOOKUP` functions, or `JOIN` processing by an external database engine.

The "jewel in the crown" of marketing is strategic analysis. Naturally, you'll want to team up with executives in engineering, customer support/services, and finance to look at the big picture and answer questions such as these:

- What are the company's most profitable products, and why? What are the correlations among product purchases, and which "loser" products actually help move the winners? What are the most likely situations for upsells and repeat business?

- What are the characteristics of the most profitable customers? What are their behaviors and growth patterns? What can the company do to find more likely candidates and stimulate their purchasing patterns?

- How is the competitive battlefield changing? Does the company need more product, better promotion, or a pricing or packaging change? How is the company's brand and reputation faring in the marketplace?

- What are the inflection points during the sales cycle? Is there a key success factor, or a failure pattern we need to fix?

- Which customers seem to be more trouble than they're worth, causing huge costs and rework in customer support? Can the company identify product or sales problems by understanding the situations involving whiners and troublemakers?

- Which marketing tactics are paying off, and how are they helping sustain the company's products and ease the sales cycle? What's the profitability of the marketing promotions?

- Which channels and partners are working, and which are just a waste of time?

Answering these kinds of questions will take solid analysis and almost certainly use of a multidimensional business intelligence tool. But the fanciest tools in the world will do no good if the source data are incomplete or misleading—and that's why it's imperative that the marketing team invest in making SFDC the authoritative source for "all things customer."

CHAPTER 11

Best Practices in Customer Support

> Waiter: *"Tea or coffee, gentlemen?"*
> First customer: *"I'll have tea."*
> Second customer: *"Me, too—and be sure the cup is clean!"*
> *(Waiter exits, returns)*
> Waiter: *"Two teas. Who asked for the clean cup?"*
>
> *—Anonymous*

T HE CUSTOMER SERVICE AND support team are often the most avid early users of SFDC. This chapter discusses how to set up and use the system to maximum advantage, which will seed the system with credible data that benefit everyone.

Support Organizations and SFDC

Many SFDC customers miss the opportunity of having their support personnel on the system nearly from day one. Of course, the system is called *Sales*force, but support staff can rapidly leverage the system and fill it with data that become immediately valuable—and therefore attractive—to the sales organization.

The members of the support organization are on the phone or in the room with customers nearly all day long, and their jobs already require good data hygiene—recording data with accuracy and good organization. Further, support people are in contact with the company's riskiest asset: upset customers. Making a customer happy one hour sooner, or with one less error, has payoffs in repeat sales and an annuity of profits.

The company's support, training, and professional services personnel also have a good perspective on who are mission-critical customers and who are noisy poseurs and wannabes. They can provide context and input on `contact roles`, product usage, customer "referencability," and organizational dynamics. Encouraging the support and services people to adopt the SFDC system early pays for itself with dramatic reductions in cost and internal errors, measurable improvements in customer satisfaction, and increased renewal and re-up rates for customers—which collectively spells higher profits. Enough said?

Support organizations, roles, titles, and responsibilities vary greatly across the SFDC customer base. Nevertheless, five basic types of support team should be leveraging the system on a routine basis:

- **Order Operations.** This team handles inbound calls from customers or sales reps needing assistance with getting the order right. Most of their time is spent on tricky order configurations, discounts and promotions, and service contract renewals. These personnel must have tight interactions with both SFDC and the order entry system, and they may also need to get information from the accounting system. Ideally, they will spend their quality time on big customers, but the goal in using SFDC is to streamline *all* of their order entry interactions.

- **Order Expediting, Distribution, and Shipping.** This team handles inbound calls from sales reps and customers needing assistance with orders once they have been placed, to make sure those orders are fulfilled as quickly and efficiently as possible. Things get tricky when products are on allocation, when products are bulky or difficult to ship, and when the customer has particular partial-shipment needs. This team needs direct interaction with the order management and warehouse/distribution systems, as well as SFDC, to resolve issues as smoothly as possible.

- **Technical and Warranty Support.** This team handles inbound calls from customers who are having difficulty using the product or who need to arrange for a warranty return or out-of-warranty service. Because this team is *always* dealing with unhappy customers, they need quick access to answers, resources, and escalation paths. Members of this team need to have enough technical skills to troubleshoot over the phone, or at least to direct the customer to troubleshooting resources on the Web.

- **Help Desk.** Large and consumer-oriented companies may have a group of employees who act as a lightweight customer support team. Because this call center is focused on getting quick answers to customers, members of this team don't need access to many systems beyond the knowledge base and online documentation, because they don't actually file cases or troubleshoot technical issues. However, their work can be dramatically streamlined via interaction with SFDC, and management needs to closely monitor them to assess their productivity and to detect troubling patterns in customer calls.

- **Professional Services.** Unlike all of the previously mentioned teams, this group has no call-center duties. Instead, their job is to plan and execute training and consulting projects for customers. Members of this team use SFDC to prepare and document proposals, customer responses, statements of work, and project progress. SFDC acts as a central, accessible repository of reusable content, templates, and project histories. Nevertheless, because they have personnel on site at customers' locations and are intimately involved with customers, professional services personnel can be *very* effective sensors for customer satisfaction issues, product ideas, and upsell opportunities that should be documented in SFDC.

If you haven't already done so, you should definitely check out the support and professional services business process diagrams on SFDC's Web site.[1] These brief PowerPoint presentations are a great starting point for discussing and designing your support organization's activities.

Universal Support Best Practices

No matter which part of the support organization your team is in, several SFDC essentials almost always apply:

- Anyone who is in any support call-center role should be on the SFDC system all day. There is just too much leverage to be cheap on this one!

- Integrating telephony into SFDC makes life much easier for the support people, as the computer–telephony integration (CTI) tools can automatically document the basics of the call (call wait time, calling number, time of day, and length of call). The best tools automatically display a pop-up with the customer's name and most recent case on the screen before the call is even answered—an important consideration for call-center people who are measured on number of calls handled per hour. While a few free CTI tools are available in the AppExchange (e.g., for Skype and Cisco IP phones), the more advanced tools are well worth the price when the call center is staffed by of more than a dozen people.

- Due to the time-sensitive nature of customer support, call-center personnel should make extensive use of SFDC's case queues, case teams, alerts, workflows, and approvals. Email auto-responses, templates, and workflows should be used to provide frequent customer updates.[2] Cases must be responded to within time-specified windows of the customer's business hours, or else automatically pushed to the next level via escalation rules. The system's web2case, email2case, and case assignment features should be configured from day one to speed interactions and responses. Tasks should be used to handle action items, and attachments[3] should be used to hold log files and other troubleshooting information. SFDC has a number of great features that can help streamline the cycle time for any person in support or consulting.

---

1. SFDC keeps moving these diagrams around, so I can't give you the URLs here. Just do a Google search to find these diagrams.
2. These emails need to be in plain-text format, and should be informative and specific enough (using mail merge techniques, including embedded links to the customer's case record) to escape spam filters and provide the customer with a sense that progress is being made.
3. SFDC's free storage space is becoming more accommodating and powerful, particularly for the Enterprise edition. If your company has a huge document library, however, you'll probably want to check out one of the document manager plugins available in the AppExchange.

- Special attention should be given to the `Agent Console`, which provides a consolidated view of customer and support information. In addition to saving screen real-estate, the `Agent Console` can decrease the number of call-center personnel clicks by 50%.

- In most industries, the actual time to resolve or remedy a customer problem is *not* the determining factor for customer satisfaction. In fact, a support team that resolves issues more slowly, yet more smoothly and completely, will score much better than a team that resolves issues quickly but leaves customers in the dark. Most customers are happiest if the support team responds quickly with initial (partial) information and then sets expectations correctly about when the next level of response will come. The SFDC system can be the cornerstone for optimizing smooth and complete support communications.

- At the conclusion of any customer interaction, the support person should survey the customer about the experience, even if the transaction was not successful. The SFDC system should be configured to initiate an email-based survey engine, Web-based survey, or phone-based set of questions to be answered. This information should be stored in the relevant `opportunity` or `case` record.

- In most industries, a well-executed customer self-service portal can achieve higher customer satisfaction scores than "more people on the phone." Particularly in high-tech industries, customers become very comfortable over time interacting with portals. Many can use these portals to get the information they need into or out of the system much faster than they could through a phone person. However, *do not implement a self-service portal as a "slash cut"* in which phone support is eliminated—you will face a customer revolt! Introduce the idea gradually, and have customers naturally drift over to the customer self-service portal. As more of the support volume shifts to the portal, you'll get suggestions for refinements to make it even easier and faster for customers. Implement these suggestions! Once 80% of the "call volume" is handled through the portal, you can provide some incentives (such as lower costs or better service levels) to cement the customer behavior.

A well-executed customer portal lowers the company's costs, gives customers 24 × 365 access to the information they need, and reduces the error rate[4] associated with support information. It doesn't come cheap, but the payoffs can be remarkable. Ideally, the portal should include access to the following information:

- ➥ Customer name, address, phone, and account information. Do *not* include credit card numbers here!

- ➥ Order history, invoices, and shipment history.

---

4. A customer is much less likely to misspell his or her own name than a phone service rep would be.

- ➥ Warranty information and support entitlements.

- ➥ Licenses or serial numbers.

- ➥ Frequently asked questions (FAQs).

- ➥ Product documentation and manuals.

- ➥ Solutions and a knowledge base[5] with really good categorization and full search capabilities.

- ➥ IM-with-a-support-person or chat bots.

- ➥ Case (problem) submittal, tracking, and updates.

- ➥ Renewal of a support contract or extension of a warranty.

- ➥ Accessories, parts, and upgrades.

- ➥ Training and certification options.

- ➥ SFDC's Ideas application, which provides a great way to capture and prioritize customer suggestions.

- ➥ Survey/feedback center.

- ➥ User preferences, time zone, business hours, language, currency, email format, and newsletter selection.

- The support personnel will need access to lots of information that's outside the purview of basic SFDC, so you will almost certainly need to use the Enterprise edition to facilitate integration with external systems. If your company has been able to stay at the Professional edition level up to now, support will be the compelling reason to upgrade to a higher SFDC level. Ideally, the support organization will need to have access to the following items in SFDC:

  - ➥ Opportunities

  - ➥ Accounts

  - ➥ Contacts

  - ➥ Products/Price Book

  - ➥ Contracts

  - ➥ Assets

  - ➥ Cases

---

5. SFDC's knowledge base is a great place to start when implementing this feature, but it can be supplemented with document libraries and blogs that should be fully searchable by customers.

➡ Information from marketing: call scripts, suggested renewal/upsell packages, and short-term promotions

➡ Information integrated from accounting: order history, invoices, and payments

➡ Information integrated from manufacturing: shipments, serial numbers, inventory, backlog, replacement parts availability, return merchandise authorization (RMA) numbers, reverse-logistics information, and warranty information

➡ Information integrated from engineering: defect reporting/tracking, resolutions, licenses, and repair/rework status

- Don't measure things too narrowly. Of course you want productivity and SLA metrics, but the SFDC system can provide a lot more important information about customer interactions. Spend some time optimizing the company's operations by figuring out the characteristics of failure: Who are the most troublesome customers? What are the most likely cases to be delayed? Why are certain situations more likely to result in multiple callbacks? Identify the trouble spots, and you may be able to fix underlying product, service, or "attitude" issues that can radically improve the cost, effort, and excellence of the company's services.

- And now a caveat: be aware that external integrations will add significant costs and potentially delay the project. Attempt such integrations only after you've solidified the basic functionality of the SFDC system. There are a variety of ways to handle the integration requirements, so make sure to read the relevant section in Chapter 7 before you make any firm decisions on this score.

The Customer Order Support Center

The ordering component of customer support may be a shared responsibility with inside sales, due to the nature of the work: helping customers get their orders into the system the right way. This job is focused on order entry, order configuration, and order correction. If you haven't already done so, read the "Order Operations for Outside Sales" section in Chapter 9.

Everyone who touches an order in SFDC needs to be working with coherent rules, business processes, and controls to ensure that orders are not corrupted or mishandled. Nothing angers customers more than incomplete or inconsistent "assistance" when they call in for help.

The first challenge in most order-support implementations is making a correct and complete order history available to the customer support reps. This is particularly true if the call center must handle orders from several business units, channels, or countries. In some cases, several systems and databases may have to be integrated before they are presented to SFDC users at all. The results of these integrations can initially be presented as read-only data, but even these "light-weight" integrations can entail a significant amount of work.

In most cases, the phone representatives need to go further than just reviewing the customer's order history. The order support center may also be involved with selling service items that other company representatives don't sell, such as support renewals, warranty extensions, manuals, and replacement supplies or parts. For this reason, they'll need full access to the order management system. For example, these reps need access to "internal only" order capabilities, such as partial shipments, co-terminating contracts, special-order items, adjustments, and special discounts. They also need access to the invoicing system, and they may even need access to parts of the ERP system to see shipment schedules. Ensuring this kind of across-the-board access can represent a significant investment, but it doesn't take long to pay for itself with lower costs and reduced error rates.

In addition to following the best universal practices discussed in the previous section, the order support center should leverage SFDC to help with the warranty/service renewal cycle in these ways:

- During the opportunity close process, a contract object should be created within SFDC, recording the appropriate warranty and support coverage information in custom fields. Contractual terms, signature pages, licenses, and invoices should be stored in the contract object. SFDC should be set up to lock down fields and records so that only members of the Finance department can modify opportunity and contract records once the deal is signed.

- As soon as an opportunity is closed, a new opportunity should be automatically opened for the anniversary of the purchase date, or whatever time is appropriate for renewals of support contracts. Most of the fields of the new opportunity should be prepopulated with data to streamline the renewal sales process. Further, at least one task should be created to remind the appropriate renewal rep to start calling the customer 60 days before the end of the warranty or support period.

- Automatic reminder emails should go out to customers about support or warranty expiration, starting 60 days before the expiry date. This communication can be done via the email blasting system, if it is tightly integrated with SFDC campaigns and activities.

- Because the order support reps will have to handle tricky orders that may include upsell opportunities, the team should use call scripting features (a free AppExchange plugin) to guide them through the order-handling call.

- The opportunity record should include a custom field to indicate customer problem areas. It should consist of a pull-down list with the 10 most common problem areas, supplemented by notes regarding specific instances. These fields should be populated manually and via survey engines.

- The order support reps should create new contacts for people with whom they interact in purchasing, legal, or other customer departments. They should also set contact roles for accounts, opportunities, or cases they are working on, thereby helping the company document the political overtones that exist in its large customers.

Order support teams should be measured along the following lines, with reports and dashboards being created for managers:

- Number of calls handled per rep per day

- Average wait time or call queue length

- Average call time

- Number of order fixes (e.g., reconfiguration, repricing) processed per day

- Number of upsells or renewals closed per day

- Value of orders fixed per day

- Number of orders escalated per day

Order Expediting, Distribution, and Shipping

Due to the nature of the order expediting, distribution, and shipping work, this part of customer support may be a shared responsibility with the manufacturing planning, distribution, or shipping functions. The focus here is on allocating inventory to achieve the best results in revenue recognition, customer satisfaction, and profitability. This role is most critical for products that are in short supply, have high shipping and storage costs, or carry very high price tags.

The first challenge in most SFDC order expediting implementations is to make the current orders list and inventory commitment/routing information available to the expediting representatives. This is particularly true if the customer support center has to handle orders from several business units, channels, or countries—in some cases, several systems and databases may have to be integrated before they are presented to SFDC users at all.

In most cases, the phone representatives need to go further than just seeing the orders and inventory. Specifically, they need to be able to edit records so they can expedite shipments, reallocate inventory to orders, or arrange for partial shipments. Achieving this goal requires two-way integration with order history, ERP, distribution, and other systems, along with appropriate controls and security. Clearly, such integration entails a significant project.

In addition to following the best practices discussed in the "Universal Support Best Practices" section, the order expediters should leverage SFDC in these ways:

- SFDC should be set up with `alerts` and `time-dependent workflows` to remind order expediters and the shipping departments of overdue orders. This consideration is particularly important for products coming in bulk shipments from Asia, where the exact contents and timing of a shipment may not be known until it is about to arrive in-country.

- The expediting and shipment information should be attached to the `opportunity` or `contract` record in SFDC—*not* delivered in an email. Given that sales reps will often have to manage customer expectations, they need to be able to see the best and most complete information available, all in one place.

Order expediters should be measured along the following lines, with reports and dashboards for managers:

- Number of calls handled per rep per day
- Average wait time or call queue length
- Average call time
- Number of orders resolved per day
- Value of orders resolved per day
- Number of orders escalated per day

Technical and Warranty Support

The technical and warranty support team is the front line for dealing with unhappy customers and providing a shield for engineering, sales, and product marketing. Members of this team need to respond quickly and courteously to bring down customer emotions, so they need access to systems that can move the resolution process along as quickly as possible. Some customers will have a service level agreement (SLA) or other support-response guarantee, with contractual penalties if time limits are exceeded.

This team will benefit most from a `customer self-service portal`. Spend money on this feature, to improve customer satisfaction and reduce support costs!

While the tech support team doesn't really need to access the opportunity, account, or other SFDC data, they do need to see assets (to determine support entitlement or warranty eligibility[6]) and create or update cases throughout the day. They also need access to a range of systems that other SFDC users almost never use: the knowledge base, bug/defect tracking system, and fix/upgrade database.

The first challenge in most SFDC tech support implementations is making a correct and complete case history available to the reps. This is particularly true if the customer support center has to handle products from several business units or countries—it's not unusual for several systems and databases to need to be integrated before they are presented to SFDC users at all. Expect to spend some money here.

In addition to following the best practices discussed in the "Universal Support Best Practices" section, the technical and warranty support team should leverage SFDC in these ways:

- SFDC should be configured to show SLA requirements and response times as part of the account, opportunity, and contract records. A workflow trigger should be set up so that cases automatically inherit the SLA deadline information from the appropriate contract.

- The technical and warranty support reps should create contacts for any new customer personnel with whom they interact. They should have a page layout that hides the total amount of the opportunity, as they don't have a need to know this information. These reps should update opportunities with information about the way the customer is using the product, including any custom referencability fields or custom objects that are appropriate there. They should also set contact roles for cases they are working on, thereby helping the company document the political overtones that exist in its large customers.

- SFDC case records should be expanded with custom fields for cross-reference information to bug/defect databases, service bulletins, RMA numbers, license/serial numbers, warranty/shipment numbers, and related information. If your company's products are heavily regulated, additional information about lot numbers and distribution channels may have to be recorded as well, in either the case, opportunity, or contract record.

- The SFDC system should be integrated with the company's defect or bug tracking system, using plugins or general-purpose integration tools from the AppExchange. For the technical support rep, these systems need to look like a seamless part of

---

6. If the company has chosen not to implement assets, these data should be attached to contracts. In B2C companies where there aren't any contracts, eligibility or entitlement data must be attached to opportunities.

SFDC. That said, for the rest of the engineering department (which will almost certainly *not* have SFDC access), the defect/bug tracking system's records need to contain complete details of the customer situation.

- If the company sells hardware, SFDC should be integrated with its RMA and reverse-logistics system so that shipping authorizations and related warranty paperwork can be issued on the fly. For post-warranty repairs, the technical support rep needs access to the repair work-order system. Implementing these custom integration projects will require the use of the general-purpose integration tools found in the AppExchange.

- Because the technical and warranty support reps are trying to solve customer problems in real time, they need to troubleshoot, run diagnostics, and provide advice on the fly. With products or services of any complexity, each rep needs access to highly scripted question/response sequences throughout the call. The free plugin from SFDC should be used to handle the "first pass" questions that are posed to all customers. Soon after the initial volley, however, the rep will need to switch to more detailed information. Depending on the company's style, these data may be provided as a set of PDF documents, intranet pages, or wiki articles. No matter which format is used, the tech support reps will need to be able to rapidly search by topic and keyword. This kind of functionality is usually kept in totally separate systems, but is best accessed via its own `tab` in SFDC. Reps need to *rapidly* navigate across the functional areas they need to use.

- `Cases` should be configured to use `record types` for different product lines, thereby keeping screen content as uncluttered and relevant as possible under each situation.

- As much information as is relevant should be attached to the `case` record. In some product categories (particularly software), however, the attached information may be several megabytes in length. Instead of using the `file attachment` feature in the SFDC system, the reps should store these large files in standard file servers and put the path to a specific file in a `note` attached to the relevant case. In this way, engineering or other personnel can get access to the diagnostic file even if they don't have SFDC user accounts.

- The `case` record should include a `custom field` to indicate customer problems. This field should take the form of a `pull-down list` with the 10 most common problem areas, supplemented by `notes` regarding specific instances. These fields should be populated manually and via survey engines.

OFFSHORING SUPPORT CENTERS

Offshoring or outsourcing parts of customer support is a continuing trend, particularly in highly competitive, high-volume operations with manufacturing overseas. There are a few key SFDC practices to consider before the company makes the decision to offshore its customer support functions.

SFDC is fully internationalized and can be easily configured to be user friendly for support operations in several countries, languages, currencies, and time zones simultaneously. The offshore personnel will need to have full access not only to the SFDC system, but also to the support-relevant systems with which SFDC is integrated. For this reason, the company should implement a fine-grained security plan, to make sure that the support people can see everything they need, but only what they *really* need. The company will also need to set up a virtual private network (VPN) if it has multiple support centers.

We recommend implementing record types, sales processes, and page layouts for each major order entry region (such as the Euro Zone or Asia), as the case-handling workflows within these regions will probably be slightly different from their U.S. counterparts. Using this approach allows spelling and other variations to fit the sales and support customs in each area. The company may also need to develop different approval cycles to fit local management chains—a need that goes double if the company uses distributors or channel partners in some countries.

We also recommend setting the offshore system's time zone to the main time zone for the customers being covered, not the reps' local time zone. This consideration is important when trying to manage tight SLA deadlines across support centers, and it can be critical during the end-of-quarter rush, when the last-minute order push can be very hectic.

Case escalation rules and workflows need to be flawless, and fit with the realities of the local workforces.[7] It is particularly important that escalated cases be smoothly handed off at the end of the local workday, so that those cases move to the top of the list of the remote "morning shift." It can be quite difficult to create reports that accurately capture these cross-site performance metrics.

Although many offshore operations use VoIP phones, we discourage the use of Skype buttons in SFDC for support operations because of marginal call quality. Skype can become quite congested, leaving a bad customer impression. This warning goes double for technical support operations that need to access and transfer large amounts of data to headquarters' engineering staff. Because SFDC's screens themselves depend on low latency and infrequent "lost packets," the last thing the team needs is more competition for Internet bandwidth.

---

7. For example, if an escalation will occur during the lunch hour in Spain or France, the escalation needs to be triggered before the support team leaves the office.

Technical support should be measured along the following lines, with reports and dashboards being made available for managers:

- Number of calls handled per day per rep

- Average wait time or queue depth

- Percent of hang-ups (or "abandon rate," indicating that the customer gave up because of the wait time)

- Average call time

- Average number of calls required to resolve an issue

- Number of cases by severity

- Average time spent by severity

- Number of cases opened per day per rep

- Number of cases closed per day per rep

- Number of cases escalated per day per rep

- Average time to resolve

- Top 10 problem categories

- SLA compliance percentage

- Customer loyalty percentage

- Customer re-up percentage

- Customer satisfaction (likely to buy again, recommend, and so forth) percentage

The technical and warranty support system should also be configured to present real-time alerts (e.g., emails, pages) to line managers, allowing them to avert building problems such as excessive wait times, pending escalations and SLA violations, and other trouble spots. Using SFDC workflows, multisite technical support operations can do load shedding to maintain high levels of customer service despite large variations in support load.

The Customer Help Desk

Large companies—particularly those with consumer products—have a customer assistance center to provide the first line of defense for confused customers. Their job is to help customers who haven't read the manual, need basic questions answered, or aren't sure whether they bought the right product. Consequently, the focus of this team is assistance and quick information access, not heavy transactions. Its goal is to immediately help the customer with the problem, or quickly identify problems that must be escalated to tech support.

Some innovative companies have developed software systems using chat bots, email, artificial intelligence, and interactive voice responder (IVR) technologies to dramatically decrease the human element of the help desk function, or eliminate it altogether. Although few—if any—of these systems are currently in production with a high level of integration to SFDC, that trend is certainly on the horizon.

In terms of SFDC access, the help desk team should open (and rapidly close or escalate) `cases` and `tasks` with annotations from phone or IM conversations. They should change `contact` records with updated information as appropriate. They need access to the SFDC `knowledge base`. But mostly, help desk personnel need access to product documentation, service bulletins, and FAQs held in document management systems, wikis, or plain old file systems outside of SFDC.

Finally, the customer help desk management needs nonintrusive measurement systems to make sure the call center is running smoothly:

- Number of calls handled per day per rep

- Average wait time or queue depth

- Percent of hang-ups (abandon rate caused by excessive wait times)

- Average call time

- Top 10 problem categories

- Survey results regarding call satisfaction (percentage of customers satisfied or very satisfied)

Professional Services

The professional services teams that provide training and carry out consulting projects are often ignored in SFDC planning, but there are very good reasons to include them. These personnel see customers for longer periods than anyone else in the corporation, and they can act as early warning sentinels for both beneficial and damaging trends.

Training

Courses should be included in the SFDC system as standard price-list products, and their order history should be maintained along with the rest of products in the `opportunity` and `contract` records. As customers subscribe to the courses, a `custom field` in the `opportunity` record should be updated to indicate the number of course tickets remaining. The certificates of course completion should be kept in `custom fields` and `notes` for the individual `contacts` who have completed the course; it's also a good idea to annotate them as notes attached to the relevant opportunity. If you want to get fancy, a workflow and some APEX code could be set up to keep a tally of the available course chits remaining at the opportunity level.

For custom courses (which are typically delivered on an on-site basis for major customers or partners), a price-list item should be created with a "standard" price and description that are modified for each situation. Even though the product roll-ups will be somewhat misleading, the opportunity records will indicate the number of companies whose employees have taken custom courses.

Consulting

Although some consulting projects can be sold as fixed-price packages, most consulting work is custom projects. Most consulting organizations create price-list items such as "Senior Consulting Day" or "Business Analyst Day," and the opportunity products will show the total number of person-days required for each category of consultant to complete the project. The statement of work, acceptance criteria, and other consulting artifacts should be attached to the customer's opportunity or contract record.

Once a project has been brought under contract, large consulting teams need to use a project management and consultant-time management system. These professional services automation (PSA) systems are typically stand-alone products, but Open Air and QuickArrow have good integrations with SFDC that reduce the amount of redundant information. Companies that don't have a PSA system typically use Microsoft Project and Excel to manage their consulting teams. If you use this approach, create a projects custom object that hangs off the opportunity or contract record, and attach these project management files to the projects object. At least one AppExchange module (offered for free) can get you started down this path.

Given the nature of consulting projects, it's important that action items be visible to all team members. Consequently, consultants should not use personal calendars for project action items and deadlines; instead, they should use SFDC for this purpose. Using tasks, workflows, alerts, and escalations, SFDC can do a lot to coordinate the work of the consulting team and ensure that deadlines and milestones are not missed by individuals or upper management.

Project progress reports (e.g., progress versus milestones, budgets, variances, and consultant's time-card summaries) and engineering documents (e.g., specifications, tests) should also be stored as attachments to the projects custom object. Given that these documents have a tendency to multiply rapidly, it's a good idea to use one of the document offloading plugins available in the AppExchange to avoid running up against SFDC's free-storage limits.

As the project comes to completion, the consultants need to update as much contact information as they can. They will also have the latest insights about contact roles, project politics, customer satisfaction, and referencability information associated with the opportunity that spawned the project. These updates will be invaluable to both sales and marketing personnel in their pursuit of renewal and upsell business.

CHAPTER 12

Best Practices in Finance and Legal

> *It's accrual world.*
> *—Anonymous*

T HIS CHAPTER COVERS THE point where "the rubber meets the road": signed contracts and money. Administrative and operational users need to understand how to use the system to streamline processes and avoid the duplicate data that frustrate all users. SFDC should be the hub of a comprehensive system for managing and storing the customer relationship over time.

Driving the Investment Decision

For companies large enough to have a CFO—and the vast majority of SFDC customers fall into this category—the investment decision to convert SFA systems or expand the system the company already has deserves your attention. It may be the company's first foray into the world of software as a service (SaaS), and many people at the company may have trepidations about the financial and IT security impact of a commitment to *any* SaaS vendor.

The good news is that SFDC is the most popular SaaS application for a reason: it has done a lot of things right, and the company does well by its customers. The SFDC infrastructure is strong enough to comfort even the most curmudgeonly IT department, the security is solid, and the business model is proven. SFDC also has staying power, with nearly 50,000 customers providing a revenue annuity.

That's all very nice, but you want to make sure that *your company* won't be contributing excessively to SFDC's annuity. The project team should be able to provide good estimates for the three-year costs, expenses foregone, and revenue potential associated with adopting an SFDC system (as described in Chapter 1). Of course, you'll need to help the team members organize the spreadsheets so they fit with your standard model for evaluating investments, but the raw materials should be there already.

Because SFDC and most of the third-party products geared toward SFDC are sold using a recurring revenue model, the ROI evaluation will look different from what your company's financial personnel might be used to when dealing with hardware and enterprise software products. Nevertheless, it's important that they consider *the* key advantage of SaaS: no shelfware. Enterprise software sales teams are famous for providing terrific "discounts" on their products because they know that the day after the purchase is done, the customer will consider it a sunk cost. There will be little direct incentive to actually use the software, and entire companies have made their fortunes by selling software for which 80% of the purchases sit collecting dust on the shelf. Perhaps the most infamous case involved a State of California purchase of Oracle products—a $130 million transaction where only a handful of users ever implemented the product. With recurring-revenue products, this kind of fall-off doesn't happen. Because it's a pay-as-you-go model, if your users don't like the software or if your company decides not to use it, you simply turn the system off.[1] This strategy provides a built-in insurance policy for the purchaser, providing protection against bad sales behaviors and changing internal priorities.

In evaluating the ROI for the SFDC decision, try to keep the big picture in mind. Financial personnel will have solid figures on procurement and operational costs, as well as savings from cost avoidance and reduced labor. The more interesting value from SFDC comes from subtler things:

- **Sales effectiveness:** Benefits include shortening the sales cycle; increasing the win rate; increasing the upsell/resell/renewal rates; increasing the number of transactions a representative can handle without errors.

- **Marketing efficiency:** Benefits include increasing the number of fully qualified leads; decreasing the number of dud leads; decreasing the risk of a CAN SPAM violation; identifying and decreasing the use of poor-performing campaigns.

- **Better customer support:** Benefits include lowering the cost of customer support; improving responsiveness, resulting in higher customer satisfaction numbers; increasing customer renewal/retention rates; better visibility into repeat purchase patterns. *Do not skimp on this area,* as a well-executed customer self-service portal can yield dramatic improvements in both support costs and customer satisfaction.

- **Streamlined internal operations:** Benefits include decreasing the amount of paper generated by and handled in the organization; eliminating "wild goose chases" caused by misplaced documents; decreasing search time for legal, financial, or marketing analysts.

- **Better executive decisions:** Because you'll have a 360-degree view of the customer, and much better metrics on sales and marketing, executive decisions will be driven more by facts and less on opinions; resource allocations will be more easily

---

1. If you do cancel, you might as well wait until the end of the year, because the vendors won't let you out of your contract or provide any refunds. This is, after all, the software industry.

evaluated; and investment decisions on issues such as sales travel, loaner equipment, and proof-of-concept projects will be more rational.

- **Coordination and control:** SFDC, when properly used, becomes a kiosk for information, a central repository for all things relating to the customer. When done right, it can lower internal email by as much as 10%—and it's not possible to be "left off the distribution list." This means it's much easier to bring people up to speed on a customer situation, and learning curves are shortened. After the first few quarters of working with the system, SFDC users get a bit of time back on their calendars. Meanwhile, executives get better visibility into what their organizations are doing, and more measurability overall.

- **Compliance:** SFDC has a number of features that support better compliance with customer-facing business processes and internal controls. In comparison with every other SaaS offering—and even most conventional on-premises SFA/CRM software packages—SFDC's internal security, workflow, control, and auditability features are top-notch.

When it comes to negotiating the deal with SFDC and any third-party vendors, know that they won't offer the discounts with which you might be familiar. Of course, if you're buying 10,000 seat licenses for SFDC's Unlimited edition, you can get a heck of a discount. Most customers represent a much more modest deal, and SFDC can't afford to bend over backward for a 50-seat transaction. To get the best deal, try these tactics:

- Negotiate for the number of seats you'll need a year from now, but at the end of the day purchase and enable only those seats you need immediately.

- Know that SFDC is happy to do a pro-rata upgrade at any time, but will not do downgrades except at renewal time (and may not allow downgrading even then).

- Find out if your company is eligible to use Platform Seats to supplement Enterprise Seats, as they can significantly lower your average per-seat charge.

- Be willing to prepay fees for the first year or more, and be willing to contractually commit for three years or more (longer than this period doesn't seem to make much difference).

- If you are converting from a system offered by one of SFDC's big competitors, negotiate some favors in exchange for using you as a public reference.

- Use the standard end-of-quarter tricks, but know that SFDC's quarters are one month off from standard fiscal quarters (for medium-size deals, even end-of-month effects can shave a point or two off the price).

SFDC has changed the formula for the product costs, but implementation can easily cost your company more than the licenses in the first year or two during which you run the system. The real cost of your SFDC implementation may take the form of consulting fees if users have lots of requirements for integrating the SFDC system with existing systems across the enterprise. Watch out for excessive requirements for integration—and read the section in Chapter 7 to gather ammunition to use in internal arguments.

Once the initial investment in the SFDC system has been made, we generally recommend that extensions and improvements to the system be charged to the main user[2] department's budget. It's too easy for users (particularly in the Sales department, which is often the leading user of the system) to ask for things when they are free. When their "great ideas" are paid for out of their department's own budget, they'll tend to be more rational.

Keeping Expectations Reasonable

The SFDC project is likely to be championed by the head of sales, the head of marketing, and maybe even the CEO. This kind of clout is essential to ensuring the system's credibility and success, but it also tends to lead to over-optimism. One of finance's most valuable roles in the SFDC development process is to keep expectations reasonable, so that people and departments do not become overtaxed.

Here are the key issues to consider when guiding executive expectations for the SFDC project:

- **Your organization's[3] risk tolerance.** SFDC should not be used simply as a way of automating things the way they are now; its whole value lies in the ways it can improve business processes and change the rules of your business, both internally and competitively. But with this opportunity comes uncertainty. You may discover that some departments want to limit their risk, which means that some of the more aggressive expectations must be toned down.

- **Your organization's agility and change-management abilities.** Some companies thrive on change, using alacrity as a competitive weapon. Others view change in a far more limited way. The better your organization is at adapting to and profiting from change, the better it will be at managing business process change. These "type A" organizations can set more aggressive SFDC goals.

---

2. Typically, the biggest users of SFDC are the Sales, Marketing, and Customer Support departments. The easiest way to identify the big users is the number of seats the department has active in the system. Apportioning the budgetary "hits" should be done based on either the number of users or the functional benefit that will be achieved by each group. For example, an improvement to quoting should be paid for by sales and perhaps operations, but not marketing or customer support.

3. By "organization," I mean the overall business or department here, not "the finance organization."

- **The intransigence of existing business processes.** In some organizations, customers, suppliers, and partners will enforce constraints on the organization's business processes, no matter how good it might be at internally adapting to change. If your supply-chain partners' "business rules" are inextricably tied to your organization's business processes, you need to tone down the more aggressive goals for SFDC. Here are some questions to calibrate the impact of these external entanglements:

  ➤ Which business processes could be eliminated, or at least radically simplified, through automation? Which processes must stick around, no matter what?

  ➤ Where could you simply remove paper and human intervention from a business process? Who would be upset if you did?

  ➤ How many trading partners insist on *not* changing the mechanisms and checkpoints of transactions? How many of them unilaterally mandate standards and dictate changes that impinge upon your company's internal business processes?

  ➤ Which regulations or compliance issues can be satisfied only in a narrowly prescribed way? Where do you have freedom in the details of *how* you comply?

Once you've reined in the wilder expectations, it's time for triage. Sort business processes into three buckets: the ones you are trying to replace/eliminate/automate, the ones you are trying to extend/optimize, and the ones that must be left totally alone.

It's also a good idea to shepherd the creation of a set of specific success metrics at the executive level. For an SFDC project metric to be meaningful, you need an "as is" (before) measurement and a "to be" (after) metric of success. Don't let people fudge on defining these metrics—if it can't be quantified realistically, it's a "desirable goal" rather than a "success criterion."

The Path to Project Success

Although the SFDC project team will span many departments, it's important that members of the Finance department play the role of referee in the politics that may develop around the project. This warning goes double if the IT organization reports into finance.

Once the decision has been made to undertake an SFDC implementation, three critical success factors determine project success:

- The consistent enthusiasm and support of the executive champion(s).

- The choice of project lead. This person needs to have a passion for SFA/CRM, a good understanding of the company's business, some political credibility, and experience in how to manage an ambitious project that spans several departments.

- Unswerving focus on user adoption. Without users, the system is just an empty shell. With user enthusiasm, its business impact soars.

Make sure that the *right* champion and team leader are chosen and dedicated to the SFDC implementation—and raise red flags if these roles are delegated too far down in the organization. These key people will make the difference between a solid ROI and a wasted investment.

Accounting and Ongoing Operations

Once the SFDC system is up and running, there are some things financial personnel need to do, and things you need other members of the company to do, to ensure clean, consistent operations in finance.

The Quote to Cash Cycle

The most involved interactions between finance and sales personnel occur during the quote to cash cycle, and you should be pushing for controls as early as possible in this business process. As discussed in detail in Chapter 9:

- Special requests—for features, consulting, discounts, or contractual terms—should be requested via the SFDC system, rather than through ad hoc emails. Putting these requests in the system lets finance personnel apply approval cycles to make sure that the right management reviews have been done before a commitment is made. More importantly, by attaching these requests to SFDC opportunities, analysis of the effect of approved "specials" on the win rate, deal size, and profitability becomes possible. Setting up these approval cycles up takes a few days' time, but can make a big difference in the amount the company spends on variances.

- Quotes should not be available for printing (or transmittal via email) until they are complete and have gone through an SFDC-enforced financial or legal approval cycle for out-of-bounds discounts or custom terms and conditions. Quotes should be generated and rendered entirely within the SFDC system. Quotes should be saved in a read-only format such as PDF that can't be edited by mischievous sales reps.

- Once a quote has been approved, it should not be editable without another SFDC automatic screening for discounting and terms (if the screening fails, another approval cycle will be automatically initiated).

- Once an order has been received, parts of the record must be locked down to prevent meddling. The administrative part of the deal-closing process (legal confirmation, posting of the contract, generation of the invoice) should be handled through SFDC's automatic workflows, with an increasing proportion of fields being locked down at each step.

- The company may want to have the `contract` be automatically generated from the SFDC system (in conjunction with Word or other application) to minimize the labor and error rate associated with data reentry. SFDC has very powerful template and external-system interfaces, and it can be integrated with nearly any application.[4]

- Using products from Adobe, DocuSign, and EchoSign, the entire `contract` generation and `approval process` can be configured to be automated and paperless. While considerable care should be taken in implementing this integration, the cost savings can be dramatic, particularly if financial personnel have to manage hundreds of contracts.

- At the end of the close cycle, the order information and `contract` should not be editable by anyone except auditors or system administrators.

Here are several important best practices regarding financial details and SFDC, which are particularly important if you integrate SFDC with your order entry, order management, or accounting system:

- SFDC has a standard `account name` field, which should be used as the "friendly name" that most users would tend to search for (e.g., "Du Pont"). The system should be extended with a `custom field` that holds the customer's legal entity name, which should match the name used by legal and finance personnel (e.g., "E. I. DuPont de Nemours, Inc.").

- SFDC's `account` object should have a `custom field` pointing to the corresponding customer records in the order entry, order management, or accounting system. If these are all separate systems, SFDC should have three fields for pointers.

- The accounting and order entry systems (and the order management system, if it is yet another system) should have pointers to the SFDC record. SFDC's `account` record identifier is an 18-character alphanumeric[5] value that is *case sensitive.*

- SFDC's `opportunity` object is the parent of all `quotes`, and the `opportunity` is where the most interesting customer data are found. Consequently, the pointer to the accounting system's order record should be stored there. SFDC's `opportunity` record identifier (again, an 18-character case-sensitive alphanumeric called a UOID) should be stored in the accounting system's order record.

- SFDC's `account` and `opportunity` objects need to follow a fairly strict naming convention. This name should be used in the accounting/order entry/order

---

4. All it takes is time and money.
5. Some SFDC reports and views will present a truncated 15-character version of the UOID. These identifiers work, but it's better (for compatibility purposes) to record the full 18-character version.

management system as the start of the "description" or "comments" field for customers and orders.

- If you use Excel extensively, watch out for its auto-mangling features for numbers, particularly if your company uses the CSV format for its data exchange. Read the discussion in the "Joy of Regex" sidebar in Chapter 3!

- SFDC is usually deployed in a single-currency mode, but (as discussed in Chapter 10) switching the system to a multi-currency mode is fairly straightforward. Within the system, all users will see all transactions and reports in their local currency and language, irrespective of the currency in which the transaction was done.

- SFDC has settings for `fiscal year` and `business hours`. Make sure they agree with the settings in the other systems the company uses!

- SFDC provides a sophisticated and robust `forecasting` system, but it works only at the level of bookings. SFDC's `products` and `price list` functionality can be used to hold flags and schedules for revenue recognition at the stock-keeping unit (SKU—that is, line-item) level, but the system does not in itself manage revenue-recognition events or calculate schedules. Consequently, SFDC will need to export these data into your accounting system to create a proper GAAP forecast of products and services.

- SFDC can store all of the company's products, orders, and everything else the accounting personnel need for calculating commissions—but the system does not offer any internal incentive or compensation management functionality. Most customers do their commissions work on external spreadsheets fed by SFDC data, and this is often the best answer to this dilemma. Several powerful and elegant third-party incentive management systems may be nicely integrated into SFDC, but they are expensive and can be hard to manage. Check out Chapter 7 if you want to know more.

- SFDC is very easily extended to accommodate new fields and new kinds of records. Before you attach new data to the system, however, you need to make sure the data are in the right place so they will be well behaved over time. This means a bit of analysis prior to taking action—check out "A Guided Tour of the SFDC Object Model" in Chapter 2.

- SFDC also has some features (e.g., user data entry screens, email alerts, reports, dashboards) that can be leveraged by other applications. If you want to know more about what's possible, check out Chapter 7.

- If you integrate SFDC with the accounting, order entry, or order management system, `accounts` must be created and updated in SFDC weeks before they appear in the financial system(s). The integration logic should not attempt to create a customer record in the financial system(s) until a valid order has been placed.

- If your company has grown through acquisition and has several SFA and financial systems, double-check any integration logic that may create `accounts` in SFDC or customers in the financial system(s). At my company, we have witnessed nightmarish situations where duplicate `account` (customer) names are created on a daily basis due to poor business process integration.

Once an order is received, SFDC offers several areas of functionality that help record and organize information that accounting, finance, customer support, and legal personnel will want to see over time. SFDC can act as a centralized repository for the following items:

- RFI, RFQ, and quote information
- Statements of work (SOWs), schedules, milestones, and work-breakdown structures
- Service level agreements (SLAs)
- Licenses, authorizations, certificates, and serial numbers
- Contracts, exhibits, non-disclosure agreements, and addenda
- Engineering change orders (ECOs)
- Purchase orders
- Invoices
- Call notes
- Payment history
- Follow-up or callback tasks

If you want to do detailed searches or create `alerts`, `reports`, or `workflows` about a piece of information, the information needs to be stored in an SFDC field. As mentioned previously in this book, attached documents stored in SFDC are not searchable. Thus, even if three documents show a contractual milestone date, if you need to see it or search for that date from within SFDC, you'll need to add the data item as an explicit SFDC field. For example, renewal dates, price expiration dates, and renegotiation windows would need to be entered into SFDC's `contract` object.

Out of the box, SFDC provides very few roll-up views or fields. Instead, details about each `contract` are visible only from the `contract` record. For `account` management (such as when dealing with a customer who has a history of payments problems), it is very useful to create custom `roll-up fields` at the `account` level that summarize the overall situation, such as the following elements:

- Total number of orders
- Total value of orders
- `InArrears` flag
- Date of last order

To help manage the quote to cash cycle (particularly if you've integrated SFDC with the accounting, invoicing, order entry, and order management systems), you'll want to design several SFDC workflow `approval processes`, as well as `views`, `reports`, and `dashboards` to see items such as these:

- Discounts by product line
- Discounts by sales rep
- Discounts by region
- Billings by size
- Invoices by customer
- Days' sales outstanding
- Top 10 customers
- Top 10 in-arrears customers
- Top 10 nonrenewing customers

Profitability Analysis

The company's P&L history can provide good clues about its product and service profitability. Even so, depending on sales and cost data alone paints an incomplete and sometimes misleading picture of the company's success. Product profitability can be distorted by politically driven cost allocations, and customer behavior is completely masked by conventional product sales analysis.

The whole point of an SFA/CRM system is to be able to track and analyze patterns of customer interactions. Work with the marketing team to identify correlations among purchases (such as "80% of the time when we sell profitable product A is when we sell unprofitable product B"), profiles of customer profitability (such as "Our highest-profit customers are never our highest-volume customers"), and inflection points in the sales cycle (such as "70% of the time when we do a free proof of concept (POC), we win the deal—but only if the POC is done before stage 5"). Marketing people love to analyze and discover trends, and the real pros will be more objective than either engineering or sales personnel when it comes to product or promotion investment decisions.

Workflows and Streamlining

When properly implemented, SFDC is a great way to streamline a company's marketing, sales, order, and customer support operations. Its workflow system can be extended to go even further. If you're interested in the business process streamlining that's possible with SFDC, check out Chapter 8 for more information.

Even if you're not interested in workflow, a few principles should be followed as SFDC is implemented:

- The model of sales, marketing, and support information should be centralized whenever possible. SFDC provides worldwide, secure access via a Web browser, and the simple act of making information more consistently accessible can mean a big difference in internal efficiency.

- You should set an explicit goal to reduce your company's internal email by 10%, because each piece of information stored in SFDC should be able to save a couple of last-minute "Anybody know what's going on?" emails. SFDC pushes companies toward a "kiosk" model of information—where anything users need to know is available on demand, in a consistent, reliable place—and frees them from the tyranny of email (which uses an "interruption model").

- For anything relating to sales and marketing (and perhaps customer service), you should insist on the elimination of external spreadsheets and paper. Aside from adding costs, external spreadsheets are not subject to audit trails, access controls, or approval cycles. SFDC's built-in controls take you a long way toward regulatory compliance.

- Move quickly down the path from SFA to true CRM functionality, as that is where the biggest payoffs happen. Integration converts an SFA tool into a full CRM system. SFDC is among the easiest applications in the world to integrate with, and unifying sales, marketing, support, order operations, and other groups' customer information can be the basis for obtaining a true 360-degree view of the customer.

Cost Containment

Although your company probably already has an expense-tracking system, SFDC has a free add-on application that makes it easy for sales and field support personnel to put in expense claims and attribute their expenses to individual customers, projects, or contracts. For the field force, having this functionality in SFDC is ideal for two reasons:

- These reps are already in the system and have no excuse to not enter a bit more data there.

- The plugin minimizes the amount of data reentry. Using SFDC's reporting engine allows for easy export of the expense data and, therefore, for integration into the company's standard expense-tracking application.

Process Controls, Security, and Compliance

SFDC has very fine-grained security, and it can be set up so that users can see or edit only the things they need to at that stage of the business process. In addition, most objects can be set up with full audit trails, so you know precisely who did what and when. SFDC also supports locking down records and approval cycles that ensure process compliance. While configuring and maintaining all these controls can be tiresome, that's what security's all about, right?

Here are our recommendations for SFDC's security system:

- As a matter of company policy, no one should be allowed to delete anything in the SFDC system. Users may be able to flag records as bad data or a dead deal, but the organization can never improve (or really comply) if these records can actually be expunged from the system. By prohibiting deletion, you'll have an extra measure of process assurance.

- For auditability, we recommend that `field history` be turned on for all objects in the system, to provide full audit trails. Audit trails are free, and they can be turned on for as many as 20 fields per SFDC object, but they do have to be activated manually.

- Data-sharing rules should be relatively lax initially, but gradually tighten up so that reps and customer support users can see only the `accounts`, `opportunities`, and `contacts` that are within their purview. If other people need to see the `opportunity` records, consider using a `page layout` that hides the total order amount from them. The gradual tightening is needed to ensure that the security policy is not getting in the way of revenue generation. In addition, we recommend that the `view all forecasts` option be turned off to maintain a strict need-to-know hierarchy.

- For access control, we recommend that password policies—including login hours, allowed IP ranges, auto-logout, account lockout, and password aging—start out a bit lax, and then tighten up after the first few weeks of SFDC use. The reason for this path relates to system adoption: you don't want to provide *any* excuse for people to not to use the system. Once they've become familiar with SFDC, make password security a bit tighter after having notified the users of this plan (and given them a cheat sheet for when things go wrong). You'll know the policy is too strict if people are constantly getting locked out of the system because they forgot their password for the twelfth time this month.

- As a matter of policy, the number of people with administrative privileges should be kept to a bare minimum—typically between two and six people total. Because system administrators have complete visibility into every user's account, every significant action, and all the data managed by the system, this must be a highly trusted role. As with any IT system, never let an administrator become a disgruntled employee (and never let a disgruntled employee become a system admin); these unhappy people can pose serious security and compliance risks.

- Leverage the system as an aid to regulatory and standards compliance. SFDC's `workflow` system, in conjunction with `record types` and conditional `page layouts`, can provide the core for an auditable process control system. Several companies have used this system as the basis for compliance with Sarbanes-Oxley Act (SOX) Sections 404 and 409. There's even a SOX audit module available in SFDC's AppExchange, appropriately named "SOX ROX."

REPORTS: HIDE 'EM?

SFDC has a powerful and easy-to-use reporting system that gives users visibility to all their data.

That's the problem. Anyone who can access the reporting system at all can access *all* of it—and there isn't even an audit trail to indicate who has run which reports. A disgruntled or soon-to-depart sales rep can pull all of his or her contacts and contracts onto a paper, PDF, or Excel report that can walk out the door tonight.

Unfortunately, there isn't much subtlety in the choices for dealing with this issue: either let users have access, or turn reports entirely off for certain types of users. The good news is that for users who are prohibited from running reports, you can set the system up to deliver standardized reports automatically, without the user even clicking a button.

While we're at it, you need to think about Outlook synchronization. This feature is both useful and secure, but it means that employees can download all of the company's contacts at the click of a button. Again, this is an all-or-nothing decision.

These are judgment calls, but ones you should explicitly make.

Investor Relations

Wall Street analysts, private-placement firms, and other investors are a valuable constituency that must be skillfully managed. While most SFDC clients do not have a full-time person dedicated to investor relations (IR), larger companies (particularly *Fortune* 500 conglomerates) will have not only a full-time IR person, but an entire IR agency at their disposal. If your company is large enough to have these functions, or if it runs an investors' conference, SFDC can be configured to help.

The idea is to improve collaboration inside and outside the company. Outlook and Excel are the *lingua franca* of finance, but they are almost useless when it comes to cross-company collaboration (e.g., between a company and its IR firm). SFDC's Web-based functionality is a great way to coordinate and collaborate on your IR projects.

SFDC has developed a free add-on (available in the AppExchange) designed around the needs and workflow of the PR team, as discussed in Chapter 10. This add-on provides all the basics for the PR function, and it can be easily modified and extended to match the workflow of nearly any IR team.

After you've read Chapter 10's description of the free PR plugin, here are some extra considerations for managing investor relations:

- Keep all the detailed personal information on contacts in Outlook (or your favorite contact management tool). Don't try to synchronize this database with SFDC—this effort will be more trouble than it's worth in the world of IR. You will need to create IR contacts in SFDC, but these can easily be done as a one-time import of a CSV file dumped from the main contacts database. All that really needs to be imported into SFDC is each person's name and email address.

- Run the investor bulk mailings from within the SFDC system (its functionality works well with lists containing as many as 200 emails per blast). Typically, there's no point in setting up a campaign to track responses from individual mailings, but if you have the energy to do so, knock yourself out.

- For the SFDC contacts, create one or two new values for the type pick list so as to keep your IR people hidden from view of the marketing and sales people and out of ad hoc reports. Typically, these values will be something like "IR target" or "Industry analyst." If you want to be doubly safe, put a prefix on the name (along the lines of "HANDS OFF—Joe A. Investor").

- Put investor firm names in the SFDC system as accounts. Again, create one or two new values for the type pick list to keep these accounts separate from your company's prospects and customers. You will certainly want to use the same warning prefix for the account name (to keep "HANDS OFF—IR—Bank of America" separate from the "Bank of America" account in reports and other data views).

- Adjust pick lists on contacts to reflect the status of analysts and investors. You'll almost certainly want to use record types and page layouts to customize the look of SFDC for the IR team.

Mergers, Integrations, and Divestitures

This topic has two sides: the strategic work of identifying and developing the M&A, spin-off, or carve-out, and the operational work of actually making the change in corporate structure.

The Strategic Side of M&A and Divestitures

If your firm does an acquisition or divestiture only infrequently, SFDC will not add a lot of value to its corporate development group. However, if the company is constantly being pitched deals, needs to evaluate several candidates at a time, or does an acquisition or divestiture several times per year, SFDC can make life much easier for the folks charged with managing those deals. Indeed, venture capitalists and private equity firms use SFDC all the time for managing their deal flows and capital calls.

SFDC provides a free template for M&A operations that creates several custom objects that are relevant for tracking and evaluating candidates over time. Features such as those that focus on quarterly financials, sources of referrals, funding sources, and valuations can be quickly enabled. Due to the confidential nature of this information, it is imperative that you implement record types and page layouts to keep this strategic information safe from prying eyes. That said, the centralized nature of SFDC—and the fact that most executives will have logins to the system already—make it an ideal way to share information among the people with a need to know.

With a small amount of VisualForce development, specially formatted screens can be created for the corporate development team. VisualForce can even generate deal-summary "one pagers" at the click of a button for strategic review meetings.

The Operational Side of M&A or Divestitures

The operational aspects of mergers, acquisitions, and divestitures constitute a big topic requiring some special attention with respect to SFDC, particularly when the system is highly integrated with other systems across the enterprise.

Any large structural change in the sales and marketing department will necessitate significant reworking of the SFDC system. Do not underestimate the effort required to cope with a merger—updating SFDC as the result of such a deal can be just as a big a project as the initial system implementation.

If you need to integrate another company's data with your company's existing SFDC system, there is an easy path: if both companies use SFDC already, you can use the `Salesforce to Salesforce` feature (it's free) to span the two instances. If, however, the other company has a different SFA system, it may be less disruptive to convert that company's data to its own SFDC instance (running two instances indefinitely, spanned by `Salesforce to Salesforce`) than to bring those data directly into your company's existing SFDC instance. Talk with your SFDC sales rep and your favorite consultant for the latest guidance on this issue.

If you're going in the other direction because the company plans to divest itself of a division, there's some real work to do—but it's a lot simpler than integration. The basic approach is to buy a second SFDC instance, do a full dump of the existing instance's data, clone its configuration (using `packages` and the force.com `Eclipse` plugin), filter out only the things that are relevant to the divested division, and load all of that data in the instance. I've made this process sound much easier (and weeks shorter) than it really is, but from a purely SFDC perspective, it's a straightforward project. Integrating (or dis-integrating) SFDC's connections to external systems can involve much more serious work, however.

Fundraising

Whether you work for a pre-IPO (initial public offering) company making the funding rounds, a public firm planning a secondary offering, or a not-for-profit organization looking for institutional grants, SFDC can be a very helpful tool for its executive staff. SFDC can be used in three distinct contexts:

- As a stand-alone tool for investors (either the Professional or Enterprise edition)

- As a stand-alone tool for fundraisers (typically the Professional edition)

- As a fundraising tool in conjunction with SFDC's normal roles in sales, marketing, and customer support (must be the Enterprise edition)

SFDC provides a couple of free configurations tailored to the needs of venture capitalists and private equity, with a series of prefabricated `custom objects`, `relationships`, and `record types` that can be further customized to your company's operational needs. Due to the subtle nature of long-term relationship management that's part of the investment banking world, you'll need to do *very* careful analysis of your deal flow, business processes, and information-sharing model before any implementation work is done. In my firm's investment banking engagements, just the discovery and understanding of these factors can account for 20% of the overall SFDC implementation effort.

If you work for an investment firm, the "later stage" your investment focus is, the more important historical data will be. This means a more complex object model, and a much higher cost of migrating the existing database to the SFDC system. If your historical data are really valuable, cleansing and enriching the data can cost as much as $10 per record (double the cost of commodity SFA/CRM data).

If you work at a nonprofit organization, and particularly one that targets consumers with large numbers of postal mail, email, and phone campaigns, the cost of migrating the existing contact information is relatively small (typically, the contact information consists of just the target's name, mailing address, email address, and phone). However, if you need to import the history of your contacts and discussions with donors, the cost of properly migrating the data can reach as much as $5 per record. Do a cost–benefit analysis of large historical imports before you start—and make sure there is business value before you over-invest in preserving historical data.

Legal

In most companies, the legal function works closely with finance, particularly on contractual and policy issues. Here are the things that legal personnel should know about working with SFDC.

Information Retention

SFDC is a SaaS application that delivers all functionality from its originator's network centers. In normal operation, SFDC stores no information on any of the company's computers—it's all stored "in the cloud" of the Internet. SFDC has implemented very tight internal security, has duplicated its data centers, and runs continuous backups of all client companies' data.

On a practical level, this means that anything put into the SFDC system will be stored indefinitely. Even if your company's personnel delete data, that information resides in SFDC's archive somewhere and can be recovered as part of a discovery process (although recovery of that data would be anything but free). For this reason, legal personnel need to extend their company's information storage retention policy to cover SFDC (and to SaaS vendors in general).

The good news is that SFDC's parametric data are relatively benign (take a look at the screens and you'll see). It is a best practice to forbid the storage of personal financial or health-oriented information (such as Social Security, credit card, bank account, and insurance numbers) on this system. Go ahead and forbid with my blessing.

The less-good news is that SFDC allows the storage of arbitrary files as record attachments. As this use of SFDC is relatively expensive, for many reasons it's a good idea to forbid users from uploading photos, videos, or other large files to the SFDC system. That said, storing PDF files containing things like signature pages and installation diagrams in the system should be encouraged. Back to the good news: a number of add-on products make it easy to store documents on your own file servers, yet have links to the files appear magically within SFDC pages. Check out Chapter 7 for more on this capability.

Contract Generation

SFDC can be configured and integrated to feed customer and order information into a company's existing contract generation system (of course, it won't do so until the final approvals are in place, but the mechanism is there in SFDC). This strategy works equally well with full legal content management systems and with simple Word templates (if your organization is a small company).

If you want to exert better control over contracts, SFDC can be configured to generate contracts from a standard boilerplate without resorting to an external Word document. The system generates an uneditable digitally signed PDF document, so you have solid control over exactly what the customer receives. Any of the options mentioned here can be configured with a few days' consulting work.

Contract Storage

As discussed earlier in this chapter, it is a best practice to store customer contracts in SFDC, attached to the system's `contract` record.

Once you've gotten your mind around this idea, you'll discover that SFDC is equally useful for storing and tracking your partner and supplier contracts. Although a bit of extra customization is required to implement this process, the leverage it provides for both the financial and legal functions can pay for the consulting work[6] in just a few months. Of course, if your company already has a legal content management system, it makes more sense to leave all of the contracts where they are, and simply provide pointers to the contract locations from within SFDC's records.

Human Resources

In many companies, HR works closely with the Legal and Finance departments, and sometimes reports into the CFO. SFDC isn't a tool that HR personnel typically use very often, but there are still some considerations for the HR function when this system is implemented:

- It's a good idea to put internal contact information for all employees into the SFDC system. This database is secure, and having everyone's internal phone number, mobile phone number, location, and email address available is helpful for any SFDC user.

---

6. I have a hard time imagining which consultant you'd want to use for this kind of project.

- It is *not* a good idea to put any personal information in the SFDC system, such as employees' home address, home phone, or any financial information. If these data are stored in SFDC, you should lock down those fields with `field-level security`, `record types`, and `page layouts` to keep prying eyes away from these data.

- SFDC is not particularly appropriate for a general HR management system. Of course, SFDC could be configured to do nearly anything—but I have never seen it used that way.

- SFDC *has* been used as a recruiting database in several of my company's venture capitalist and private equity clients. Investment bankers meet a lot of talent, and SFDC can be easily extended to track recruitability of potential hires. This idea can be used by nearly any firm that comes in contact with talented partners, suppliers, or customers. The first thing to do is create `page layouts` for HR, and add five `custom pick-list fields` to their `lead` and `contact` records: current title, previous title, potential title, availability, and recruiting priority. The actual résumés should be stored as ASCII text in the "Description" text area, so they will be fully searchable from within SFDC.

- If you think about it, the recruiting process is similar to a sales process: there's prospecting, pipeline management, offer management, and closing. There are tasks to be followed up on, and a `workflow` for approvals. SFDC can be configured to match almost any recruiting process, and a free plugin available at the AppExchange can configure the system to work as a nice, Web-based recruiting tool. In addition to providing a central repository of information (so the hiring managers can see the status of all job requirements and candidates), this plugin creates nice reports, metrics, and management dashboards. Configuring SFDC to manage these HR tasks will take a few days of consulting time, but it provides a solid, secure system for you and your internal clients.

CHAPTER 13

Best Practices in IT

> *The three most dangerous things in information technology are a programmer with a soldering iron, a manager who codes, and a tech support guy who gets ideas.*
>
> *—Anonymous*

THIS CHAPTER IS FOR everyone who works in information technology—whether employees or consultants. Most IT people already have most of the skills, knowledge, experience, and attitudes they need for a smooth, successful implementation of SFDC. But if you've never worked with SFDC before, there are a few twists. This chapter explores three key issues for IT personnel: policy, data quality, and administration.

Level of IT Engagement

Although a SFDC sales reps might say that IT does not need to be involved with the SFDC system, if your company is large enough to have an IT department, it's a safe bet that those personnel should be involved with the system at least on an advisory basis. Although SFDC is "just an application," you will quickly be able to see the global ramifications of application decisions that users will miss.

If you've never deployed or worked with a significant SaaS application before, there is a bit of a learning curve, because SaaS changes a lot of the rules for applications software. The differences in SFDC include these key points:

- Initial decision making is different, because the cost functions and benefit streams have different timing. The up-front payment is low because there's no hardware or software to procure, and there are no upgrade fees for new versions. Payments are steady and predictable, not lumpy—but the fees continue forever. On the benefits side, a basic system can be operational in six weeks, so time to value is much quicker than with on-premises software.

- SFDC is almost always paid for and run out of the Sales, Marketing, or Customer Support department. Although IT personnel may be called upon to work on the system occasionally, the expenditures rarely hit their budget directly. In fact, we recommend (for clear decision making) that the budget for any work IT does on the SFDC system be a transfer *into* the IT budget, rather than a drain on it.

- In many parts of the SFDC project, there isn't that much for the IT team to actually do. While there's always an oversight role (for security, policy enforcement, and asset protection), in the first year there may be nothing for IT to deploy.

- Many development, extension, and integration projects may be done entirely without the assistance of central IT, because the required resources and interfaces are largely outside the company's network. SFDC also has a large number of plugin products that can extend and integrate the system, and half of them are free. (See Chapter 7 to find out more about these applications.)

- Almost every truly successful SFDC implementation will need to integrate with existing software in the company's network. The IT team must be intimately involved with this process, and integration usually involves just as much effort for SFDC as it would any packaged enterprise application. Keep your eyes open for the "signal flare" represented by an SFDC upgrade to the Enterprise edition, as this is the minimal version for external integration.

- After deployment, user departments can be almost entirely self-sufficient. For example, users will never call the IT department and ask for help in rebooting a machine because of SFDC issues (although they will call the help desk when they lock themselves out of the system because they forgot their passwords). Further, users can call consultants in to make system modifications or extensions without needing to call IT, because the changes are usually to SFDC's systems, not the company's internal system.

- System administration can be largely delegated to user groups (assuming, of course, that they are adequately trained). Many SFDC systems are largely stand-alone entities, so there's no intrinsic need to involve IT in their administration. Of course, once SFDC has been integrated with the company's other systems, you'll need to have a federated model for administering the systems in tandem. SFDC, fortunately, makes it pretty easy to create this model.

- Performance and operations for SaaS applications are mostly out of IT's hands, because the vendor takes care of all aspects of its application's uptime and performance. SFDC has a very good record indeed of operational continuity, and the company provides several weeks' notice for planned downtime. Most of the time, the SFDC servers respond to user interactions within 250 milliseconds.

In most cases, however, the perceived performance of SFDC in the headquarters buildings will be somewhat slower than with an on-premises application; conversely, it will be perceived as much faster in remote offices (particularly those located outside the United States). Perceived performance really takes a hit if the company's network has latency problems or drops a lot of packets during busy hours. SFDC has several Web 2.0 features that make for fairly large page sizes, and working in interrupted page refresh mode will make the system look very slow. These problems are particularly noticeable on marginal WiFi links.

- Another wrinkle on operations and performance occurs when SaaS applications are integrated with one another. There will be no end of amusing fingerpointing among the vendors when incompatibilities occur, particularly if their products compete with each other.

- Because the company's IT department doesn't deploy anything for the SFDC functionality, the IT personnel have basically no involvement in, or control over, patches and upgrades: they simply appear, and the users *can't* stick with the old version. Fortunately, SFDC's quality and compatibility have been very high, and the company gives plenty of advance notice regarding upcoming changes.

- Security and disaster recovery are also largely out of the IT department's hands. SFDC has a very solid security track record, and it has invested millions in establishing highly available, distributed data centers for disaster recovery. The company performs continuous replication and online backup, and its servers have proved very resilient to attack.

  However, security and disaster recovery issues become complicated with the addition of third-party add-ons (which are implemented as an entirely separate SaaS operation). If your company's internal IT teams have tough standards, make sure that they notify everyone on the SFDC team that all third-party SaaS products and integration adaptors must be screened prior to purchase.

  The final twist to this topic occurs when SFDC is integrated with on-premises applications. Several third-party products include thick-client tools or server interface modules that need to be installed, updated, and operated on a company's systems in a secure and predictable way. These third-party products will involve standard IT oversight, just as any on-site software would. The good news is that SFDC has done a lot with these third-party vendors to make sure that their product architectures foster IT best practices.

- Information leak protection (ILP) is a hot topic today, particularly when the information being considered consists of customer records, leads, and transaction history. For a number of reasons, throughout the book we have urgently advised that highly sensitive customer information—credit card numbers, Social Security numbers, bank account numbers, ACH/SWIFT routing numbers, FEIN or state corporation numbers, and health-related information—*not* be stored in the SFDC database. SFDC has done a good job of protecting information with fine-grained field-level access, role-based privileges, and audit trails for logins and changes. Nevertheless, if a user is authorized to see a piece of data, he or she *will* be able to pull it out of the system as an Excel spreadsheet or print it as an HTML page. It will be important for IT personnel to set up their company's ILP system to recognize SFDC .csv or .xls files, and block them from being attached to emails or downloaded to external storage media. Of course, because SFDC is available to any authorized user machine,[1] the ILP software would need to be installed on users' home machines and laptops.

Skills IT Will Need

I hate to sound like a consultant, but the skills needed for IT personnel to work with the SFDC team will depend on the nature of the implementation project. There's a continuum of SFDC usage, from simple SFA to comprehensive CRM. On the pure SFA end of this continuum is stand-alone sales, marketing, and customer support functionality. IT won't need to learn very much here. The system has extensive online documentation, and it would be hard to take more than two weeks of classes. A couple of IT people could attend these educational sessions and then do mini "train the trainer" sessions for the few things that the help desk and system administrators would need to be ready to handle once the SFDC system is implemented.

In the middle of the spectrum are simple extensions and customizations, which consist of either internal SFDC wizards or external file sharing, Excel macros, or Access queries. Again, there's almost nothing for IT personnel to learn beyond the SFDC object model (discussed in Chapter 2) and the report wizards. The most common external application integrated in this part of the spectrum will be an email blasting system (also known as marketing automation), which is itself a SaaS application; this integration/configuration task should almost always be handled by the third-party vendor.

At the CRM end of the spectrum is integration of SFDC with systems with which IT personnel are typically already familiar. Integration of the IT applications with SFDC typically follows this functional order: quoting, order entry, eCommerce, accounting, inventory/ distribution, bug tracking, professional services automation, content management, and analytics/business intelligence. Even though off-the-shelf adaptors are available for most standard applications and SFDC has a superb Web services API, the work to merge the data models that underlie the various systems can take several months and should involve the IT team. Even if your company uses consultants for this purpose, IT people need to determine

---

1. Yes, the SFDC system has IP range restrictions, time-of-day restrictions, auto-logout, and strong password and authentication mechanisms. But once users are in the system, they're in.

the architecture, the rules, and the business process implications of changing data. Most of the skills needed for this effort will likely be present among the IT personnel. But if you've never used Web services, there are some things to learn—and learning to use SFDC's API will require some homework.

There are many cases where real code needs to be developed and deployed into SFDC. This code is typically written in CSS, JavaScript, APEX (Java derivative), and VisualForce (an HTML/XML derivative). You'll need classic development and testing skills for creating and implementing this code. For further discussion of this topic, read the "IT and Web Team Organizational Readiness" section in Chapter 5 and the discussion of tools in Chapter 7.

One final area in which IT skills are needed is project management. SFDC lends itself to Agile project management techniques. Even though project or program managers may exist throughout your company, few of them will understand IT issues and almost none of them will "get" Agile techniques. At the very least, IT people should help train the project managers for the implementation and upgrade cycles, thereby ensuring that the project is deployed properly.

THE SKILL OF ACCESSIBILITY

Because most SFDC users (and their management) will be very far away from the IT group, it's doubly important that IT personnel be approachable and accessible for help with SFDC projects. The non-IT people who will be making decisions probably don't know the right questions to ask about SFDC's technical details, and won't realize the implications of their assumptions and wishful thinking.

To help the SFDC newbies, create a FAQ about IT's involvement and put it on the project wiki. Have an outreach phone conference with the project leaders (ideally, before they've signed any contracts) and get in the loop early to help the non-IT people avoid problems and bureaucratic delays. If your review boards meet only once per quarter, make sure to tell project managers about deadlines well in advance.

Planning for the Implementation

If you haven't already done so, read Chapters 2 and 3 carefully. Read the "Who Owns the Data Now?" section in Chapter 6. Also, at least skim the Introduction and Chapters 1, 7, and 8 to get some context and expectations management tips for SFDC.

In planning for implementation of the SFDC system, there are a number of issues to think through and adapt to your company policies.

Data Quality and the Continuity of Information

SFDC is destined to be the system of record for the "customer master," so it is important that customer records be as meaningful and complete as possible. There are a number of constraints and cross-currents IT personnel need to consider when developing standards for both data quality and continuity:

- Customer data should be complete for a horizon of three years or more. While "more is better," it is very unusual for anyone to care about orders or other customer interactions that are more than five years old—even the IRS and the courts won't care what happens beyond seven years.

- The company will need to develop policies for how much historical information will be brought into the SFDC system as part of the initial implementation, and for the conditions under which information should be archived. While the goal is to keep information intact as much as possible, SFDC's storage costs (beyond the gigabyte or two provided as part of the initial account and user setup) can become an annoyance. Note that SFDC has created some new storage options that improve the situation here—ask the SFDC sales reps about new pricing options.

- The rule of thumb for customer-oriented data must be "If it's not in SFDC, it doesn't exist," because that is the reality from an end user's perspective. Our Web 2.0 habits and the short-attention-span-theater management style that prevails today mean that decisions will be made long before anyone has time to unpack and process an archive file.

- Despite the immediate-term focus, there must be a standard of quality for data to be allowed in to SFDC: the new data must result in increased credibility and better ease of use for the system. Thus, if the data contain a lot of duplicates or noise, it's better to keep those data out of the system until they can be brought up to snuff. The rationale here is the need to reinforce the virtuous circle: more confidence in the system means more users of the system, who bring in more data, which results in more visibility, which builds further confidence in the system. Bad data cause this cycle to run in reverse, causing a general degradation of the system's value.

- Unique external keys are fundamental for data quality, particularly when SFDC will be integrated with external systems. The best candidates for universal keys are the email address and cookie ID (for leads and contacts); the D-U-N-S number, Web site address, and main phone number (for accounts); and the transaction ID (or time stamp) for opportunities, contracts, and cases. Of course, SFDC generates its own unique UOID for every object in the system, but those identifiers are case sensitive and may not be storable in an external system. You will need to have pointers to objective external information when doing integration or data warehousing projects.

- Certain SFDC records and artifacts cannot be deleted once they are created. Specifically, `users`, `forecast hierarchies`, `workflows`, `customizable forecasting`, `person accounts`, `custom fiscal years`, and `multi-currency` can never be removed once they are instantiated. While some of these items can be renamed, it is best that obsolete records and artifacts not be recycled because this practice can confuse historical analyses and comparisons.

- Integration between SFDC and outside systems gives users more visibility, leverage, and control. Even so, the more systems with which the SFDC system is tightly integrated, the higher the likelihood of data corruption and duplicates. In a perfect world, these problems wouldn't happen—but in the real world, the tiniest revisions to the integration code, upgrades to external applications, or business process workflow can cause new bugs to appear. Use an integration strategy that is as *loosely coupled* as possible to satisfy the company's business requirement, as a read-only mashup is far safer for the data in both SFDC and the external system than a "full-duplex" replication or synchronization scheme.

Once you've established those policies and standards, it's important to identify the owners of data quality for every phase of the SFDC project. During the initial construction and deployment, the implementation team (including the external-system integration people) will own the problem: identify those individuals and assign them the tasks of developing metrics and meeting objectives. After the system is live, the data quality problem will be owned mainly by the system administrators and architectural review team (see Chapter 4).

Support and Administration

During the planning phase, it's a good idea to specify administrative policies and think through how help desk and administrative tasks will be handled during each phase of the system life cycle. Here are recommended best practices:

- Although duplicates and noisy data are annoying, best practices call for disabling the `delete` and `merge record` functions for all standard users. While these users should be flagging records for deletion or consolidation, their flags should simply hide the bad data. System administrators need to do the data fixes promptly, but they won't be able to identify or solve root causes if users have "papered over" the problem.

- User login IDs (typically, this is the user's email address) must be unique for all users forever. For example, if a user's address is joe@shmoe.com, the system must never let that email address be used again by any SFDC customer. While this requirement is not especially onerous, if your company has a lot of employees and some of them have common names[2] before the "@," you'll want to develop some sort of a standard for these SFDC login IDs before assigning system IDs.

- Setting a policy for the user alias in SFDC will be surprisingly important, particularly if you want to develop reports that automatically filter for an individual's perspective (e.g., "Show all tasks generated by me"). The aliases need to be unique, so a scheme based on first and last initials works only in the smallest implementations—even a three-initial strategy tends to fall apart after a few hundred users.[3] For larger user bases, we recommend assigning user aliases based on a nomenclature of first initial, middle initial, and last name. If overlaps still occur, we recommend adding a single digit at the end of the last names for the overlapping users.

- The number of administrators should be kept to the bare minimum (to avoid data corruption and system misconfiguration problems), while satisfying the needs of users. In operations with one site and fewer than 100 users, a single SFDC administrator (with a backup who has privileges, but almost never logs in) is sufficient. Even in large multilocation operations, one administrator per "shift" (one for the Americas, one for Europe, Middle East, and Africa [EMEA], and one for Asia/Australia) can be enough. I can't conceive of a situation requiring more than six SFDC administrators (two for each shift).

- Irrespective of the number of administrators, each of them needs to take a week's worth of SFDC training before the administrator is allowed on the system. Even if "they've worked with it before," SFDC's administrative tasks become increasingly complex every six months or so, and administrators regularly make visible, annoying mistakes when configuring the security and access privileges, lead assignment rules, case assignment and escalation rules, and workflow approval processes. An under-educated administrator who is trying to import or cleanse data can cause an amazing amount of damage in short order. SFDC has recently introduced administrator certification tests and classes, and it's a great idea to send at least your main administrators to these sessions.

- Generally speaking, very few nonadministrative users should have access to importing tools and API access. This is an area where self-service is absolutely the wrong strategy.

---

2. Bill Gates's email address was bill@microsoft.com for more than a decade, despite the size of his company. According to industry lore, Microsoft had more than 6,000 employees before the company hired another "Bill." Most companies will not have this level of discipline about email addresses and common names.

3. Even though the namespace for three alphabetic characters could theoretically cover 17,576 individuals, the distribution frequency of letters is by no means linear with names. In an Irish or Chinese company, a large proportion of the names will converge to only a few initials, and the three-character namespace will soon be exhausted.

- SFDC supports a number of administrative models, thanks to its very flexible role-based privileges. While a "follow the sun" (shift-based) administrative model is easy to think through, it may not be flexible enough for the company's real needs (particularly at the end of the quarter, when everyone is stressed). Consider a delegated model (where "power users" local to an office can do some administrative actions and offload "administrivia" such as resetting passwords). In highly complex implementations with a lot of external integration points, it's a best practice to use a federated model, where individual administrators become subject-matter experts in particular areas of the system. To make any delegated administration model work, IT personnel will need to apply some sort of change-control aid. Take a look at the free ChangeControl plugin from the AppExchange as one possibility (see Chapter 7 for more on the tools needed by system administrators).

User Accessibility

SFDC has done a lot to make its system as friendly as possible to people with disabilities, and the "Section 508" features (required by the Americans with Disabilities Act [ADA]) may be particularly relevant if your company is a nonprofit organization or a government contractor.

As good as the SFDC system is, however, there's only so much that can be done with browser-based applications. The basic data entry and interaction pages are fairly accessible with keyboard shortcuts and "hooks" for readers and voice synthesis. To work well, the reader application must be able to handle frames, CSS, and JavaScript. Unfortunately, turning on accessibility mode inevitably disables some of the more advanced Web 2.0 features of SFDC. Further, some parts of the system—calendars, dashboards, more advanced pages, wizards, and administrative setup pages—are not really "accessible" by the standards. Although VisualForce pages that you build yourself can be made more ADA friendly, many of the third-party plugins found in the AppExchange probably do not meet the government accessibility standards.

SFDC is likely to enhance the accessibility of the system over time, but people with special accessibility needs are unlikely to be productive in the current system beyond basic sales, marketing, and call-center activities.

Security

Security is always a tradeoff. When I used to consult for the U.S. Department of Defense, the agency had A-level compliant computers that were secure, but nearly useless. B2-level compliant computers were better, but it was still easy to get caught in a corner without a meaningful escape key.

SFDC is not nearly as restrictive (indeed, the default configuration is very open), but it is based on Secure Sockets Layer (SSL) and carries an SAS 70 type II certification. SFDC can be configured for Single Sign On (SSO) through the Lightweight Directory Access Protocol (LDAP). The system can be set up to achieve a high level of commercial security, using a wide range of controls that should be thought through prior to implementation and deployment:

- Field-level access controls

- Field-level "CRUD controls"

- Field-level audit trails

- Role-specific record types

- User role hierarchies (for data visibility)

- User profiles

- User-level screen layouts and views

- Conditional "lockdown" of data

- User-level sharing of records and forecasts

- User level activity controls (e.g., reporting)

- Delegation of approvals

- Delegation of administrative privileges

- Login hours

- IP range restrictions

- Machine authorization

- Session auto-timeout

- Account lockout (after N unsuccessful logins)

- Password strength

- Password aging

The proper security tradeoff seems to be where everyone can get their jobs done, 80% of users never have a problem, and 20% are occasionally irritated. For example, password settings should be tight enough so that someone forgets his or her password once a week and gets locked out of the system. By comparison, if dozens of users get locked out during the closing week of the quarter, the security policy has probably gone too far.

An important prerequisite for good security is having the support of the boss. The boss has to show that he or she cares about protecting company information, protecting the privacy of customer information, phishing, and information leakage. The boss has to authorize the budget for end-user training on security (only about 30 minutes—but for *every user*) and set up some sort of HR policy for identifying and dealing with the security risk posed by disgruntled employees.

An important area of security planning is developing policies for on-boarding new employees and off-boarding old ones. This process requires an explicit link from the HR function, and these policies should take immediate action as soon as the HR people know that an offer letter has been accepted or an employee has given notice.

Compliance

Given that SFDC has already been deployed to nearly 50,000 companies around the world, it's a safe bet that it complies with any relevant regulations and standards. Of course, if your company has special requirements, check with your friendly SFDC sales rep. (Also, check the SFDC blogs and forums to see if there's been any chatter among the cognoscenti.)

The bigger issue is usually the company's own data and surrounding internal practices. For example, lapses in manual procedures for credit card information handling might result in a failed payment-card industry (PCI) audit. Likewise, ongoing use of external spreadsheets might mean that the company's forecasting process would fail a Sarbanes-Oxley Act audit.

Our general advice is to keep the SFDC data policy simple: any highly confidential or risky data should not be stored in the SFDC database. Even if some users need access to confidential data as part of their "SFDC activities," those data can be stored in an existing system of record and accessed via a read-only mashup or a pop-up window. Check out the discussion in Chapter 7 for more on this topic.

Integration

SFDC is one of the easiest systems to integrate with. It has a well-documented and rich API, and its solid SOAP-based Web services architecture supports both inbound and outbound messaging. Off-the-shelf adaptors are available from several companies (see Chapter 7) to link the SFDC system to dozens of application packages or to nearly any application a company's IT department has built internally.

Integration with Microsoft Outlook is available as part of a free plugin from SFDC, but it is really suited only for one-way "synching" of emails, contacts, tasks, and events. The plugin runs inside the Outlook binary running on the client PC. Although it works in two-way mode, the practical implications (in ease of use and risk of data duplication) of this mode may result in many wasted hours for users. This replication issue becomes even more obvious with Microsoft Exchange and shared folders. If your company needs ambitious and sophisticated integration between SFDC and Outlook, your IT team will probably need to write a Visual Basic or C# plugin themselves.

Integration with Microsoft Office (Excel and Word) is also available for free from SFDC, and these plugins have worked well in most customer engagements. If you need to do some fancy stuff, the Excel connector is available as an open-source version. Of course, the

Office .NET compatibility libraries let you do anything you want over Web services' SOAP calls—it's a simple matter of coding.[4]

Integration with IBM/Lotus Notes is also available as a free plugin for client PCs from the AppExchange. I have no idea exactly which Lotus products are actually covered (probably only Mail and Organizer), and I have not seen this plugin used in production. But it almost certainly works for someone—SFDC wouldn't have created the plugin if the company weren't on the hook to a big customer for this integration.

Integration with LDAP is available from several sources, providing SSO capabilities for users. These adaptors typically run on one of the company's servers, but the best way to understand their deployment and configuration options is to do a trial evaluation of the software before the implementation starts in earnest.

Deeper levels of application integration are riskier and more costly. Please read the section in Chapter 7 on this topic, as it's important for cost and security reasons to eliminate any marginal integration "requirements."

As discussed in Chapters 1 and 4, it's important to do some "value engineering" analysis before committing to an ambitious integration program. The ongoing costs of integration can be just as significant as they are for custom application development.

Implementation

If you haven't done so already, read all of Chapters 4 and 6 and their guidance on project management, deployment cycles, and the political side of user adoption. Even if members of the IT department aren't directly involved with all the topics described, knowing how the SFDC team is working will help the IT professionals and SFDC mavens collaborate better.

During the SFDC implementation, the IT team may not need to do much directly in the system. Usually, SFDC's own professional services team is used, or a specialist consultant is brought in. The reason: the core implementation is surprisingly short, and it's often not worth IT's time to gain the knowledge required.

That said, IT personnel should be involved to make sure that key requirements and standards are being taken care of—and to make sure that "nice to have" features aren't being assigned an unnecessary high priority. The biggest enemies of a clean implementation are these three items:

- Spurious requirements

- Anything that will detract from system credibility (in particular, unneeded fields or "featuritis")

- Anything that will cause scope creep

---

4. And localization. And testing. And documentation. And maintenance. And the help desk.

Here are some specific things to watch out for so as to keep the implementation team on track:

- Keep pages as sparse as possible. Use `hidden fields`, `page layouts`, `record types`, and `collapsible sections`.

- Remove buttons that are ill-advised or "training wheels" options, such as `delete`, `merge`, and `QuickCreate`.

- Use typed fields, pick lists, and lookup fields as often as possible. Avoid long-text fields.

- Use field `validation rules` for manual entry; auto-populate as many fields as possible with `formula fields`, `rollup fields`, `workflow rules`, and APEX code.

- Use `matrix reports` to quickly find data exceptions and problem trends; use Excel pivot tables to find even more data anomalies before they become problems.

- Prune the number of reports and report folders. The initial set of reports that comes with the SFDC system is overwhelming.

- Deploy a single instance of SFDC unless the company has some very unusual requirements. For a multidivisional company with international operations, one comprehensive instance should be all it needs. Of course, the (free) `Salesforce to Salesforce` feature can bridge implementations, but over the long run a multi-instance deployment will be more costly and inflexible than it needs to be.

- Avoid frivolous use of `APEX` and `VisualForce` code. If the features are really required, go for it. But for every function or page built using these technologies, there will be operational consequences and sacrifices of self-maintainability over time.

- Make sure that the item-level, `user-defined help` items are populated with information that's comprehensible by real users. The system is self-documenting if you use it properly. Also make sure that user cheat sheets are written and stored both in the system's `documents` area and in the project wiki.

- Implement the `Ideas` application for internal users. This free SFDC application is a great way to collect user feedback and understand ongoing priorities.

Implementing Data Quality

During the architecture and design phase, the most highly leveraged step the IT team can take is to remove unnecessary data items and restructure the data model to match the company's business processes. Left to their own devices, users tend to make several classic errors:

- Too-lax security settings
- Too many system administrators
- Incorrect `role` and `forecast hierarchies`
- `Custom fields` attached to the wrong objects
- Incorrect `custom objects`
- Erroneous `assignment rules`, `autoresponse rules`, `formulas`, and `data validation`
- Bogus reports and dashboards

The good news is that fixing these issues is typically a one-time job. There won't be a lot of ongoing need for system fixes from users—particularly if you lock most of the system down so that they can't hurt themselves.

During the construction phase, the team needs to build in as much data quality as possible (particularly using human-factors engineering) and invest in self-corrective mechanisms (particularly in system integration interfaces). For example:

- Building a `customer self-service` Web portal with an "account maintenance" page will enable customers to fix data quality problems and make updates on their own. Even though the customers and prospects will be updating only a few fields (e.g., contact information), the cumulative effect of all those data fixes can be amazing. Portals are the *only* economical way to do things if your company is a consumer-facing business with millions of records.

- Use of an email-validation loop for new `lead` creation, cookies to identify return registration (as discussed in Chapter 10), and `campaigns` is a great way to cut down on the number of low-quality `leads` and `contact` duplication—perhaps by as much as 50%.

- Developing "check first" code for all external system integration (particularly the Web site) can prevent the creation of duplicate `leads`, `contacts`, `accounts`, `opportunities`, and `cases`. As these records typically represent 80% of the records in the system, preventing duplication in these areas can yield a dramatic improvement in data quality.

- Implementing a data-enrichment service for `leads`, `contacts`, and `accounts` can mean important improvements in perceived data quality and completeness. These services, which can be implemented as a Web service in real time or on a nightly basis, can automatically validate data and correct typos.

- For external system integrations, a data queuing mechanism can be used to handle SFDC timeouts or busy periods.

- Improving the data import and cleansing/enrichment processes will make a big difference in the value of the data, particularly for `leads`. Spend time developing templates, macros, scripts, and checklists that turn the `lead` preprocessing cycle into a repeatable, bug-free process. See Chapter 10 for more discussion of this topic.

Even before the SFDC implementation team creates user reports and dashboards, its members should create data quality reports, dashboards, and monthly metrics. In addition to using SFDC's data quality dashboards, create reports that can measure the following items:

- Number of incomplete records (to identify fields that are habitually left blank)

- Number of records marked as "bad data" (particularly `leads`)

- Number of new unread/neglected records (particularly `leads`)

- Number of `accounts` with no child objects (i.e., `contacts`, `contact roles`, `opportunities`, or `cases`)

- Number of records with "data bounces" (where a single field is repeatedly changed back and forth[5] between a couple of values)

- Number of records with contradictory data (e.g., states that don't agree with countries, postal codes, email domain country identifiers, or phone city codes)

- Number of records with out-of-bounds values (e.g., 12-digit ZIP codes), silly input (a 2,000-character text entry or a 2-character `notes` record[6]), or data in the wrong field (look for email addresses or phone numbers in text fields)

- Number of records that appear to be duplicates (particularly for `leads` and `contacts`, but also for `accounts`, `cases`, and `opportunities`)

- Number of records that are out of date (particularly open `opportunities` and `cases` that haven't been updated since their deadlines)

---

5. This problem is most easily quantified by enabling `field history tracking`, and it usually indicates faulty code or integration logic.
6. SFDC's internal reports cannot "see" the `notes` object. Reports on `notes` must be done via the `Excel connector`, `Data loader`, or another API-based data access tool.

Areas Where IT Personnel Need to Be Directly Involved in SFDC

Even the most independent system implementation team will need assistance from central IT in a number of areas. For example, they'll need assistance with policy standards, review boards, and infrastructure configuration (e.g., the SFDC team may need IT to open a port in an internal firewall).

The SFDC team will also need assistance with any data that are to be imported or migrated: they need to get the schemas and metadata, understand the semantics, and be informed of any unusual behavior linked to the data. They'll need data samples to run pilot migrations, and the full data set to do the final import. They may need some assistance to properly placate external systems at certain points in their deployment.

The SFDC team will also need assistance in coding and configuring some external systems, particularly the company's Web site and eCommerce system. Some trivial work (a few lines of HTML) is required to set up the `Web2Lead` and `Web2Case` functions. In implementing the `partner portal` and `customer self-service portal`, the SFDC team will need to integrate IT's HTML, CSS, and JavaScript code with templates provided with the SFDC components. If someone builds a `Sites` application—using `VisualForce` and SFDC's deployment platform—the application will need to be linked into the company's main Web site. This effort may require writing a trivial amount of HTML and JavaScript, but somebody has to build that application and push it into the main site infrastructure.

If your company plans to use the `support` module in SFDC, some work must be done in the company's mail server to fully integrate the `Email2Case` functionality. Some integration must also be done between SFDC's `case` object and the defect reporting system (such as JIRA or Bugtraq).

If your company operates a significant call center (inbound or outbound), integrating SFDC with its phone system will require a bit of IT time. Several CTI adaptors are available as off-the-shelf products, but they still require some configuration and setup.

As users make requests for plugins found in the AppExchange (see Chapter 7), at least some setup work will be required to install those programs. Usually, this amounts to an hour or so of IT time to implement simple features, but it can be significantly longer for some of the complex external applications. The rule of thumb: the more expensive the plugin is, the more IT will need to be involved in its setup and configuration.

If the company decides to develop some custom code—either as internal `VisualForce` or `APEX`, or as external server-side functionality—the IT department will almost certainly be called upon to use the Eclipse IDE with the SFDC plugins. They really work! But beware the JavaScript, CSS, and HTML-interpreter goblins that live within your Web browser. There are literally hundreds of bizarre rendering and behavioral bugs unique to Firefox, Internet Explorer, and Safari—and the bugs seem to change with each bug patch of the browser. You might wish that these issues were merely a faded memory, but an amazing array of anomalies continues to occur with code that looks legal, particularly inside `S-controls`. The bottom line: leave lots of time for testing any browser code you deploy!

The biggest single area requiring IT effort will be any integration of the SFDC system with external systems. Even if your company can use the pure off-the-shelf adaptors, IT personnel will need to be involved with defining the business process activities and triggers for the integration, aligning the data items, and testing for corruption-free, duplicate-free operation. This analysis can entail a significant effort. If you haven't already done so, read the section on integration in Chapter 7. Unfortunately, the juiciest integration problems almost always involve external code and very tricky data manipulations. Although external consultants can help in these areas, in the long run the highest-quality and most economical outcomes will happen because of dedicated internal IT resources. As Chapters 9 through 11 suggest, executives may demand a dozen integrations for the fanciest CRM implementations.

Project Management and Deployment

Even if members of the IT department aren't asked to handle the project management for the SFDC implementation, you should know what the project managers are doing and which model they are using. As discussed in Chapter 4, we highly recommend an Agile project management style. Although SFDC rarely involves extensive development, Agile's incremental delivery style, user focus, and iterative testing are essential to ensuring the success and controlling the costs of SFDC deployments. The larger the project, the more essential Agile management and phased deployments will be.

Finally, in setting up security features and access controls, err on the side of laxness (at least initially) to maximize early adoption, collaboration, and information sharing. Over time, the controls can be easily tightened, but at the beginning do everything you can to *not* intimidate or frustrate users.

Ongoing Usage

Given Agile project management and quick deployment cycles, "ongoing usage" of the SFDC system will probably start within weeks of system procurement. Even though only a few users may be actively on the system, in the words of Emperor Palpatine, it will be a "fully armed and operational battle station."

As users are set up and activated, it's often best to log in to their accounts before you hand them over, so you can configure things for the users before they "dip a toe into the water." To do so, when you first create the user account, set the user email address to your own address and log in to the account. Unfortunately, there are a few settings in the account that can be tailored only if you log in as the user:

- `Grant login access` for administrators; this date can be set to several years in the future if you want indefinite access.

- Set the `application` for the user (assuming that it needs to be one of the non-default applications).

- Set the default `dashboard` for the user.

- Set the `report` lists (folder contents and ordering) for the user.

- Tailor the `UI options` for the user (e.g., should the user see hovering items?).

- Collapse or expand `collapsible sections`.

Once you've taken these step, reset the email address to the user's address and reset the account password. You'll still be able to log in to the account indefinitely, but the user will now have control of his or her own password.

One little issue that often turns into a full-blown nuisance is SFDC's user authentication system. The first computer a user logs in from doesn't need to be authenticated, but all subsequent ones do. The authentication drill can be done in 60 seconds, but it generates an amazing amount of static from users. So here's a trick: set the system's network security feature to exempt all computers within your company's IP address range. You'll find this feature in SFDC's `Administrative Setup` area, and it's largely self-explanatory. The address range you put in can consist of two major address increments (e.g., 66.0.0.0 to 68.0.0.0), but don't set it wider than is needed to cover all of the business's locations (as this would unduly weaken login security).

Encouraging Adoption

Users will be coming on to the SFDC system in waves. The goal from day one is to get people using the system, filling it with the data they need to complete their own tasks. It is essential that users not be asked to put in data that "would be great," because they will view this request as a tax unless it helps them directly in some way.

Entering good data is the number one way to improve adoption and the level of utilization for the SFDC system. If you implemented data quality and enrichment features (discussed earlier), turn them on as early as practicable. Make sure that people are trained in how to use the data quality features. Set expectations properly, and then please the users with how much better things get every few weeks.

Start using the data quality reports as early as you can. Look for trends in the data, to understand where problems are occurring. When an obvious data entry problem crops up, use (or tighten up) field validation rules to prevent the problem from spreading. Whenever you discover data pollution from outside sources, don't fix the records until you have also fixed the external source of the pollution.

The SFDC project team will be focusing on "good news" generation and politics. At the same time, it is essential to have solid metrics on how groups are adopting the system.

THE VIRTUAL HELP DESK

Help desks are important to users (so they can get simple answers from friendly/non-IT people) and IT teams (so they can avoid the dumbest questions) alike. Even so, most SFDC customers don't have a help desk function.

The first line of defense is the SFDC system itself: fully populated "bubble help" for items on the screen, a documents section full of cheat sheets, a FAQ, and helpful links within each of the major page types.

The next line of defense is the project wiki, which should include reference documents, cheat sheets, podcasts (5-minute training sessions), and ScreenCam tutorials (keep them to less than 15 minutes in length).

Even with all of this documentation available at users' fingertips, you have to be ready for people who don't read or who are clever enough to discover problems you didn't anticipate. To do so, you need some sort of virtual help desk.

The help desk won't really be staffed, and it's not really a desk. Rather, it's an email address and a voicemail box at which users can report problems. Someone in IT needs to check these sources *very* frequently—ideally, twice an hour. Most of the time, they'll be empty, but you never want to have users hanging in the wind for more than 30 minutes.

SFDC's built-in `adoption dashboard` isn't a bad place to start. You can then go even further by creating some weekly reports that provide a bit more detail:

- Number of logins and length of login per user
- Number of `lead`, `contact`, `account`, `opportunity`, and `case` records created and updated
- Number of fields changed per user, as indicated by `field history tracking` entries
- Number of `tasks` created and updated

Administration

Even though much of the SFDC administration may be done by people who don't work for the central IT department, this section pulls together guidelines for all administrators.

For small to medium-size operations, SFDC administration is usually a part-time job. It's nowhere near as challenging or specialized as the administration of SAP, Oracle, or even

WHAT IS OBJECT HYSTERESIS?

Hysteresis is a term used to describe hardware that has nondeterministic behavior, for which outputs are time dependent. Let me be the first to introduce you to this phenomenon as it applies to software.

SFDC is a SaaS application that is delivered as a set of Web services. Most of the time, results from instantiating or modifying things appear (essentially) instantly to all users of the system.

However, because of SFDC's loosely coupled services and replication delay, some complex objects may not appear to all users and services at the same instant. For example, if you have successfully created a new report, it may not show up instantaneously when you search for it. Updating `custom objects` and clicking some buttons are actions that generate a "We'll send you an email when we're done" message (e.g., use of the `forecast hierarchy`, recalculating `object sharing rules`, updating `S-controls`, pushing updates to the `sandbox`, and updating `dashboards`); these messages may take a minute or more to be available to all users, even if they appear available to the individual making the change.

While the object update is being propagated, the system will pretend to have performed the update even though it hasn't completed. For a minute or more of the hysteresis, the system will demonstrate uncertain behavior. These effects can be quite annoying to developers who are trying to debug something.

The best antidote for this problem is to chill out, work on some other detail, or just grab a cappuccino. Make it a decaf. Sometimes the bugs are due to hysteresis; at other times they occur because you've made a minor mistake and just need to take a break. Either way, why sweat it if the system may behave properly in a couple of minutes?

Microsoft applications. Real training is required for you to be effective, but most of the time this is a job that makes sense for people who have a technical bent but *not* IT depth.[7]

The first order of business for administrators is to create a virtual help desk to handle the most basic questions. Create and collect as many cheat sheets as you can for users, and post all of them in SFDC's documents area. Also publish these documents, as well as FAQs and other helpful documents (e.g., user guides for the Outlook and Notes plugins), in the project wiki. Obtain any needed training materials (including audio tracks for podcasts and WebEx sessions for Web replay) and post them, along with links to SFDC's online tutorials, in the project wiki as well. The joy you'll get from the first time you say the administrator's mantra—"RTFM[8]"—will make it worth all the effort.

---

7. Of course, if your company has 1,000 users and has integrated SFDC with SAP accounting and outsourced payroll and distribution applications, at least one of the SFDC system administrators will need to be an IT professional.

8. In a book such as this, I'm not allowed to spell out this acronym. All you need to know is that R stands for "read," T stands for "the," and M stands for "manual."

One topic deserves special mention. You will most likely receive calls from power users who claim to need system administrator access. Almost invariably, adding a "cowboy" system administrator is a serious mistake. Just say no.

Weekly Activities

SFDC's typical administrative duties seem to follow a weekly cycle: a lot of things will go wrong Monday morning (don't ask me why), and a couple of tasks need to be done once a week on the day of your choice. These cyclical duties include the following tasks:

- Running and storing a weekly snapshot of the system data and attachments

- Doing data updates to the `sandbox` (assuming your company has bought the full data `sandbox`)[9]

- Running deduping tools such as RingLead or DemandTools

- Running adoption dashboards

- Running data quality reports

  ➡ If you find fields that are consistently blank more than 30% of the time, consider removing them from page views.

  ➡ If you find a set of bad data records, don't delete them; instead, quarantine them until you've been able to troubleshoot the problem and fix its root cause.

- Deactivating users (either due to departure from the company or transfer to a new job that does not require SFDC access)

- Transferring records due to changes in job responsibility or territory coverage

- Modifying roles or record-sharing rules

- Importing leads and contacts

- Modifying price lists (particularly if your company does a lot of promotions and limited-time offers)

- Changing delegation and escalation paths to account for absences or extended travel

A bit of elaboration is required regarding the mass-record transfers that are needed whenever a new user starts in the system, a territory is split, or a user is assigned to new accounts. Generally speaking, the `accounts`, `leads`, `contacts`, and open `opportunities` should be reassigned to the new user. `Closed opportunities`, however, should not be transferred to the new user, as this change will lead to erroneous calculation of commissions

---

9. Make *sure* to coordinate the timing of these updates with the work of any developers who are using the sandbox, lest you blow away some of their work.

BACKUPS AND SNAPSHOTS AND REPLICAS, OH MY!

Although SFDC performs continuous replication and online backup, restoring a system based on those data means entering into a lengthy and expensive consulting contract (unless you can prove the data loss was SFDC's fault . . . good luck on that one). Read those words again, and take heed.

Make a complete system snapshot—including attachments—at least once per month, and make weekly snapshots of all system records. This kind of backup requires only the click of a link, so there's no excuse not to make these copies. You can also use SFDC's `Data loader` tool to perform a scripted data dump to your company's own servers.

Keep several months' worth of archives on a company-owned disk. Storage is cheap, so use it to lower the cost of mistakes. You'll thank me for this advice someday.

It's also very helpful to keep backups of the system configuration, metadata, and setup. This can be done through the `sandbox`, but the data can also be exported to a local storage system via SFDC's free `Eclipse` plugin. Having these data available can also be very helpful for cloning your system if you need to set up a second instance.

You should also consider investing in a replication tool like those available from Pervasive, Relational Junction, or Informatica. These tools can be used to create local replicas of your company's SFDC database for disaster recovery, real-time data warehousing, or other purposes.

(and may propagate problems to the accounting system or data warehouse). Further, `closed opportunities` should be completely locked down so that neither the new rep nor the old rep can modify them. If the new rep wants to see old `opportunities`, use the `sales teams` function to give him or her visibility into the records. To perform these reassignments, if just one or two changes must be made, use the wizards found in the SFDC system. By contrast, if the entire salesforce is being redesigned, it's usually better to use the `Data loader` tool and Excel to make all these changes.

If you have implemented significant add-on applications to SFDC (such as an email blaster, document management system, or commissions/incentive management system), these third-party products will likely have administrative needs of their own. I won't cover the issues here, but someone on *your staff* will need to take care of these responsibilities. This means taking the vendor's class in configuration and administration, and setting aside time for the care and feeding of the third-party application on a weekly basis.

On-Demand Activities

You will occasionally need to resolve user problems in real time.

- Unlocking user accounts or resetting passwords due to user forgetfulness.

- Troubleshooting email campaigns or auto-responders that generate excessive bounced emails.

- Adding exempted IP ranges, to free specific users from the authentication-email-and-ridiculous-certificate drill.

- Using login privileges temporarily granted to rapidly troubleshoot problems and configure the user interface to be much more approachable. As there are a half-dozen little things that can make a big difference to end users—and most of them are poorly documented—the ability to "log in as you" lets the administrator improve the user experience in less time than it would take to explain to the users how to fix it themselves.

Maintaining Data Quality

No matter which tasks you perform as part of your regular duties, you as the administrator serve as the first line of defense for ensuring data quality in the SFDC system. Spend the right amount of time to do these things correctly—everyone will notice errors, or thank you for solving their problems.

If only a small number of records needs to be merged, use SFDC's Merge Lead button. Due to the complexity of contacts, however, you are more likely to need to use SFDC's merge function—a wizard that is accessed via a 120-character URL. Grab it by visiting the www.SFDC-secrets.com site.

SFDC's internal features dedupe only leads against leads or contacts against contacts, using a fairly simple matching algorithm. For more sophisticated deduping, you will need to use CRMfusion's or RingLead's deduping tools. They provide some very advanced features (such as fuzzy logic) to find a wider range of candidate duplicate records. However, harnessing the power and speed of these tools requires some discipline on the administrator's part, because there isn't an effective "undo" mechanism that you can employ after you merge a false duplicate. (As always, make a full backup of all potentially affected records before you run the deduping tool.) Do the deduping in several passes, by starting with the strictest matching criteria, merging those records, and gradually loosening the criteria. Once your match criteria produce more than 20% spurious matches, stop using the tool for this cycle. In most SFDC implementations, anything less than 10% duplication is perfectly acceptable (and anything less than 3% seems almost unattainable).

Accounts should sometimes be merged, if they really are the same entity. Before you go there, think about whether the accounts should be merged in the first place. Are these accounts related in some way—do they have a parent, child, or sibling relationship? SFDC's parent account functionality was specifically designed to create account hierarchies, which can be very helpful for understanding company politics and purchasing department behavior. If the two accounts in question are siblings (say, GE Jet Engines and GE Medical), create a parent account (in this example, GE HQ) with nothing in it (for the time being), and have both of the existing accounts point to it as the parent. Check out the discussion in Chapter 9 about this process. Creating this kind of structure provides much more

428   CHAPTER 13 ■ BEST PRACTICES IN IT

information and context to the customer relationship, so don't merge `accounts` until you've understood this issue. You can use SFDC's internal wizard (with an 80-character URL—grab it at www.SFDC-secrets.com) if you're cheap, or fancy deduping features from RingLead or CRMfusion.

Archiving Data

If your company's SFDC system is overflowing with data or it's time to archive old records, here are guidelines of how to prepare for the archiving:

- Only archive records if you know they are the cause of storage problems, as it's a task you'd like to avoid. Most SFDC records are quite small; it's the attached files and emails that fill up the system.

- You can't delete an object from the system unless its dependent objects are removed first. Tracking all of these relationships down can be time-consuming, so don't plan on completing an archive operation in 20 minutes.

- You may be able to archive just `notes`, `tasks`, and `attached files` to free up the space you need. Because `notes`, `tasks`, and `attachments` are always attached to a record, make sure to capture the UOIDs of the objects they are attached to, to facilitate future searches and joins. Check out the Case Detachifier plugin found in the AppExchange, and use the `view top files by size` feature in the `storage management` area of SFDC `setup`.

- `Leads` are typically never deleted from the system, because you will lose metrics on marketing and `campaigns`. Normally, `leads` are merely transferred to queues that render them invisible to most users. If you plan to remove `leads` from the system, make sure to archive `activities`, `notes`, `attachments`, and `campaign` membership tables that point to each of the archived `leads`.

- `Accounts` should never be deleted from the system. These records are tiny, but they are the top level in an information pyramid that cannot be safely removed. If you need to have old `accounts` disappear from view, use the `type` pick list to create `filters` for `views`, `reports`, and other user touchpoints.

- `Contacts` should follow the same rules as `accounts`, unless a `contact` has been created in the system with no updates to data or related lists. These still-born `contacts` can be safely archived.

- `Opportunities` should follow the same rules as `contacts`. Never let a sales rep convince you to remove an `opportunity` because it's irrelevant.

- Quotes and line items should follow the same rules as opportunities.

- Cases should never be deleted, unless they were spuriously created by an errant piece of internal software. Even then, make sure that the software bug has been resolved before you remove the case.

- Campaigns should never be deleted or archived.

- Users can never be deleted or removed from the system. They can, however, be renamed to indicate that they are deactivated. In addition to deactivating idled users, I recommend changing the name Joe Blow to be {Joe Blow} and the alias to be {JBlow}, as this puts the name at the bottom of alphabetized lists and provides an easy way to filter these names in reports and views. Do *not* recycle individual user accounts (by changing the name entirely), as this will greatly complicate all kinds of historical analysis. Once you have deactivated the user, his or her license will be available for use with a new user account.

Management of the Administrative Function

Once the SFDC system is up and running, the administrators should set up and review a user "suggestion box" forum either using the project wiki or the SFDC Ideas feature. By engaging users to come up with solutions, and polling them on their preferences, the administrative staff can be much more responsive to the users' real needs. This wins big points for the IT department as well as for SFDC itself.

As discussed in Chapter 4, SFDC administrators need to act as or deputize a set of data architects who make decisions about which additions or corrections to the system object model (particularly custom objects and relations) are necessary, which reports should be removed from the system, which AppExchange goodies should be added to the system, and how to best implement user requests.

In a large, multidivisional company, the administrators should also set up a change control board (CCB) to review the list of user requests and allocate resources for the requested changes. If the users are really asking for something big (like a new subsystem or an additional system integration), the CCB would be the vehicle for arbitrating and formalizing budget requests. Figure 13-1 illustrates an example CCB process. The CCB typically meets on a weekly basis when the system is first being deployed, but eventually can move to monthly meetings once the system is stabilized.

Every few quarters, the system needs "meta-administration"—the management of system management. The administrators need to think through how they'll work as a team, whether they should use a federated model of administration, and which kinds of privileges should be delegated to power users.

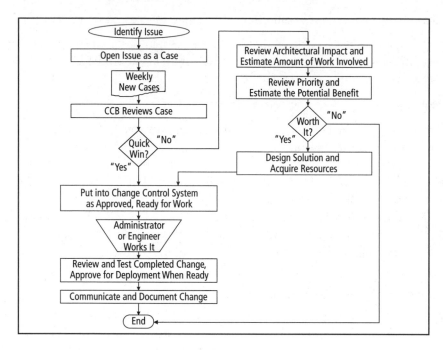

FIGURE 13-1   A change control board review process

APPENDIX A

Tools to Prioritize Requirements

B USINESS DECISIONS ARE DRIVEN by priorities, with tradeoffs being made that allow for sensible allocations of budget and time. All too often, prioritization is a purely political process that yields inconsistent or even illogical results. The tools discussed in this appendix are designed to produce prioritization that incorporates the input of lots of users, yet produces consistent (and maybe even defendable) results for SFDC projects.

Prioritizing Project Requirements

Prioritizing requirements for IT work is something of a black art, but there can be no more important thing to get right in a project. It doesn't matter how tightly executed or beautifully presented a feature is, if it is an unimportant feature. Given that the number one cause of scope creep is a weak or erratic prioritization mechanism, getting this process right produces dividends throughout the entirety of the SFDC implementation project.

No single prioritization tool or method will be appropriate for all companies and situations. This appendix describes a few alternative approaches that you can try with your teams and executives.

Here are questions to ask to evaluate the efficacy of a prioritization method:

- Is the tool easy to understand and use?

- Does the tool elicit the right kind of input from users?

- Does the method produce predictable, credible rankings of features?

- Does the method realistically balance costs versus benefits, or does it lead to over-optimism that blindly leads toward high expectations?

- Do people—particularly management—follow the rankings, or do they overrule them within a few weeks?

An important ingredient of good priority calls is making sure everyone is aware of both the *true* costs and the hoped-for benefits of any choice. It's tempting to focus on the benefits and assume that the costs will be somebody else's problem, so make sure to include *both sides* of the equation in priority discussions. Cost categories include these types of expenditures:

- External fees and expenses (dollars required to satisfy the requirement)

- Internal staff time (person-weeks required to complete the tasks)

- Delay (calendar time required to complete the task)

- Team morale (tough to quantify, but look at unpaid overtime and unrecognized effort)

- Effect on overall SFDC reputation/credibility (tough to quantify, but can work with a scale such as "-- - 0 + ++")

Benefit categories include these types of rewards:

- Revenue increases (expected extra dollars per quarter)

- Cost decreases (expected external cost savings per quarter)

- Time savings (expected person-hours per quarter)

- Error reduction (tough to quantify, so use a scale such as "n/a small medium large")

- Flexibility/responsiveness (from the customer's or user's perspective; use a scale such as "n/a small medium large")

The Delphi Method

The Delphi Method was developed by the RAND Corporation years ago when members of that company noticed that forecasts made in a bureaucratic setting weren't as accurate as they should be. Indeed, the larger the group, the less accurate the forecast. The ability of important or eloquent people to sway the group's opinion overwhelmed "the wisdom of crowds." In extreme cases, the collective IQ of groups sank to the lowest common denominator of its members.

The Delphi Method is able to make forecasts and tradeoffs *more reliable* as the number of people involved in planning grows. One of the innovations of this method is to ask participants what level of confidence they have in their own forecasts, so that less-certain inputs are given less weight.

We've adapted this model for prioritizing requirements at the start of an SFDC project.

1. Create a column on the spreadsheet to indicate the importance of the requirement ("importance" needs to be a number from 1 to 10 indicating the business significance of the requirement).

2. Create another column to indicate the rank or management level of the main champion of the requirement (higher is better, as it's an indicator of internal political visibility).

3. Add a column on the spreadsheet for each of the cost and benefit areas mentioned previously, and fill in as many of the rows as you can.

4. Create a column on the spreadsheet to indicate the responder's level of confidence about the information on that row. (This level should be ranked from 1 to 10, with 1 indicating "We really don't know" and 10 indicating "We are very sure.")

5. Use formulas in Excel to create a weighted average that includes each of these factors to form a total score for each requirement line item.

You can find an example of the results on the book's Web site (www.sfdc-secrets.com).

You will want to have one of these spreadsheet scores for each major SFDC stakeholder group. The total number of spreadsheets should be kept to less than 20 for manageability, and preferably there will be fewer than 10 spreadsheets. The final step is to aggregate (with one last weighted average) the "final scores" across all stakeholders, producing a single composite score for each line item. Use these scores to create an initial ranking of the requirements.

Of course, this scoring system will not make any decision, but it does provide insight into what the organization thinks is important. It can at least be a starting point for discussion and negotiation, as it weighs the costs, benefits, importance of the item, and level of confidence in the information. See this book's Web site for example Delphi Method prioritization spreadsheets.

Even if you don't believe in the Delphi Method for ranking requirements, go through the exercise anyway to create composite "scores" for the costs and benefits of the line items. These cost–benefit indices can then serve as inputs for the simpler prioritization techniques discussed in the rest of this appendix.

Prioritize via Investment

In this prioritization method, you do not attempt to collect or evaluate preferences from a large number of people. Instead, you just ask a few executives to play an investment game, and then generate a weighted average of their responses. It's moderately fun to play this game, and it can be done in as little as 5 minutes of an executive's time.

The setup for this investment game is simple: each participant is given a hypothetical $100,000 to invest in SFDC in the way that would provide the best value for his or her group (or personal agenda). Each individual must invest the entire $100,000 in SFDC, allocating it to those features that will make the most difference, either by yielding the most benefit or avoiding the most pain. You can see an example of what the voting form looks like on the book's Web site, www.sfdc-secrets.com.

After you've collected the input from the participants (there should be a separate spreadsheet or piece of paper for each person), ask them to do the exercise a second time, but this time to apportion the $100,000 according to what they believe the business impact would be *for the company overall*. Don't let the executives see their old votes—give them a blank piece of paper. The instructions are along this line: "Suppose that investing in SFDC will result in $1 million (or, for a really big business, $100 million) of additional profits over the next three years. If that were true, which features on the list below would be responsible for that profit increase? Apportion your $100,000 based on which line items caused the increased profit." Some negative profit impact *is* allowed in this round,[1] because it's quite possible that some features (such as security controls and regulatory compliance) will actually detract from company performance, even if they are a good idea.

Typically, the answers from the two rounds will be quite different. Once you have collected the inputs, calculate a straight average to create the composite vote for the group.

Weakest/Strongest Elimination

This exercise doesn't use spreadsheets or parametric analysis. Instead, it's a sort of *American Idol* combined with *The Weakest Link*. This method isn't very precise, but it's useful for short-term priority calls because it's relatively quick and intuitive.

This prioritization method is done as a group exercise, typically around a conference table or via videoconferencing. The list of features is put in a spreadsheet, initially in "best guess" order of preference (with the no-brainers at the top of the list). The process is simple triage, and the goal is to divide the list into three groups:

- Features that are "above the line"—they are safe from questioning and sure to be done.

- Features that are alternates in case one of the "above the line" items can't be done or needs to be delayed.

- Features that are "below the line"—they won't be done this time, so there's no point in reviewing them any further now.

---

1. If negative profit impacts are assigned to some features, then the positive impact will be larger than the $100,000 to balance out the math.

The list (see Table A-1 for an example) is used as a crucible for several rapid rounds of voting, along these lines (typically using a moderator[2] to keep things going quickly):

1. Ask the audience to spend 20 seconds looking at the top part of the list to find the most obvious no-brainer feature.

2. Ask the audience to shout out their favorite "no-brainer," and see if the group can quickly be brought to consensus that the nominee should, indeed, be kept above the line. As soon as this item's status is resolved (20–30 seconds), move to the next item on the list.

3. Ask the audience to find an item in the top of the list that should be demoted to the second category. Move that item below the line in the Excel spreadsheet so everyone can see it. There's a cute Excel macro that performs line-item moves with a single keystroke—pick it up at www.SFDC-secrets.com.

4. Repeat this "beauty contest" cycle until you've gone through all items in the top of the list.

5. Switch to "the weakest link" cycle: start at the bottom of the list, and ask the crowd to nominate the most useless or uninteresting feature. As soon as there's consensus, move that item to the very bottom of the list.

6. Ask the audience if any items in the bottom area of the list should be promoted to the second category. Repeat the "weakest link" cycle until you've run through all items in the bottom area of the list

7. Look at the middle part of the list for items that should be demoted or promoted.[3] Move these items as the decisions go, so that everyone sees the consequences.

8. Repeat the whole cycle *just on the above-the-line features,* dividing them into three groups (high, medium, and low priority, but all to be done).

Using this technique you can get through a prioritization cycle in 20–30 minutes.

---

2. It's best *not* to have the CEO or other executive lead this exercise because it's tough not to telegraph personal priorities to the audience, even in just reading the items on a voting list. The project manager or other neutral party should moderate these votes so that the resulting prioritization will be perceived as unbiased.

3. Generally, it's easier for people to vote down marginal items than to decide which item is "the most important," so collect more demotion votes than promotion votes.

TABLE A-1   Above/Below-the-Line Voting

Item Number	Description	Cost Index*	Benefit Index*
1	Advanced forecasting	1	6
2	Advanced forecasting reports and alerts	1	6
3	Dashboards	2	9
4	Lead capture and routing	2	4
5	Lead scoring and qualification	4	4
6	Opportunity creation	1	0
7	Basic forecasting reports	1	1
	Above here are the must-do items		
8	Opportunity aging and backtrack alerts	1	4
9	Order-level quoting	1	0
10	Line-item-level quoting	3	4
11	Historic opportunity import, 1 year	6	3
12	Contract import, 1 year	6	7
13	Support ticket integration	7	6
	*Below here are the won't-do items***		
14	Contract import, 3 year	7	8
15	Historic opportunity import, 3 year	8	4
16	Quote approval	2	9
17	Customer portal	7	6
18	Automatic quoting	1	0
19	Mobile sales rep and support access	8	7
20	Call center integration	3	1
21	Data warehouse/business intelligence	2	7
22	Multi-currency support	1	3
23	Automatic license key generation	3	1

*   The cost index and benefit index are meant to indicate the relative sizes of the costs and benefits of each line item.

** The middle range of this list includes the prioritized alternates for must-do items that can't fit within the schedule or run into problems.

Popular Votes

Some types of organizations prefer using popular voting to drive decisions, as a matter of culture and management style. Popular votes are easy to conduct, but can be problematic when it comes to meaning and wisdom. Not everyone who votes is equally competent or knowledgeable about SFA issues, and some voters just won't have as much at stake as others will.

If you use a popular voting mechanism and are willing to put up with the problems of "one person, one vote," you should seriously consider using SFDC's own Ideas application: it's perfect for this kind of dynamic popularity contest.

In most cases, it is preferable to use *unequal* voting: VPs should have bigger votes than worker bees, and the Sales department should have a bigger vote than the Accounting department. The vote weighting issue is particularly important when sales territories disagree violently about the importance of features. The idea of unequal voting may rub some people the wrong way, but the bills are going to be paid mainly by the Sales VP, and he or she has the most to gain from a great SFDC implementation.

Be sure to set up the apportionment of voting *before* you actually take any votes, so as to maintain the appearance of neutrality. The weighing of different people's "importance" may be a very touchy issue, so play nice.

Example Requirements Statements

A S DISCUSSED IN CHAPTERS 1 and 4, the statement of requirements drives budgetary decisions and helps shape the waves of features that will be deployed in each delivery cycle. This appendix gives some example requirements for company situations, assuming that they don't have an existing SFA/CRM system in place.

The requirements statements here are kept at a management level: they're not very detailed, but they have enough context to help drive business decisions. Once the project is under way, a completely different level of requirement would be created, delving into the technical details, user specifics, and task interdependencies. Because the details of technical requirements would confound nearly any business person, however, they should be left out during the prioritization and tradeoff phase of decision making.

Example Project Requirements: Smaller Company

Company profile: A manufacturing company has grown to have sales of $30 million/year, with 15 sales reps, 5 sales support people, 2 full-time marketers, and several contractors who touch leads. The organization has been using ACT for contact management, Outlook for email campaigns, and spreadsheets for pipeline management, forecasting, order promise dates, and deliveries. It uses QuickBooks for accounting.

Problems driving an SFDC decision: The way the company works right now, too many things fall through the cracks. Leads aren't followed up on, and marketing can't tell which activities are producing the leads that really count—the ones that drive sales. Forecasting is manual, unreliable, and very inaccurate. The executives were embarrassed at a recent board meeting when the week-10 bookings forecast included nonsensical data, and the company badly missed its target at the end of the quarter. End-of-quarter revenues are a mess because important customers aren't getting their orders filled while incomplete shipments sit on the factory floor at the end of the quarter.

People driving the decision: The CEO and VP of Sales are the main drivers. The CFO and the factory workers make a lot of noise, but this issue is not their domain. The marketing personnel are big supporters, but they have little political clout.

Overview of requirements: There are several problems to solve, but they should be fixed in order. The main issues for the executive drivers are forecasting accuracy, missed deals, and weak sales management. While there are clearly other requirements for the system, if the major problems aren't solved first, the executives in the company will not view the project as a success.

The main phases of the project requirements would likely follow this order:

1. Get SFDC up and running for pipeline management and forecasting.

   ↪ Clean and import all `contacts`, `accounts`, and `opportunities` from existing spreadsheets and import them into SFDC.

   ↪ Implement basic SFDC functionality (no `advanced forecasting` module for now).

   ↪ Train the sales reps on how to enter and update deals.

   ↪ Create a forecasting spreadsheet that's driven by SFDC data.

2. Move off of ACT for `lead` and `contact` management.

   ↪ Clean and import all reps' ACT `leads` into the system.

   ↪ Integrate SFDC with the Web site so all registrants automatically become `leads` in the system.

   ↪ Create processes and templates for all external `lead` sources to be imported into SFDC.

   ↪ Train the sales reps, inside sales, sales support, and marketing people on how to enter and manipulate `leads` and `contacts`.

   ↪ Create management reports on `lead` handling and `contact` conversion rates.

3. Use `opportunities` to track deals.

   ↪ Establish `sales stages` and `probability` percentages.

   ↪ Create `opportunity page layouts`.

   ↪ Create reports that replace off-board pipeline and forecasting spreadsheets.

   ↪ Train the sales reps on how to enter and edit deals.

4. Develop end-of-quarter forecasting for pipeline and shipments.

   ↪ Start using SFDC for basic quoting and storage of `contract` data.

   ↪ Extend SFDC records to include `quote` line items, shipment promise dates, willingness to accept partial orders, and other data.

➥ Develop reports to analyze bookings forecasts over time.

➥ Develop reports to show shipment requirements during the quarter.

➥ Train reps, finance personnel, marketing staff, and executives on how to enter and interpret these data.

5. Start using `campaigns` to increase marketing effectiveness.

➥ Implement the `campaigns` module.

➥ Add a deduping service to prevent duplicate data.

➥ Develop multiple landing pages on the Web site and integrate them into SFDC.

➥ Start using the `Google for Campaigns` feature for online ads.

➥ Start using a standard email blasting service for online marketing.

➥ Develop reports to analyze marketing effectiveness.

➥ Train marketers and contractors on the proper use of the SFDC system, and executives on interpreting marketing metrics.

6. Integrate the SFDC system with QuickBooks for order management, invoicing, and revenue recognition.

➥ Buy an adaptor to connect SFDC with QuickBooks.

➥ Synchronize all the existing customer and account names between the systems.

➥ Import and reconcile the order history from the last two years.

➥ Develop reports for financial analysts.

➥ Train order operations and finance people in the proper use and interactions between the two systems.

Note that the phases of the system would likely be implemented over several quarters, with only the first two phases as "hard priorities" and the later requirements being reordered depending on their perceived priority after initial usage and experience with the SFDC system.

Example Project Requirements: Larger Company

Company profile: A worldwide products company sells more than $1 billion in product and services in more than 10 countries. Its field force includes 500 sales reps, hundreds of sales support people, 300 consultants, 100 marketers, and dozens of contracting companies that touch leads around the world. The company has been using both Seibel and Upshot for CRM, both in the United States and in other countries. It uses Eloqua for online and offline marketing, Outlook for email and schedule management, and a complex series of spreadsheets for forecasting. The company uses Oracle for accounting.

Problems driving an SFDC decision: Far too many things are not working properly. Accounts and deals are not being handled correctly, particularly when an opportunity straddles geographic territories. Key information seems to get lost in the system, frustrating everyone from sales reps (who know they put the information in) to sales managers (who can't understand the status of a deal).

Sales personnel complain that there aren't enough leads, even though marketing personnel claim to produce thousands of leads every quarter. Marketers have noticed there are lots of duplicates and a significant amount of bad data in the system, and they suspect that users are deleting records when they are confused or merely trying to hide a lost deal. Marketing has no idea which lead-generation activities are actually working. Leads are being "flipped" over to partners so the channel can work more deals, but no one can tell whether the leads are being followed up on, or even what "follow-up" should really measure.

The pipeline forecast is partially automated, but there's a lot of manual manipulation of the forecast on a weekly basis. The finance group runs its own forecast that second-guesses the sales forecast. No one trusts the existing SFA/CRM data for analysis, and the system isn't sufficiently integrated with other corporate systems to drive the business in a coordinated way.

People driving the decision: The VP of Sales is under pressure to improve performance, as well as visibility and predictability of results. The VP of Marketing is under scrutiny because of questions about the effectiveness of the marketing expenditures. The CEO thinks that the SFA/CRM problems are lowering the company's stock price, and the board of directors wants to see action.

Overview of requirements: There is a very wide range of problems to be solved here, both inside the existing SFA/CRM systems and in the surrounding systems and processes. Because of the number of data-related problems (duplication, junk data, lost entries, and possible data deletion), several changes to external processes and user procedures will be needed—and each of these changes requires a political driver. The order in which problems should be solved will depend on the priority as perceived by the management team. The high-priority items right now are directly related to revenue: the ability to find, update, and close deals, and the ability to generate consistently credible forecasts. Even with all the other requirements, if the forecast problems aren't solved first, the executives in the company will not view the project as a success.

At the same time, everyone needs to use the existing systems. Given this constraint, like the New York City subway rebuilding project, the new system will need to operate in parallel with the old one. The "parallel play" period will involve a lot of manual work (both users and system administrators will have to deal with this issue) to keep the systems more or less synchronized. The beneficial side of this approach is that the systems analysts will be able to use the two systems to cross-check each other to more rapidly fix problems.

The early phases of project requirements might follow this path:

1. Get SFDC up and running as the system of record for basic opportunity entry and updating.

   ➡ Dedupe and reconcile all SFA/CRM account information with the company financial system; transition these account names to the new SFDC system.

   ➡ Dedupe and reconcile all opportunity names with the company financial system; transition these opportunities to the new system.

   ➡ Create custom fields and pick lists for the specific types of deals the company does.

   ➡ Populate the price list with domestic prices.

   ➡ Implement basic security and access hierarchy.

   ➡ Do not attempt to get product-level detail, advanced forecasting, or quoting in this first phase.

   ➡ Train the inside reps, sales reps, and sales operations people on how to enter and update deals.

2. Develop end-of-quarter forecasting for pipeline and shipments.

   ➡ Create a forecasting spreadsheet driven by SFDC data; create spreadsheets that cross-check this information with finance and other systems on a monthly basis.

   ➡ Start using SFDC for basic quoting; enable the products module and populate the price list (domestic only in this phase).

   ➡ Extend SFDC records to include quote line items, shipment promise dates, willingness to accept partial orders, and other data.

   ➡ Add quote approval workflows to check for unusual discounts, payment terms, or other variations.

   ➡ Link approved quotes to financial systems.

   ➡ Add order approval workflows, and link completed orders to the company's financial system.

   ➡ Integrate the current inventory and available-to-promise dates from the company's ERP system.

   ➡ Develop reports to analyze bookings forecasts over time.

➥ Develop reports to show shipment requirements during the quarter.

➥ Extend `workflows` and lockdown logic for Sarbanes-Oxley Act compliance.

➥ Train reps and executives on how to enter and interpret these data.

3. Extend the system for international users.

➥ Implement more advanced security and access hierarchies.

➥ Implement `sales teams`.

➥ Create a safe testing area using the SFDC `sandbox`.

➥ Populate the `sandbox` with deduped and reconciled `account` information and `opportunity` names from the foreign accounting systems.

➥ Populate the `price list` with international pricing.

➥ Use the `translation workbench` to facilitate localized text of all system areas.

➥ In the `sandbox`, turn on the `multi-currency mode` to make sure that none of the system extensions or integrations with external systems breaks.

➥ Implement special requirements for international quoting and sales cycles.

➥ Turn on the `multi-currency mode` in the operational system.

➥ Write reports that provide global roll-ups for `forecasting` and `quoting`.

➥ Train international users and executives on how to enter and interpret the data.

4. Extend the system to professional services.

➥ Add sales engineers, support engineers, trainers, and consultants to the system.

➥ Start using `cases` and `solutions` for technical support.

➥ Add professional services items into the `price list` and start quoting them in the system.

➥ Add special `workflows` for approving professional services `quotes`.

➥ Use `workflows` for `case` escalation.

➥ Create reports for technical support and consulting management.

➥ Train all professional services personnel on how to use the system.

5. Integrate SFDC with other key operational systems.

➥ Integrate SFDC `contracts` with the Oracle accounting system and the company's existing document management system.

➥ Integrate SFDC into the company's business intelligence/data analytics tools.

6. Convert marketing personnel to SFDC.

- Clean, enrich, and dedupe all `leads` and `contacts` from existing systems and migrate them to SFDC.

- Develop naming standards for `campaigns` and respondents; import all `campaigns` from existing systems and processes into SFDC.

- Integrate Eloqua with SFDC.

- Extend the company's Web site integration into SFDC.

- Develop templates for importing `leads` from each of the lead-producing venues and services.

- Start using SFDC `campaigns` for all marketing activities, particularly Google advertising.

- Develop marketing reports and scorecards.

- Train marketing users and contractors on how to use the SFDC system, and marketing executives on how to interpret the data.

In large projects, technical or process issues discovered during the project will almost inevitably cause a reordering of the later phases of the SFDC system implementation. In addition, perceived business needs may change during the life of the project. However, it's important that the executive sponsors understand that each major change of priorities will cause some delay and wasted effort. Communicating this message clearly but pleasantly is one of the key challenges for the project leader, because the executives are as vulnerable to "happy ears" as anyone else.

Index

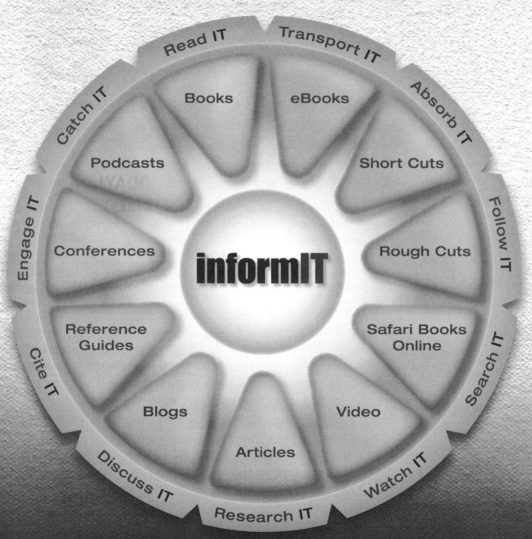

FREE Online Edition

Your purchase of **Salesforce.com® Secrets of Success** includes access to a free online edition for 45 days through the Safari Books Online subscription service. Nearly every Prentice Hall book is available online through Safari Books Online, along with more than 5,000 other technical books and videos from publishers such as Addison-Wesley Professional, Cisco Press, Exam Cram, IBM Press, O'Reilly, Que, and Sams.

SAFARI BOOKS ONLINE allows you to search for a specific answer, cut and paste code, download chapters, and stay current with emerging technologies.

Activate your FREE Online Edition at www.informit.com/safarifree

> **STEP 1:** Enter the coupon code: IVBVNGA.

> **STEP 2:** New Safari users, complete the brief registration form.
> Safari subscribers, just log in.

If you have difficulty registering on Safari or accessing the online edition, please e-mail customer-service@safaribooksonline.com